COMPLETE OUR SURVEY AND LET
US KNOW WHAT YOU THINK!

☐ Please do NOT send me information about VIZ products, news and events, special offers, or other information.

☐ Please do NOT send me information from VIZ's trusted business partners.

Name: _____

Address: _____

City: _____ **State:** _____ **Zip:** _____

E-mail: _____

☐ **Male**   ☐ **Female**   **Date of Birth** (mm/dd/yyyy): ____ / ____ / ____   (Under 13? Parental consent required)

What race/ethnicity do you consider yourself? (please check one)

☐ Asian/Pacific Islander   ☐ Black/African American   ☐ Hispanic/Latino

☐ Native American/Alaskan Native ☐ White/Caucasian   ☐ Other: _____

What VIZ product did you purchase? (check all that apply and indicate title purchased)

☐ DVD/VHS _____

☐ Graphic Novel_____

☐ Magazines_____

☐ Merchandise_____

Reason for purchase: (check all that apply)

☐ Special offer   ☐ Favorite title   ☐ Gift

☐ Recommendation   ☐ Other_____

Where did you make your purchase? (please check one)

☐ Comic store   ☐ Bookstore   ☐ Mass/Grocery Store

☐ Newsstand   ☐ Video/Video Game Store ☐ Other:_____

☐ Online (site: _____)

What other VIZ properties have you purchased/own? _____

_____

How many a[illegible] many were VIZ titles? **(please check one from each column)**

ANIME	MANGA	VIZ
☐ None	☐ None	☐ None
☐ 1-4	☐ 1-4	☐ 1-4
☐ 5-10	☐ 5-10	☐ 5-10
☐ 11+	☐ 11+	☐ 11+

I find the pricing of VIZ products to be: (please check one)

☐ Cheap ☐ Reasonable ☐ Expensive

What genre of manga and anime would you like to see from VIZ? (please check two)

☐ Adventure ☐ Comic Strip ☐ Science Fiction ☐ Fighting

☐ Horror ☐ Romance ☐ Fantasy ☐ Sports

What do you think of VIZ's new look?

☐ Love It ☐ It's OK ☐ Hate It ☐ Didn't Notice ☐ No Opinion

Which do you prefer? (please check one)

☐ Reading right-to-left

☐ Reading left-to-right

Which do you prefer? (please check one)

☐ Sound effects in English

☐ Sound effects in Japanese with English captions

☐ Sound effects in Japanese only with a glossary at the back

THANK YOU! Please send the completed form to:

VIZ Survey
42 Catharine St.
Poughkeepsie, NY 12601

All information provided will be used for internal purposes only. We promise not to sell or otherwise divulge your information.

Author's Profile
Yukie Nasu

Born: Tokyo, Japan
Star Sign: Aries
Blood Type: A
Debuted in Hana to Yume, Winter
Publication with the story "U.F.
Chance." In 1986, her first
continuing series, the boy's-life story
"Here is Greenwood," became an
enormously popular signature series.
She has also published quite a few
fantasy and science fiction stories,
including "Flower Destroyer," "Yōma
Shūrai Fukushū-ki," "Gekkō," "Illusion
Food Master," and many others.

Here is
Greenwood.

Contents

Guide to Honorifics

"sempai"
Used to address more senior members of an organization. In a school, students in grades higher than the speaker would be addressed by [their name here]-sempai, as would more senior employees in a company.

"Sempai/kohai relationship"
Since HERE IS GREENWOOD takes place in a school, the sempai/kohai relationship is a crucial aspect of the life of the students. It is much like the Western mentor/protégé relationship, but on a school-wide scale. Sempai, the senior students, are expected to look after the interests of their kohai, guide them, help them with their problems, give them referrals, and be their counselor. Kohai are expected to respect their sempai, do chores or menial tasks, follow orders, and learn.

Diminutives and nicknames
Like Western nicknames, most Japanese nicknames are shortened versions of their regular names, sometimes with the honorific -chan or -kun tacked at the end. Sumire calls her husband "Hiro-kun," shortened from Kazuhiro-kun and, similarly, she calls her brother-in-law "Yakkun," shortened and slightly changed from Kazuya-kun. "Suka-chan" (pronounced ska-chahn) is a similar diminutive taken from Hasukawa, except the word "suka" is also a not-so-common insult approximately equivalent to "baka" (fool).

—William Flanagan

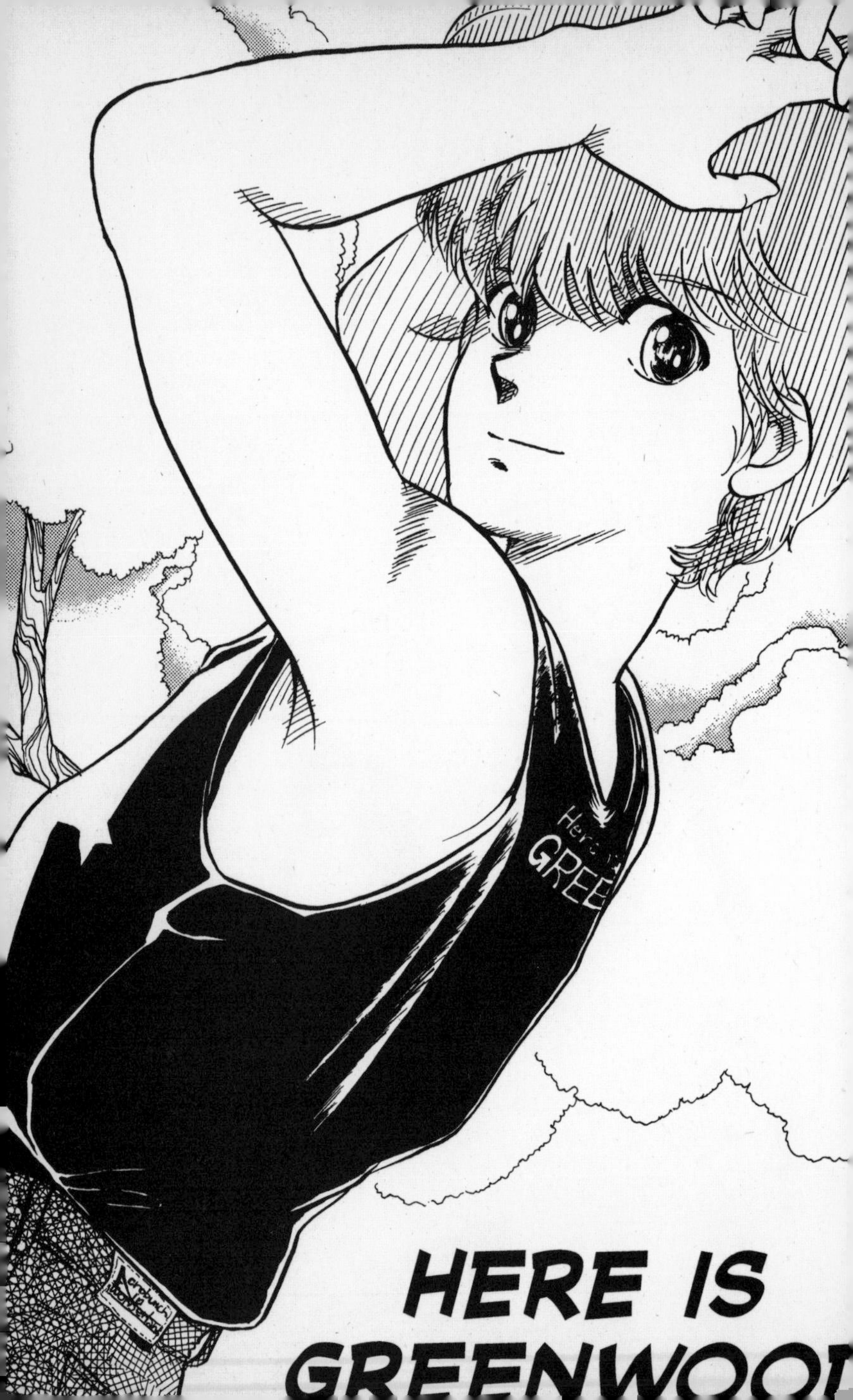
HERE IS
GREENWOOD

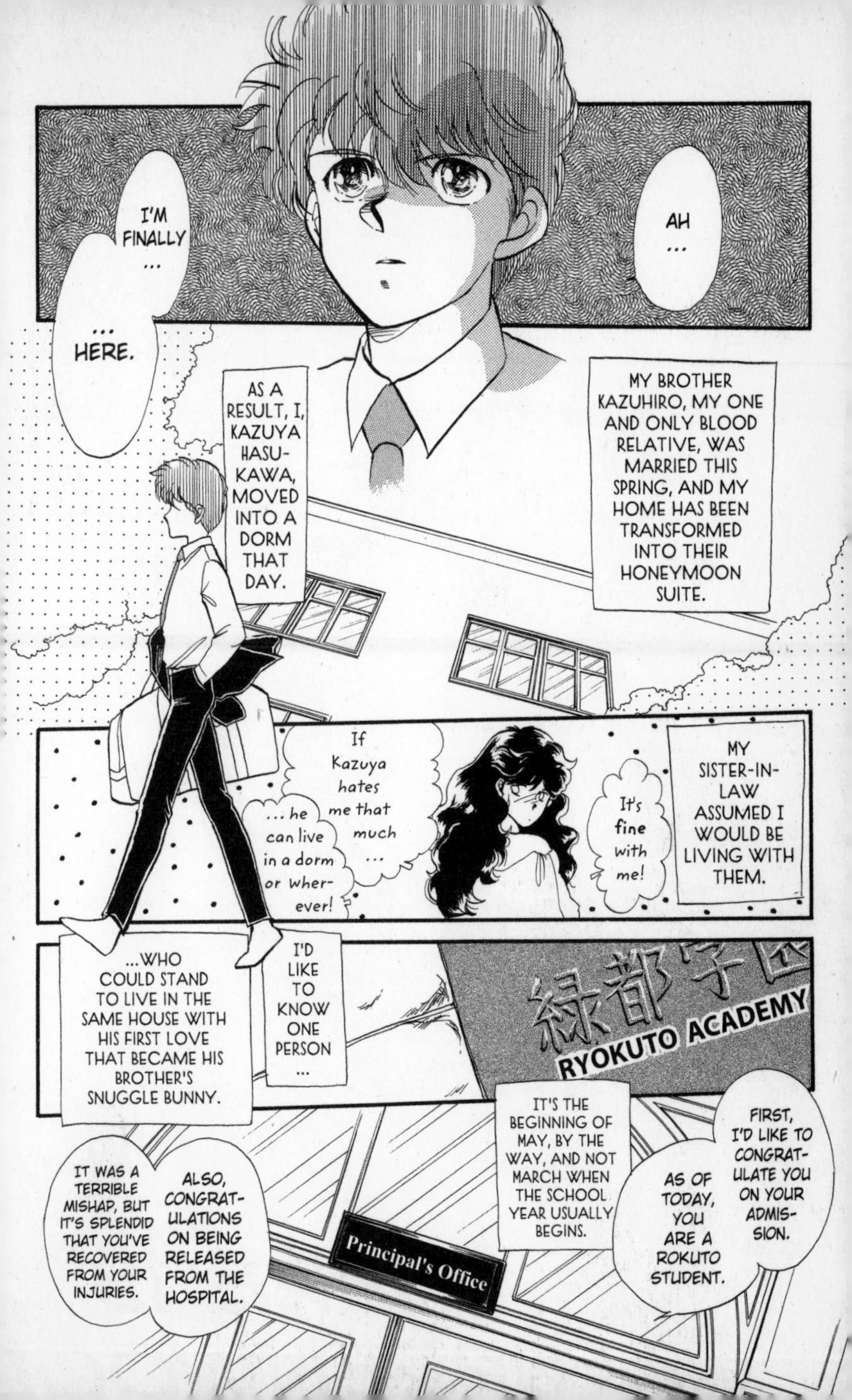
AH ...
I'M FINALLY ...
... HERE.
MY BROTHER KAZUHIRO, MY ONE AND ONLY BLOOD RELATIVE, WAS MARRIED THIS SPRING, AND MY HOME HAS BEEN TRANSFORMED INTO THEIR HONEYMOON SUITE.
AS A RESULT, I, KAZUYA HASU-KAWA, MOVED INTO A DORM THAT DAY.
MY SISTER-IN-LAW ASSUMED I WOULD BE LIVING WITH THEM.
It's fine with me!
If Kazuya hates me that much ...
... he can live in a dorm or wher-ever!
緑都学園
RYOKUTO ACADEMY
I'D LIKE TO KNOW ONE PERSON ...
...WHO COULD STAND TO LIVE IN THE SAME HOUSE WITH HIS FIRST LOVE THAT BECAME HIS BROTHER'S SNUGGLE BUNNY.
FIRST, I'D LIKE TO CONGRAT-ULATE YOU ON YOUR ADMIS-SION.
AS OF TODAY, YOU ARE A ROKUTO STUDENT.
IT'S THE BEGINNING OF MAY, BY THE WAY, AND NOT MARCH WHEN THE SCHOOL YEAR USUALLY BEGINS.
Principal's Office
ALSO, CONGRAT-ULATIONS ON BEING RELEASED FROM THE HOSPITAL.
IT WAS A TERRIBLE MISHAP, BUT IT'S SPLENDID THAT YOU'VE RECOVERED FROM YOUR INJURIES.

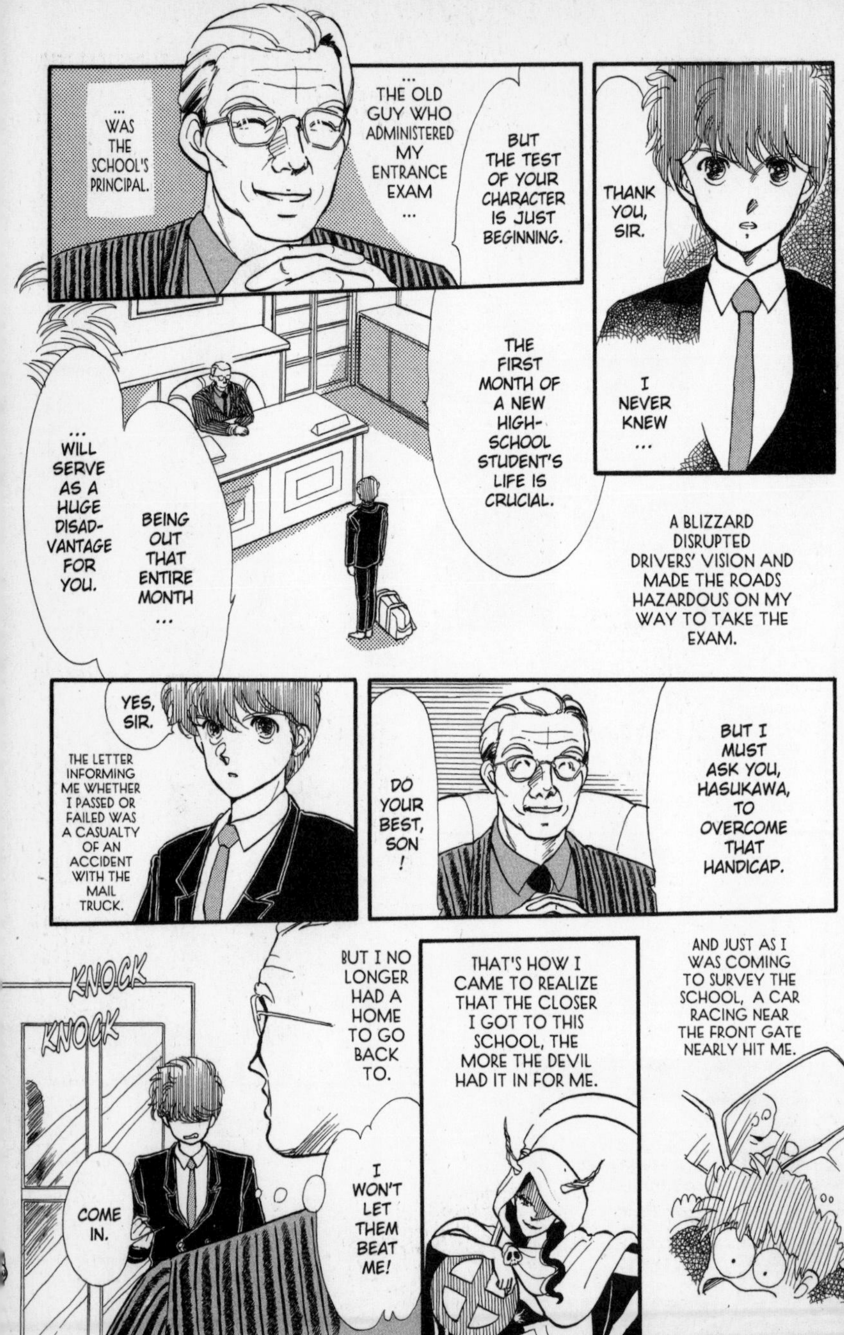
THANK YOU, SIR.
I NEVER KNEW ...
BUT THE TEST OF YOUR CHARACTER IS JUST BEGINNING.
... THE OLD GUY WHO ADMINISTERED MY ENTRANCE EXAM ...
... WAS THE SCHOOL'S PRINCIPAL.
THE FIRST MONTH OF A NEW HIGH-SCHOOL STUDENT'S LIFE IS CRUCIAL.
BEING OUT THAT ENTIRE MONTH ...
... WILL SERVE AS A HUGE DISADVANTAGE FOR YOU.
A BLIZZARD DISRUPTED DRIVERS' VISION AND MADE THE ROADS HAZARDOUS ON MY WAY TO TAKE THE EXAM.
BUT I MUST ASK YOU, HASUKAWA, TO OVERCOME THAT HANDICAP.
DO YOUR BEST, SON!
YES, SIR.
THE LETTER INFORMING ME WHETHER I PASSED OR FAILED WAS A CASUALTY OF AN ACCIDENT WITH THE MAIL TRUCK.
AND JUST AS I WAS COMING TO SURVEY THE SCHOOL, A CAR RACING NEAR THE FRONT GATE NEARLY HIT ME.
THAT'S HOW I CAME TO REALIZE THAT THE CLOSER I GOT TO THIS SCHOOL, THE MORE THE DEVIL HAD IT IN FOR ME.
BUT I NO LONGER HAD A HOME TO GO BACK TO.
I WON'T LET THEM BEAT ME!
KNOCK
KNOCK
COME IN.

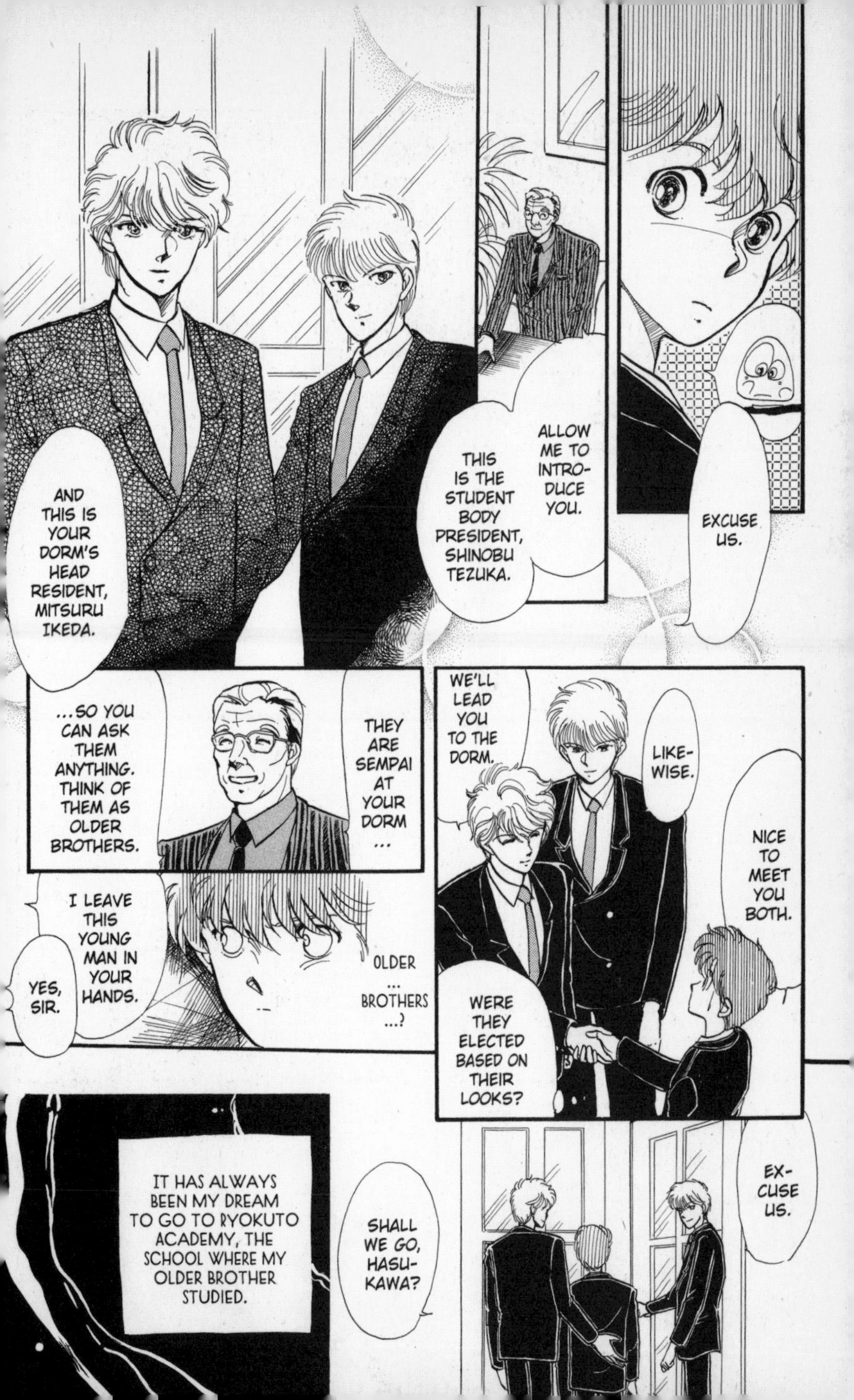
EXCUSE US.
ALLOW ME TO INTRODUCE YOU.
THIS IS THE STUDENT BODY PRESIDENT, SHINOBU TEZUKA.
AND THIS IS YOUR DORM'S HEAD RESIDENT, MITSURU IKEDA.
LIKEWISE.
WE'LL LEAD YOU TO THE DORM.
NICE TO MEET YOU BOTH.
WERE THEY ELECTED BASED ON THEIR LOOKS?
THEY ARE SEMPAI AT YOUR DORM ...
...SO YOU CAN ASK THEM ANYTHING. THINK OF THEM AS OLDER BROTHERS.
OLDER ... BROTHERS ...?
I LEAVE THIS YOUNG MAN IN YOUR HANDS.
YES, SIR.
EXCUSE US.
SHALL WE GO, HASUKAWA?
IT HAS ALWAYS BEEN MY DREAM TO GO TO RYOKUTO ACADEMY, THE SCHOOL WHERE MY OLDER BROTHER STUDIED.

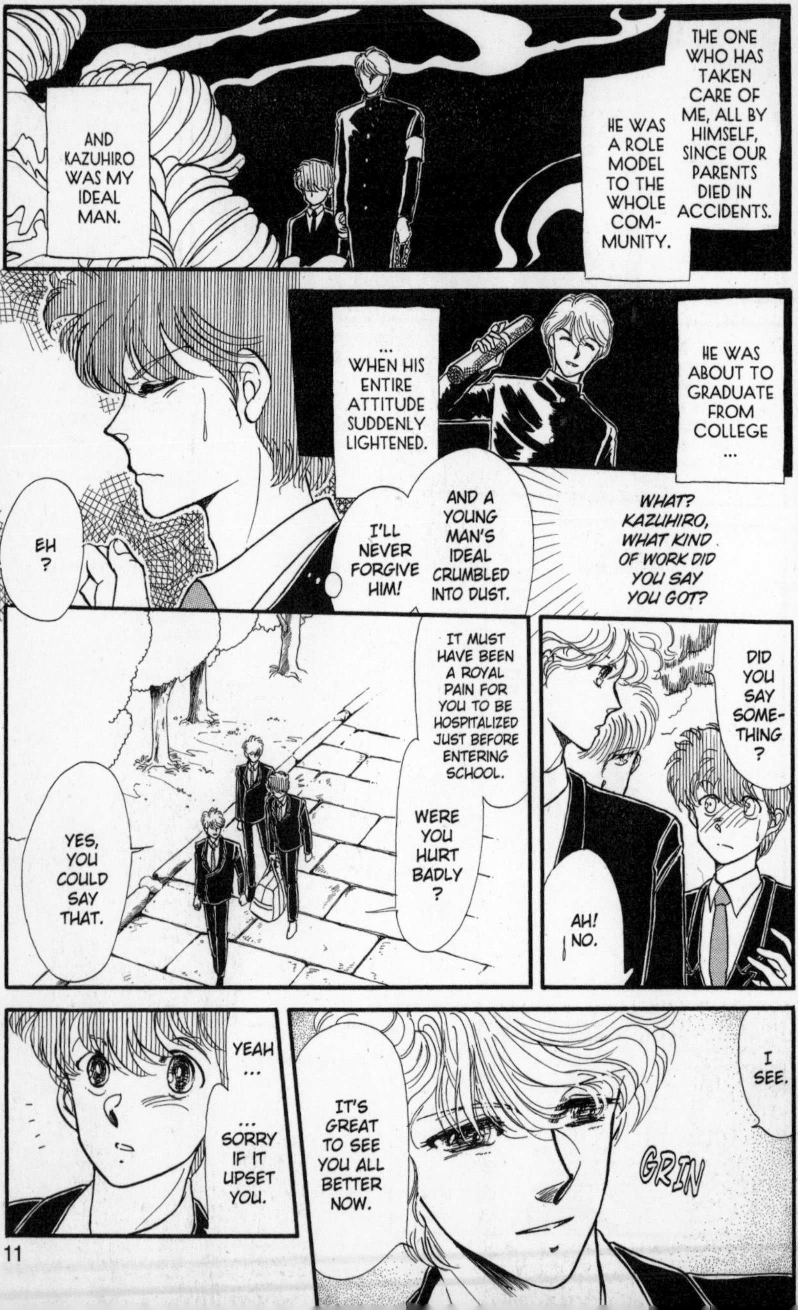
THE ONE WHO HAS TAKEN CARE OF ME, ALL BY HIMSELF, SINCE OUR PARENTS DIED IN ACCIDENTS.
HE WAS A ROLE MODEL TO THE WHOLE COM-MUNITY.
AND KAZUHIRO WAS MY IDEAL MAN.
HE WAS ABOUT TO GRADUATE FROM COLLEGE ...
... WHEN HIS ENTIRE ATTITUDE SUDDENLY LIGHTENED.
WHAT? KAZUHIRO, WHAT KIND OF WORK DID YOU SAY YOU GOT?
AND A YOUNG MAN'S IDEAL CRUMBLED INTO DUST.
I'LL NEVER FORGIVE HIM!
EH?
DID YOU SAY SOME-THING?
AH! NO.
IT MUST HAVE BEEN A ROYAL PAIN FOR YOU TO BE HOSPITALIZED JUST BEFORE ENTERING SCHOOL.
WERE YOU HURT BADLY?
YES, YOU COULD SAY THAT.
I SEE.
GRIN
IT'S GREAT TO SEE YOU ALL BETTER NOW.
YEAH ...
... SORRY IF IT UPSET YOU.

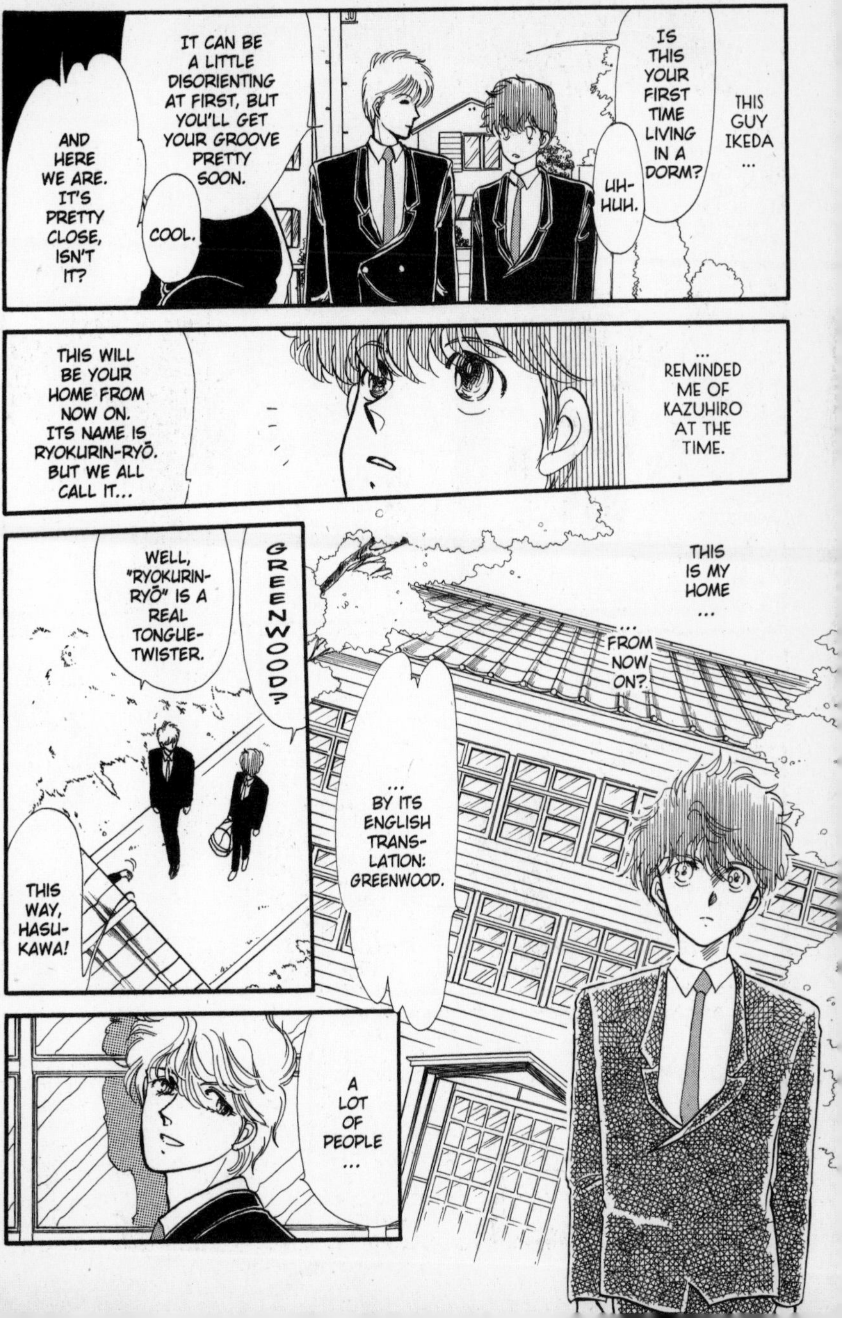
THIS GUY IKEDA ...
IS THIS YOUR FIRST TIME LIVING IN A DORM?
UH-HUH.
IT CAN BE A LITTLE DISORIENTING AT FIRST, BUT YOU'LL GET YOUR GROOVE PRETTY SOON.
COOL.
AND HERE WE ARE. IT'S PRETTY CLOSE, ISN'T IT?
... REMINDED ME OF KAZUHIRO AT THE TIME.
THIS WILL BE YOUR HOME FROM NOW ON. ITS NAME IS RYOKURIN-RYŌ. BUT WE ALL CALL IT...
THIS IS MY HOME ...
... FROM NOW ON?
GREENWOOD?
WELL, "RYOKURIN-RYŌ" IS A REAL TONGUE-TWISTER.
THIS WAY, HASU-KAWA!
A LOT OF PEOPLE ...
... BY ITS ENGLISH TRANS-LATION: GREENWOOD.

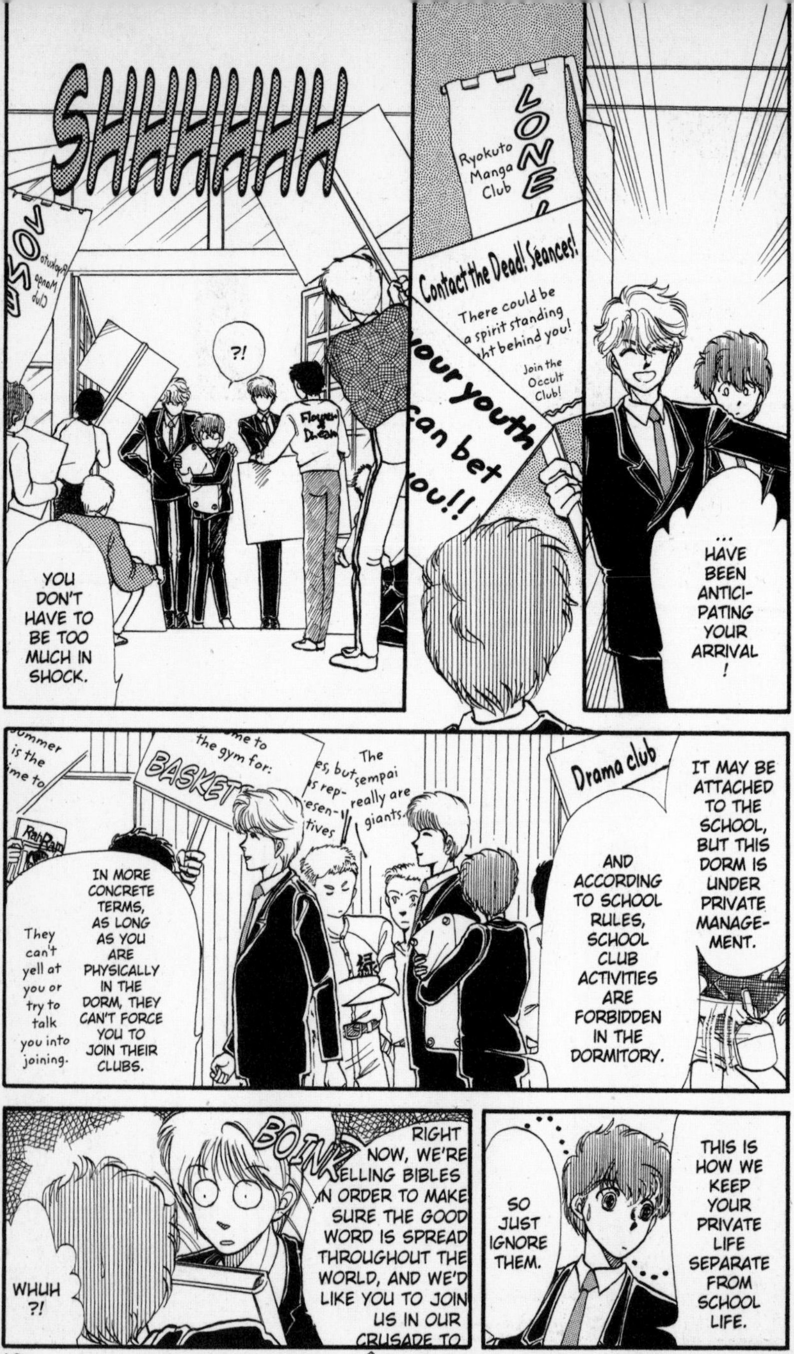

... HAVE BEEN ANTICIPATING YOUR ARRIVAL!
Ryokuto Manga Club
Contact the Dead! Séances!
There could be a spirit standing
Join the Occult Club!
SHHHHHHH
Ryokuto Manga Club
?!
YOU DON'T HAVE TO BE TOO MUCH IN SHOCK.
IT MAY BE ATTACHED TO THE SCHOOL, BUT THIS DORM IS UNDER PRIVATE MANAGEMENT.
Drama club
AND ACCORDING TO SCHOOL RULES, SCHOOL CLUB ACTIVITIES ARE FORBIDDEN IN THE DORMITORY.
The sempai really are giants.
IN MORE CONCRETE TERMS, AS LONG AS YOU ARE PHYSICALLY IN THE DORM, THEY CAN'T FORCE YOU TO JOIN THEIR CLUBS.
They can't yell at you or try to talk you into joining.
THIS IS HOW WE KEEP YOUR PRIVATE LIFE SEPARATE FROM SCHOOL LIFE.
SO JUST IGNORE THEM.
BOING
RIGHT NOW, WE'RE SELLING BIBLES IN ORDER TO MAKE SURE THE GOOD WORD IS SPREAD THROUGHOUT THE WORLD, AND WE'D LIKE YOU TO JOIN US IN OUR CRUSADE TO
WHUH ?!

↑Too many words for the balloon.

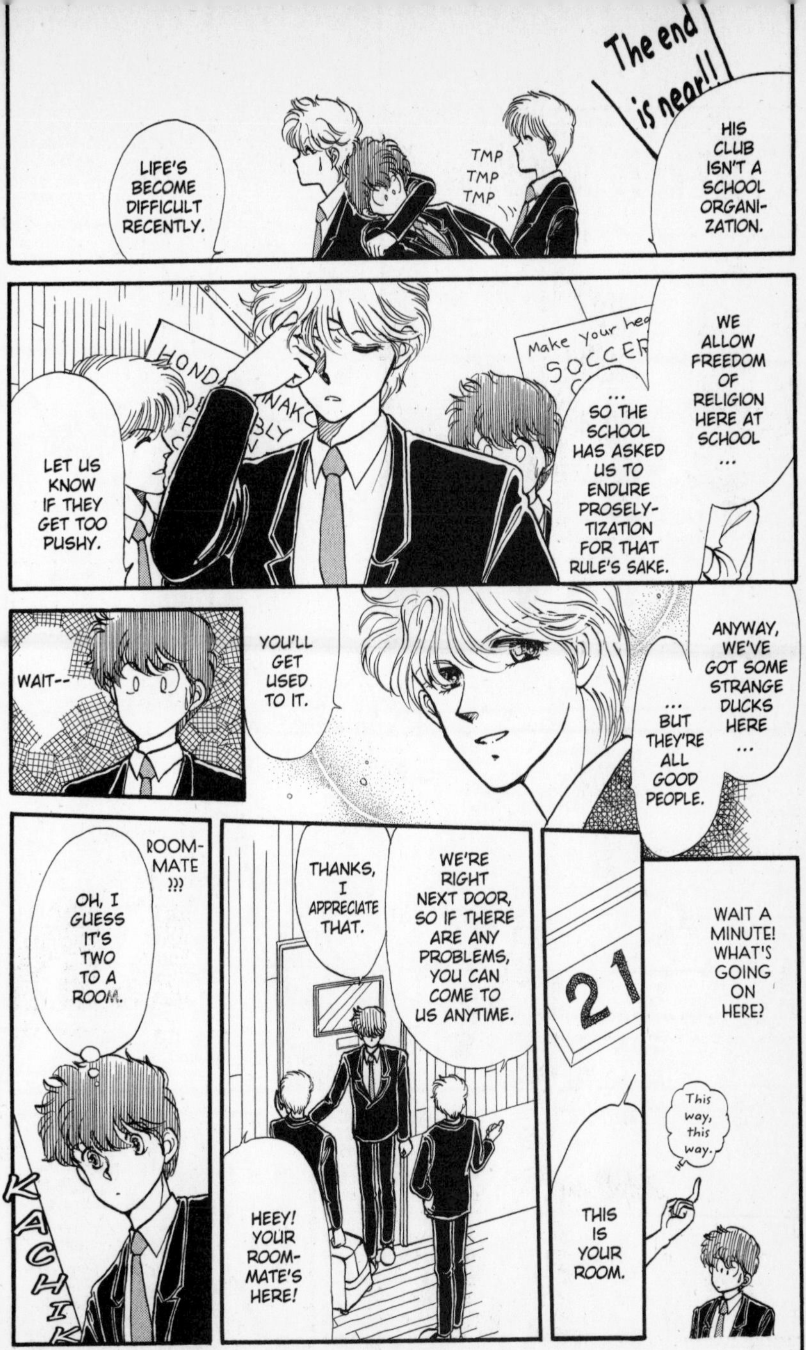
The end is near!!
HIS CLUB ISN'T A SCHOOL ORGANIZATION.
TMP TMP TMP
LIFE'S BECOME DIFFICULT RECENTLY.
WE ALLOW FREEDOM OF RELIGION HERE AT SCHOOL ...
... SO THE SCHOOL HAS ASKED US TO ENDURE PROSELYTIZATION FOR THAT RULE'S SAKE.
LET US KNOW IF THEY GET TOO PUSHY.
ANYWAY, WE'VE GOT SOME STRANGE DUCKS HERE ...
... BUT THEY'RE ALL GOOD PEOPLE.
YOU'LL GET USED TO IT.
WAIT--
WAIT A MINUTE! WHAT'S GOING ON HERE?
This way, this way.
21
THIS IS YOUR ROOM.
WE'RE RIGHT NEXT DOOR, SO IF THERE ARE ANY PROBLEMS, YOU CAN COME TO US ANYTIME.
THANKS, I APPRECIATE THAT.
HEEY! YOUR ROOMMATE'S HERE!
ROOMMATE ???
OH, I GUESS IT'S TWO TO A ROOM.
KACHIK

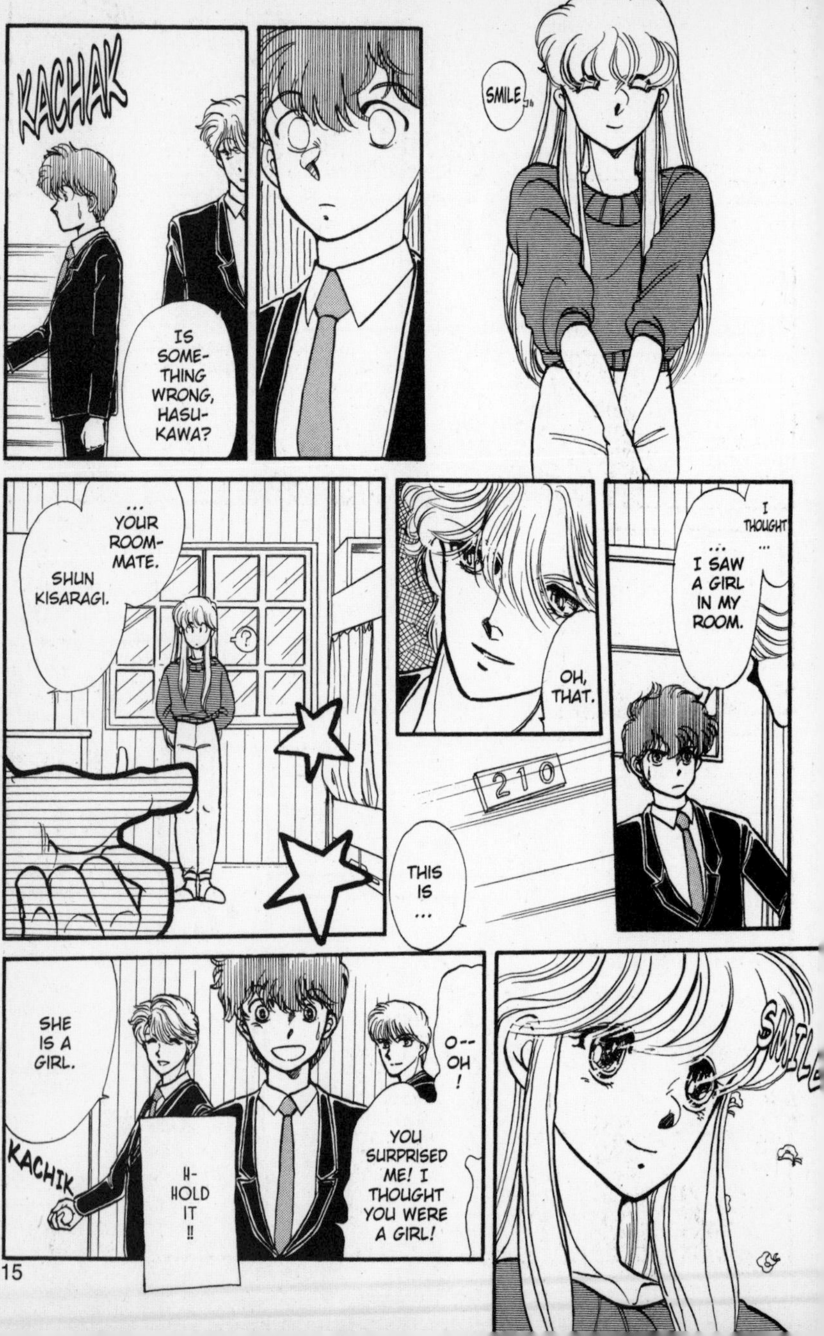
SMILE
KACHAK
IS SOMETHING WRONG, HASUKAWA?
I THOUGHT ... I SAW A GIRL IN MY ROOM.
OH, THAT.
THIS IS ...
... YOUR ROOMMATE.
SHUN KISARAGI.
SMILE
O-- OH!
SHE IS A GIRL.
YOU SURPRISED ME! I THOUGHT YOU WERE A GIRL!
H- HOLD IT !!
KACHIK

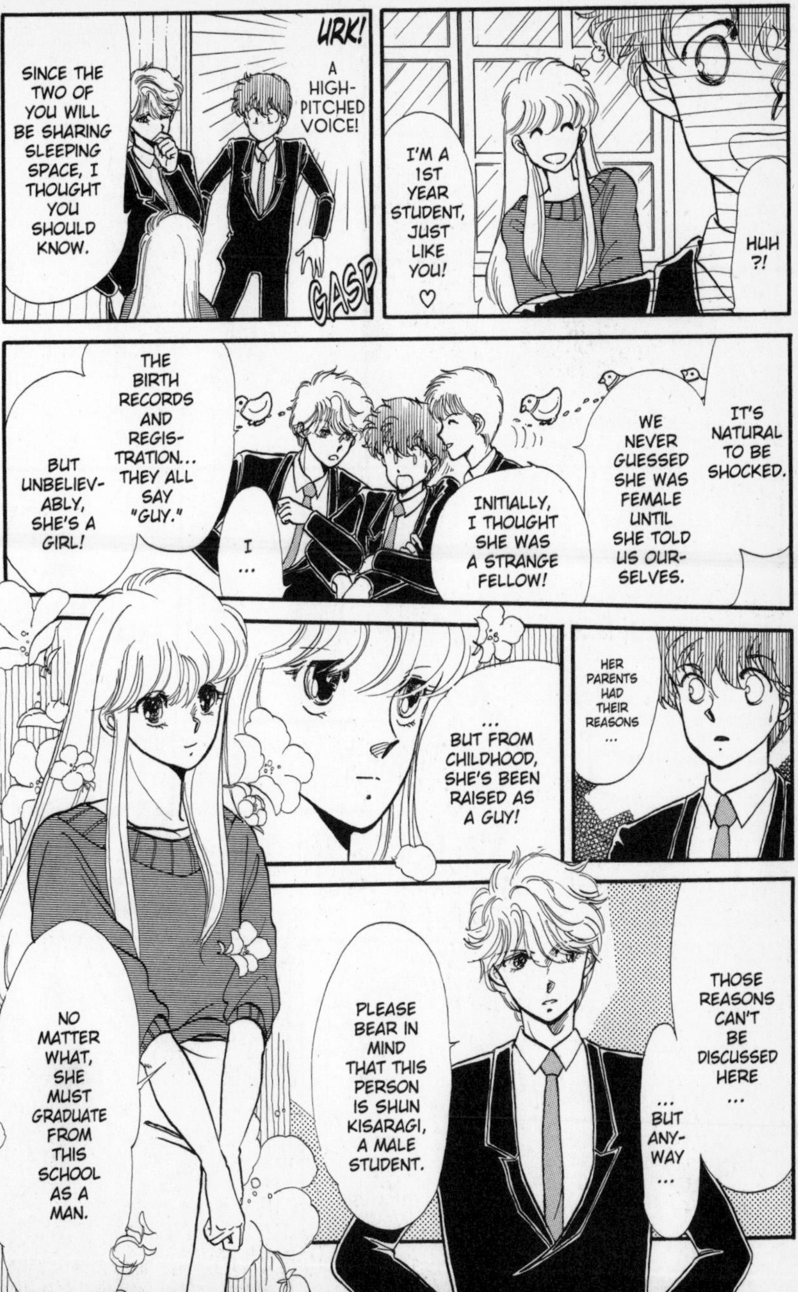
I'M A 1ST YEAR STUDENT, JUST LIKE YOU! ♡
HUH ?!
URK!
A HIGH-PITCHED VOICE!
GASP
SINCE THE TWO OF YOU WILL BE SHARING SLEEPING SPACE, I THOUGHT YOU SHOULD KNOW.
IT'S NATURAL TO BE SHOCKED.
WE NEVER GUESSED SHE WAS FEMALE UNTIL SHE TOLD US OURSELVES.
INITIALLY, I THOUGHT SHE WAS A STRANGE FELLOW!
I ...
THE BIRTH RECORDS AND REGISTRATION... THEY ALL SAY "GUY."
BUT UNBELIEVABLY, SHE'S A GIRL!
HER PARENTS HAD THEIR REASONS ...
... BUT FROM CHILDHOOD, SHE'S BEEN RAISED AS A GUY!
THOSE REASONS CAN'T BE DISCUSSED HERE ...
... BUT ANYWAY ...
PLEASE BEAR IN MIND THAT THIS PERSON IS SHUN KISARAGI, A MALE STUDENT.
NO MATTER WHAT, SHE MUST GRADUATE FROM THIS SCHOOL AS A MAN.

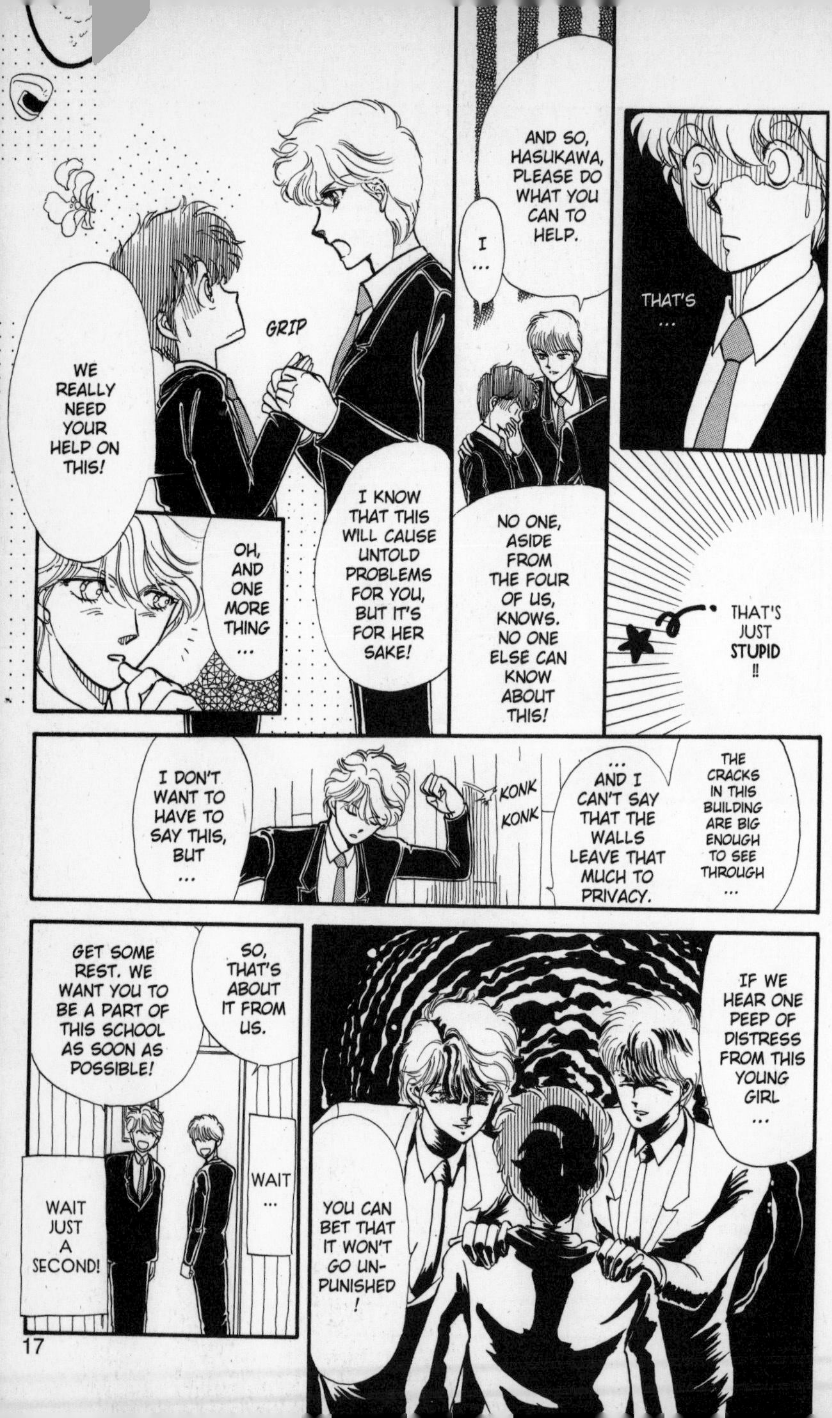
THAT'S ...
THAT'S JUST STUPID !!
AND SO, HASUKAWA, PLEASE DO WHAT YOU CAN TO HELP.
I ...
NO ONE, ASIDE FROM THE FOUR OF US, KNOWS. NO ONE ELSE CAN KNOW ABOUT THIS!
GRIP
I KNOW THAT THIS WILL CAUSE UNTOLD PROBLEMS FOR YOU, BUT IT'S FOR HER SAKE!
WE REALLY NEED YOUR HELP ON THIS!
OH, AND ONE MORE THING ...
THE CRACKS IN THIS BUILDING ARE BIG ENOUGH TO SEE THROUGH ...
... AND I CAN'T SAY THAT THE WALLS LEAVE THAT MUCH TO PRIVACY.
KONK
KONK
I DON'T WANT TO HAVE TO SAY THIS, BUT ...
IF WE HEAR ONE PEEP OF DISTRESS FROM THIS YOUNG GIRL ...
YOU CAN BET THAT IT WON'T GO UN-PUNISHED!
SO, THAT'S ABOUT IT FROM US.
GET SOME REST. WE WANT YOU TO BE A PART OF THIS SCHOOL AS SOON AS POSSIBLE!
WAIT ...
WAIT JUST A SECOND!

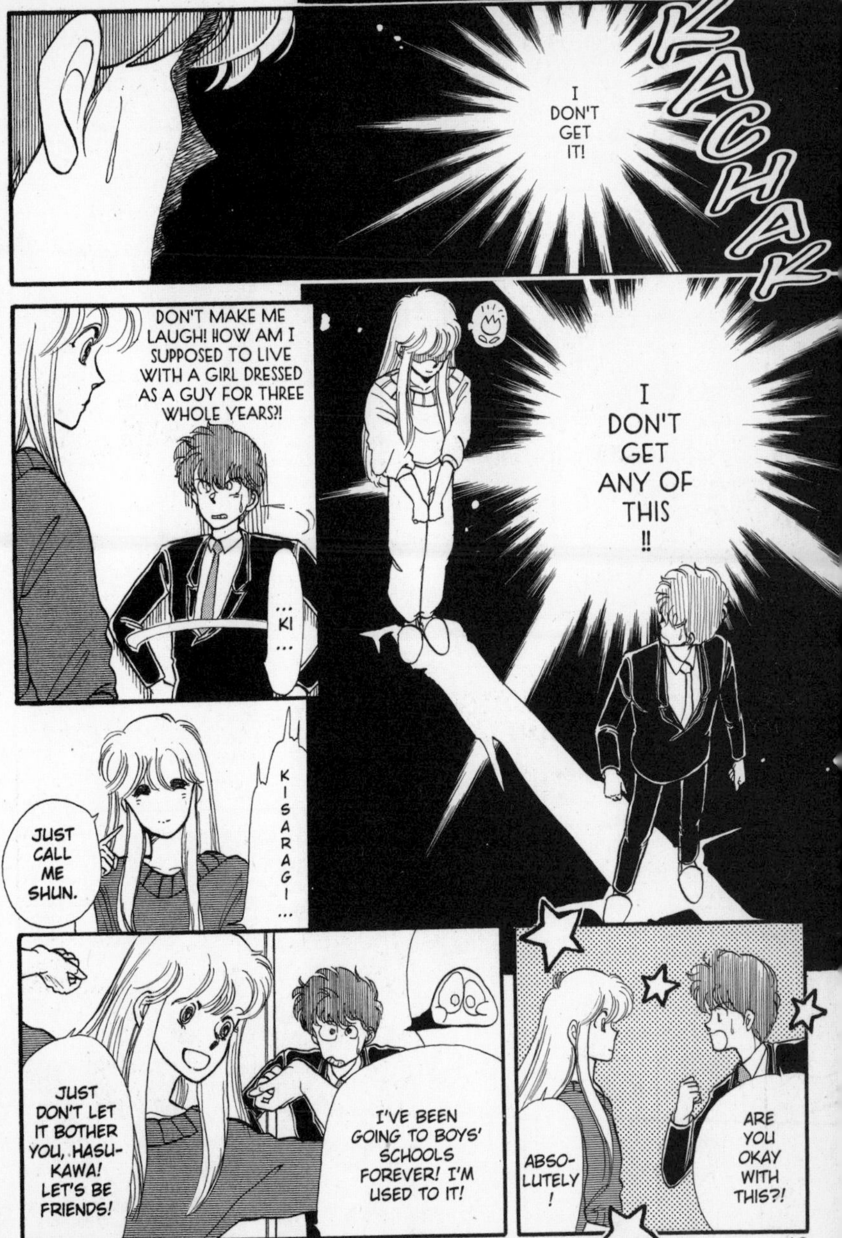
YACHAK
I DON'T GET IT!
I DON'T GET ANY OF THIS!!
DON'T MAKE ME LAUGH! HOW AM I SUPPOSED TO LIVE WITH A GIRL DRESSED AS A GUY FOR THREE WHOLE YEARS?!
...KI...
KISARAGI...
JUST CALL ME SHUN.
ARE YOU OKAY WITH THIS?!
ABSOLUTELY!
I'VE BEEN GOING TO BOYS' SCHOOLS FOREVER! I'M USED TO IT!
JUST DON'T LET IT BOTHER YOU, HASUKAWA! LET'S BE FRIENDS!

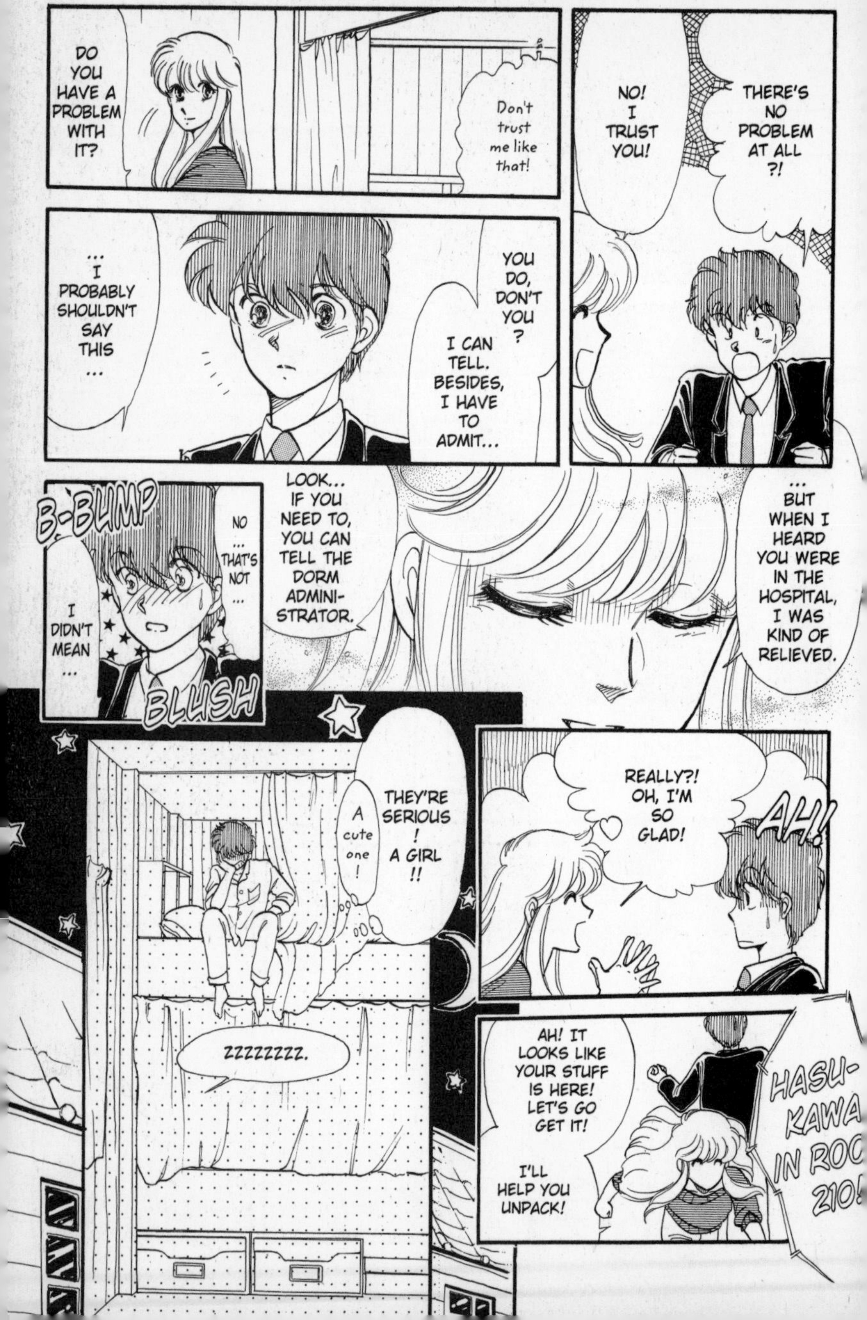
THERE'S NO PROBLEM AT ALL ?!
NO! I TRUST YOU!
DO YOU HAVE A PROBLEM WITH IT?
Don't trust me like that!
YOU DO, DON'T YOU ?
I CAN TELL. BESIDES, I HAVE TO ADMIT...
... I PROBABLY SHOULDN'T SAY THIS ...
... BUT WHEN I HEARD YOU WERE IN THE HOSPITAL, I WAS KIND OF RELIEVED.
LOOK... IF YOU NEED TO, YOU CAN TELL THE DORM ADMINI-STRATOR.
NO ... THAT'S NOT ...
B-BUMP
I DIDN'T MEAN ...
BLUSH
AH!
REALLY?! OH, I'M SO GLAD!
HASU-KAWA IN ROO 210!
AH! IT LOOKS LIKE YOUR STUFF IS HERE! LET'S GO GET IT!
I'LL HELP YOU UNPACK!
THEY'RE SERIOUS ! A GIRL !!
A cute one !
ZZZZZZZZ.

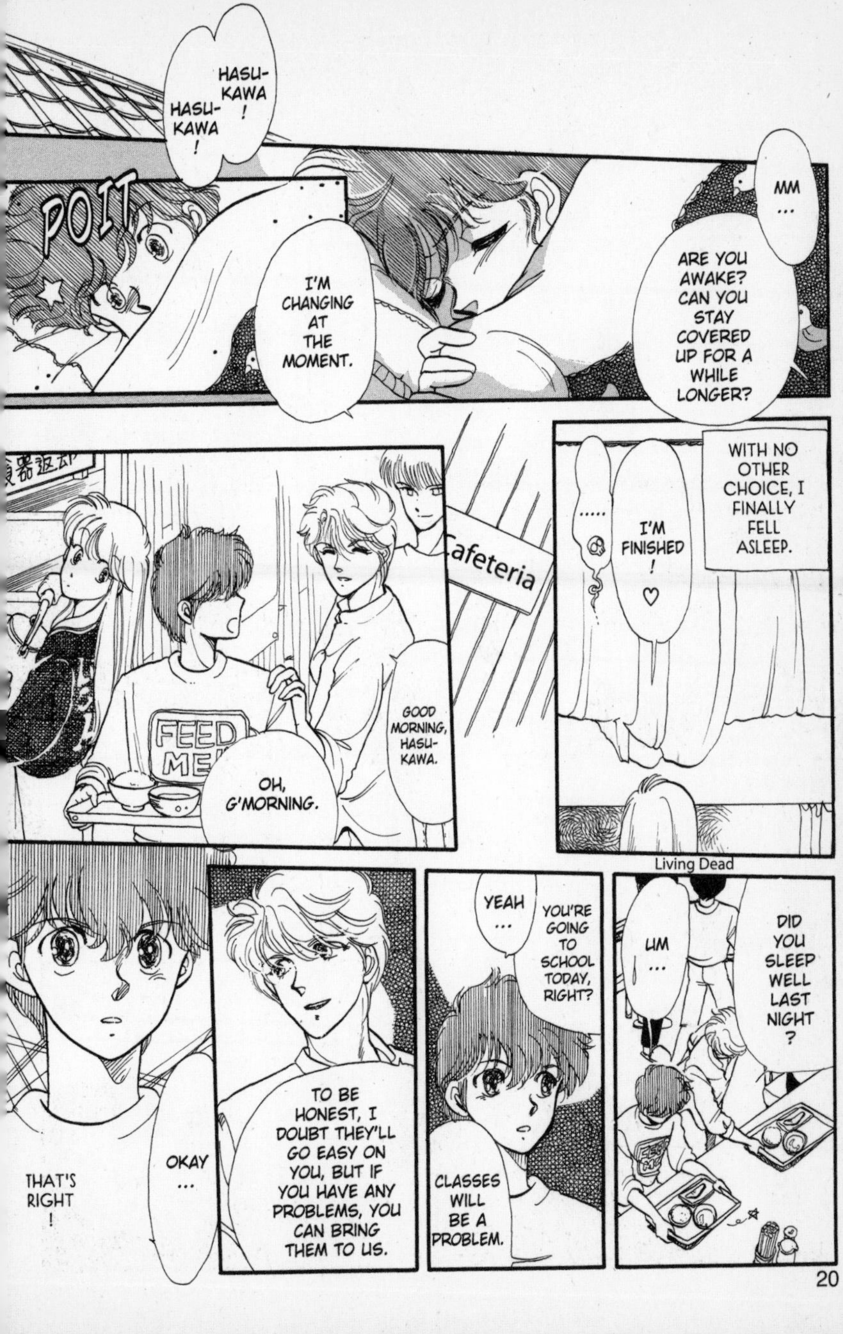
HASU-KAWA!
HASU-KAWA!
POIT
MM ...
ARE YOU AWAKE? CAN YOU STAY COVERED UP FOR A WHILE LONGER?
I'M CHANGING AT THE MOMENT.
WITH NO OTHER CHOICE, I FINALLY FELL ASLEEP.
I'M FINISHED! ♡
.....
Cafeteria
GOOD MORNING, HASU-KAWA.
OH, G'MORNING.
DID YOU SLEEP WELL LAST NIGHT?
UM ...
YOU'RE GOING TO SCHOOL TODAY, RIGHT?
YEAH ...
CLASSES WILL BE A PROBLEM.
TO BE HONEST, I DOUBT THEY'LL GO EASY ON YOU, BUT IF YOU HAVE ANY PROBLEMS, YOU CAN BRING THEM TO US.
OKAY ...
THAT'S RIGHT!
Living Dead

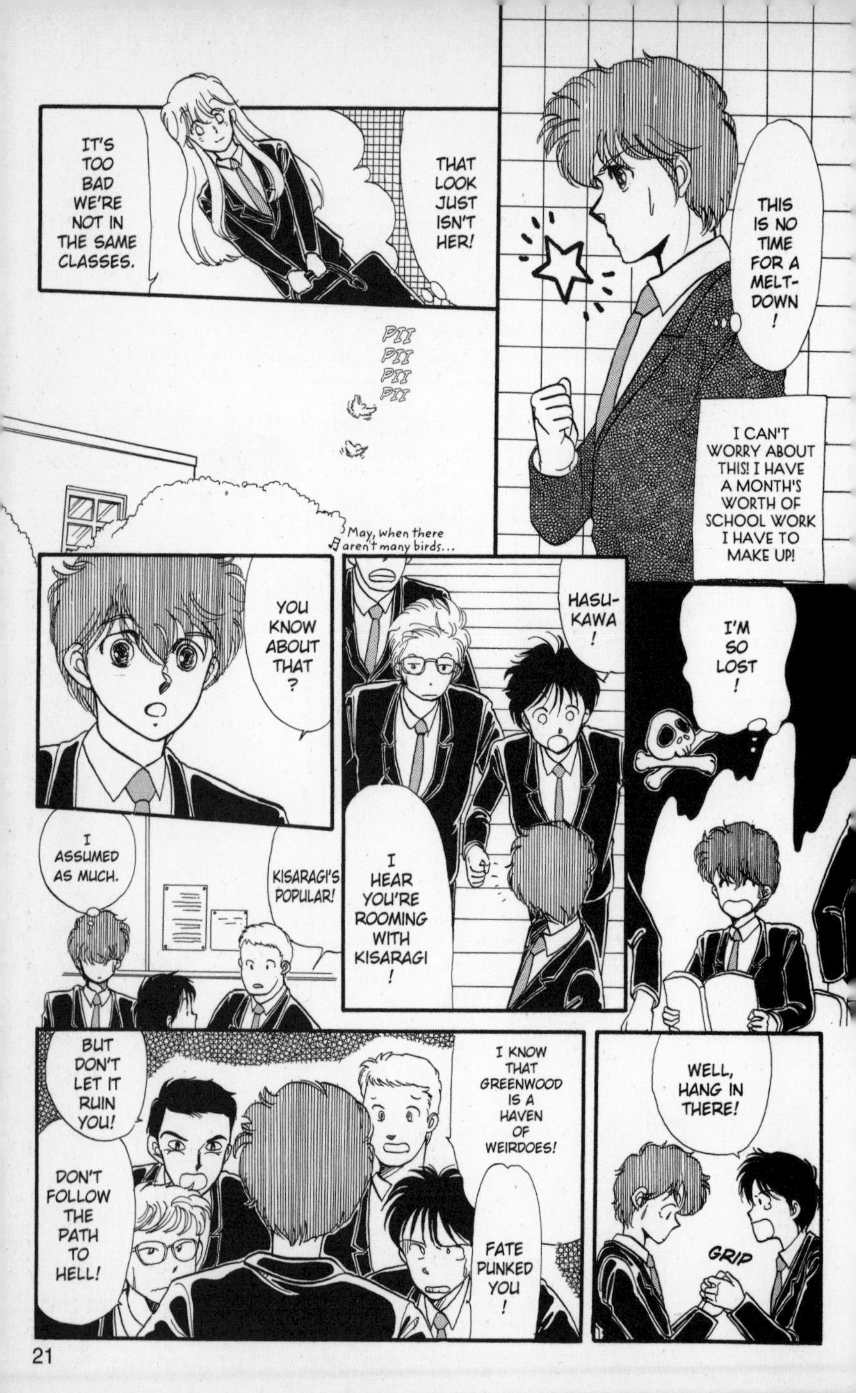
THIS IS NO TIME FOR A MELT-DOWN!
I CAN'T WORRY ABOUT THIS! I HAVE A MONTH'S WORTH OF SCHOOL WORK I HAVE TO MAKE UP!
THAT LOOK JUST ISN'T HER!
IT'S TOO BAD WE'RE NOT IN THE SAME CLASSES.
PII PII PII PII
May, when there aren't many birds...
I'M SO LOST!
HASU-KAWA!
I HEAR YOU'RE ROOMING WITH KISARAGI!
YOU KNOW ABOUT THAT?
KISARAGI'S POPULAR!
I ASSUMED AS MUCH.
WELL, HANG IN THERE!
GRIP
I KNOW THAT GREENWOOD IS A HAVEN OF WEIRDOES!
FATE PUNKED YOU!
BUT DON'T LET IT RUIN YOU!
DON'T FOLLOW THE PATH TO HELL!

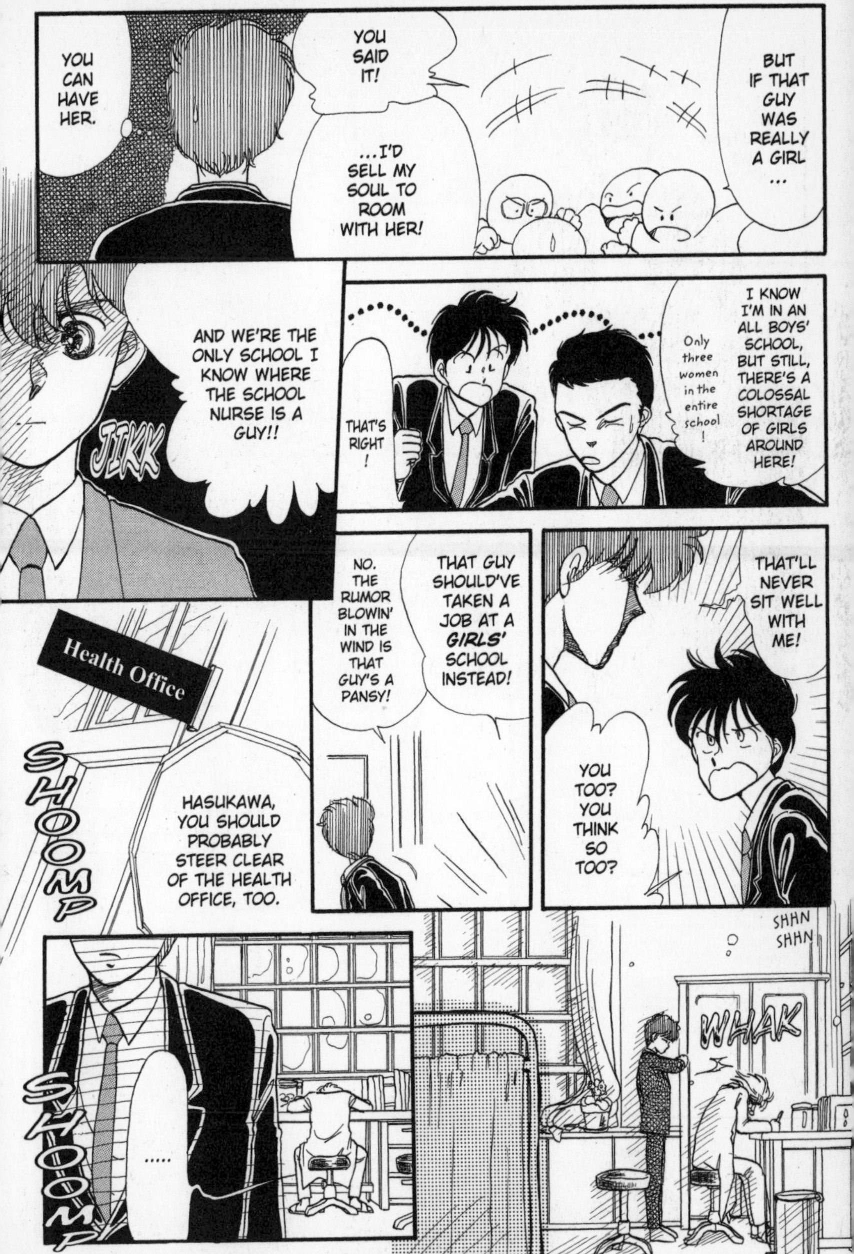

BUT IF THAT GUY WAS REALLY A GIRL ...
YOU SAID IT!
...I'D SELL MY SOUL TO ROOM WITH HER!
YOU CAN HAVE HER.
I KNOW I'M IN AN ALL BOYS' SCHOOL, BUT STILL, THERE'S A COLOSSAL SHORTAGE OF GIRLS AROUND HERE!
Only three women in the entire school!
THAT'S RIGHT!
AND WE'RE THE ONLY SCHOOL I KNOW WHERE THE SCHOOL NURSE IS A GUY!!
JIKK
THAT'LL NEVER SIT WELL WITH ME!
YOU TOO? YOU THINK SO TOO?
THAT GUY SHOULD'VE TAKEN A JOB AT A GIRLS' SCHOOL INSTEAD!
NO. THE RUMOR BLOWIN' IN THE WIND IS THAT GUY'S A PANSY!
Health Office
SHOOMP
HASUKAWA, YOU SHOULD PROBABLY STEER CLEAR OF THE HEALTH OFFICE, TOO.
SHHN SHHN
WHAK
SHOOMP
.....

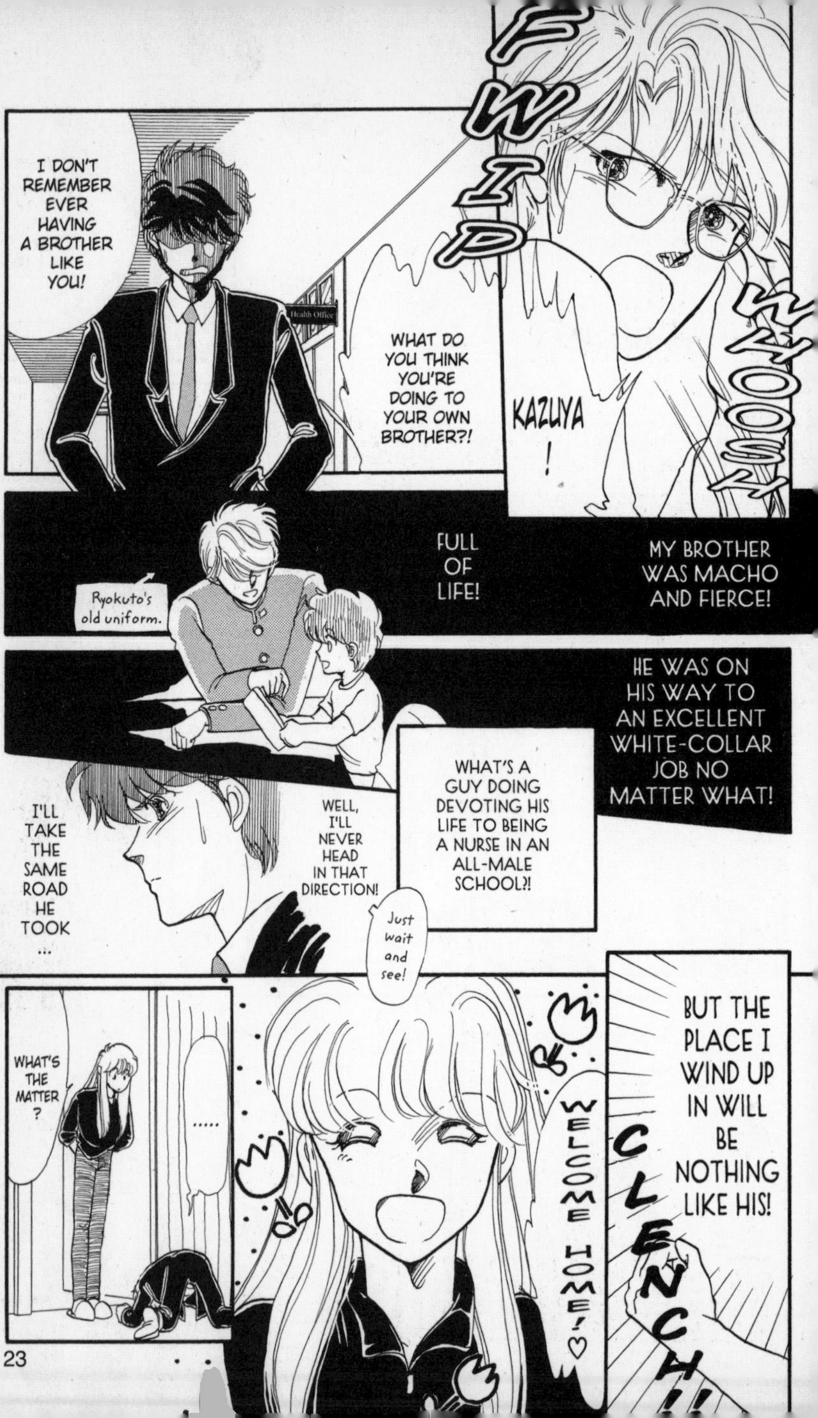
FWIP
WHOOSH
KAZUYA!
WHAT DO YOU THINK YOU'RE DOING TO YOUR OWN BROTHER?!
I DON'T REMEMBER EVER HAVING A BROTHER LIKE YOU!
Health Office
MY BROTHER WAS MACHO AND FIERCE!
FULL OF LIFE!
Ryokuto's old uniform.
HE WAS ON HIS WAY TO AN EXCELLENT WHITE-COLLAR JOB NO MATTER WHAT!
WHAT'S A GUY DOING DEVOTING HIS LIFE TO BEING A NURSE IN AN ALL-MALE SCHOOL?!
WELL, I'LL NEVER HEAD IN THAT DIRECTION!
I'LL TAKE THE SAME ROAD HE TOOK ...
Just wait and see!
BUT THE PLACE I WIND UP IN WILL BE NOTHING LIKE HIS!
CLENCH!!
WELCOME HOME!♡
.....
WHAT'S THE MATTER ?

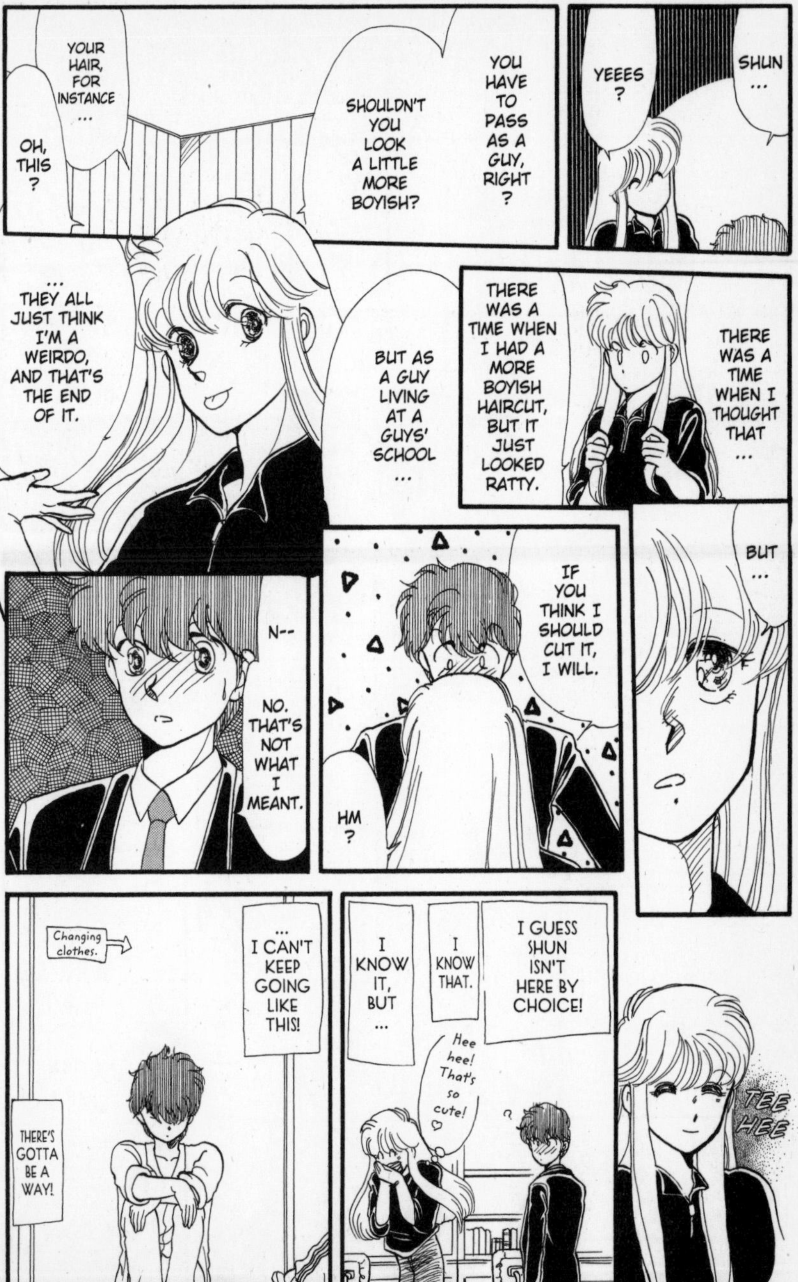
SHUN ...
YEEES ?
YOU HAVE TO PASS AS A GUY, RIGHT ?
SHOULDN'T YOU LOOK A LITTLE MORE BOYISH?
YOUR HAIR, FOR INSTANCE ...
OH, THIS ?
THERE WAS A TIME WHEN I THOUGHT THAT ...
THERE WAS A TIME WHEN I HAD A MORE BOYISH HAIRCUT, BUT IT JUST LOOKED RATTY.
BUT AS A GUY LIVING AT A GUYS' SCHOOL ...
... THEY ALL JUST THINK I'M A WEIRDO, AND THAT'S THE END OF IT.
BUT ...
IF YOU THINK I SHOULD CUT IT, I WILL.
HM ?
N--
... NO. THAT'S NOT WHAT I MEANT.
TEE HEE
I GUESS SHUN ISN'T HERE BY CHOICE!
I KNOW THAT.
I KNOW IT, BUT ...
Hee hee! That's so cute!
... I CAN'T KEEP GOING LIKE THIS!
Changing clothes.
THERE'S GOTTA BE A WAY!

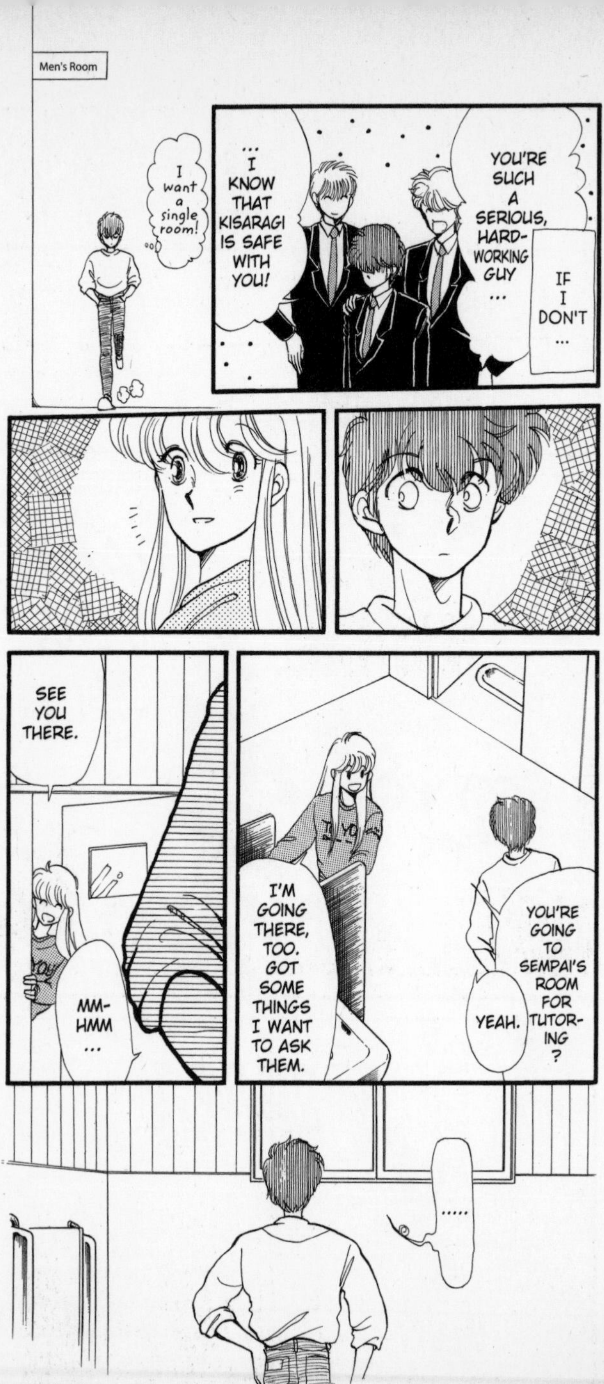
YOU'RE SUCH A SERIOUS, HARD-WORKING GUY ...
IF I DON'T ...
... I KNOW THAT KISARAGI IS SAFE WITH YOU!
Men's Room
I want a single room!
YOU'RE GOING TO SEMPAI'S ROOM FOR TUTORING?
YEAH.
I'M GOING THERE, TOO. GOT SOME THINGS I WANT TO ASK THEM.
SEE YOU THERE.
MM-HMM ...
.....
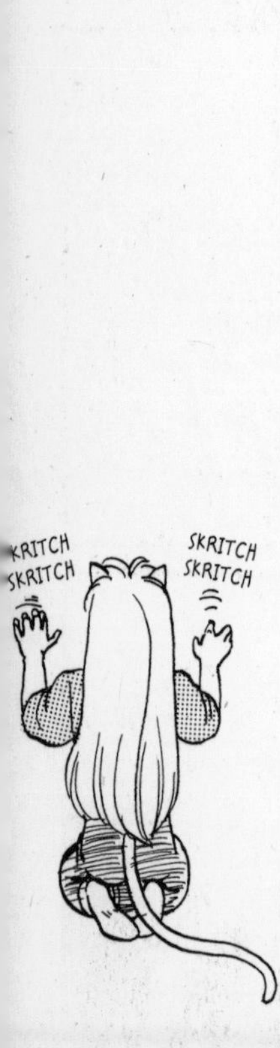
SKRITCH SKRITCH
KRITCH SKRITCH

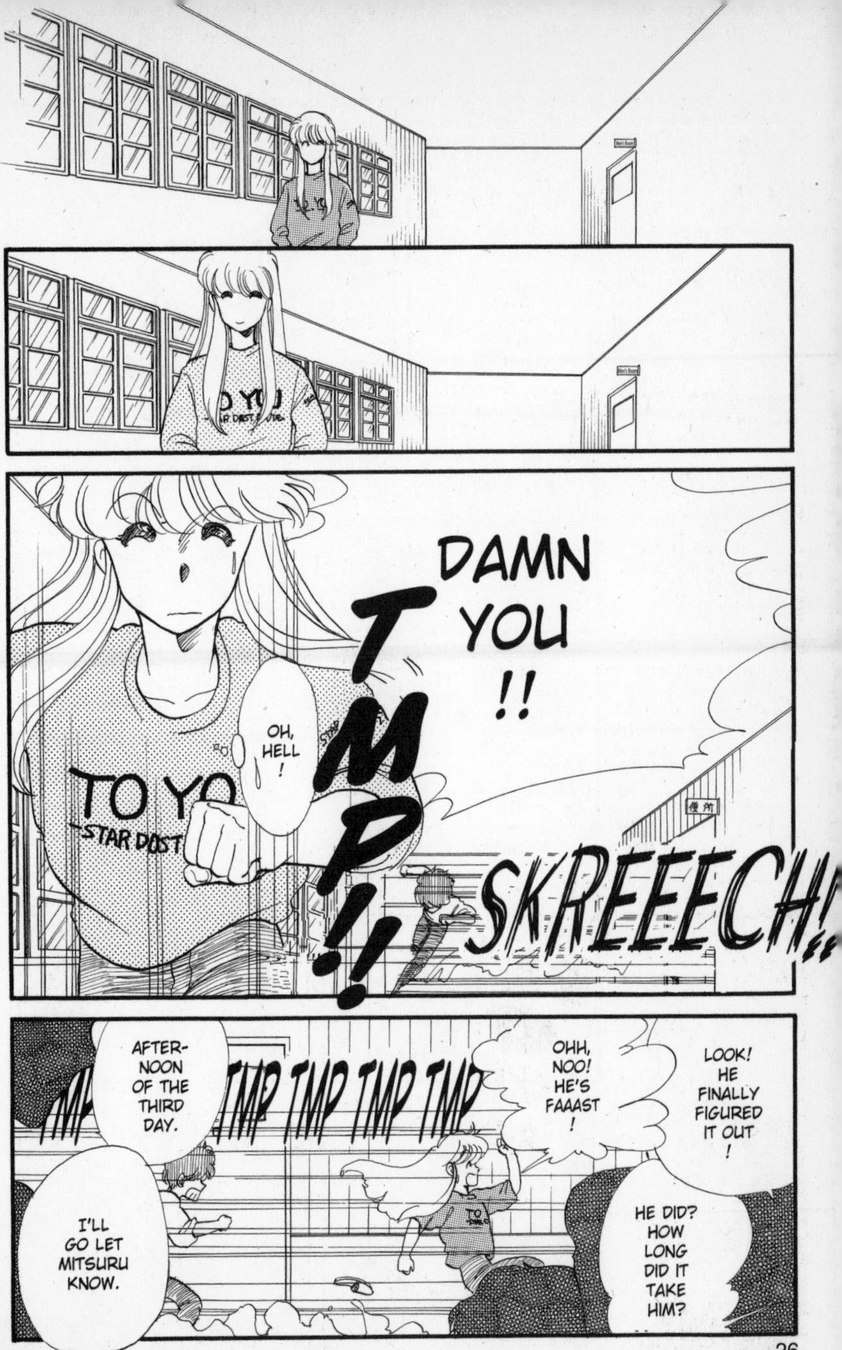
DAMN YOU !!
TMP!!
SKREEECH!!
OH, HELL!
LOOK! HE FINALLY FIGURED IT OUT!
OHH, NOO! HE'S FAAAST!
TMP TMP TMP TMP TMP
AFTERNOON OF THE THIRD DAY.
HE DID? HOW LONG DID IT TAKE HIM?
I'LL GO LET MITSURU KNOW.

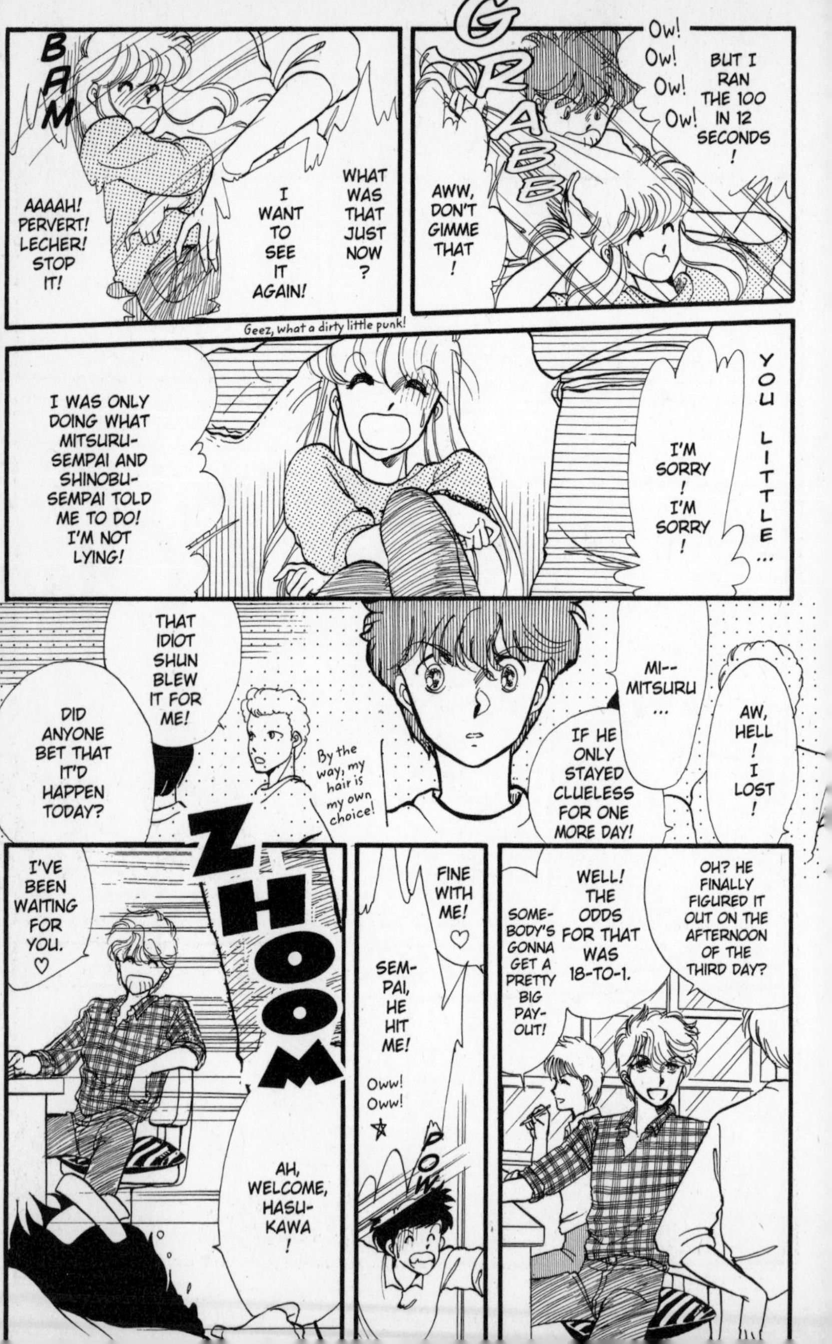
GRABB
Ow! Ow! Ow! Ow!
BUT I RAN THE 100 IN 12 SECONDS!
AWW, DON'T GIMME THAT!
WHAT WAS THAT JUST NOW?
I WANT TO SEE IT AGAIN!
AAAAH! PERVERT! LECHER! STOP IT!
BAM
Geez, what a dirty little punk!
YOU LITTLE...
I'M SORRY! I'M SORRY!
I WAS ONLY DOING WHAT MITSURU-SEMPAI AND SHINOBU-SEMPAI TOLD ME TO DO! I'M NOT LYING!
MI--MITSURU...
AW, HELL! I LOST!
IF HE ONLY STAYED CLUELESS FOR ONE MORE DAY!
THAT IDIOT SHUN BLEW IT FOR ME!
By the way, my hair is my own choice!
DID ANYONE BET THAT IT'D HAPPEN TODAY?
OH? HE FINALLY FIGURED IT OUT ON THE AFTERNOON OF THE THIRD DAY?
WELL! THE ODDS FOR THAT WAS 18-TO-1.
SOME-BODY'S GONNA GET A PRETTY BIG PAY-OUT!
FINE WITH ME! ♡
SEM-PAI, HE HIT ME!
Oww! Oww!
POW
ZHOOM
I'VE BEEN WAITING FOR YOU. ♡
AH, WELCOME, HASU-KAWA!

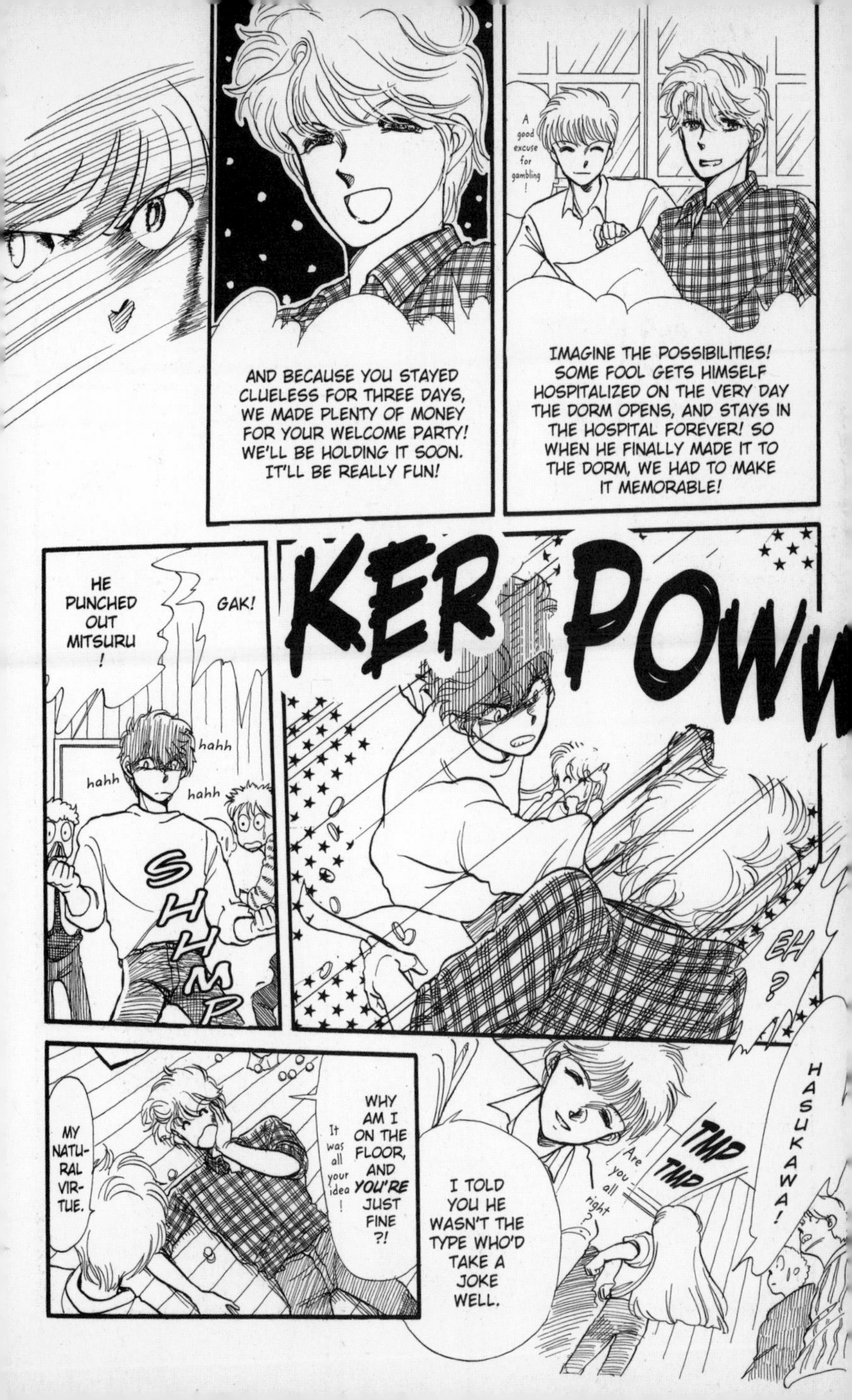
A good excuse for gambling!
IMAGINE THE POSSIBILITIES! SOME FOOL GETS HIMSELF HOSPITALIZED ON THE VERY DAY THE DORM OPENS, AND STAYS IN THE HOSPITAL FOREVER! SO WHEN HE FINALLY MADE IT TO THE DORM, WE HAD TO MAKE IT MEMORABLE!
AND BECAUSE YOU STAYED CLUELESS FOR THREE DAYS, WE MADE PLENTY OF MONEY FOR YOUR WELCOME PARTY! WE'LL BE HOLDING IT SOON. IT'LL BE REALLY FUN!
KER POWW
EH?
GAK!
HE PUNCHED OUT MITSURU!
hahh
hahh
hahh
SHHMP
HASUKAWA!
TMP TMP
Are you all right?
I TOLD YOU HE WASN'T THE TYPE WHO'D TAKE A JOKE WELL.
WHY AM I ON THE FLOOR, AND *YOU'RE* JUST FINE?!
It was all your idea!
MY NATURAL VIRTUE.

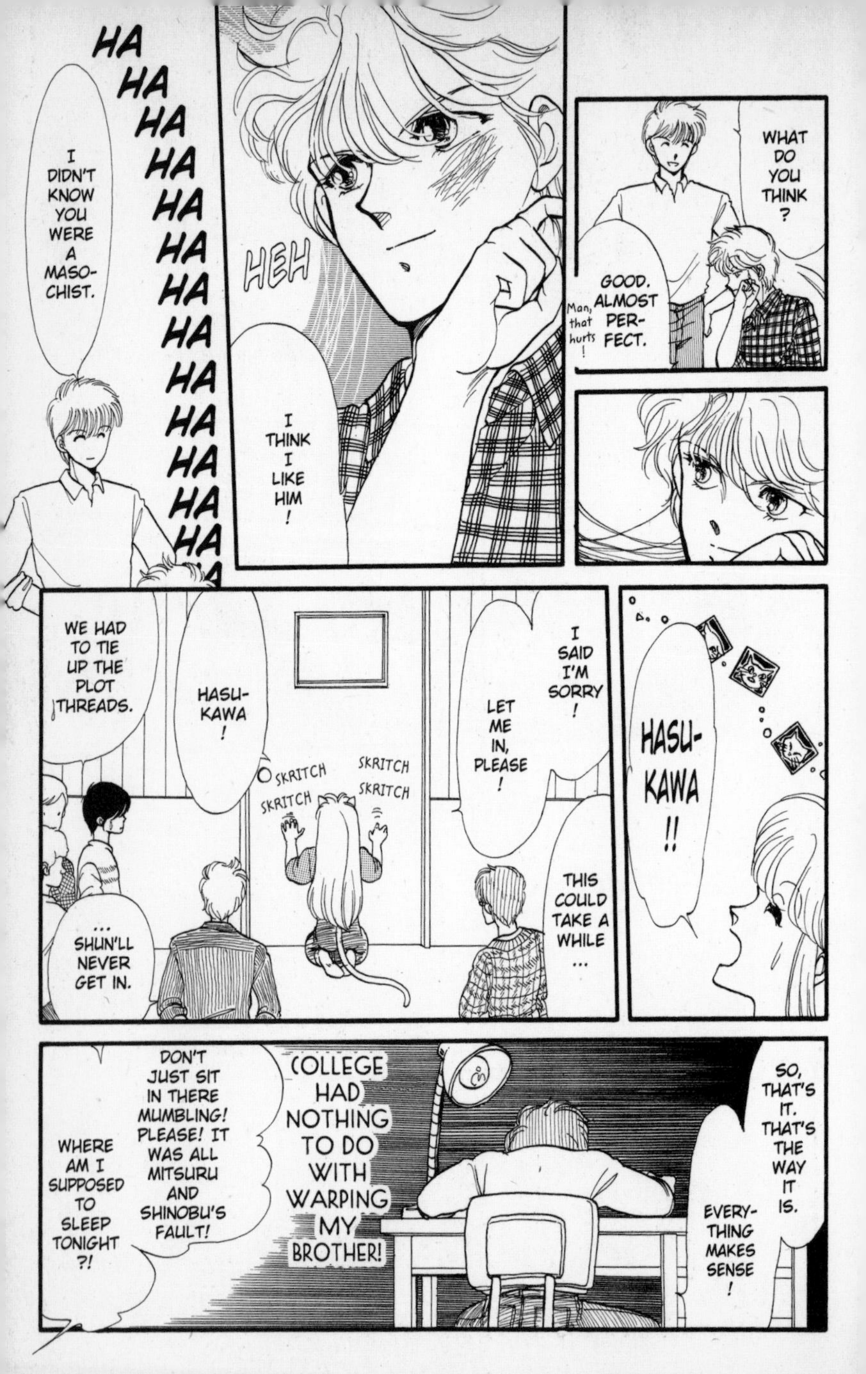
WHAT DO YOU THINK?
GOOD. ALMOST PERFECT.
Man, that hurts!
HEH
I THINK I LIKE HIM!
HA HA HA HA HA HA HA HA HA HA HA HA HA
I DIDN'T KNOW YOU WERE A MASOCHIST.
HASU-KAWA!!
I SAID I'M SORRY!
LET ME IN, PLEASE!
THIS COULD TAKE A WHILE...
SKRITCH SKRITCH
SKRITCH SKRITCH
HASU-KAWA!
WE HAD TO TIE UP THE PLOT THREADS.
...SHUN'LL NEVER GET IN.
SO, THAT'S IT. THAT'S THE WAY IT IS.
EVERYTHING MAKES SENSE!
COLLEGE HAD NOTHING TO DO WITH WARPING MY BROTHER!
DON'T JUST SIT IN THERE MUMBLING! PLEASE! IT WAS ALL MITSURU AND SHINOBU'S FAULT!
WHERE AM I SUPPOSED TO SLEEP TONIGHT?!

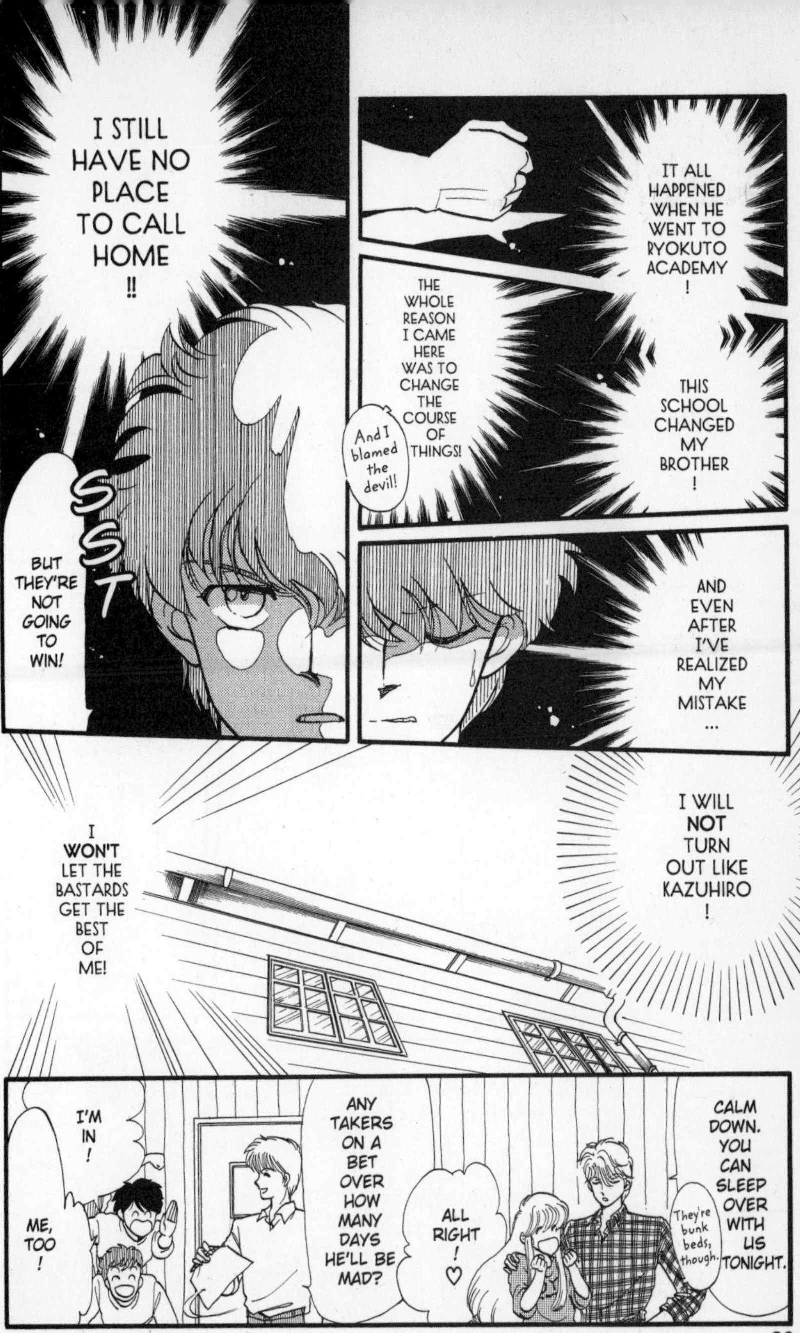
IT ALL HAPPENED WHEN HE WENT TO RYOKUTO ACADEMY!
THIS SCHOOL CHANGED MY BROTHER!
THE WHOLE REASON I CAME HERE WAS TO CHANGE THE COURSE OF THINGS!
And I blamed the devil!
AND EVEN AFTER I'VE REALIZED MY MISTAKE...
I STILL HAVE NO PLACE TO CALL HOME!!
SSST
BUT THEY'RE NOT GOING TO WIN!
I WILL NOT TURN OUT LIKE KAZUHIRO!
I WON'T LET THE BASTARDS GET THE BEST OF ME!
CALM DOWN. YOU CAN SLEEP OVER WITH US TONIGHT.
They're bunk beds, though.
ALL RIGHT! ♡
ANY TAKERS ON A BET OVER HOW MANY DAYS HE'LL BE MAD?
I'M IN!
ME, TOO!

HERE IS GREENWOOD

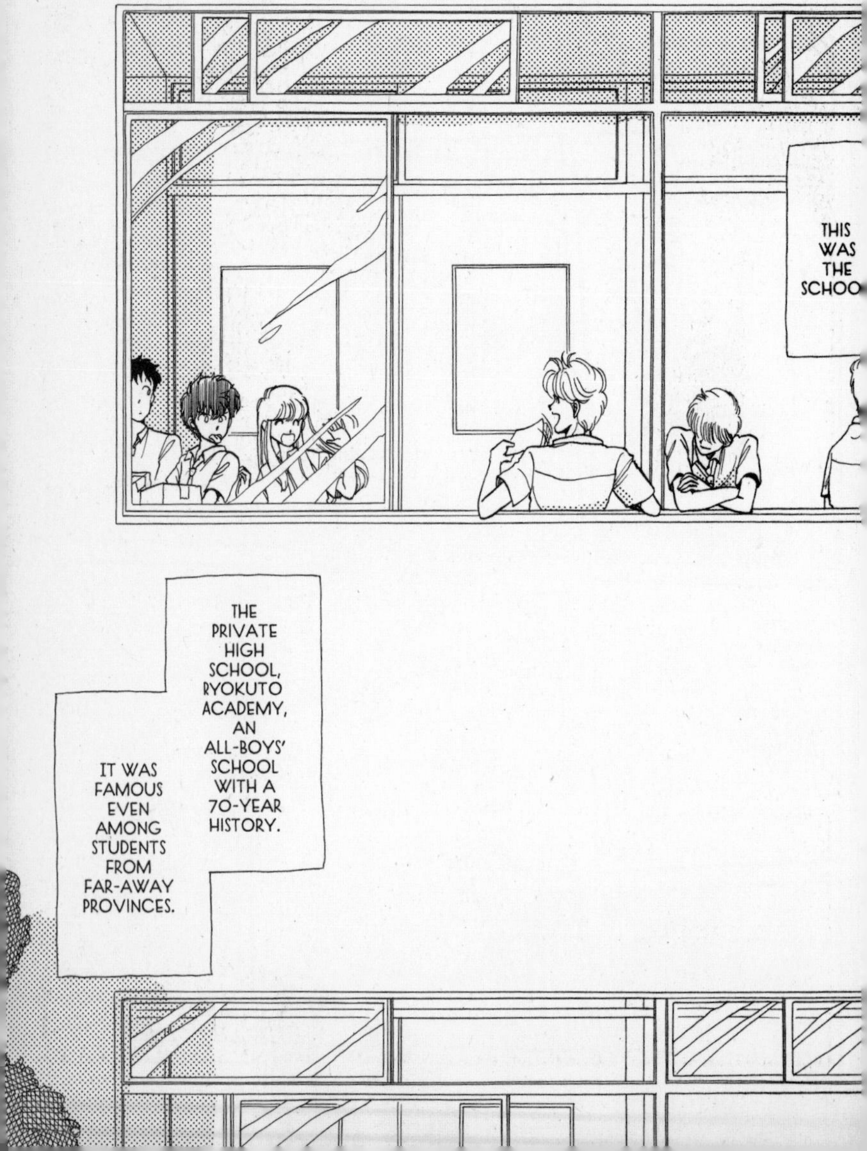
THIS WAS THE SCHOO
THE PRIVATE HIGH SCHOOL, RYOKUTO ACADEMY, AN ALL-BOYS' SCHOOL WITH A 70-YEAR HISTORY.
IT WAS FAMOUS EVEN AMONG STUDENTS FROM FAR-AWAY PROVINCES.

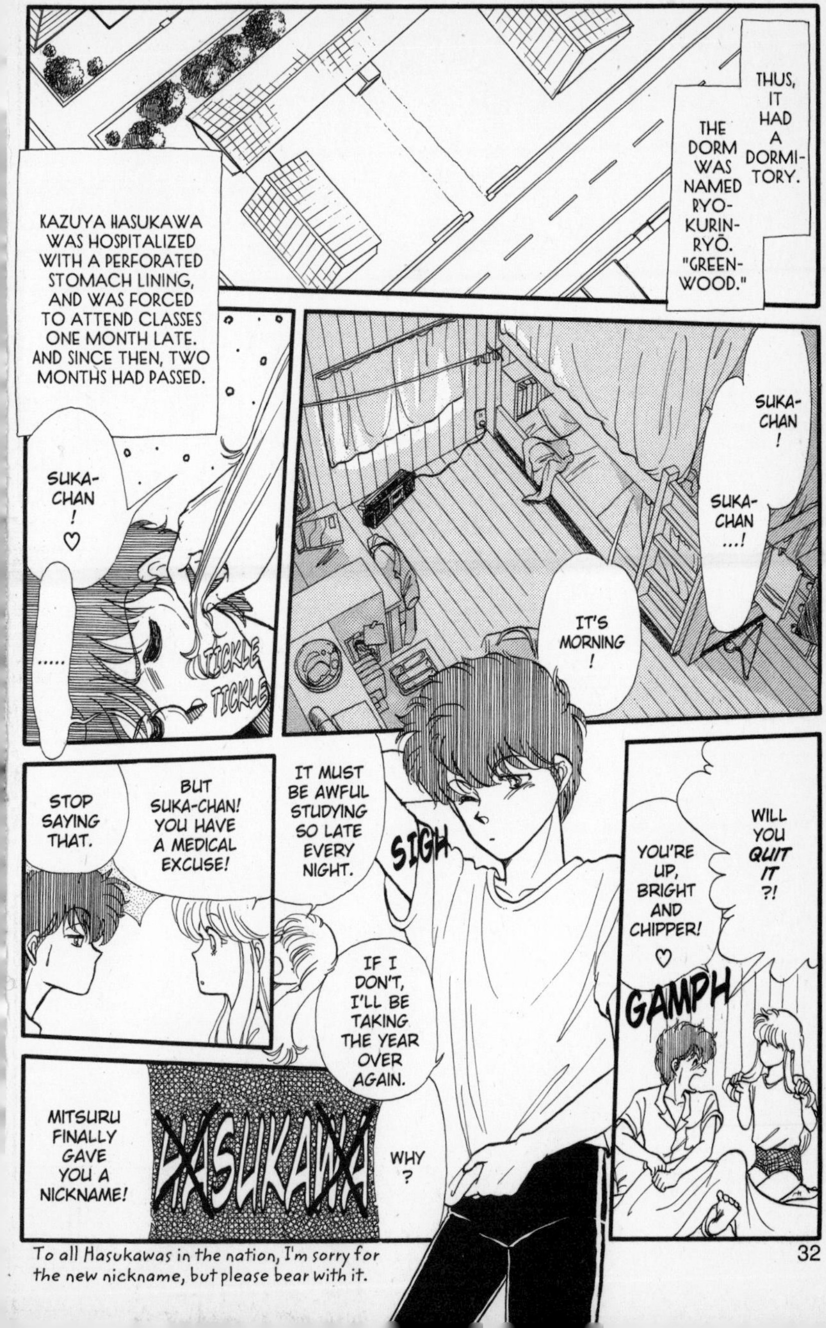
THUS, IT HAD A DORMITORY.
THE DORM WAS NAMED RYO-KURIN-RYŌ. "GREEN-WOOD."
KAZUYA HASUKAWA WAS HOSPITALIZED WITH A PERFORATED STOMACH LINING, AND WAS FORCED TO ATTEND CLASSES ONE MONTH LATE. AND SINCE THEN, TWO MONTHS HAD PASSED.
SUKA-CHAN!
SUKA-CHAN...!
IT'S MORNING!
SUKA-CHAN! ♡
.....
TICKLE TICKLE
WILL YOU QUIT IT?!
YOU'RE UP, BRIGHT AND CHIPPER! ♡
GAMPH
IT MUST BE AWFUL STUDYING SO LATE EVERY NIGHT.
SIGH
IF I DON'T, I'LL BE TAKING THE YEAR OVER AGAIN.
BUT SUKA-CHAN! YOU HAVE A MEDICAL EXCUSE!
STOP SAYING THAT.
WHY?
HASUKAWA
MITSURU FINALLY GAVE YOU A NICKNAME!

To all Hasukawas in the nation, I'm sorry for the new nickname, but please bear with it.

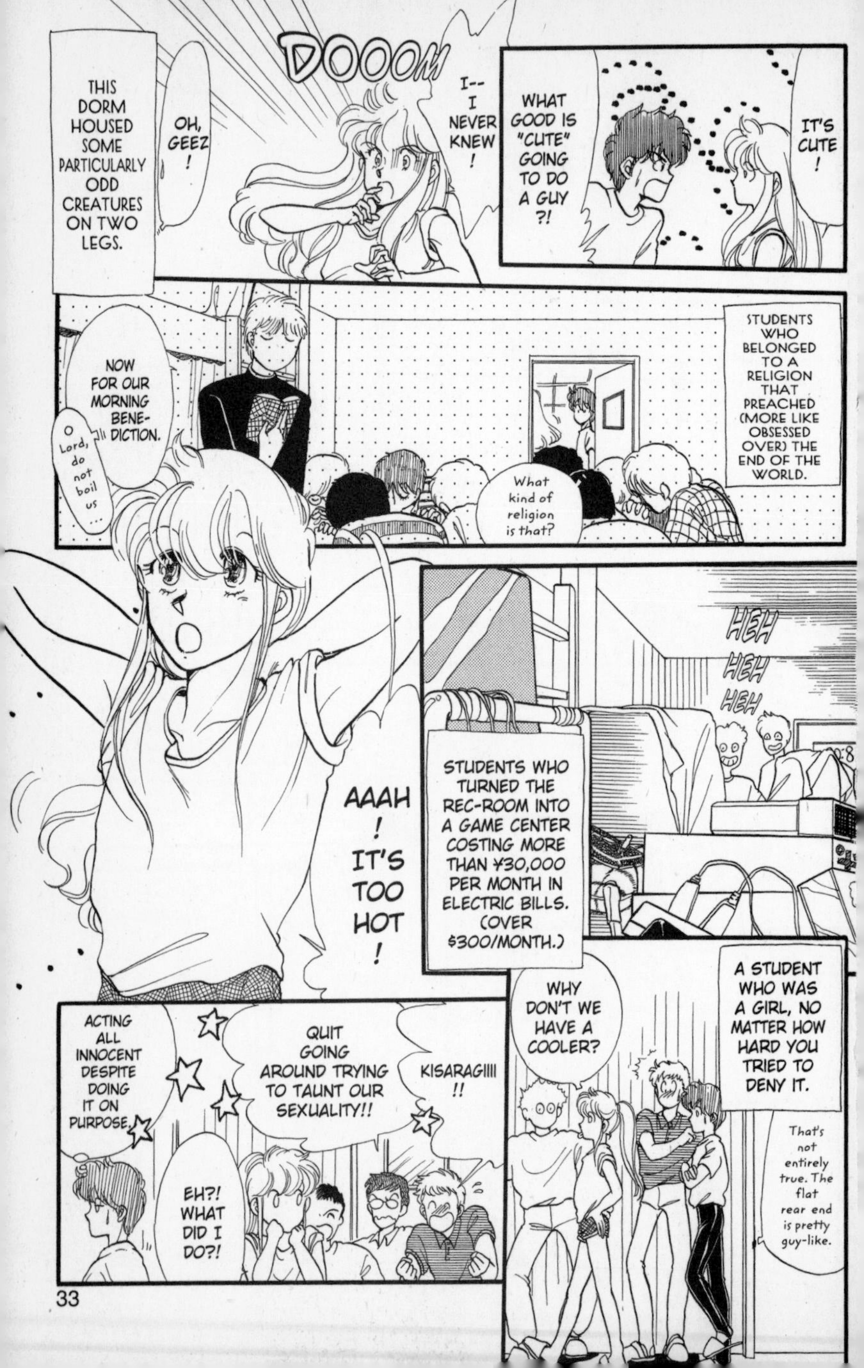
IT'S CUTE!
WHAT GOOD IS "CUTE" GOING TO DO A GUY?!
DOOOM
I-- I NEVER KNEW!
OH, GEEZ!
THIS DORM HOUSED SOME PARTICULARLY ODD CREATURES ON TWO LEGS.
STUDENTS WHO BELONGED TO A RELIGION THAT PREACHED (MORE LIKE OBSESSED OVER) THE END OF THE WORLD.
NOW FOR OUR MORNING BENE-DICTION.
O Lord, do not boil us...
What kind of religion is that?
HEH HEH HEH
STUDENTS WHO TURNED THE REC-ROOM INTO A GAME CENTER COSTING MORE THAN ¥30,000 PER MONTH IN ELECTRIC BILLS. (OVER $300/MONTH.)
A STUDENT WHO WAS A GIRL, NO MATTER HOW HARD YOU TRIED TO DENY IT.
WHY DON'T WE HAVE A COOLER?
That's not entirely true. The flat rear end is pretty guy-like.
AAAH! IT'S TOO HOT!
KISARAGIIII!!
QUIT GOING AROUND TRYING TO TAUNT OUR SEXUALITY!!
ACTING ALL INNOCENT DESPITE DOING IT ON PURPOSE.
EH?! WHAT DID I DO?!

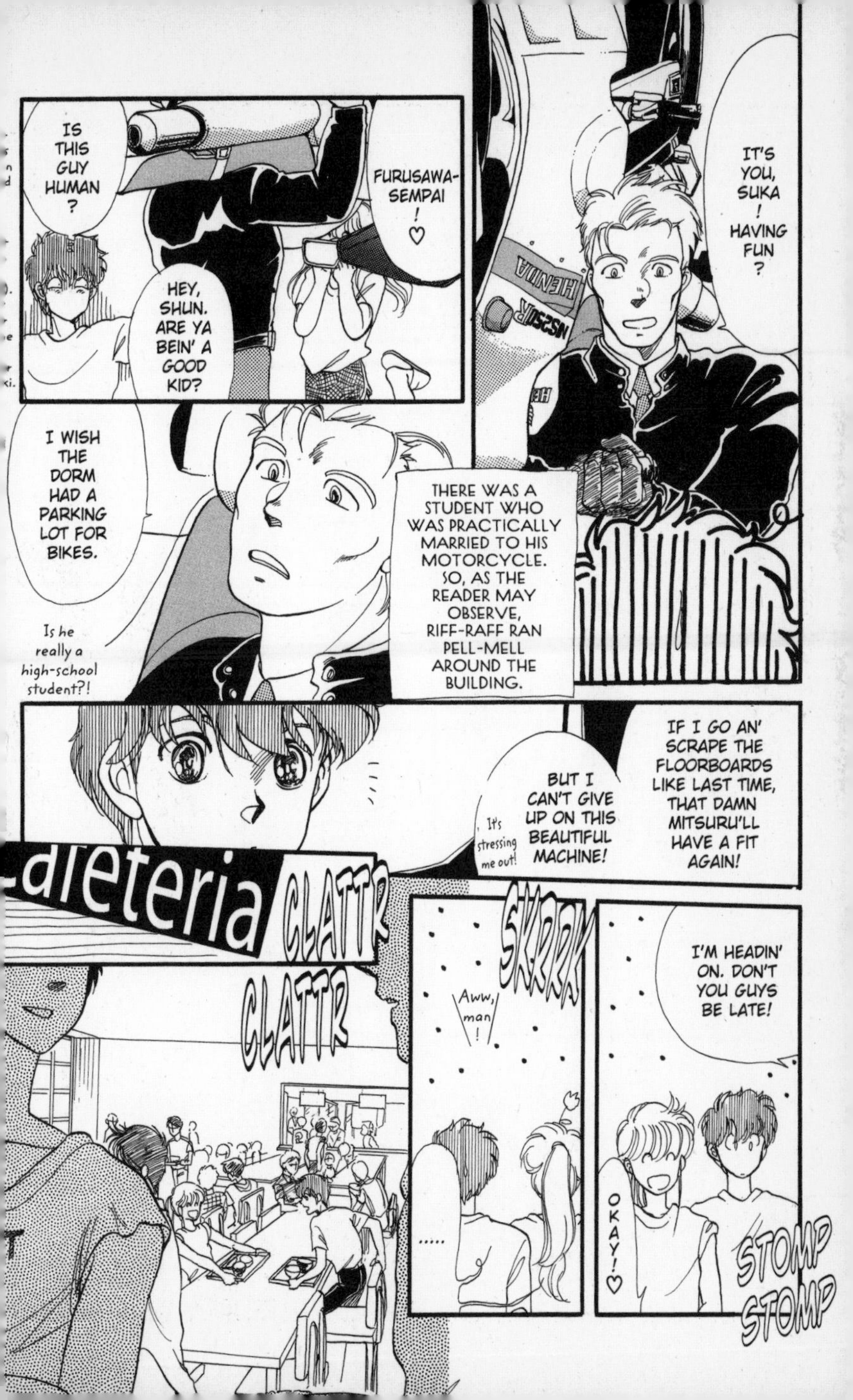

IT'S YOU, SUKA! HAVING FUN?
FURUSAWA-SEMPAI! ♡
IS THIS GUY HUMAN?
HEY, SHUN. ARE YA BEIN' A GOOD KID?
THERE WAS A STUDENT WHO WAS PRACTICALLY MARRIED TO HIS MOTORCYCLE. SO, AS THE READER MAY OBSERVE, RIFF-RAFF RAN PELL-MELL AROUND THE BUILDING.
I WISH THE DORM HAD A PARKING LOT FOR BIKES.
Is he really a high-school student?!
IF I GO AN' SCRAPE THE FLOORBOARDS LIKE LAST TIME, THAT DAMN MITSURU'LL HAVE A FIT AGAIN!
BUT I CAN'T GIVE UP ON THIS BEAUTIFUL MACHINE!
It's stressing me out!
I'M HEADIN' ON. DON'T YOU GUYS BE LATE!
OKAY! ♡
STOMP STOMP
SKRRK
Aww, man!
.....
afeteria
CLATTR CLATTR

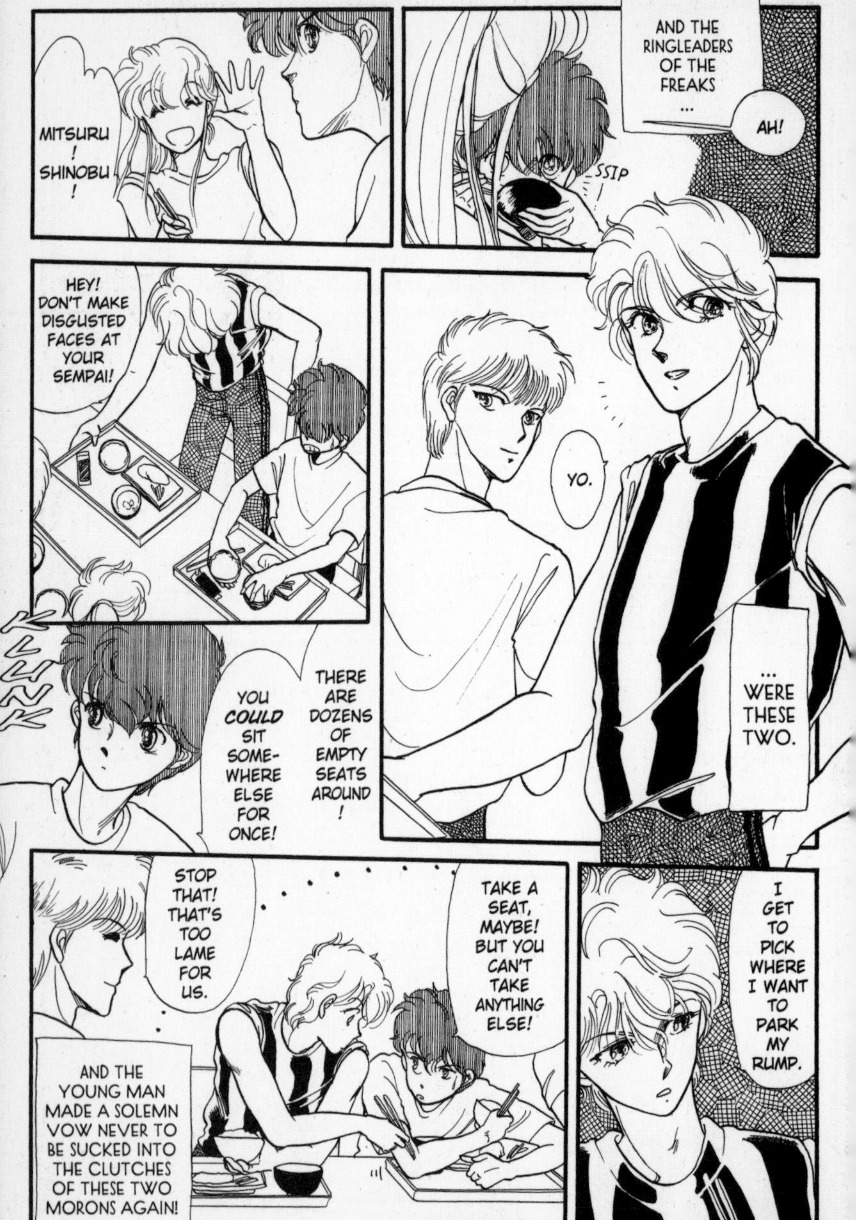
AND THE RINGLEADERS OF THE FREAKS ...
AH!
SSIP
MITSURU! SHINOBU!
YO.
... WERE THESE TWO.
HEY! DON'T MAKE DISGUSTED FACES AT YOUR SEMPAI!
KLUNK
THERE ARE DOZENS OF EMPTY SEATS AROUND!
YOU **COULD** SIT SOMEWHERE ELSE FOR ONCE!
I GET TO PICK WHERE I WANT TO PARK MY RUMP.
TAKE A SEAT, MAYBE! BUT YOU CAN'T TAKE ANYTHING ELSE!
STOP THAT! THAT'S TOO LAME FOR US.
AND THE YOUNG MAN MADE A SOLEMN VOW NEVER TO BE SUCKED INTO THE CLUTCHES OF THESE TWO MORONS AGAIN!

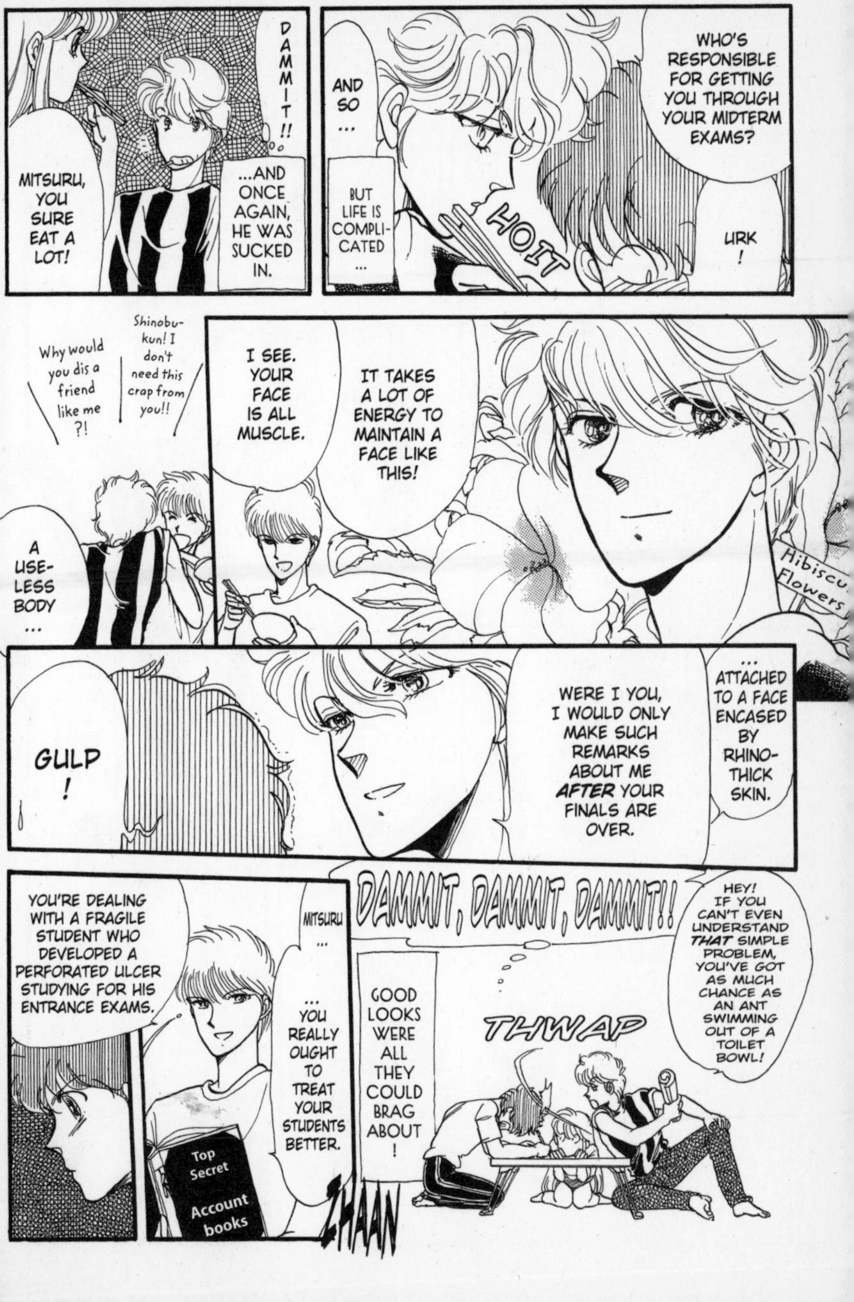

WHO'S RESPONSIBLE FOR GETTING YOU THROUGH YOUR MIDTERM EXAMS?
URK!
HOIT
AND SO ...
BUT LIFE IS COMPLICATED ...
DAMMIT!!
...AND ONCE AGAIN, HE WAS SUCKED IN.
MITSURU, YOU SURE EAT A LOT!
IT TAKES A LOT OF ENERGY TO MAINTAIN A FACE LIKE THIS!
Hibiscu Flowers
I SEE. YOUR FACE IS ALL MUSCLE.
Shinobu-kun! I don't need this crap from you!!
Why would you dis a friend like me ?!
A USELESS BODY ...
... ATTACHED TO A FACE ENCASED BY RHINO-THICK SKIN.
WERE I YOU, I WOULD ONLY MAKE SUCH REMARKS ABOUT ME AFTER YOUR FINALS ARE OVER.
GULP!
HEY! IF YOU CAN'T EVEN UNDERSTAND THAT SIMPLE PROBLEM, YOU'VE GOT AS MUCH CHANCE AS AN ANT SWIMMING OUT OF A TOILET BOWL!
DAMMIT, DAMMIT, DAMMIT!!
THWAP
GOOD LOOKS WERE ALL THEY COULD BRAG ABOUT!
MITSURU ...
... YOU REALLY OUGHT TO TREAT YOUR STUDENTS BETTER.
YOU'RE DEALING WITH A FRAGILE STUDENT WHO DEVELOPED A PERFORATED ULCER STUDYING FOR HIS ENTRANCE EXAMS.
Top Secret Account books
ZHAAN

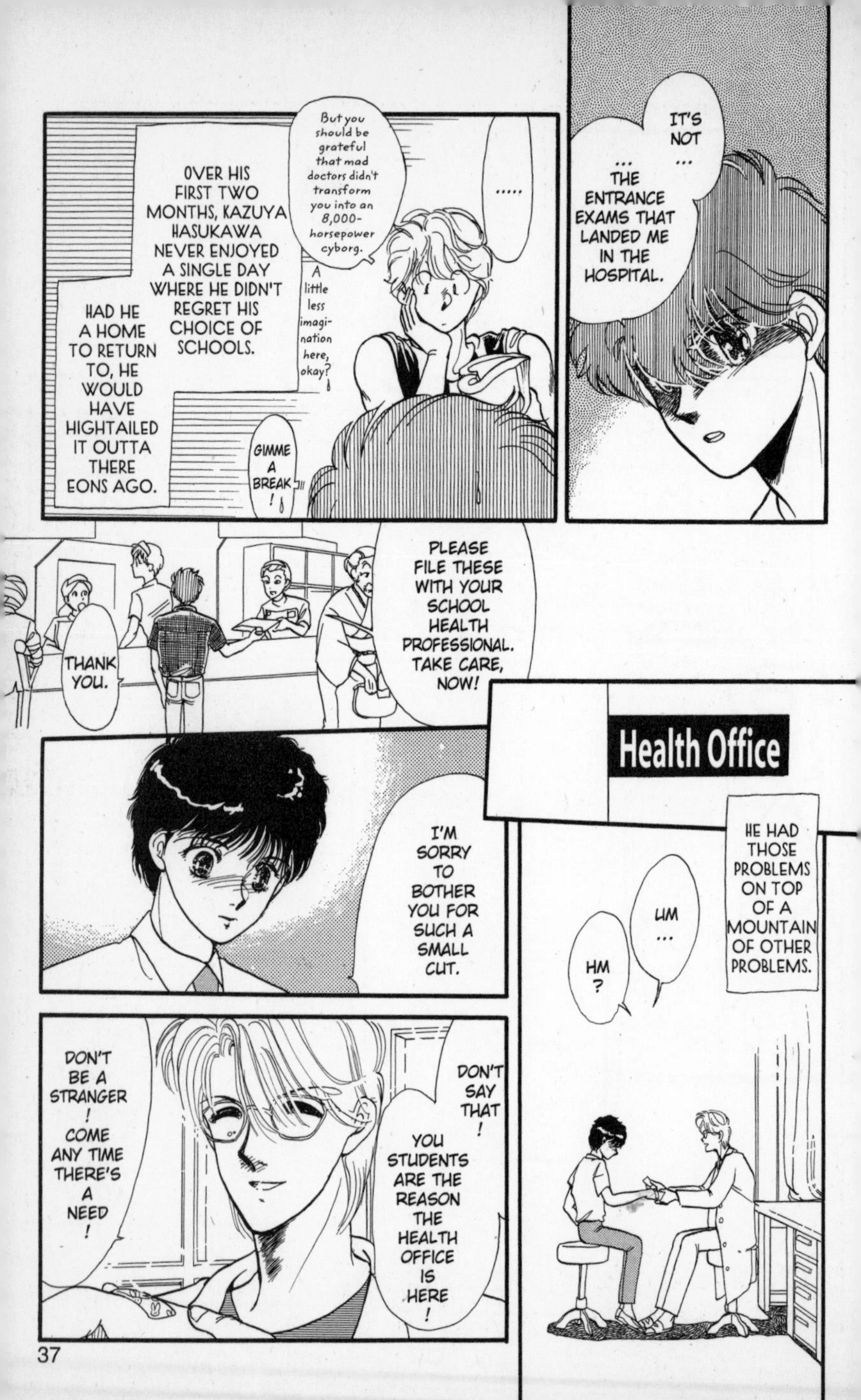
IT'S NOT ... THE ENTRANCE EXAMS THAT LANDED ME IN THE HOSPITAL.
.....
But you should be grateful that mad doctors didn't transform you into an 8,000-horsepower cyborg.
A little less imagination here, okay?
OVER HIS FIRST TWO MONTHS, KAZUYA HASUKAWA NEVER ENJOYED A SINGLE DAY WHERE HE DIDN'T REGRET HIS CHOICE OF SCHOOLS.
HAD HE A HOME TO RETURN TO, HE WOULD HAVE HIGHTAILED IT OUTTA THERE EONS AGO.
GIMME A BREAK!
PLEASE FILE THESE WITH YOUR SCHOOL HEALTH PROFESSIONAL. TAKE CARE, NOW!
THANK YOU.
Health Office
HE HAD THOSE PROBLEMS ON TOP OF A MOUNTAIN OF OTHER PROBLEMS.
UM ...
HM?
I'M SORRY TO BOTHER YOU FOR SUCH A SMALL CUT.
DON'T SAY THAT!
YOU STUDENTS ARE THE REASON THE HEALTH OFFICE IS HERE!
DON'T BE A STRANGER! COME ANY TIME THERE'S A NEED!

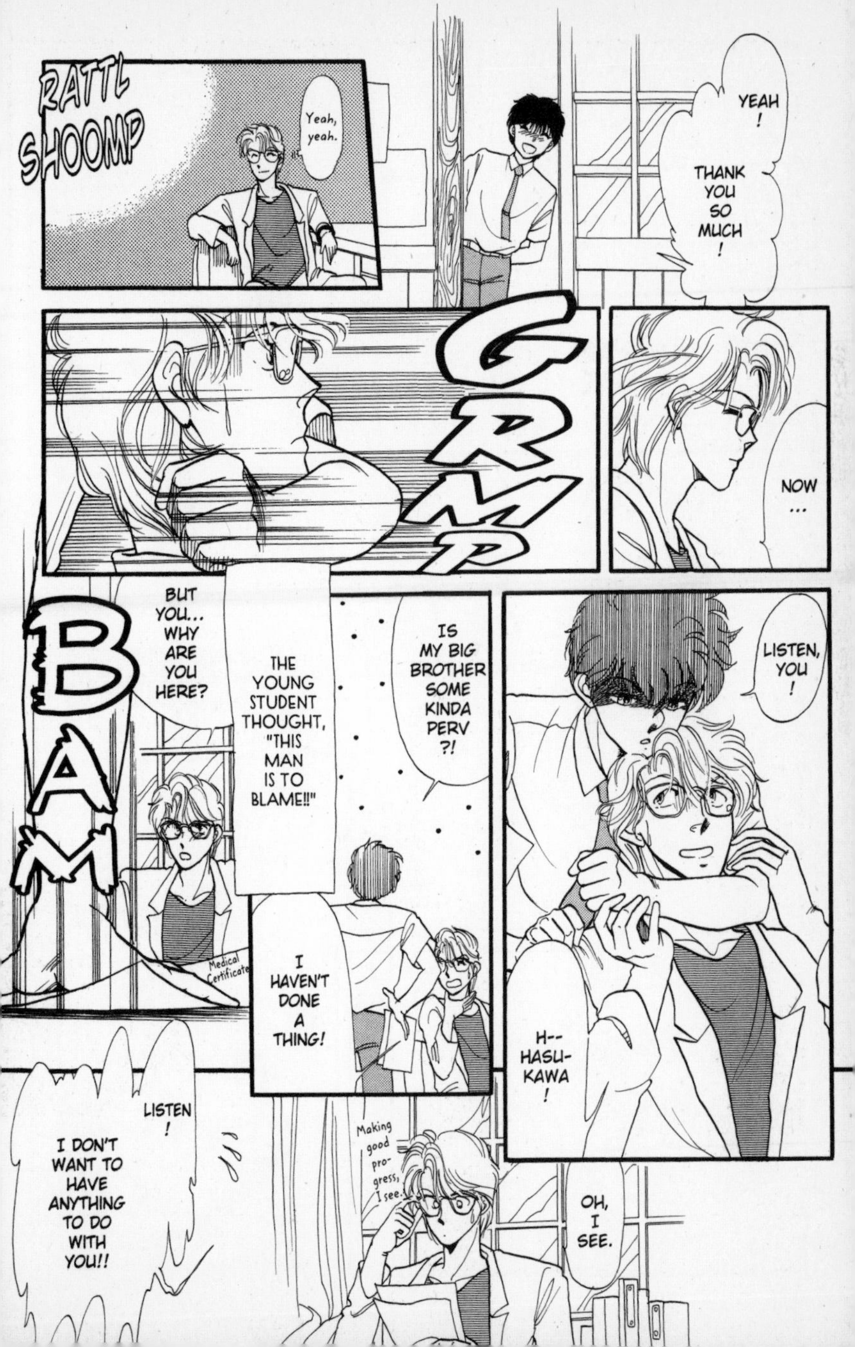
YEAH! THANK YOU SO MUCH!
RATTL SHOOMP
Yeah, yeah.
NOW...
GRMP
LISTEN, YOU!
H--HASU-KAWA!
IS MY BIG BROTHER SOME KINDA PERV?!
THE YOUNG STUDENT THOUGHT, "THIS MAN IS TO BLAME!!"
I HAVEN'T DONE A THING!
BAM
BUT YOU... WHY ARE YOU HERE?
Medical Certificate
OH, I SEE.
Making good progress, I see.
LISTEN! I DON'T WANT TO HAVE ANYTHING TO DO WITH YOU!!

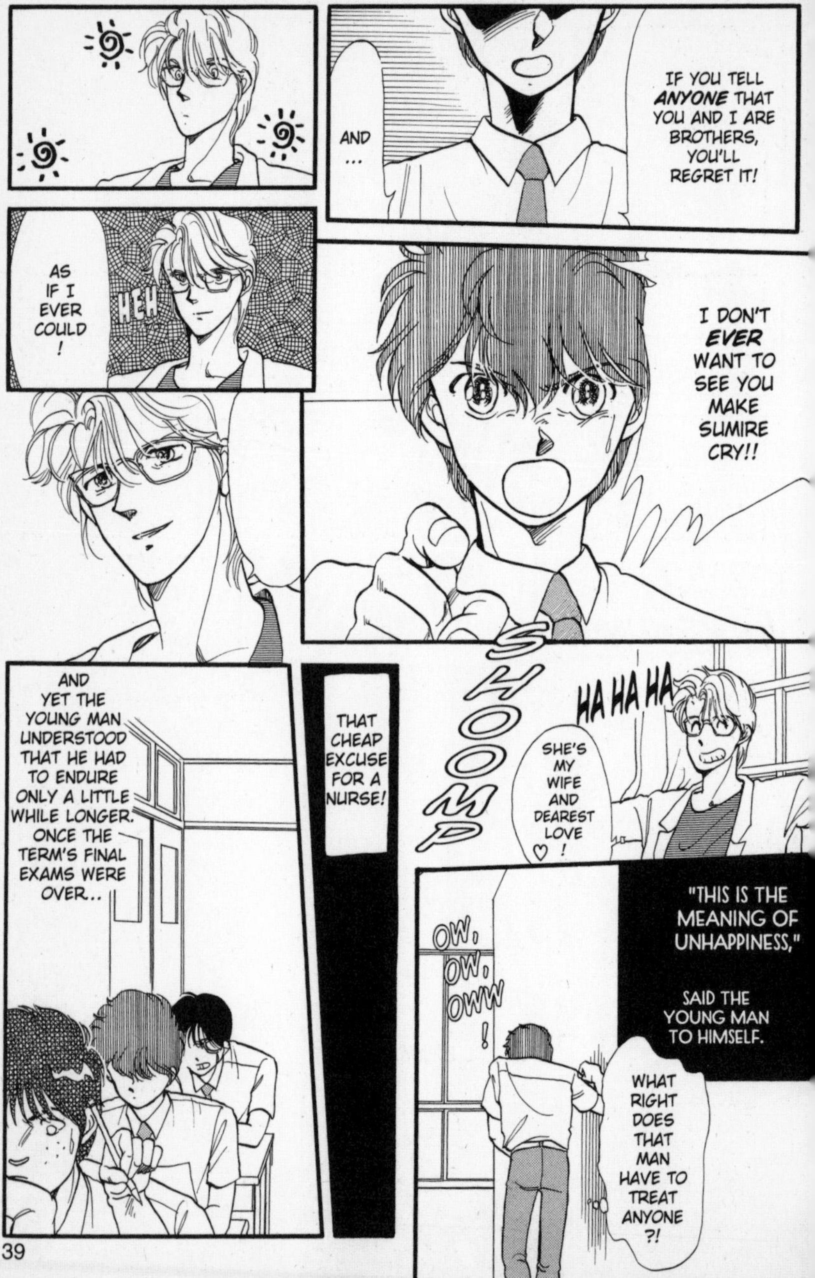
AND ...
IF YOU TELL ANYONE THAT YOU AND I ARE BROTHERS, YOU'LL REGRET IT!
I DON'T EVER WANT TO SEE YOU MAKE SUMIRE CRY!!
AS IF I EVER COULD!
HEH
SHOOMP
HA HA HA
SHE'S MY WIFE AND DEAREST LOVE ♡ !
"THIS IS THE MEANING OF UNHAPPINESS,"
SAID THE YOUNG MAN TO HIMSELF.
OW, OW, OWW!
WHAT RIGHT DOES THAT MAN HAVE TO TREAT ANYONE ?!
THAT CHEAP EXCUSE FOR A NURSE!
AND YET THE YOUNG MAN UNDERSTOOD THAT HE HAD TO ENDURE ONLY A LITTLE WHILE LONGER. ONCE THE TERM'S FINAL EXAMS WERE OVER..

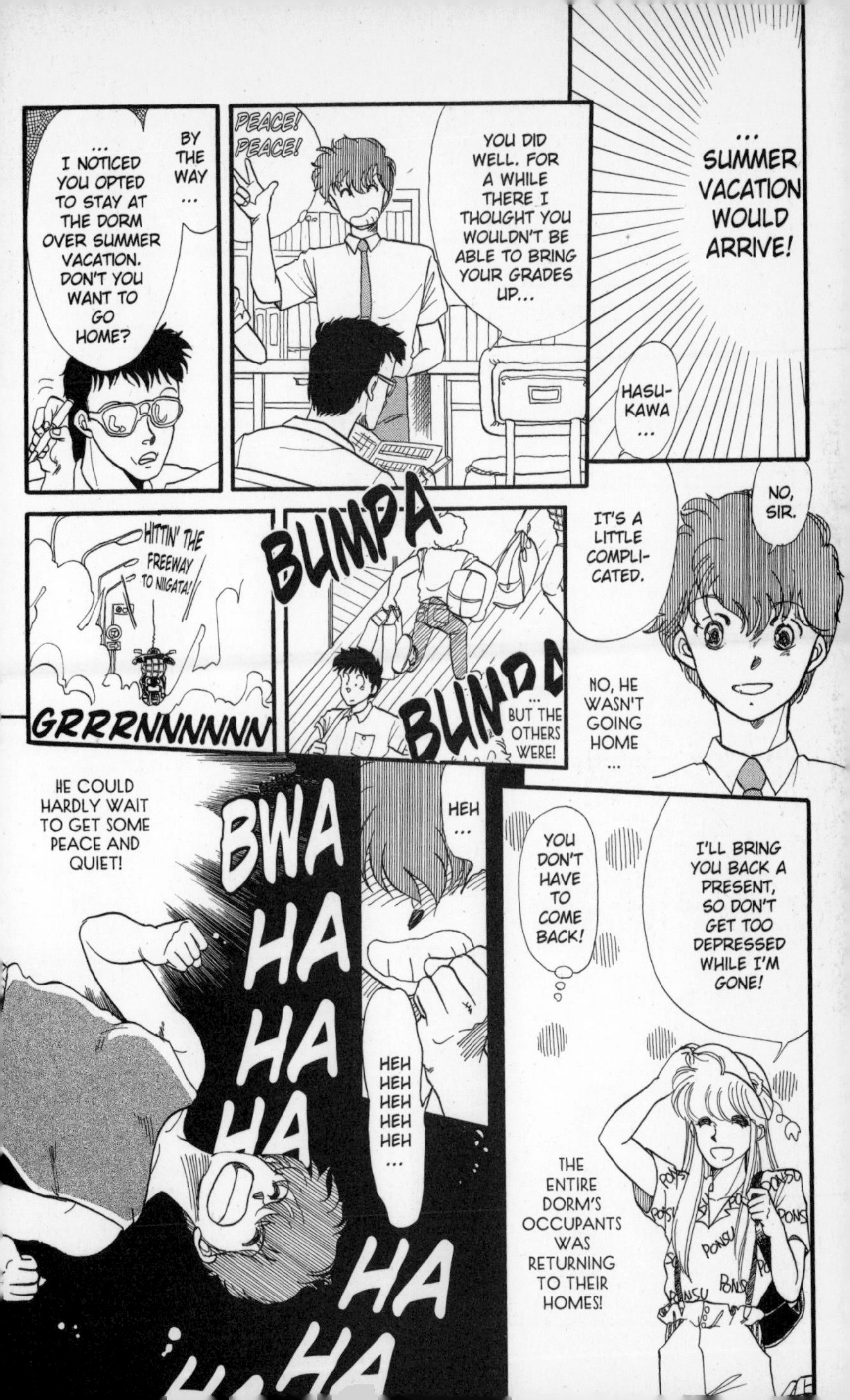
... SUMMER VACATION WOULD ARRIVE!
HASU-KAWA ...
PEACE! PEACE!
YOU DID WELL. FOR A WHILE THERE I THOUGHT YOU WOULDN'T BE ABLE TO BRING YOUR GRADES UP...
BY THE WAY ...
... I NOTICED YOU OPTED TO STAY AT THE DORM OVER SUMMER VACATION. DON'T YOU WANT TO GO HOME?
NO, SIR.
IT'S A LITTLE COMPLICATED.
NO, HE WASN'T GOING HOME ...
BUMPA
BUMD
... BUT THE OTHERS WERE!
HITTIN' THE FREEWAY TO NIIGATA!
GRRRNNNNNNN
I'LL BRING YOU BACK A PRESENT, SO DON'T GET TOO DEPRESSED WHILE I'M GONE!
YOU DON'T HAVE TO COME BACK!
THE ENTIRE DORM'S OCCUPANTS WAS RETURNING TO THEIR HOMES!
HEH ...
HEH HEH HEH HEH HEH ...
BWA HA HA HA HA HA
HE COULD HARDLY WAIT TO GET SOME PEACE AND QUIET!

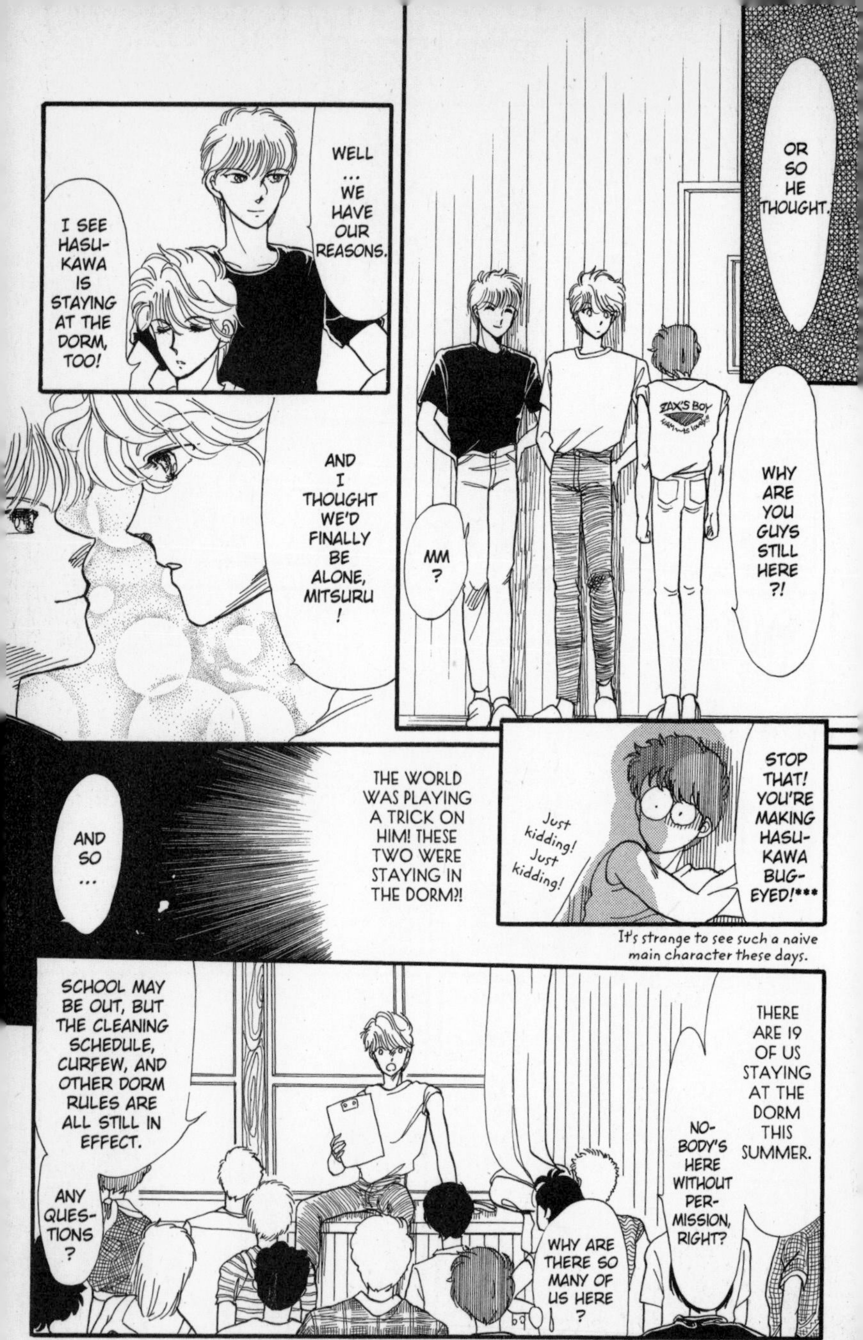
OR SO HE THOUGHT.
WHY ARE YOU GUYS STILL HERE?!
MM?
WELL ... WE HAVE OUR REASONS.
I SEE HASUKAWA IS STAYING AT THE DORM, TOO!
AND I THOUGHT WE'D FINALLY BE ALONE, MITSURU!
ZAX'S BOY
STOP THAT! YOU'RE MAKING HASUKAWA BUG-EYED!***
Just kidding! Just kidding!
THE WORLD WAS PLAYING A TRICK ON HIM! THESE TWO WERE STAYING IN THE DORM?!
AND SO ...
It's strange to see such a naive main character these days.
THERE ARE 19 OF US STAYING AT THE DORM THIS SUMMER.
NOBODY'S HERE WITHOUT PERMISSION, RIGHT?
WHY ARE THERE SO MANY OF US HERE?
SCHOOL MAY BE OUT, BUT THE CLEANING SCHEDULE, CURFEW, AND OTHER DORM RULES ARE ALL STILL IN EFFECT.
ANY QUESTIONS?

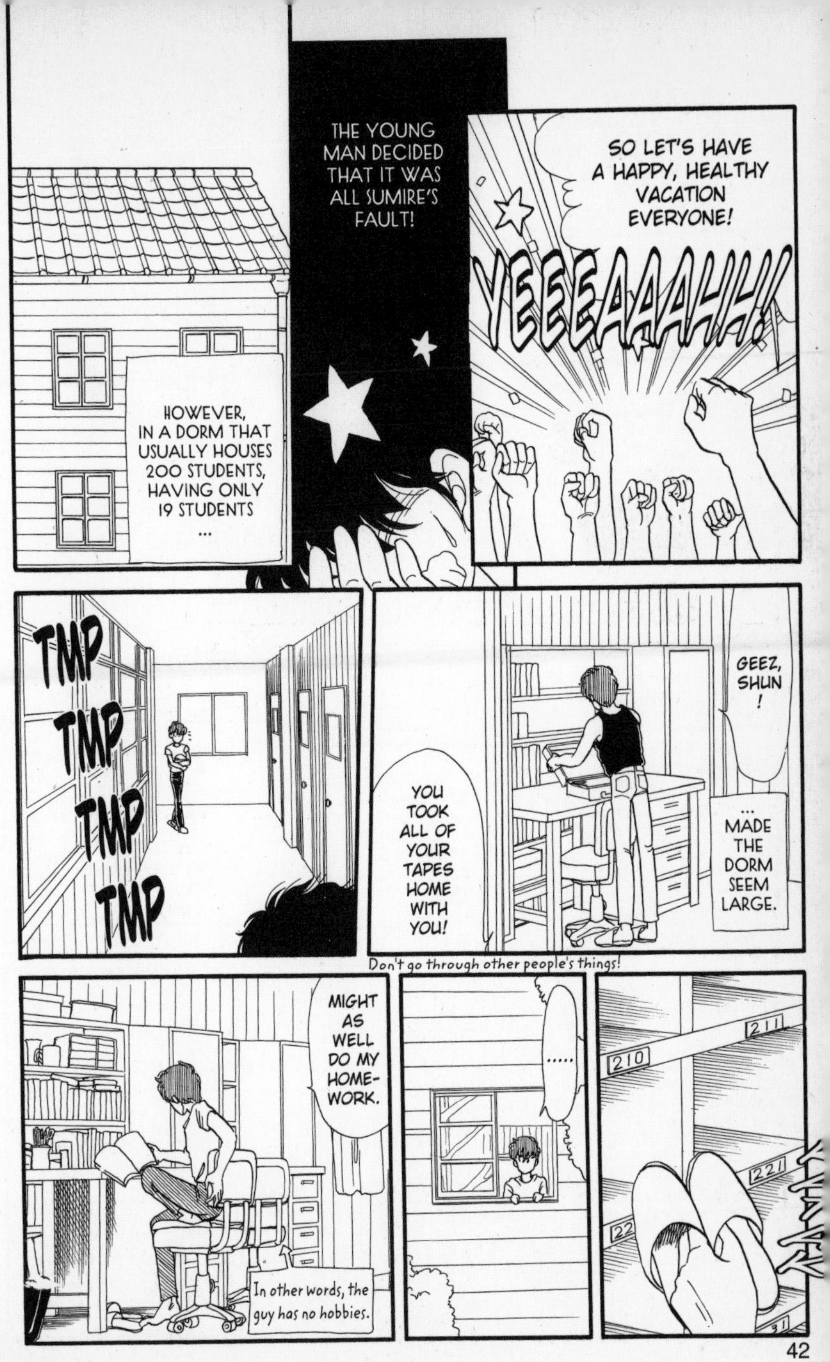
SO LET'S HAVE A HAPPY, HEALTHY VACATION EVERYONE!
YEEEAAAHH!!
THE YOUNG MAN DECIDED THAT IT WAS ALL SUMIRE'S FAULT!
HOWEVER, IN A DORM THAT USUALLY HOUSES 200 STUDENTS, HAVING ONLY 19 STUDENTS ...
GEEZ, SHUN!
... MADE THE DORM SEEM LARGE.
YOU TOOK ALL OF YOUR TAPES HOME WITH YOU!
TMP TMP TMP TMP
Don't go through other people's things!
211
210
221
.....
MIGHT AS WELL DO MY HOME-WORK.
In other words, the guy has no hobbies.

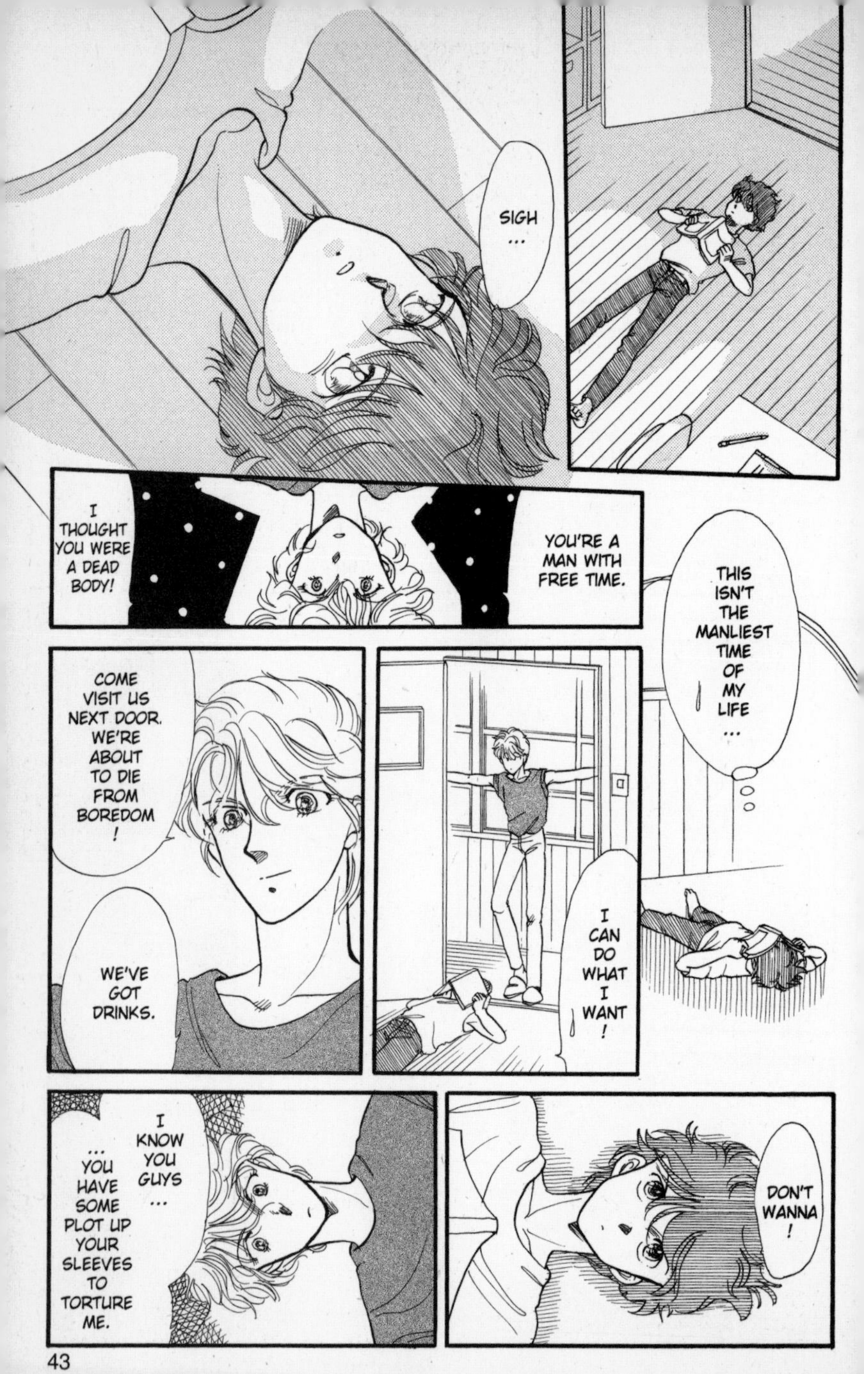
SIGH ...
THIS ISN'T THE MANLIEST TIME OF MY LIFE ...
YOU'RE A MAN WITH FREE TIME.
I THOUGHT YOU WERE A DEAD BODY!
I CAN DO WHAT I WANT!
COME VISIT US NEXT DOOR. WE'RE ABOUT TO DIE FROM BOREDOM!
WE'VE GOT DRINKS.
DON'T WANNA!
I KNOW YOU GUYS ...
... YOU HAVE SOME PLOT UP YOUR SLEEVES TO TORTURE ME.

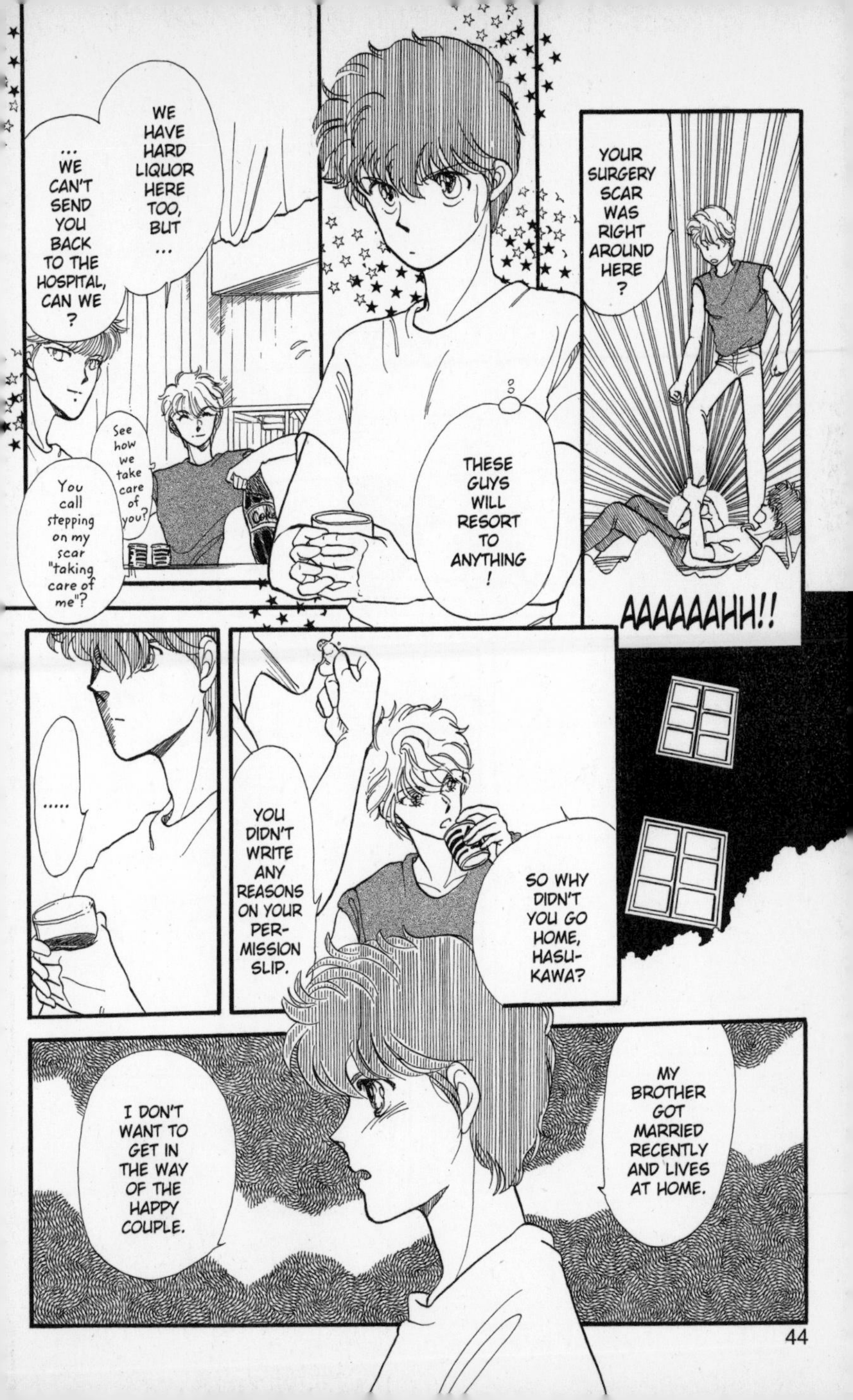
YOUR SURGERY SCAR WAS RIGHT AROUND HERE?
AAAAAAHH!!
THESE GUYS WILL RESORT TO ANYTHING!
WE HAVE HARD LIQUOR HERE TOO, BUT...
...WE CAN'T SEND YOU BACK TO THE HOSPITAL, CAN WE?
See how we take care of you?
You call stepping on my scar "taking care of me"?
SO WHY DIDN'T YOU GO HOME, HASUKAWA?
YOU DIDN'T WRITE ANY REASONS ON YOUR PER-MISSION SLIP.
.....
MY BROTHER GOT MARRIED RECENTLY AND LIVES AT HOME.
I DON'T WANT TO GET IN THE WAY OF THE HAPPY COUPLE.

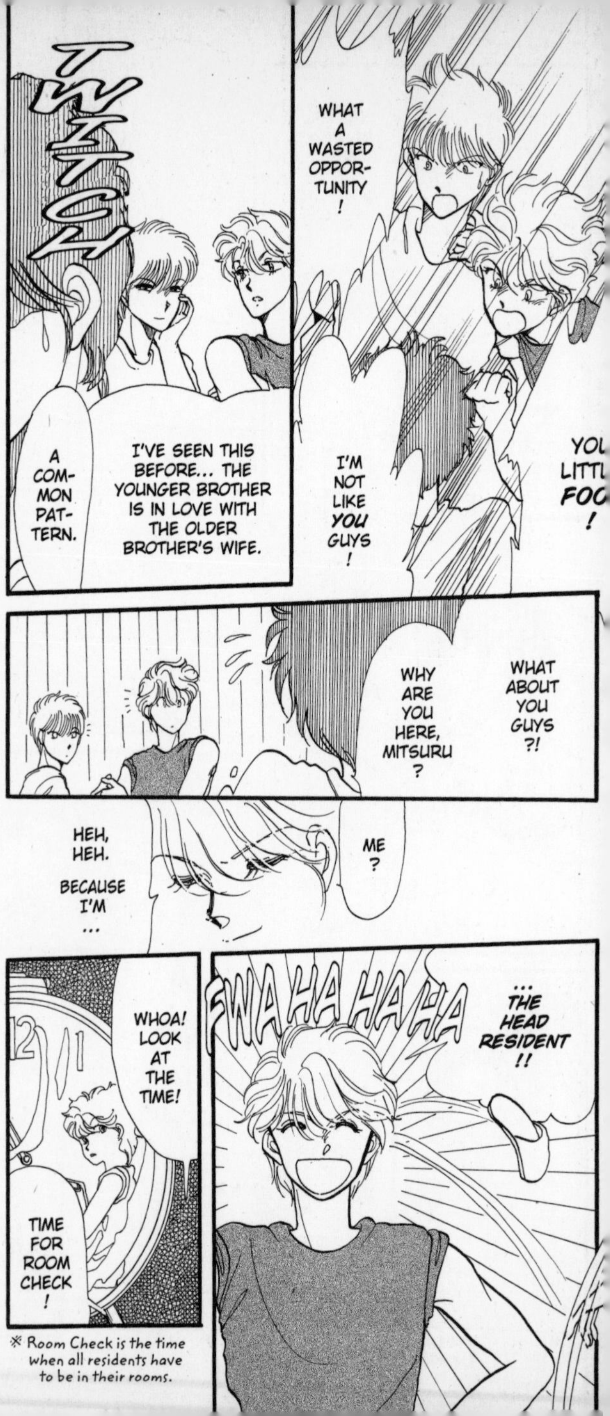
WHAT A WASTED OPPOR-TUNITY!
YOU LITTL FOO !
I'M NOT LIKE YOU GUYS!
TWITCH
I'VE SEEN THIS BEFORE... THE YOUNGER BROTHER IS IN LOVE WITH THE OLDER BROTHER'S WIFE.
A COM-MON PAT-TERN.
WHAT ABOUT YOU GUYS?!
WHY ARE YOU HERE, MITSURU?
ME?
HEH, HEH.
BECAUSE I'M ...
... THE HEAD RESIDENT!!
FWA HA HA HA HA
WHOA! LOOK AT THE TIME!
TIME FOR ROOM CHECK!

※ Room Check is the time when all residents have to be in their rooms.

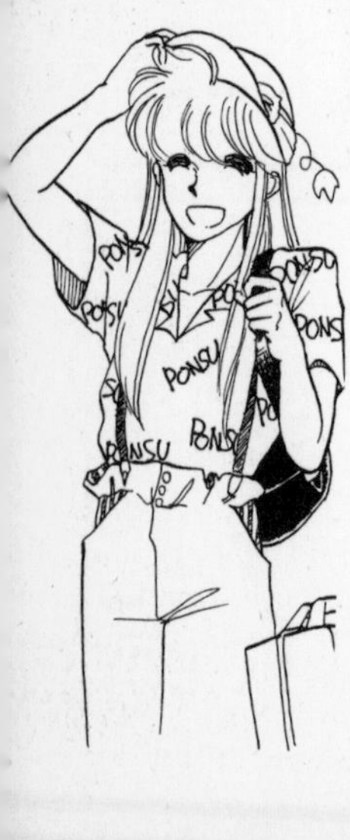

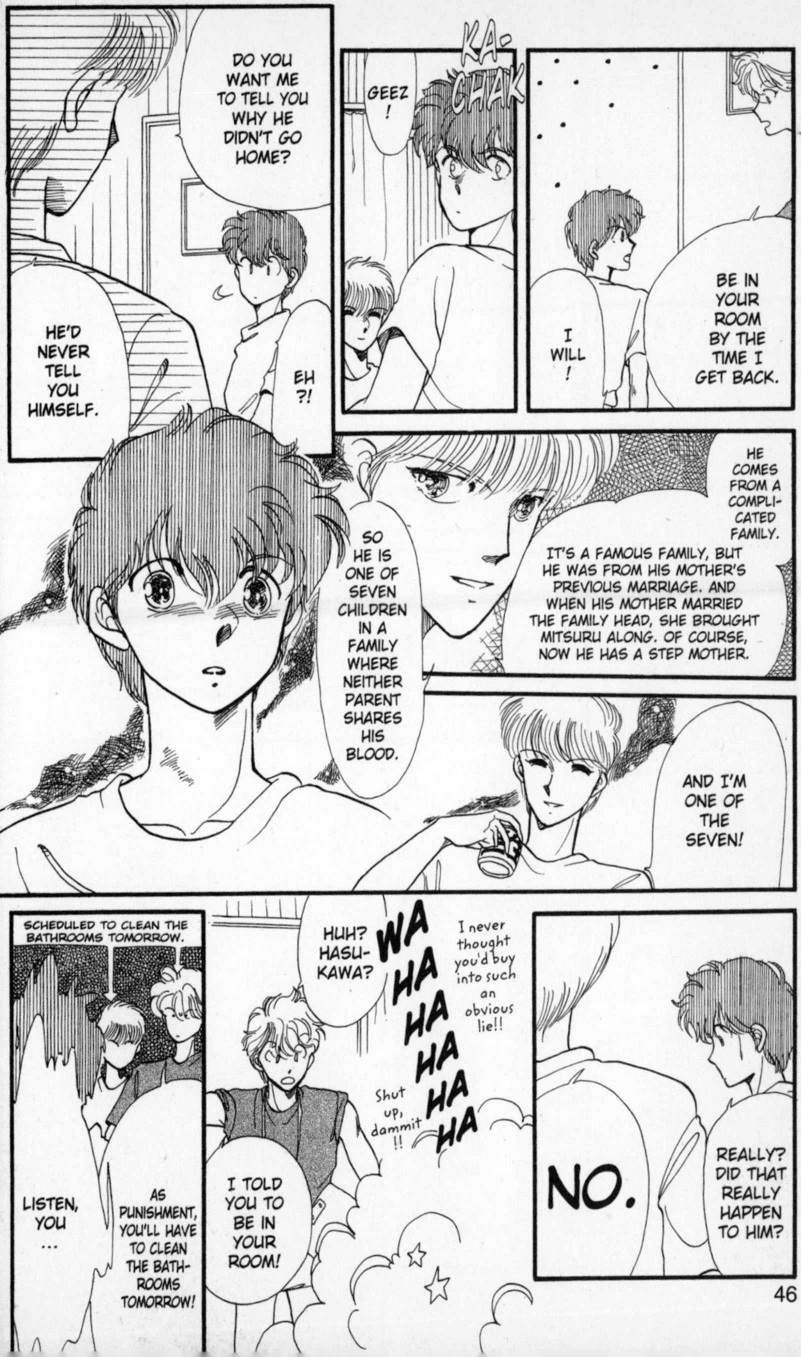

BE IN YOUR ROOM BY THE TIME I GET BACK.
I WILL!
KA-CHAK
GEEZ!
DO YOU WANT ME TO TELL YOU WHY HE DIDN'T GO HOME?
EH?!
HE'D NEVER TELL YOU HIMSELF.
HE COMES FROM A COMPLI-CATED FAMILY.
IT'S A FAMOUS FAMILY, BUT HE WAS FROM HIS MOTHER'S PREVIOUS MARRIAGE. AND WHEN HIS MOTHER MARRIED THE FAMILY HEAD, SHE BROUGHT MITSURU ALONG. OF COURSE, NOW HE HAS A STEP MOTHER.
SO HE IS ONE OF SEVEN CHILDREN IN A FAMILY WHERE NEITHER PARENT SHARES HIS BLOOD.
AND I'M ONE OF THE SEVEN!
REALLY? DID THAT REALLY HAPPEN TO HIM?
NO.
HUH? HASU-KAWA?
WA HA HA HA HA HA HA
I never thought you'd buy into such an obvious lie!!
Shut up, dammit!!
I TOLD YOU TO BE IN YOUR ROOM!
AS PUNISHMENT, YOU'LL HAVE TO CLEAN THE BATH-ROOMS TOMORROW!
LISTEN, YOU...
SCHEDULED TO CLEAN THE BATHROOMS TOMORROW.

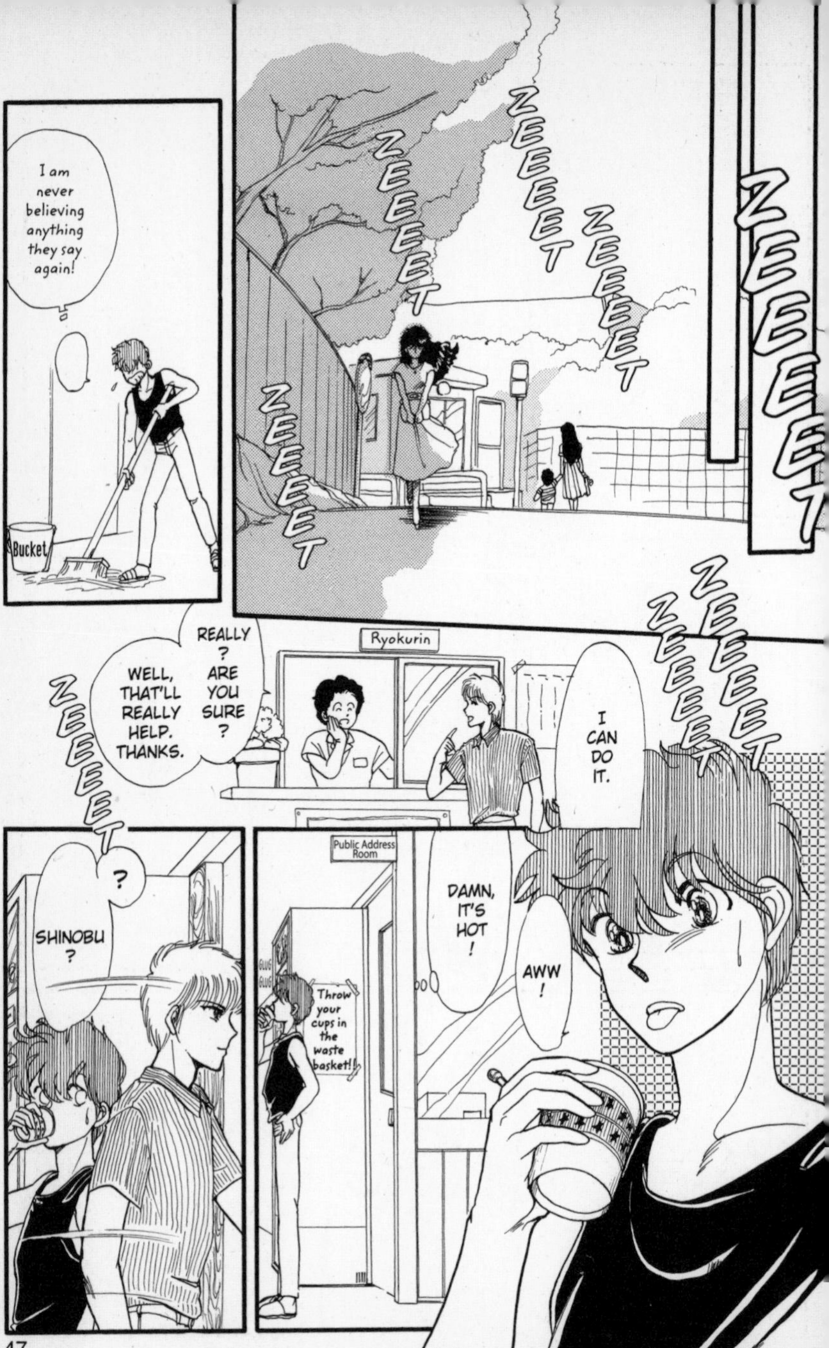
ZEEEEET
ZEEEEET
ZEEEEET
ZEEEET
ZEEEEET
I am never believing anything they say again!
Bucket
ZEEEEET
ZEEEEET
I CAN DO IT.
Ryokurin
REALLY? ARE YOU SURE?
WELL, THAT'LL REALLY HELP. THANKS.
ZEEEEET
AWW!
DAMN, IT'S HOT!
Public Address Room
GLUG GLUG
Throw your cups in the waste basket!!
?
SHINOBU?

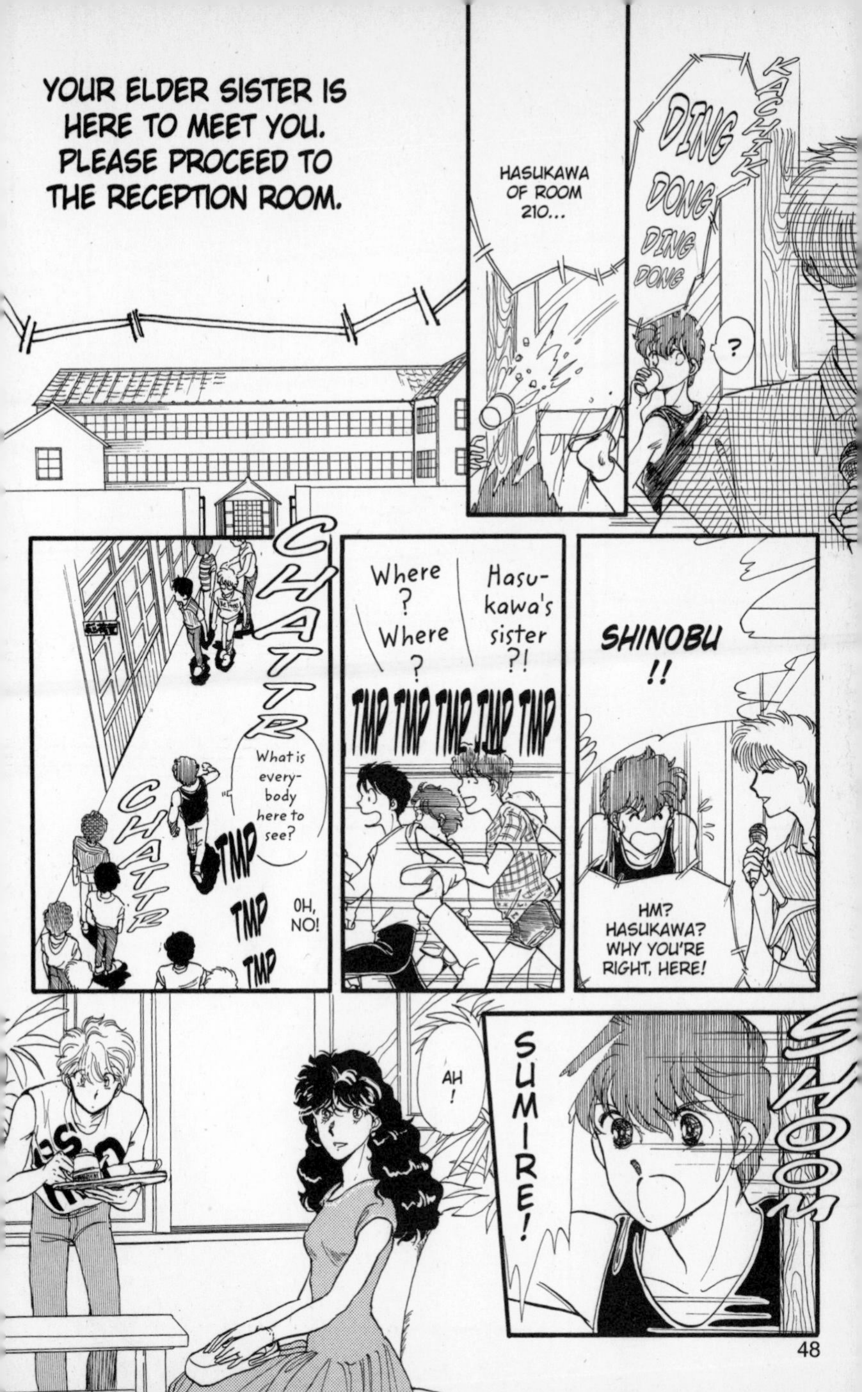
KACHIK
DING DONG DING DONG
?
HASUKAWA OF ROOM 210...
YOUR ELDER SISTER IS HERE TO MEET YOU. PLEASE PROCEED TO THE RECEPTION ROOM.
SHINOBU!!
HM? HASUKAWA? WHY YOU'RE RIGHT, HERE!
Hasu-kawa's sister?!
Where? Where?
TMP TMP TMP TMP TMP
CHATTR
What is every-body here to see?
TMP
TMP
TMP
OH, NO!
CHATTR
SHOOM
SUMIRE!
AH!

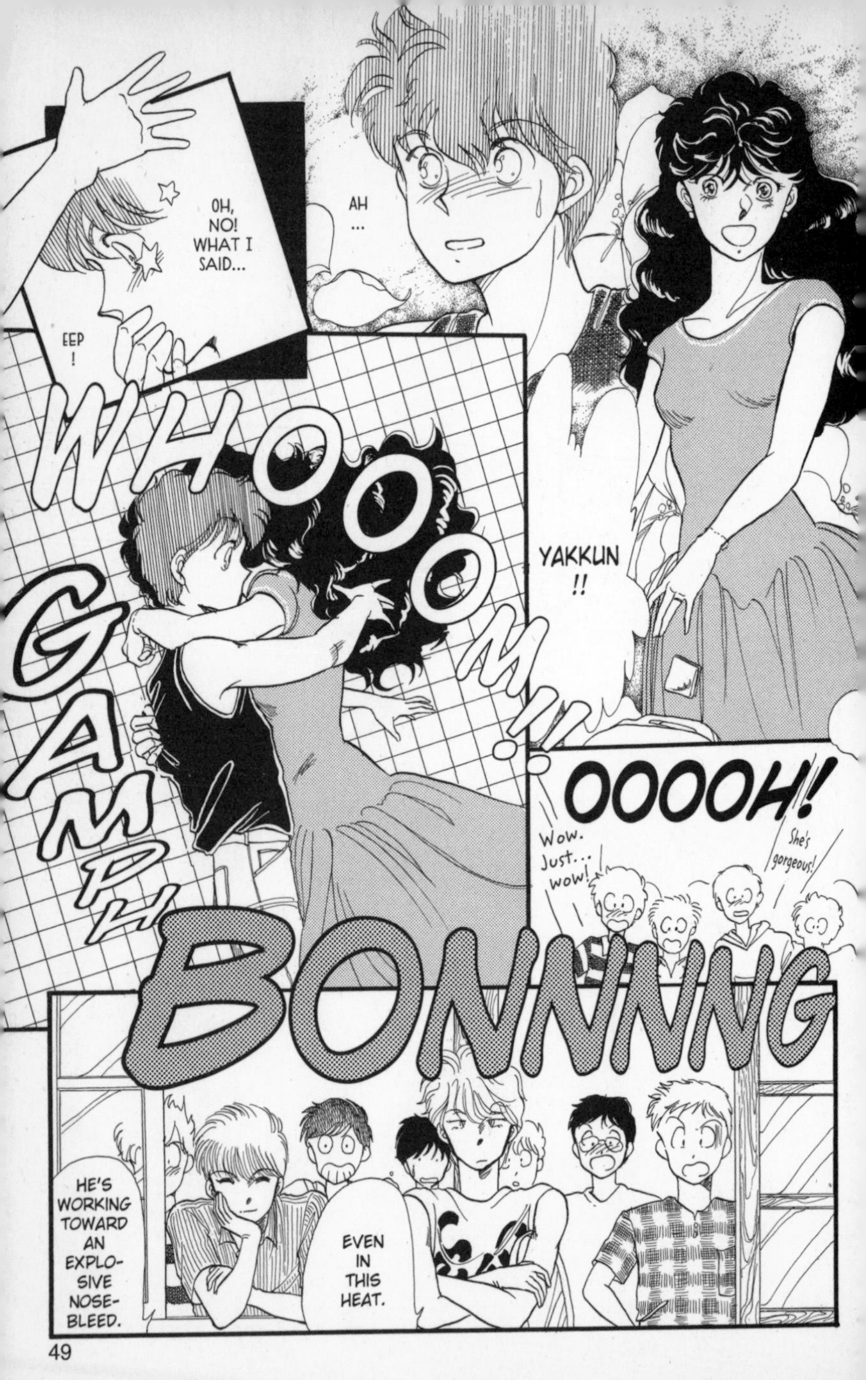
YAKKUN!!
AH ...
OH, NO! WHAT I SAID...
EEP!
WHOOOOM!!!
GAMPH
OOOOH!
She's gorgeous!
Wow. Just... wow!
BONNNG
EVEN IN THIS HEAT.
HE'S WORKING TOWARD AN EXPLO-SIVE NOSE-BLEED.

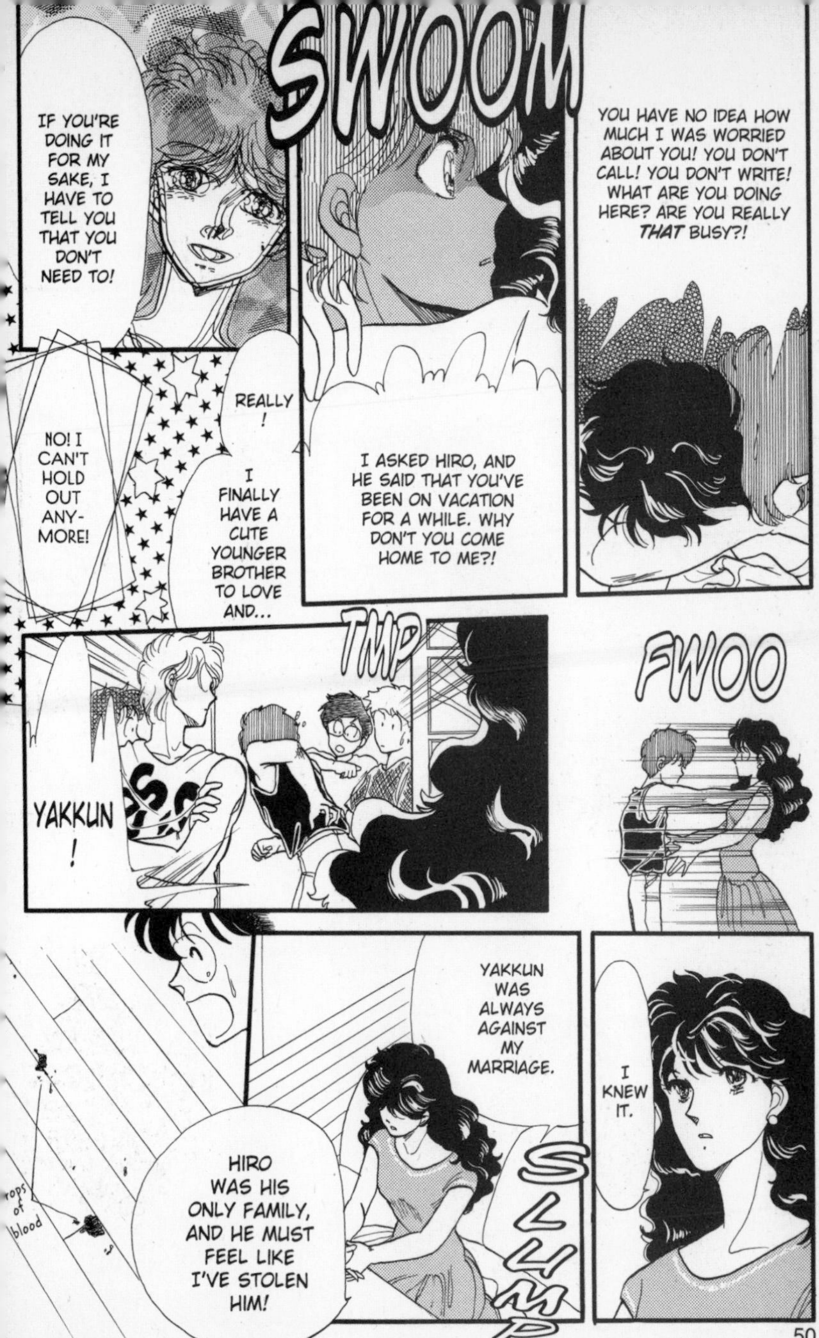

YOU HAVE NO IDEA HOW MUCH I WAS WORRIED ABOUT YOU! YOU DON'T CALL! YOU DON'T WRITE! WHAT ARE YOU DOING HERE? ARE YOU REALLY *THAT* BUSY?!
SWOOM
I ASKED HIRO, AND HE SAID THAT YOU'VE BEEN ON VACATION FOR A WHILE. WHY DON'T YOU COME HOME TO ME?!
IF YOU'RE DOING IT FOR MY SAKE, I HAVE TO TELL YOU THAT YOU DON'T NEED TO!
REALLY!
I FINALLY HAVE A CUTE YOUNGER BROTHER TO LOVE AND...
NO! I CAN'T HOLD OUT ANY-MORE!
FWOO
TMP
YAKKUN!
I KNEW IT.
YAKKUN WAS ALWAYS AGAINST MY MARRIAGE.
SLUMP
HIRO WAS HIS ONLY FAMILY, AND HE MUST FEEL LIKE I'VE STOLEN HIM!
rops of blood

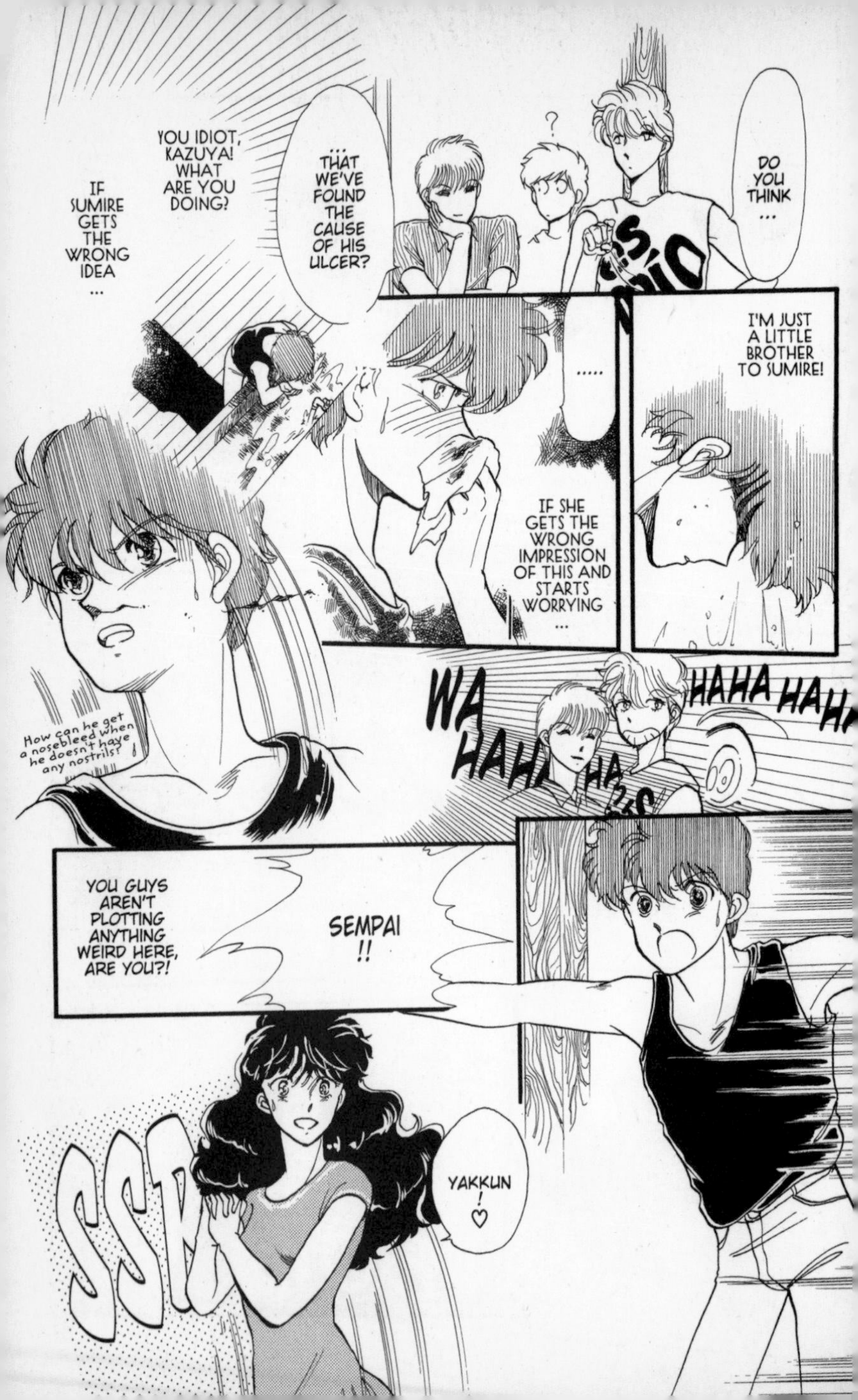
DO YOU THINK ...
... THAT WE'VE FOUND THE CAUSE OF HIS ULCER?
?
YOU IDIOT, KAZUYA! WHAT ARE YOU DOING?
IF SUMIRE GETS THE WRONG IDEA ...
I'M JUST A LITTLE BROTHER TO SUMIRE!
.....
IF SHE GETS THE WRONG IMPRESSION OF THIS AND STARTS WORRYING ...
How can he get a nosebleed when he doesn't have any nostrils?
HAHA HAHA
WA HAHA HAHA
SEMPAI !!
YOU GUYS AREN'T PLOTTING ANYTHING WEIRD HERE, ARE YOU?!
YAKKUN! ♡
SSR

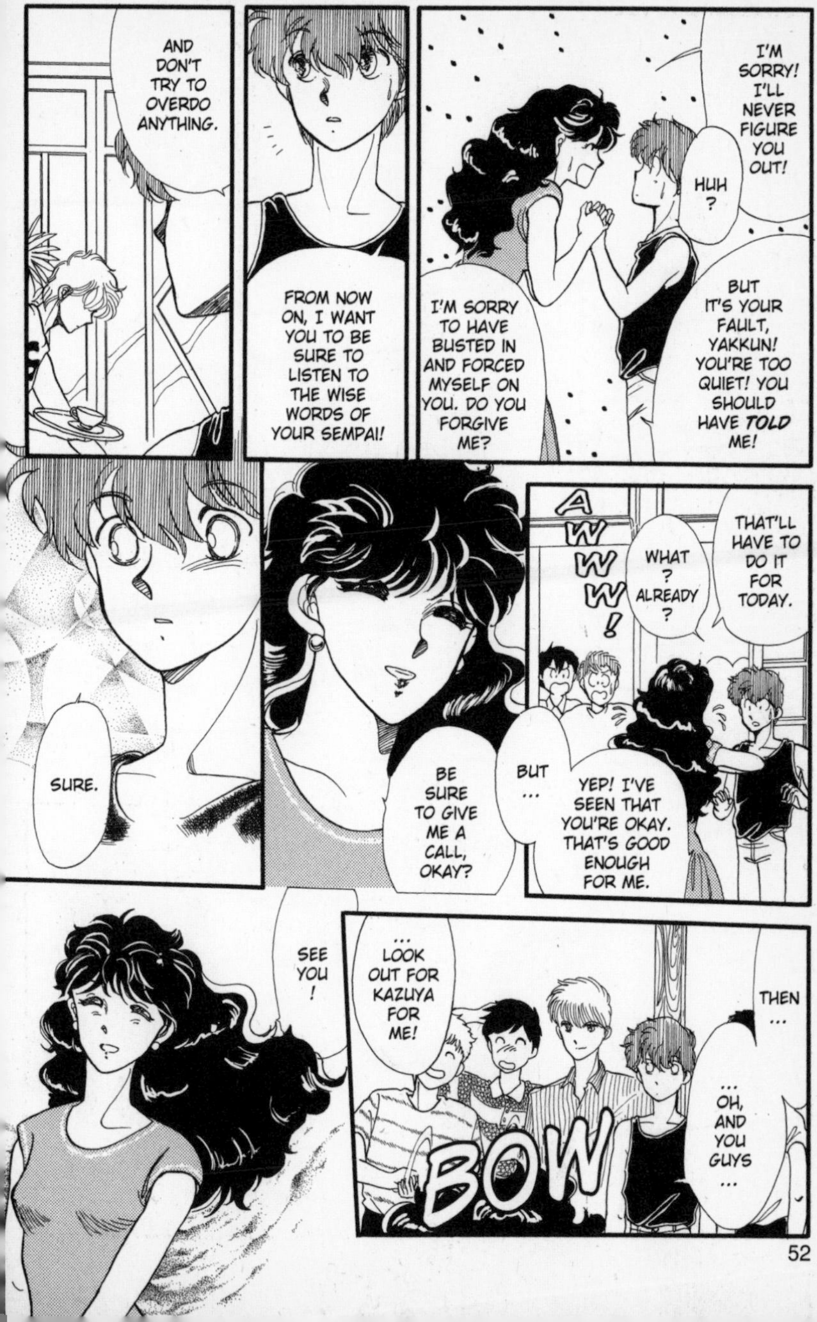
I'M SORRY! I'LL NEVER FIGURE YOU OUT!
HUH?
BUT IT'S YOUR FAULT, YAKKUN! YOU'RE TOO QUIET! YOU SHOULD HAVE *TOLD* ME!
I'M SORRY TO HAVE BUSTED IN AND FORCED MYSELF ON YOU. DO YOU FORGIVE ME?
FROM NOW ON, I WANT YOU TO BE SURE TO LISTEN TO THE WISE WORDS OF YOUR SEMPAI!
AND DON'T TRY TO OVERDO ANYTHING.
AWWW!
THAT'LL HAVE TO DO IT FOR TODAY.
WHAT? ALREADY?
YEP! I'VE SEEN THAT YOU'RE OKAY. THAT'S GOOD ENOUGH FOR ME.
BUT...
BE SURE TO GIVE ME A CALL, OKAY?
SURE.
THEN...
...OH, AND YOU GUYS...
...LOOK OUT FOR KAZUYA FOR ME!
BOW
SEE YOU!

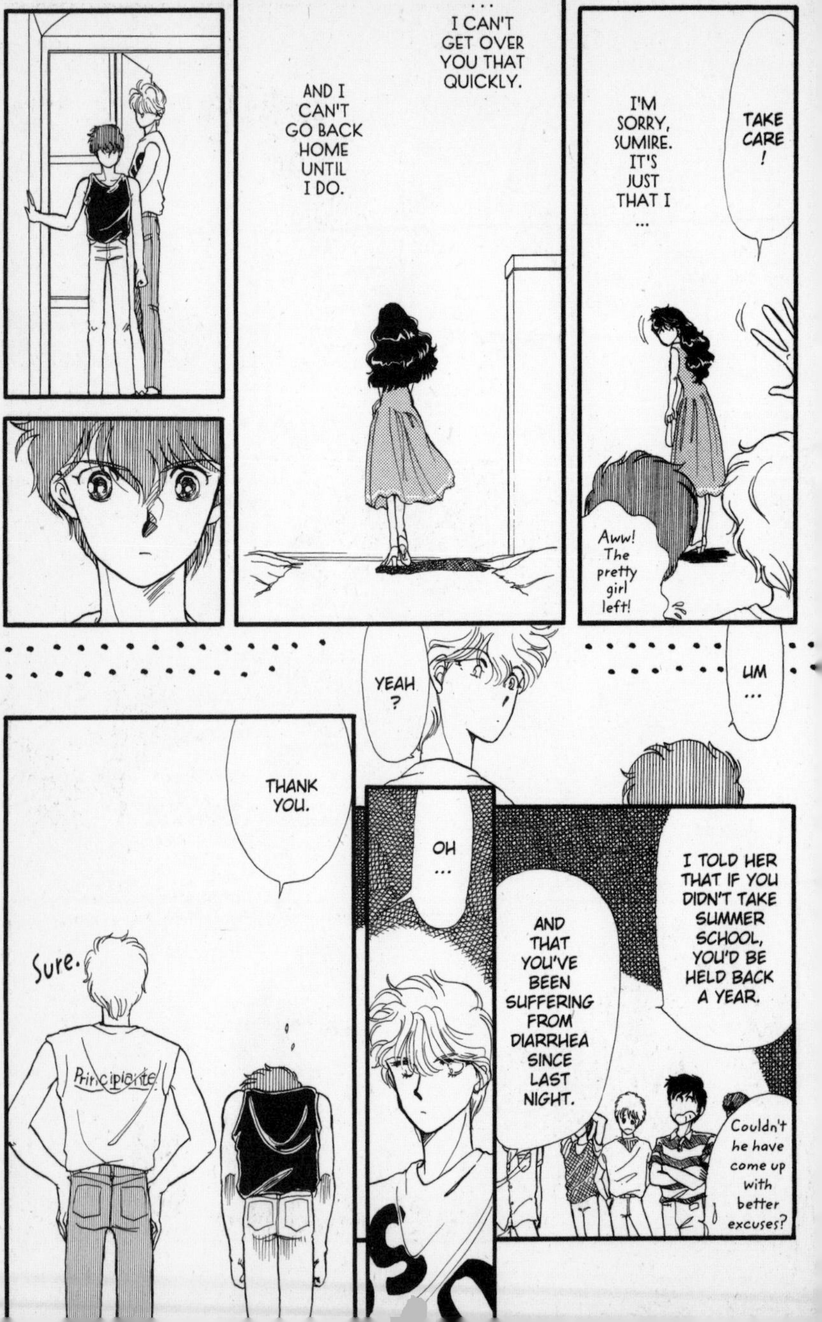
TAKE CARE!
I'M SORRY, SUMIRE. IT'S JUST THAT I ...
Aww! The pretty girl left!
... I CAN'T GET OVER YOU THAT QUICKLY.
AND I CAN'T GO BACK HOME UNTIL I DO.
UM ...
YEAH?
I TOLD HER THAT IF YOU DIDN'T TAKE SUMMER SCHOOL, YOU'D BE HELD BACK A YEAR.
AND THAT YOU'VE BEEN SUFFERING FROM DIARRHEA SINCE LAST NIGHT.
Couldn't he have come up with better excuses?
OH ...
THANK YOU.
Sure.
Principiante

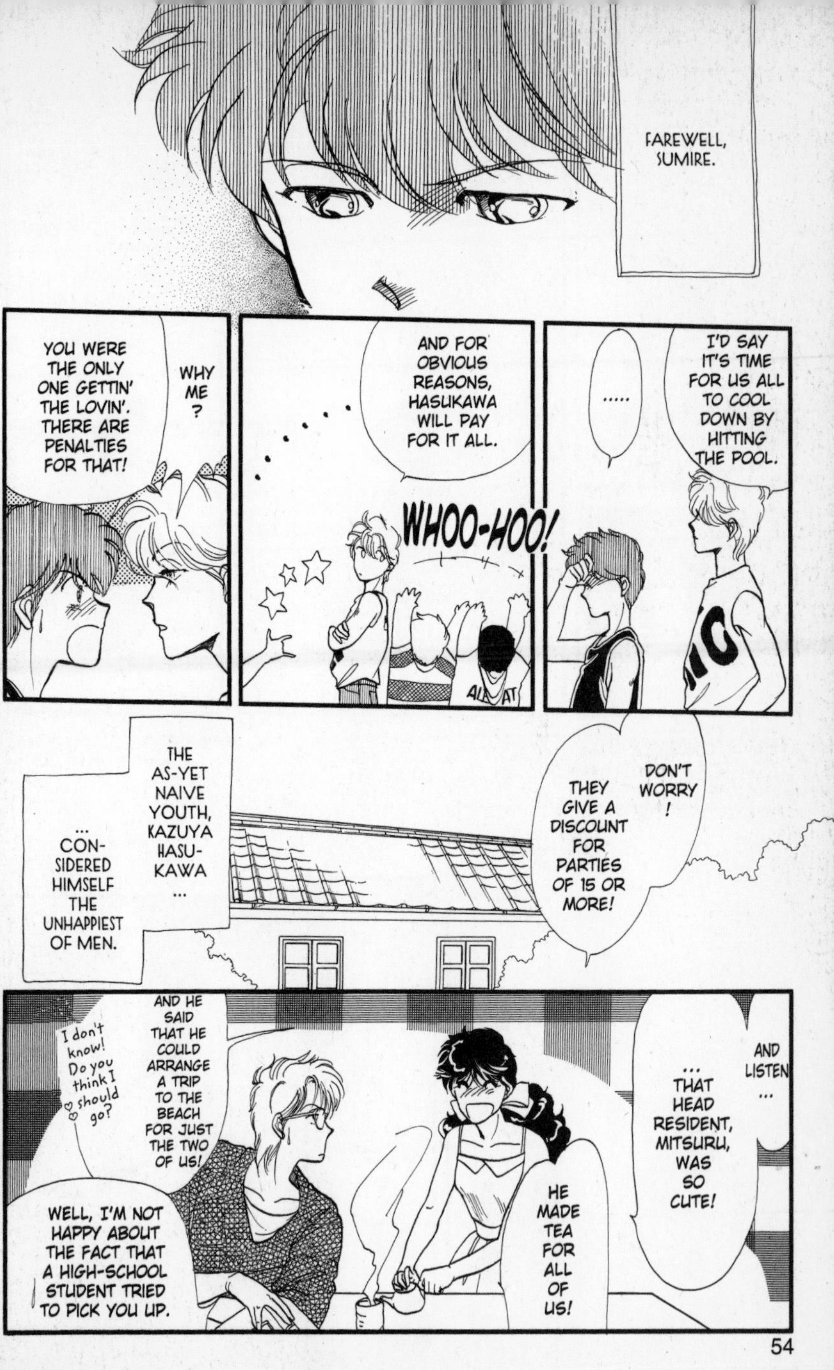
FAREWELL, SUMIRE.
I'D SAY IT'S TIME FOR US ALL TO COOL DOWN BY HITTING THE POOL.
.....
AND FOR OBVIOUS REASONS, HASUKAWA WILL PAY FOR IT ALL.
WHOO-HOO!
WHY ME?
YOU WERE THE ONLY ONE GETTIN' THE LOVIN'. THERE ARE PENALTIES FOR THAT!
DON'T WORRY!
THEY GIVE A DISCOUNT FOR PARTIES OF 15 OR MORE!
THE AS-YET NAIVE YOUTH, KAZUYA HASU-KAWA ...
... CON-SIDERED HIMSELF THE UNHAPPIEST OF MEN.
AND LISTEN ...
... THAT HEAD RESIDENT, MITSURU, WAS SO CUTE!
HE MADE TEA FOR ALL OF US!
AND HE SAID THAT HE COULD ARRANGE A TRIP TO THE BEACH FOR JUST THE TWO OF US!
I don't know! Do you think I should go?
WELL, I'M NOT HAPPY ABOUT THE FACT THAT A HIGH-SCHOOL STUDENT TRIED TO PICK YOU UP.

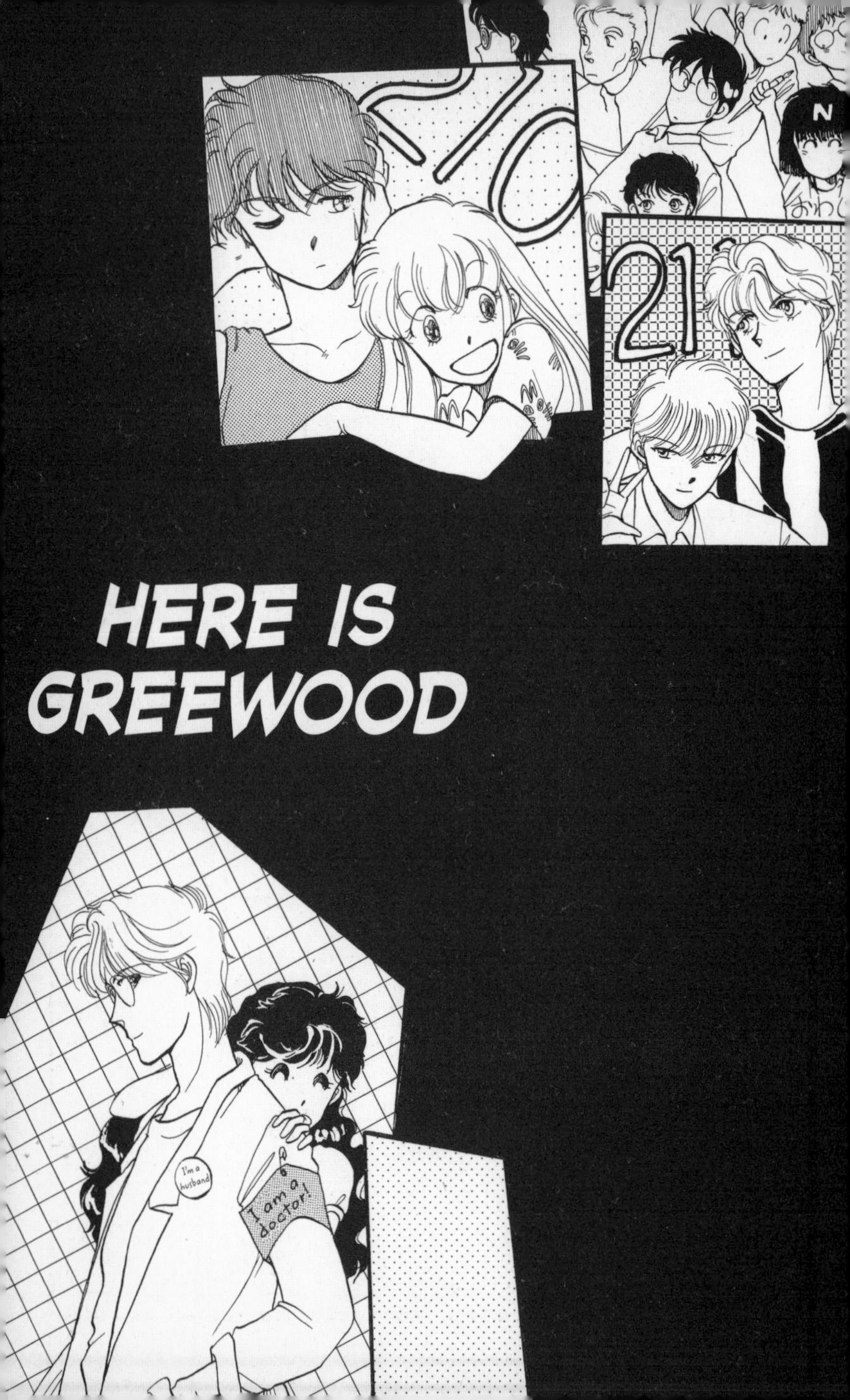
21
HERE IS GREEWOOD
I'm a husband
I am a doctor!

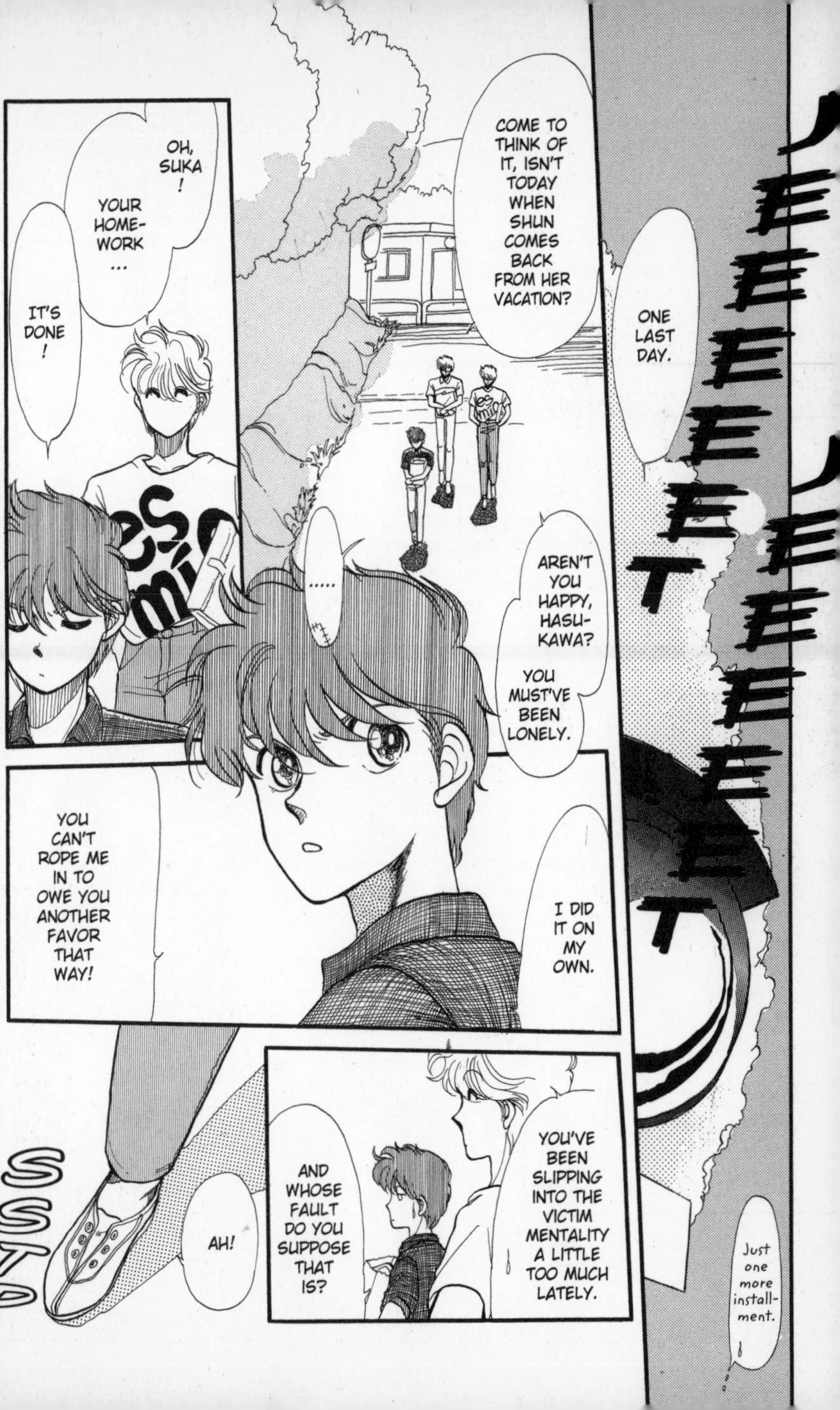

JEEEEEEEEET
JEEEEEEET
ONE LAST DAY.
COME TO THINK OF IT, ISN'T TODAY WHEN SHUN COMES BACK FROM HER VACATION?
OH, SUKA! YOUR HOMEWORK...
IT'S DONE!
.....
AREN'T YOU HAPPY, HASUKAWA?
YOU MUST'VE BEEN LONELY.
I DID IT ON MY OWN.
YOU CAN'T ROPE ME IN TO OWE YOU ANOTHER FAVOR THAT WAY!
Just one more installment.
YOU'VE BEEN SLIPPING INTO THE VICTIM MENTALITY A LITTLE TOO MUCH LATELY.
AND WHOSE FAULT DO YOU SUPPOSE THAT IS?
AH!
SSTA

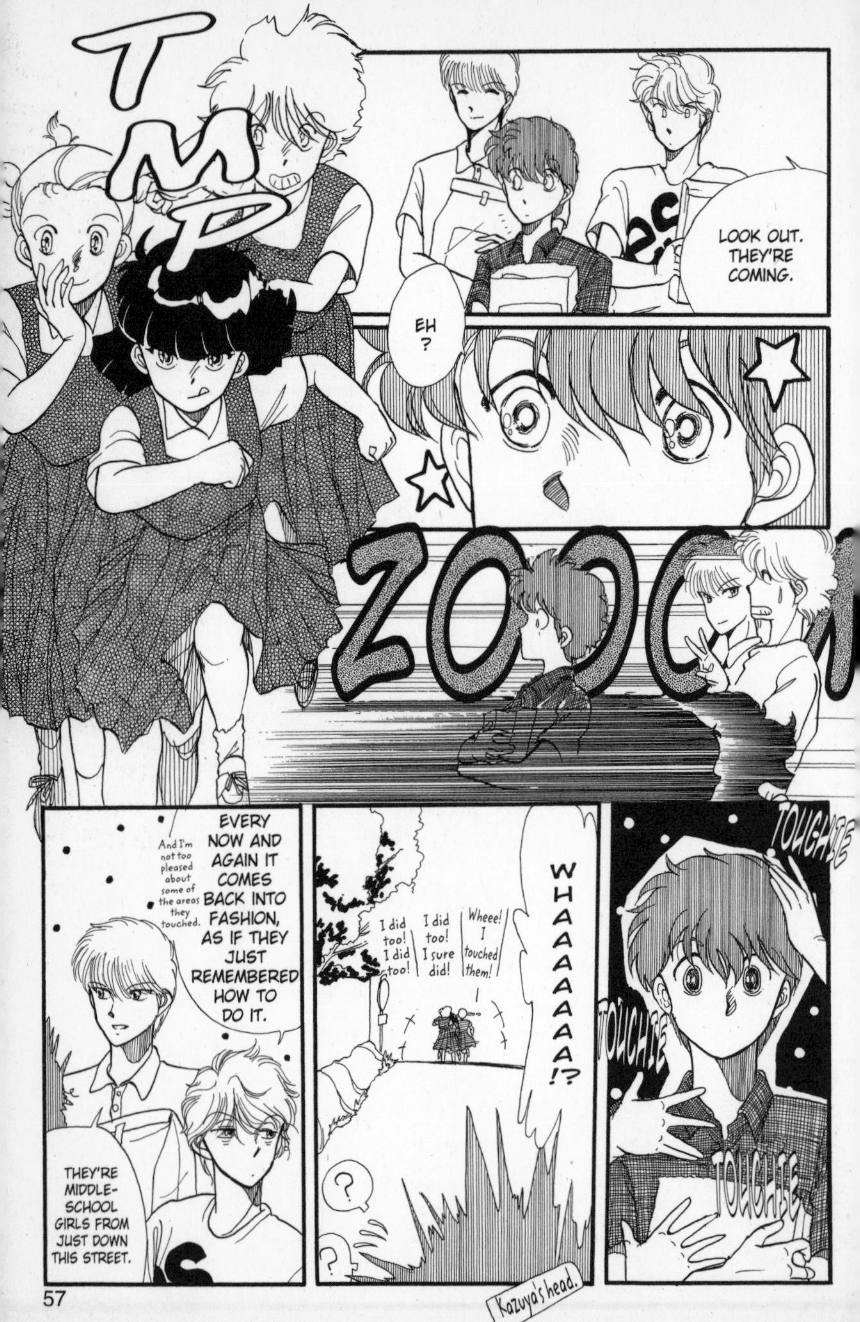
LOOK OUT. THEY'RE COMING.
EH ?
ZOOOM
TMP
TOUCHIE
TOUCHIE
TOUCHIE
WHAAAAAAAAAA!?
Wheee! I touched them!
I did too! I sure did!
I did too! I did too!
?
?
Kazuya's head.
EVERY NOW AND AGAIN IT COMES BACK INTO FASHION, AS IF THEY JUST REMEMBERED HOW TO DO IT.
And I'm not too pleased about some of the areas they touched.
THEY'RE MIDDLE-SCHOOL GIRLS FROM JUST DOWN THIS STREET.

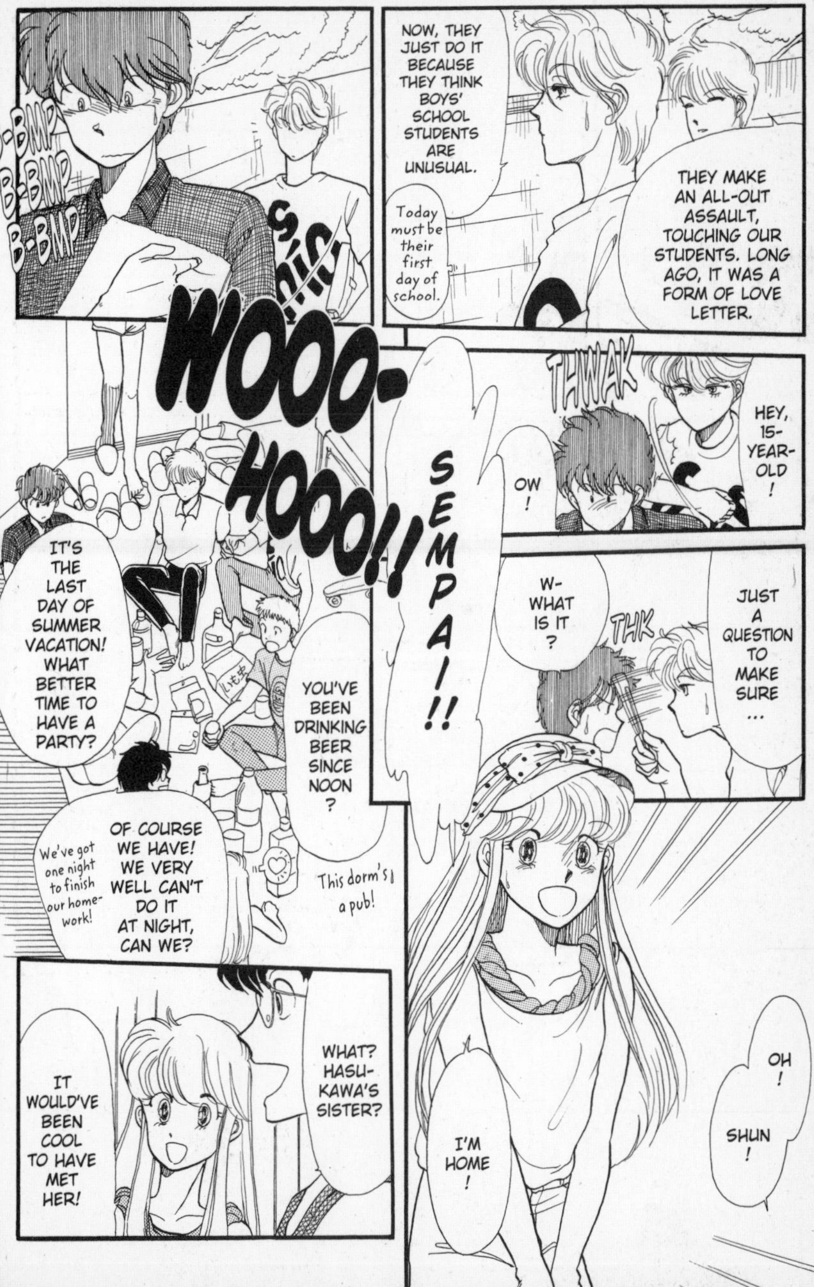
THEY MAKE AN ALL-OUT ASSAULT, TOUCHING OUR STUDENTS. LONG AGO, IT WAS A FORM OF LOVE LETTER.
NOW, THEY JUST DO IT BECAUSE THEY THINK BOYS' SCHOOL STUDENTS ARE UNUSUAL.
Today must be their first day of school.
B-BMP B-BMP B-BMP
THWAK
HEY, 15-YEAR-OLD!
OW!
JUST A QUESTION TO MAKE SURE...
THK
W-WHAT IS IT?
OH! SHUN!
I'M HOME!
SEMPAI!!
WOOO-HOOOO!!
IT'S THE LAST DAY OF SUMMER VACATION! WHAT BETTER TIME TO HAVE A PARTY?
YOU'VE BEEN DRINKING BEER SINCE NOON?
OF COURSE WE HAVE! WE VERY WELL CAN'T DO IT AT NIGHT, CAN WE?
We've got one night to finish our homework!
This dorm's a pub!
WHAT? HASUKAWA'S SISTER?
IT WOULD'VE BEEN COOL TO HAVE MET HER!

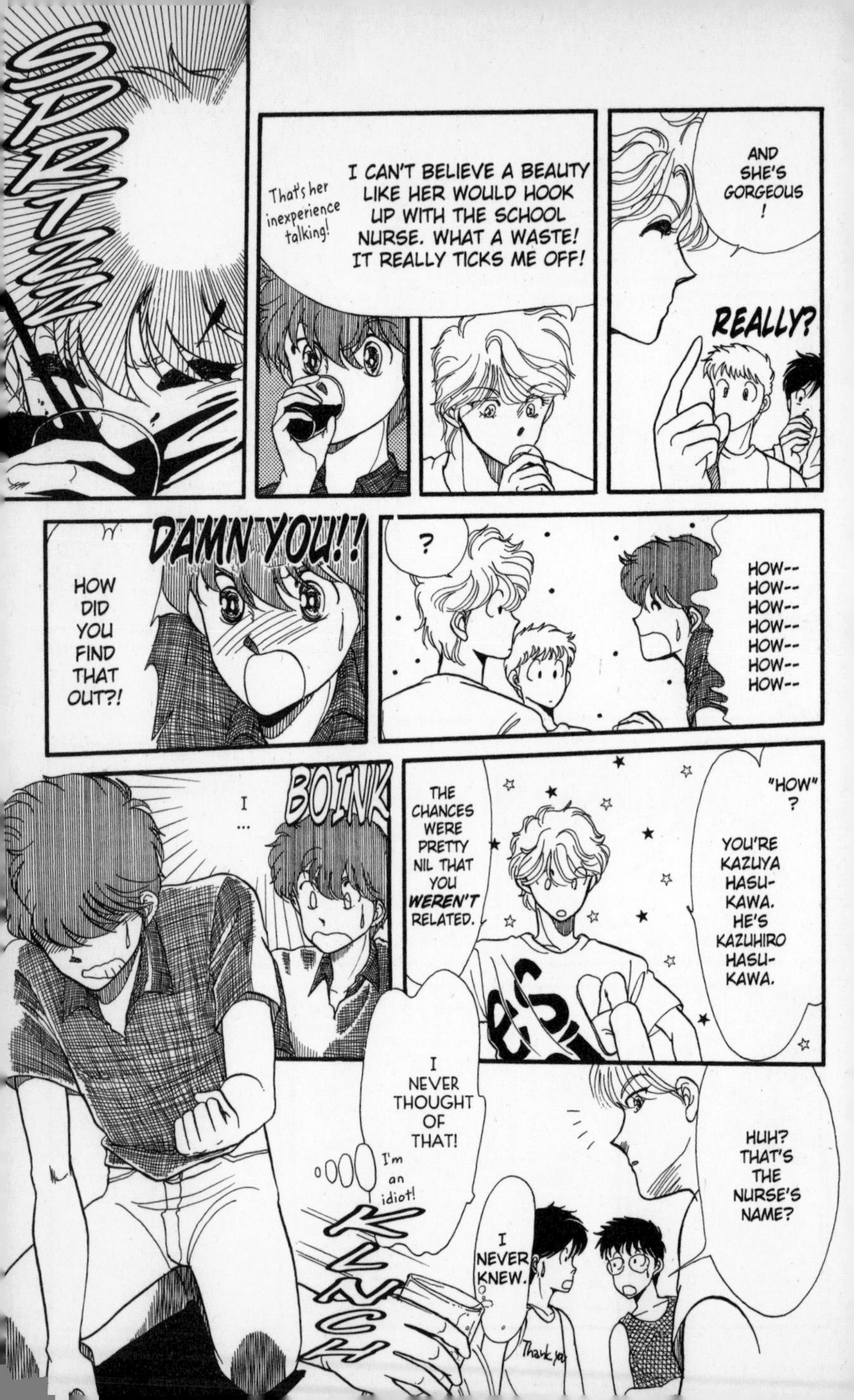
AND SHE'S GORGEOUS!
REALLY?
I CAN'T BELIEVE A BEAUTY LIKE HER WOULD HOOK UP WITH THE SCHOOL NURSE. WHAT A WASTE! IT REALLY TICKS ME OFF!
That's her inexperience talking!
SPRTMM
?
HOW-- HOW-- HOW-- HOW-- HOW-- HOW-- HOW--
DAMN YOU!!
HOW DID YOU FIND THAT OUT?!
"HOW"? YOU'RE KAZUYA HASU-KAWA. HE'S KAZUHIRO HASU-KAWA.
THE CHANCES WERE PRETTY NIL THAT YOU *WEREN'T* RELATED.
HUH? THAT'S THE NURSE'S NAME?
I NEVER KNEW.
Thank you
I NEVER THOUGHT OF THAT!
I'm an idiot!
BOINK
I ...
KLNCH

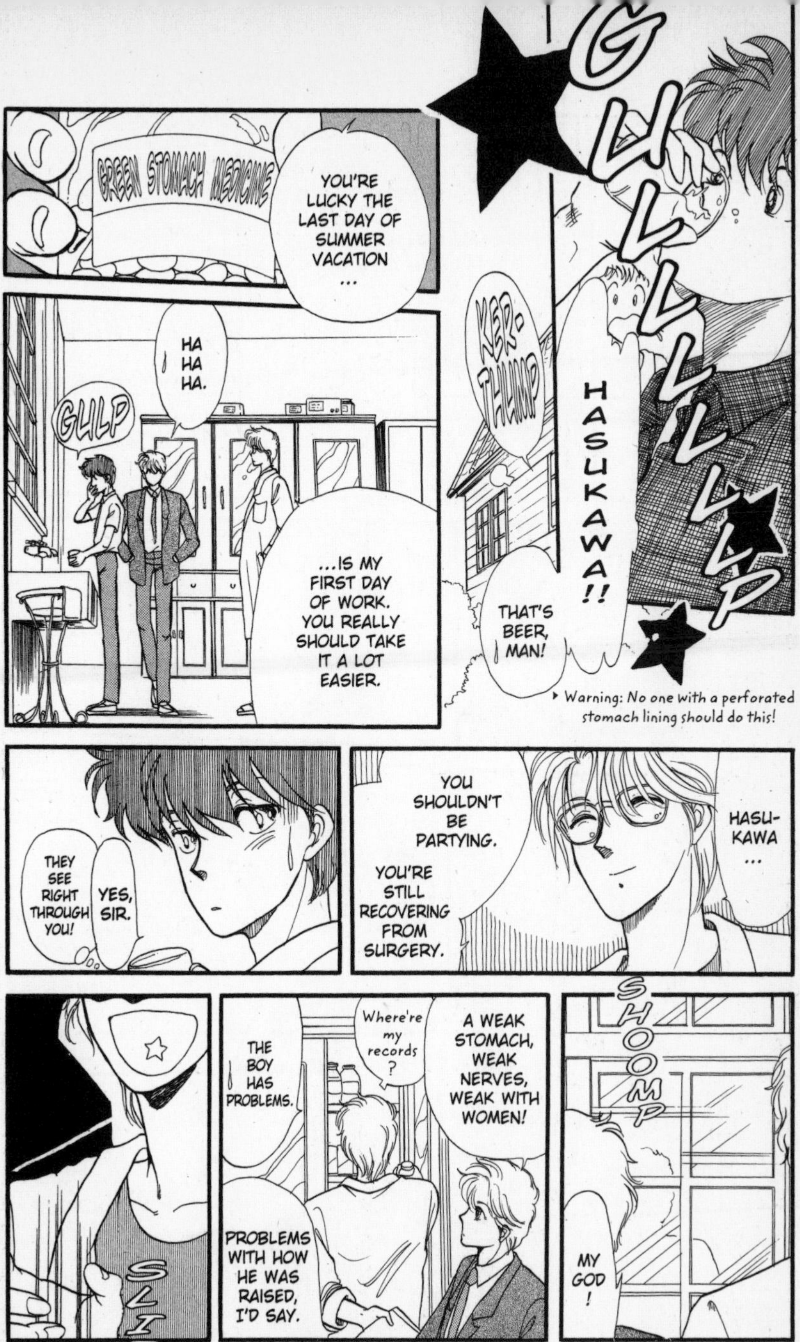
GULLLLLLP
HASUKAWA!!
KER-THUMP
THAT'S BEER, MAN!
Warning: No one with a perforated stomach lining should do this!
GREEN STOMACH MEDICINE
YOU'RE LUCKY THE LAST DAY OF SUMMER VACATION ...
HA HA HA.
GULP
...IS MY FIRST DAY OF WORK. YOU REALLY SHOULD TAKE IT A LOT EASIER.
HASU-KAWA ...
YOU SHOULDN'T BE PARTYING.
YOU'RE STILL RECOVERING FROM SURGERY.
YES, SIR.
THEY SEE RIGHT THROUGH YOU!
SHOOMP
MY GOD!
A WEAK STOMACH, WEAK NERVES, WEAK WITH WOMEN!
Where're my records?
THE BOY HAS PROBLEMS.
PROBLEMS WITH HOW HE WAS RAISED, I'D SAY.
SLIP

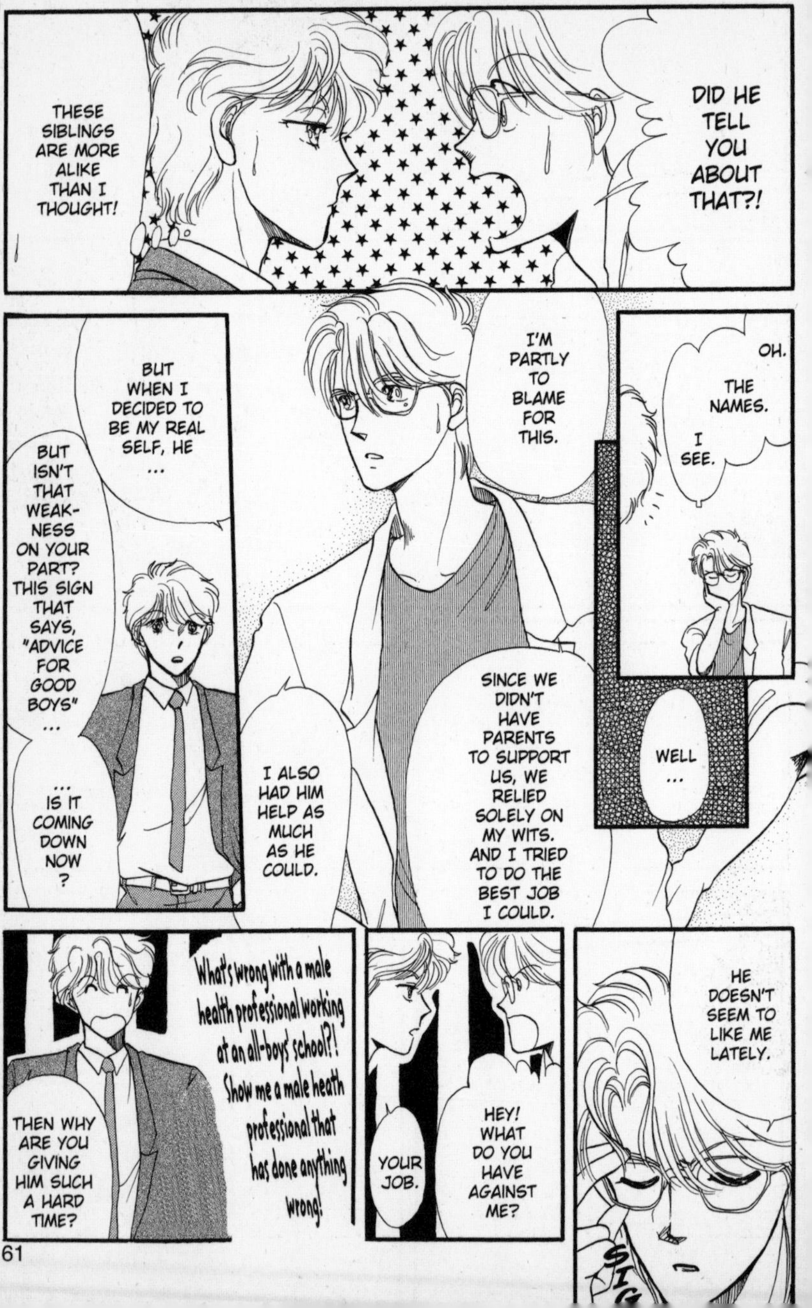
DID HE TELL YOU ABOUT THAT?!
THESE SIBLINGS ARE MORE ALIKE THAN I THOUGHT!
OH.
THE NAMES.
I SEE.
WELL ...
I'M PARTLY TO BLAME FOR THIS.
SINCE WE DIDN'T HAVE PARENTS TO SUPPORT US, WE RELIED SOLELY ON MY WITS. AND I TRIED TO DO THE BEST JOB I COULD.
I ALSO HAD HIM HELP AS MUCH AS HE COULD.
BUT WHEN I DECIDED TO BE MY REAL SELF, HE ...
BUT ISN'T THAT WEAKNESS ON YOUR PART? THIS SIGN THAT SAYS, "ADVICE FOR GOOD BOYS" ...
... IS IT COMING DOWN NOW ?
HE DOESN'T SEEM TO LIKE ME LATELY.
HEY! WHAT DO YOU HAVE AGAINST ME?
YOUR JOB.
What's wrong with a male health professional working at an all-boys' school?! Show me a male heath professional that has done anything wrong!
THEN WHY ARE YOU GIVING HIM SUCH A HARD TIME?

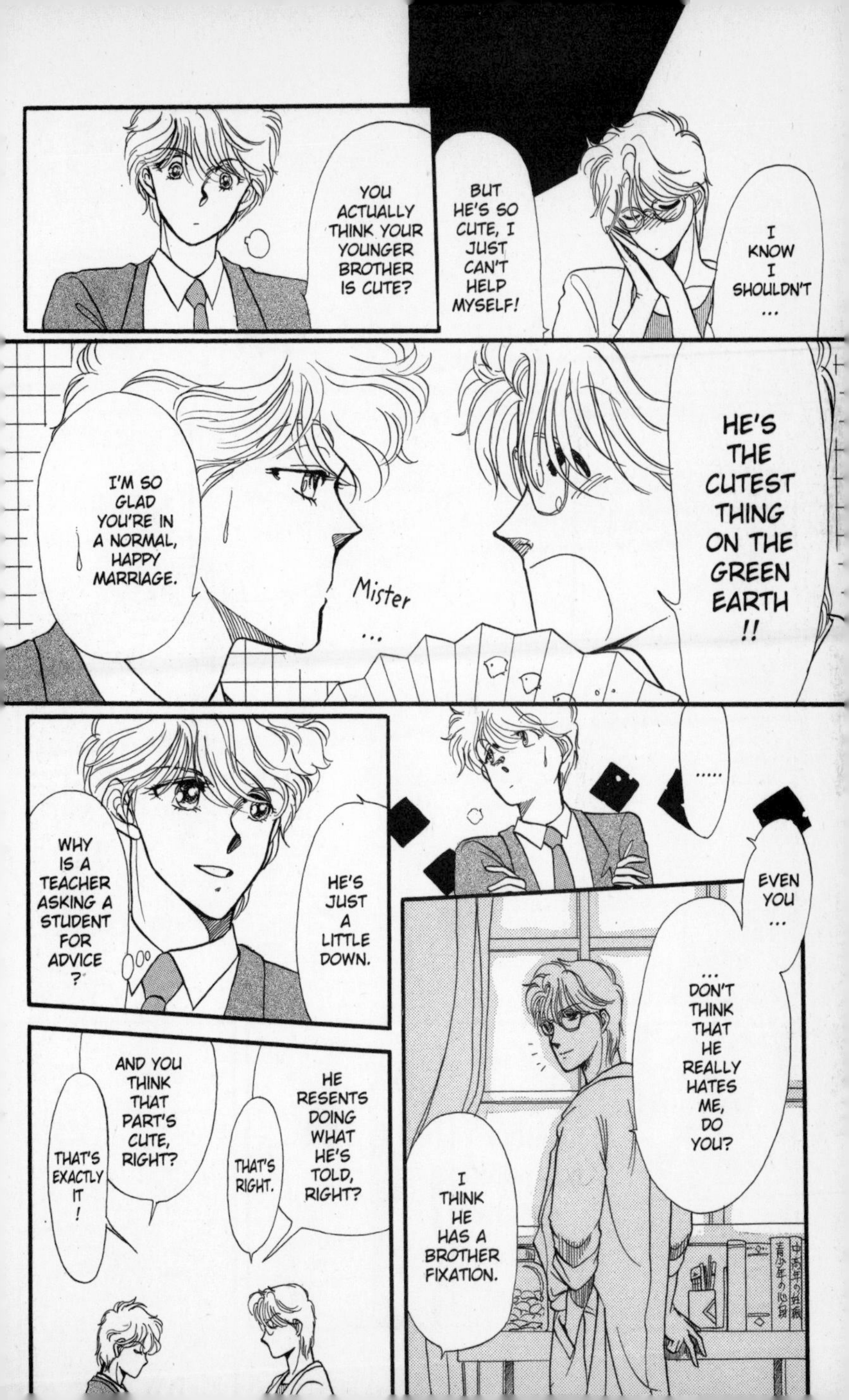
I KNOW I SHOULDN'T ...
BUT HE'S SO CUTE, I JUST CAN'T HELP MYSELF!
YOU ACTUALLY THINK YOUR YOUNGER BROTHER IS CUTE?
HE'S THE CUTEST THING ON THE GREEN EARTH!!
Mister ...
I'M SO GLAD YOU'RE IN A NORMAL, HAPPY MARRIAGE.
.....
HE'S JUST A LITTLE DOWN.
WHY IS A TEACHER ASKING A STUDENT FOR ADVICE?
EVEN YOU ...
... DON'T THINK THAT HE REALLY HATES ME, DO YOU?
I THINK HE HAS A BROTHER FIXATION.
HE RESENTS DOING WHAT HE'S TOLD, RIGHT?
THAT'S RIGHT.
AND YOU THINK THAT PART'S CUTE, RIGHT?
THAT'S EXACTLY IT!

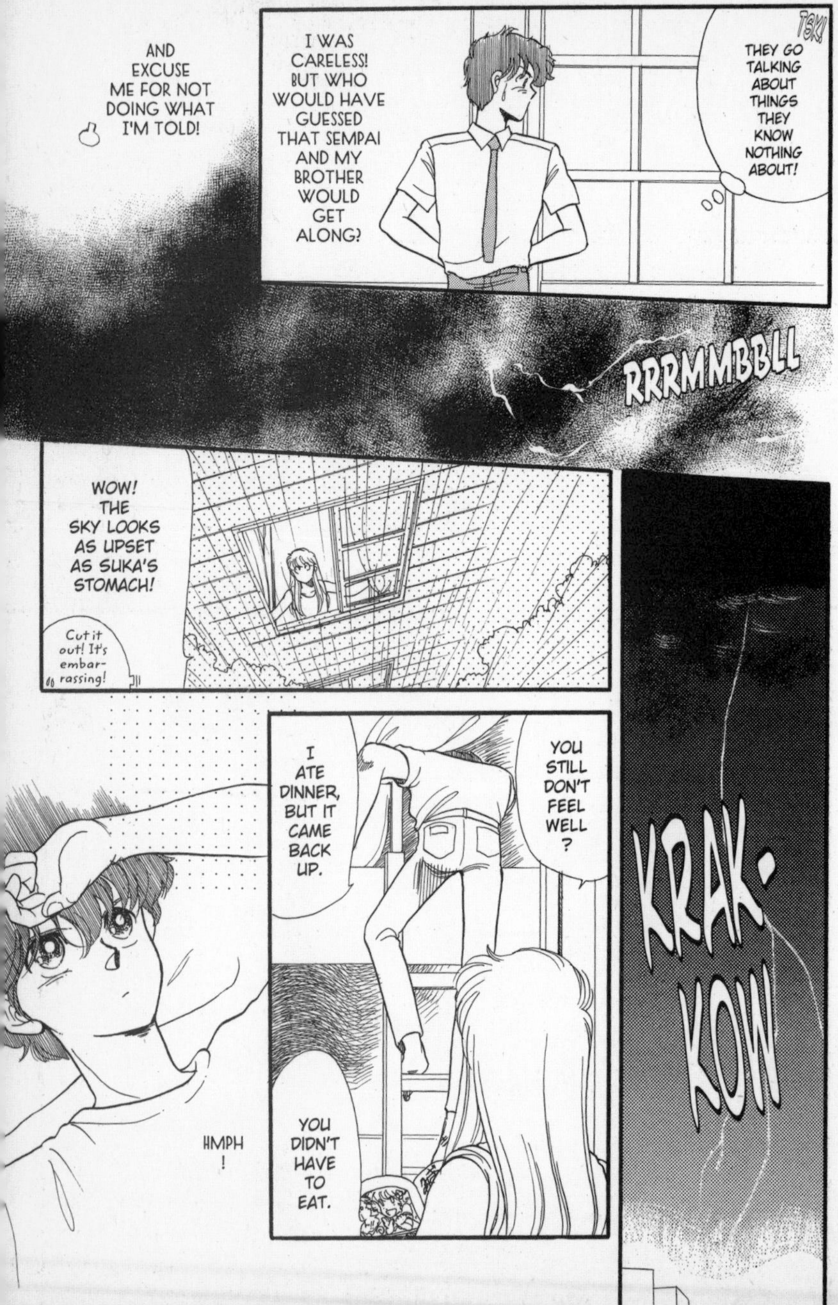
TSK!
THEY GO TALKING ABOUT THINGS THEY KNOW NOTHING ABOUT!
I WAS CARELESS! BUT WHO WOULD HAVE GUESSED THAT SEMPAI AND MY BROTHER WOULD GET ALONG?
AND EXCUSE ME FOR NOT DOING WHAT I'M TOLD!
RRRMMBBLL
KRAK-KOW
WOW! THE SKY LOOKS AS UPSET AS SUKA'S STOMACH!
Cut it out! It's embarrassing!
YOU STILL DON'T FEEL WELL?
I ATE DINNER, BUT IT CAME BACK UP.
YOU DIDN'T HAVE TO EAT.
HMPH!

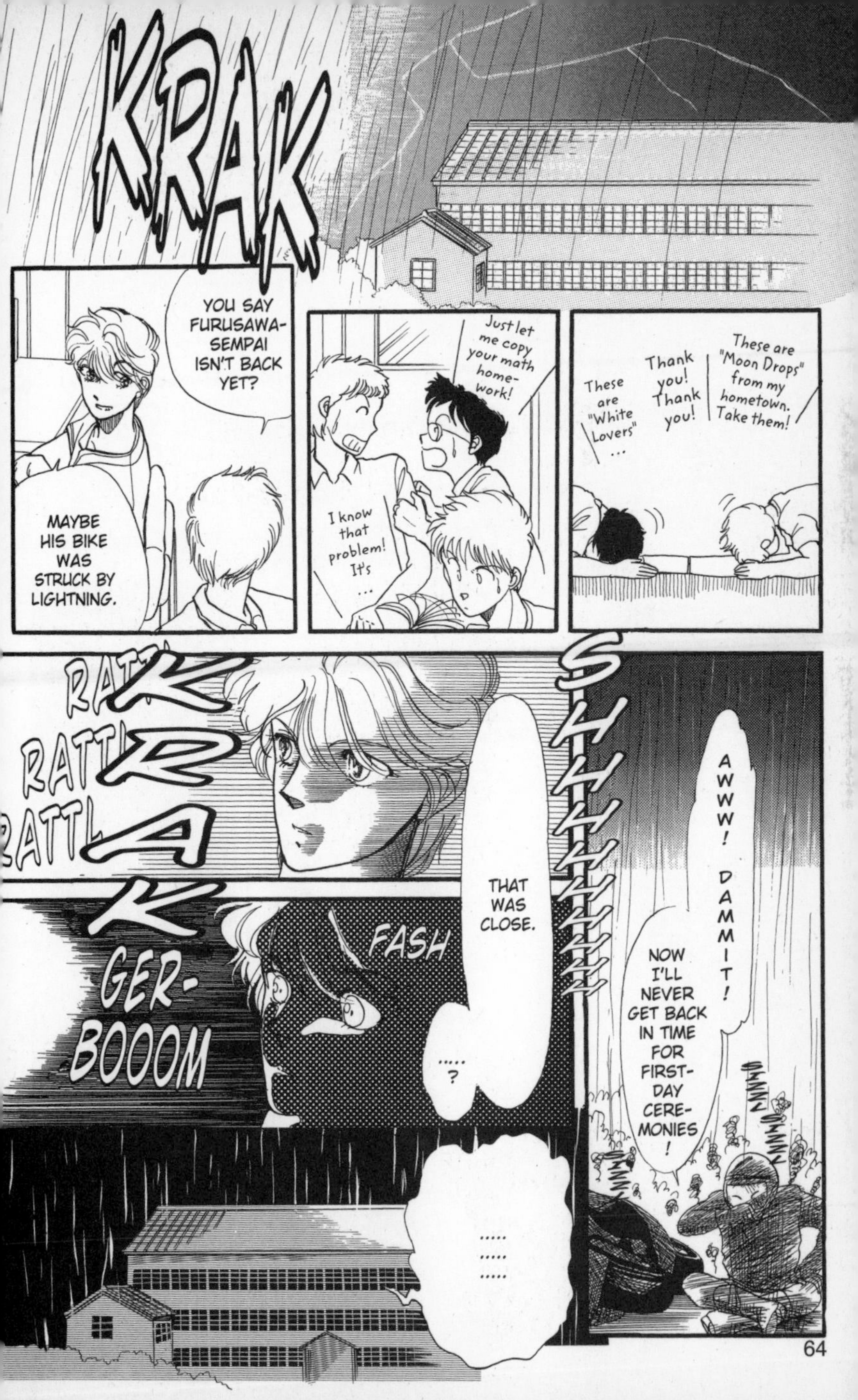
KRAK
These are "Moon Drops" from my hometown. Take them!
Thank you! Thank you!
These are "White Lovers" ...
Just let me copy your math homework!
I know that problem! It's ...
YOU SAY FURUSAWA-SEMPAI ISN'T BACK YET?
MAYBE HIS BIKE WAS STRUCK BY LIGHTNING.
SHHHHHHHHHH
AWWW! DAMMIT!
NOW I'LL NEVER GET BACK IN TIME FOR FIRST-DAY CEREMONIES!
SIZZZ SIZZZ SIZZZ
RATTL RATTL RATTL
KRAK
THAT WAS CLOSE.
FASH
GER-BOOOM
.....?
....

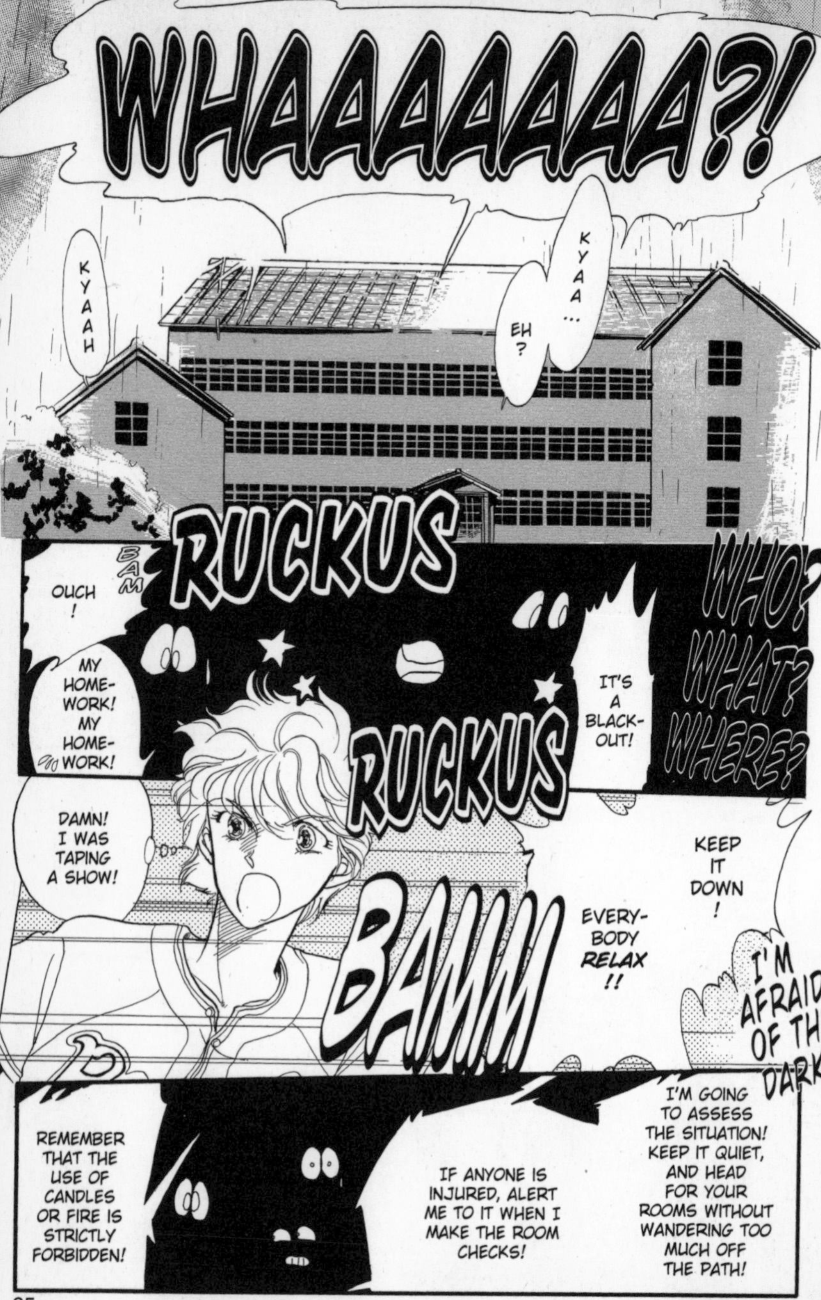
WHAAAAAAA?!
KYAA...
EH?
KYAAH
RUCKUS
BAM
WHO? WHAT? WHERE?
IT'S A BLACK-OUT!
OUCH!
MY HOME-WORK! MY HOME-WORK!
RUCKUS
KEEP IT DOWN!
I'M AFRAID OF THE DARK!
EVERY-BODY RELAX!!
BAMM
DAMN! I WAS TAPING A SHOW!
I'M GOING TO ASSESS THE SITUATION! KEEP IT QUIET, AND HEAD FOR YOUR ROOMS WITHOUT WANDERING TOO MUCH OFF THE PATH!
IF ANYONE IS INJURED, ALERT ME TO IT WHEN I MAKE THE ROOM CHECKS!
REMEMBER THAT THE USE OF CANDLES OR FIRE IS STRICTLY FORBIDDEN!

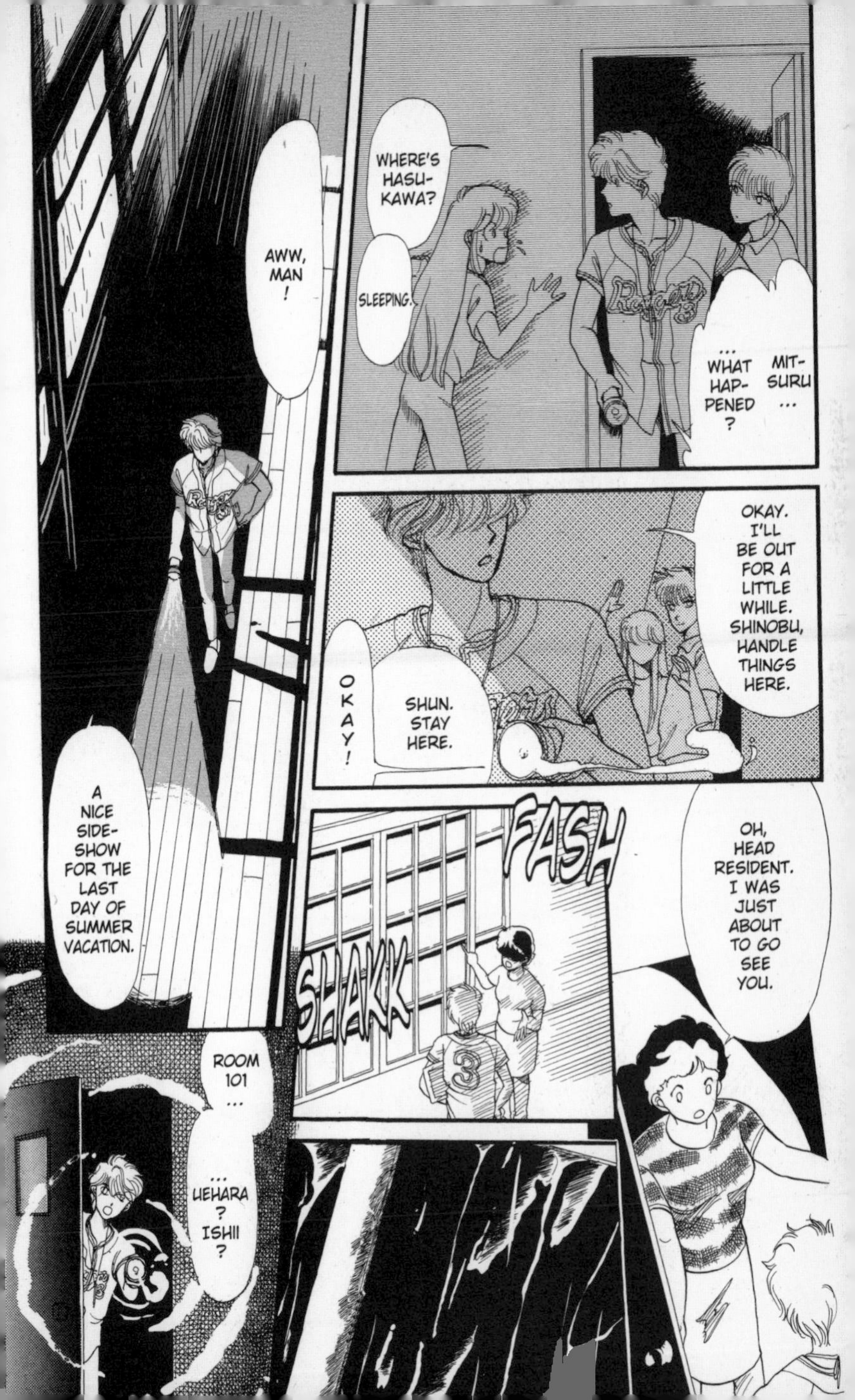
WHERE'S HASU-KAWA?
SLEEPING.
MIT-SURU ...
... WHAT HAP-PENED ?
OKAY. I'LL BE OUT FOR A LITTLE WHILE. SHINOBU, HANDLE THINGS HERE.
SHUN. STAY HERE.
OKAY!
FASH
SHAKK
AWW, MAN!
A NICE SIDE-SHOW FOR THE LAST DAY OF SUMMER VACATION.
OH, HEAD RESIDENT. I WAS JUST ABOUT TO GO SEE YOU.
ROOM 101 ...
... UEHARA? ISHII?

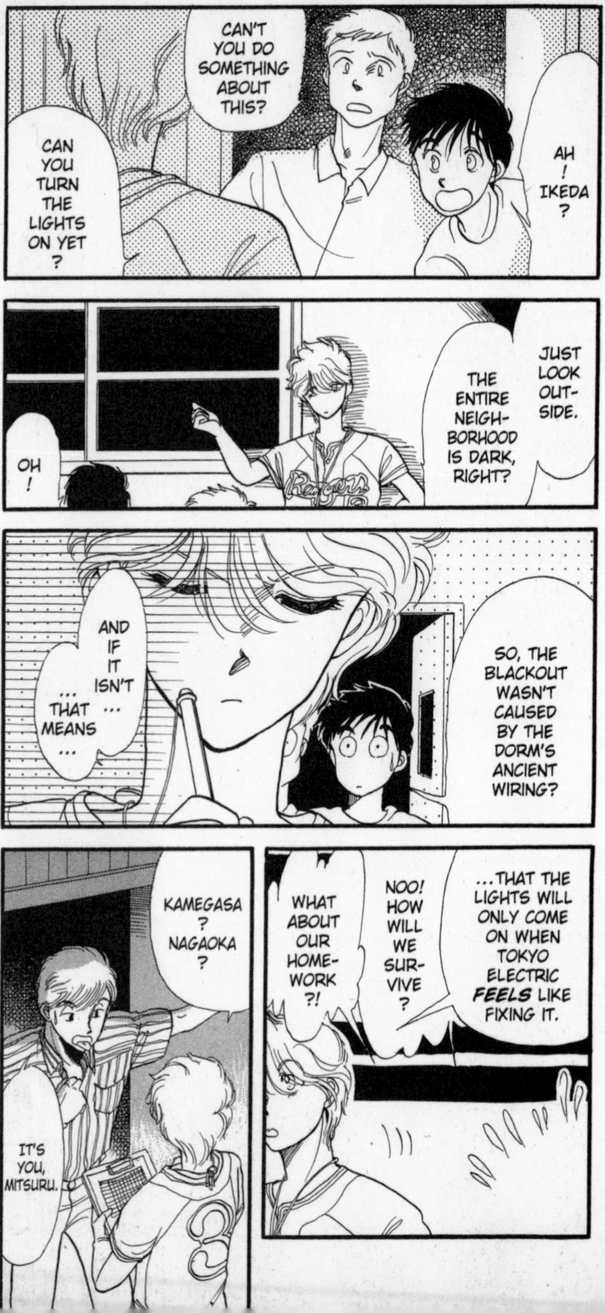
AH! IKEDA?
CAN'T YOU DO SOMETHING ABOUT THIS?
CAN YOU TURN THE LIGHTS ON YET?
JUST LOOK OUT-SIDE.
THE ENTIRE NEIGH-BORHOOD IS DARK, RIGHT?
OH!
SO, THE BLACKOUT WASN'T CAUSED BY THE DORM'S ANCIENT WIRING?
AND IF IT ISN'T ...
... THAT MEANS ...
...THAT THE LIGHTS WILL ONLY COME ON WHEN TOKYO ELECTRIC FEELS LIKE FIXING IT.
NOO! HOW WILL WE SUR-VIVE?
WHAT ABOUT OUR HOME-WORK?!
KAMEGASA? NAGAOKA?
IT'S YOU, MITSURU.

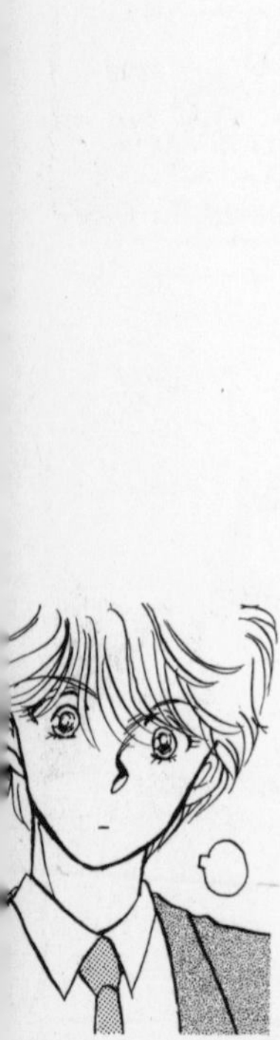

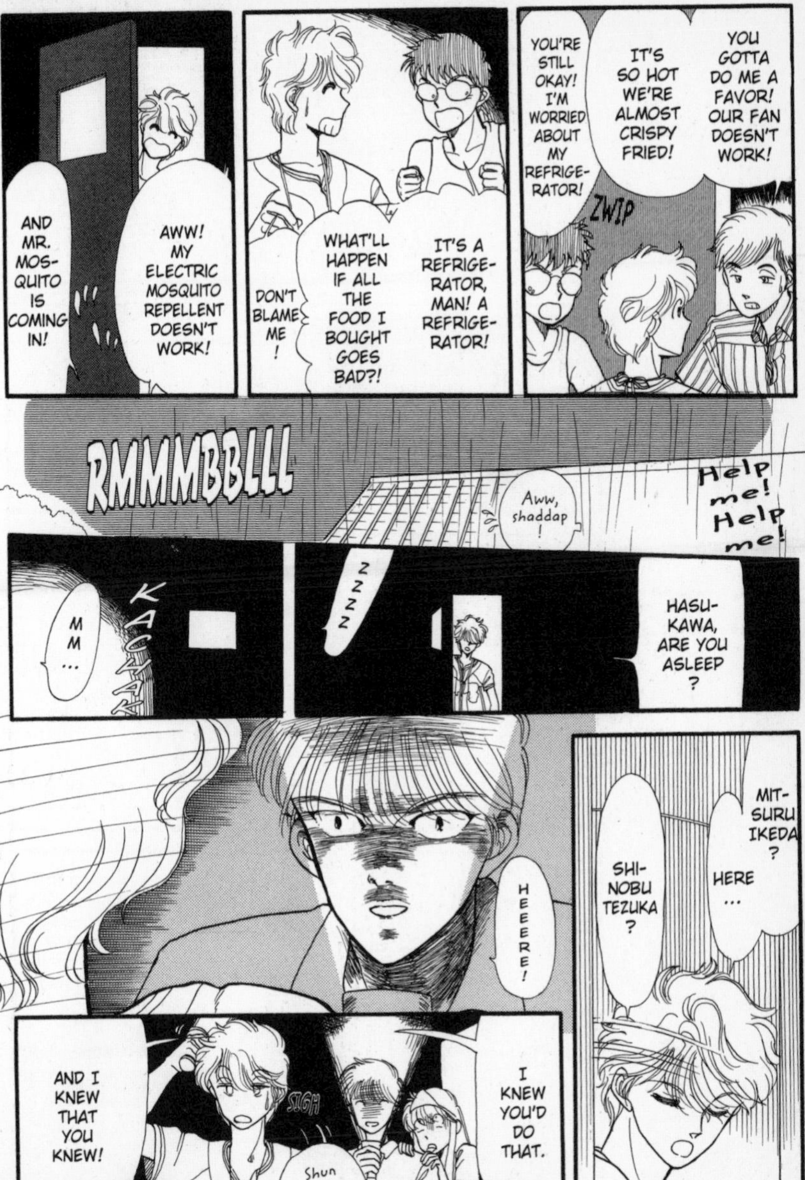
YOU GOTTA DO ME A FAVOR! OUR FAN DOESN'T WORK!
IT'S SO HOT WE'RE ALMOST CRISPY FRIED!
YOU'RE STILL OKAY! I'M WORRIED ABOUT MY REFRIGERATOR!
ZWIP
IT'S A REFRIGERATOR, MAN! A REFRIGERATOR!
WHAT'LL HAPPEN IF ALL THE FOOD I BOUGHT GOES BAD?!
DON'T BLAME ME!
AWW! MY ELECTRIC MOSQUITO REPELLENT DOESN'T WORK!
AND MR. MOSQUITO IS COMING IN!
Help me! Help me!
Aww, shaddap!
RMMMBBLLL
HASUKAWA, ARE YOU ASLEEP?
ZZZZ
MM...
MITSURU IKEDA?
HERE...
SHINOBU TEZUKA?
HEEERE!
I KNEW YOU'D DO THAT.
SIGH
Shun is here, too!
AND I KNEW THAT YOU KNEW!

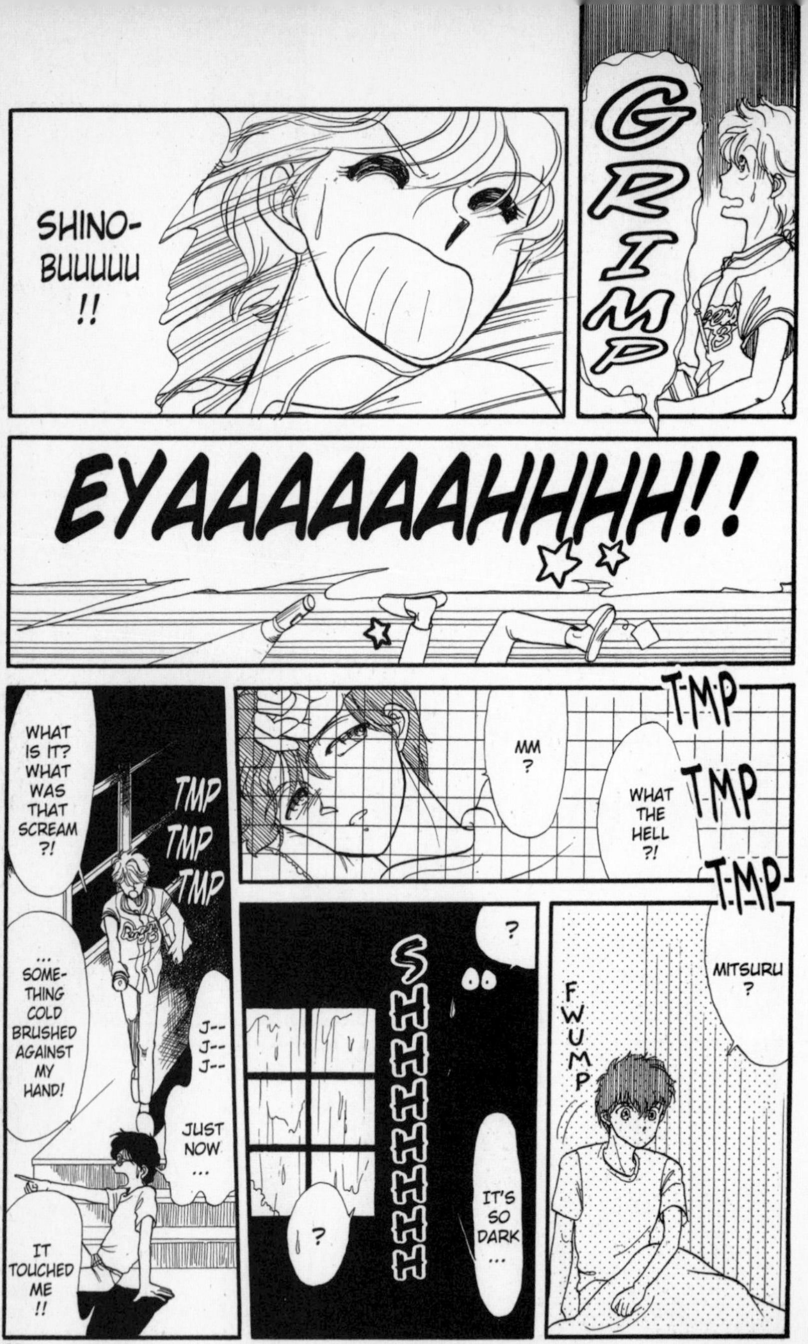
GRIMP
SHINO-BUUUUU!!
EYAAAAAAHHHH!!
T·M·P
MM?
TMP
WHAT THE HELL?!
T·M·P
MITSURU?
FWUMP
?
SHIIIIIIIII
??
IT'S SO DARK...
WHAT IS IT? WHAT WAS THAT SCREAM?!
TMP TMP TMP
...SOME-THING COLD BRUSHED AGAINST MY HAND!
J-- J-- J--
JUST NOW...
IT TOUCHED ME!!

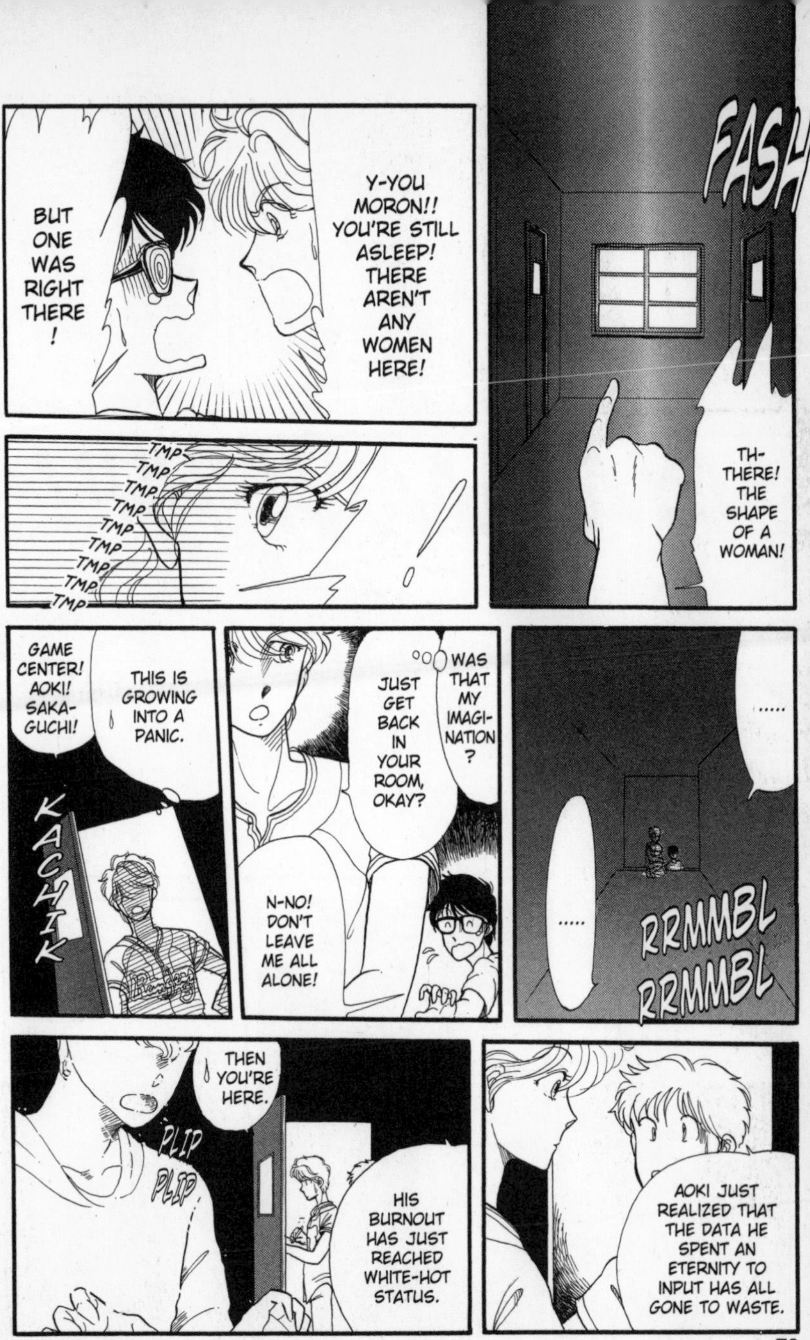
FASH
TH-THERE! THE SHAPE OF A WOMAN!
Y-YOU MORON!! YOU'RE STILL ASLEEP! THERE AREN'T ANY WOMEN HERE!
BUT ONE WAS RIGHT THERE!
!
TMP TMP TMP TMP TMP TMP TMP TMP TMP
.....
.....
RRMMBL RRMMBL
WAS THAT MY IMAGINATION?
JUST GET BACK IN YOUR ROOM, OKAY?
N-NO! DON'T LEAVE ME ALL ALONE!
THIS IS GROWING INTO A PANIC.
GAME CENTER! AOKI! SAKA-GUCHI!
KACHIK
AOKI JUST REALIZED THAT THE DATA HE SPENT AN ETERNITY TO INPUT HAS ALL GONE TO WASTE.
THEN YOU'RE HERE.
PLIP PLIP
HIS BURNOUT HAS JUST REACHED WHITE-HOT STATUS.

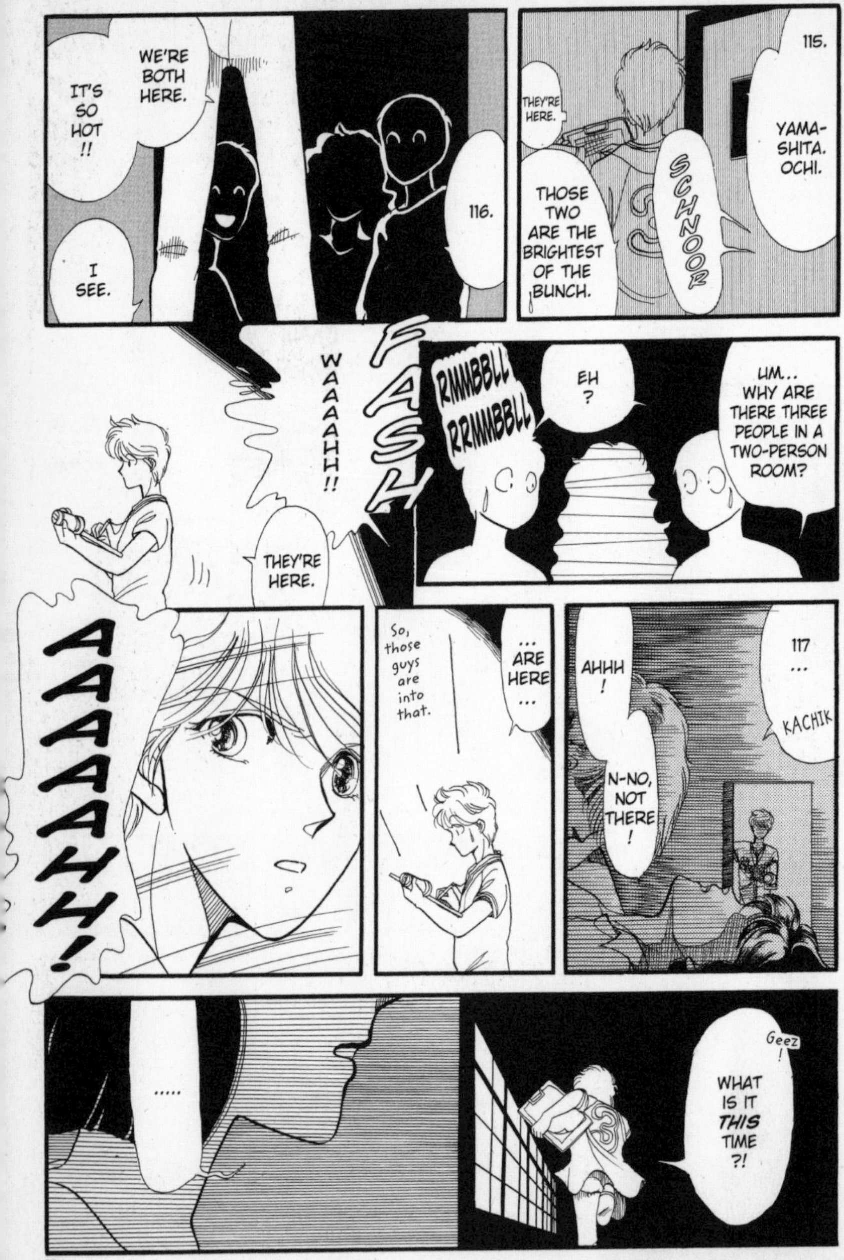
115.
YAMA-SHITA. OCHI.
SCHNOOR
THEY'RE HERE.
THOSE TWO ARE THE BRIGHTEST OF THE BUNCH.
116.
WE'RE BOTH HERE.
IT'S SO HOT !!
I SEE.
UM... WHY ARE THERE THREE PEOPLE IN A TWO-PERSON ROOM?
EH ?
RRMMBBLL RRMMBBLL
FASH
WAAAAAHH!!
THEY'RE HERE.
117 ...
KACHIK
AHHH !
N-NO, NOT THERE !
... ARE HERE ...
So, those guys are into that.
AAAAAAHH!
Geez !
WHAT IS IT *THIS* TIME ?!
.....

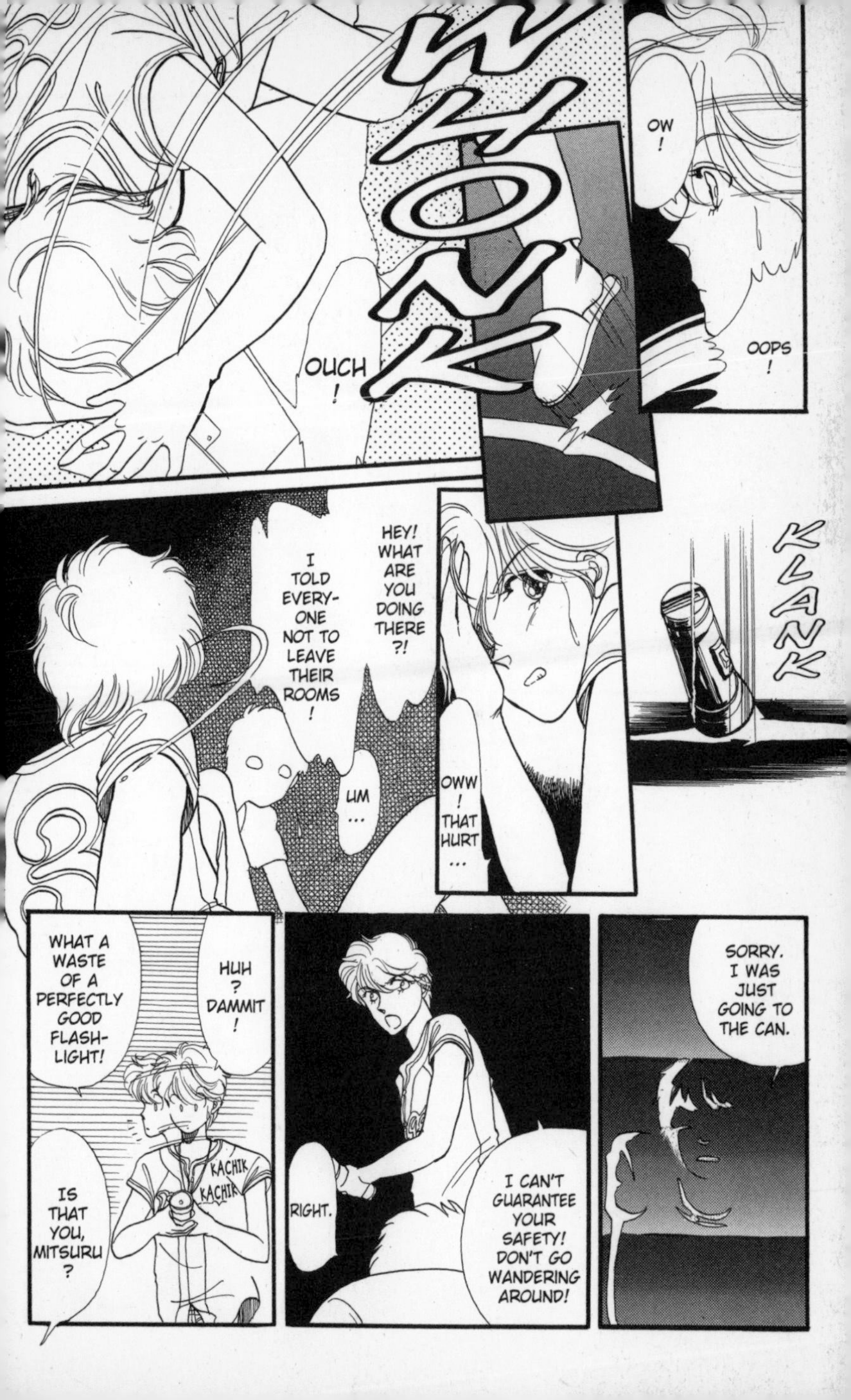
OW!
OOPS!
WHONK
OUCH!
KLANK
OWW! THAT HURT...
HEY! WHAT ARE YOU DOING THERE?!
I TOLD EVERYONE NOT TO LEAVE THEIR ROOMS!
UM...
SORRY. I WAS JUST GOING TO THE CAN.
I CAN'T GUARANTEE YOUR SAFETY! DON'T GO WANDERING AROUND!
RIGHT.
HUH? DAMMIT!
WHAT A WASTE OF A PERFECTLY GOOD FLASHLIGHT!
KACHIK KACHIK
IS THAT YOU, MITSURU?

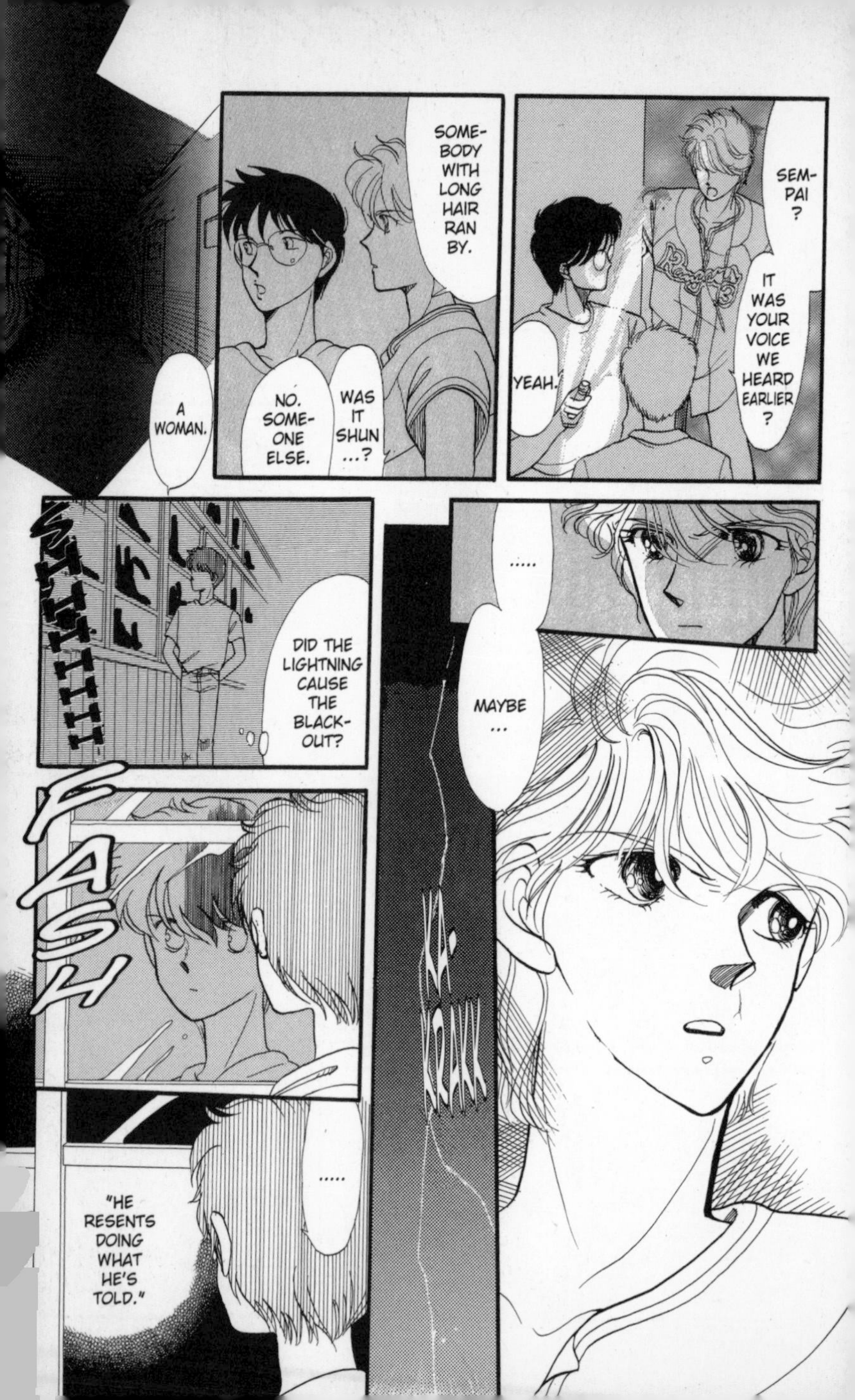
SEM-PAI?
IT WAS YOUR VOICE WE HEARD EARLIER?
YEAH.
SOME-BODY WITH LONG HAIR RAN BY.
WAS IT SHUN...?
NO. SOME-ONE ELSE.
A WOMAN.
.....
MAYBE...
DID THE LIGHTNING CAUSE THE BLACK-OUT?
FLASH
KA-KRAKK
.....
"HE RESENTS DOING WHAT HE'S TOLD."

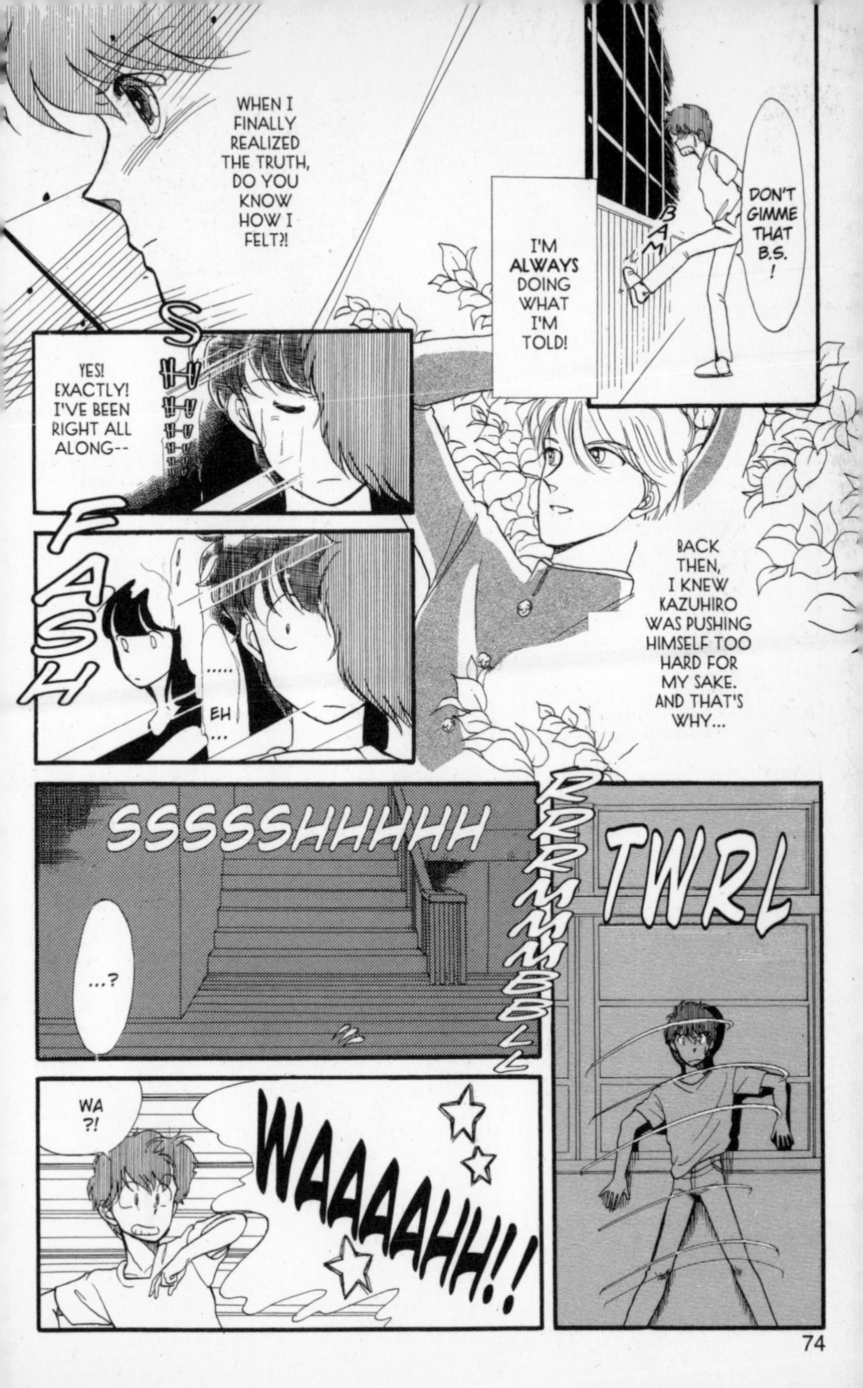
DON'T GIMME THAT B.S. !
BAM
I'M ALWAYS DOING WHAT I'M TOLD!
WHEN I FINALLY REALIZED THE TRUTH, DO YOU KNOW HOW I FELT?!
BACK THEN, I KNEW KAZUHIRO WAS PUSHING HIMSELF TOO HARD FOR MY SAKE. AND THAT'S WHY...
S
SHU
YES! EXACTLY! I'VE BEEN RIGHT ALL ALONG--
FASH
.....
EH ...
RRRUMMMBBLL
TWRL
SSSSSHHHHH
...?
WA ?!
WAAAAHH!!

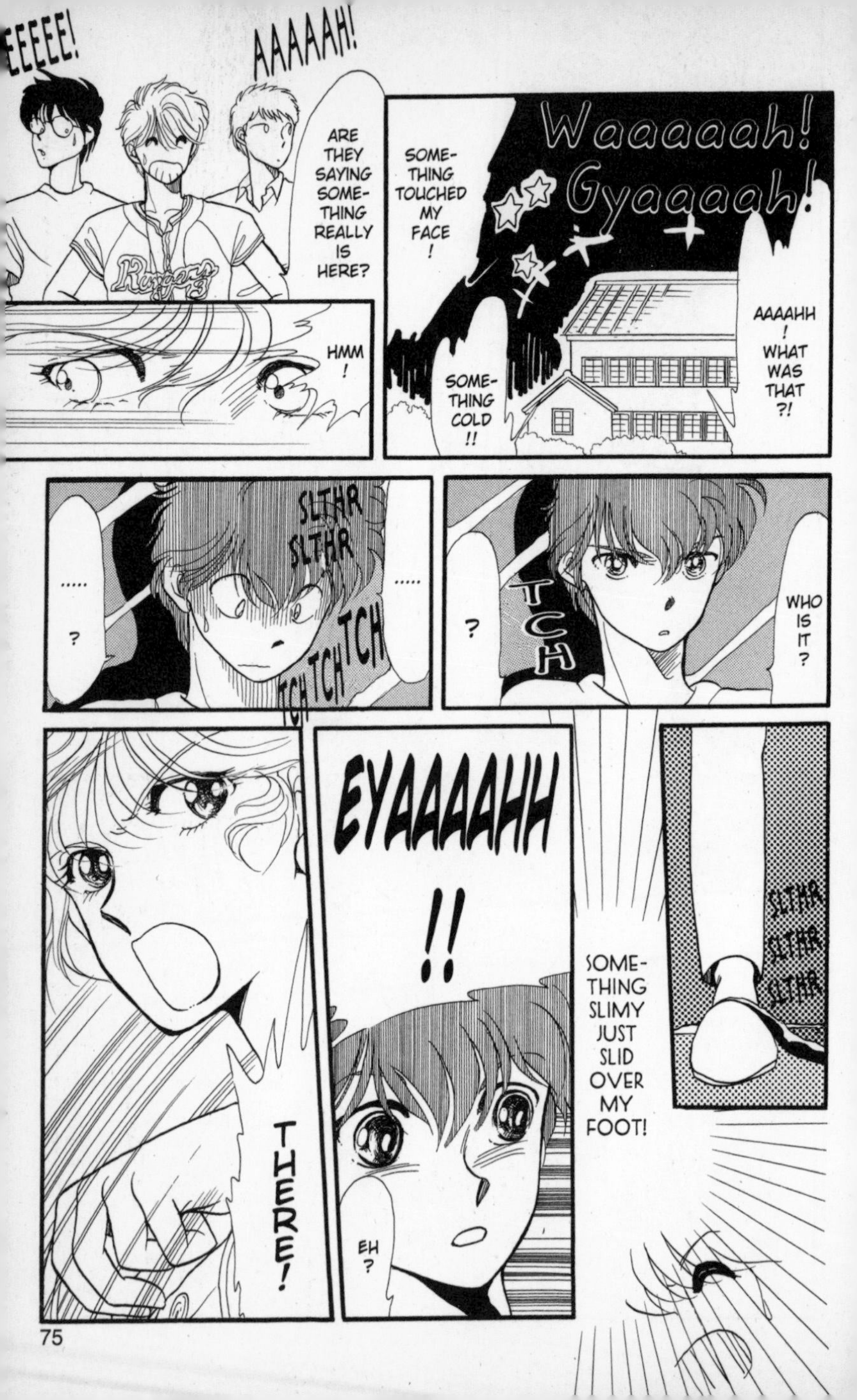
Waaaaah! Gyaaaah!
SOMETHING TOUCHED MY FACE!
AAAAHH! WHAT WAS THAT?!
SOMETHING COLD!!
AAAAAH!
EEEEE!
ARE THEY SAYING SOMETHING REALLY IS HERE?
HMM!
WHO IS IT?
TCH
?
.....
SLTHR SLTHR
TCH TCH TCH
.....
?
SLTHR SLTHR SLTHR
SOMETHING SLIMY JUST SLID OVER MY FOOT!
EYAAAAHH!!
EH?
THERE!

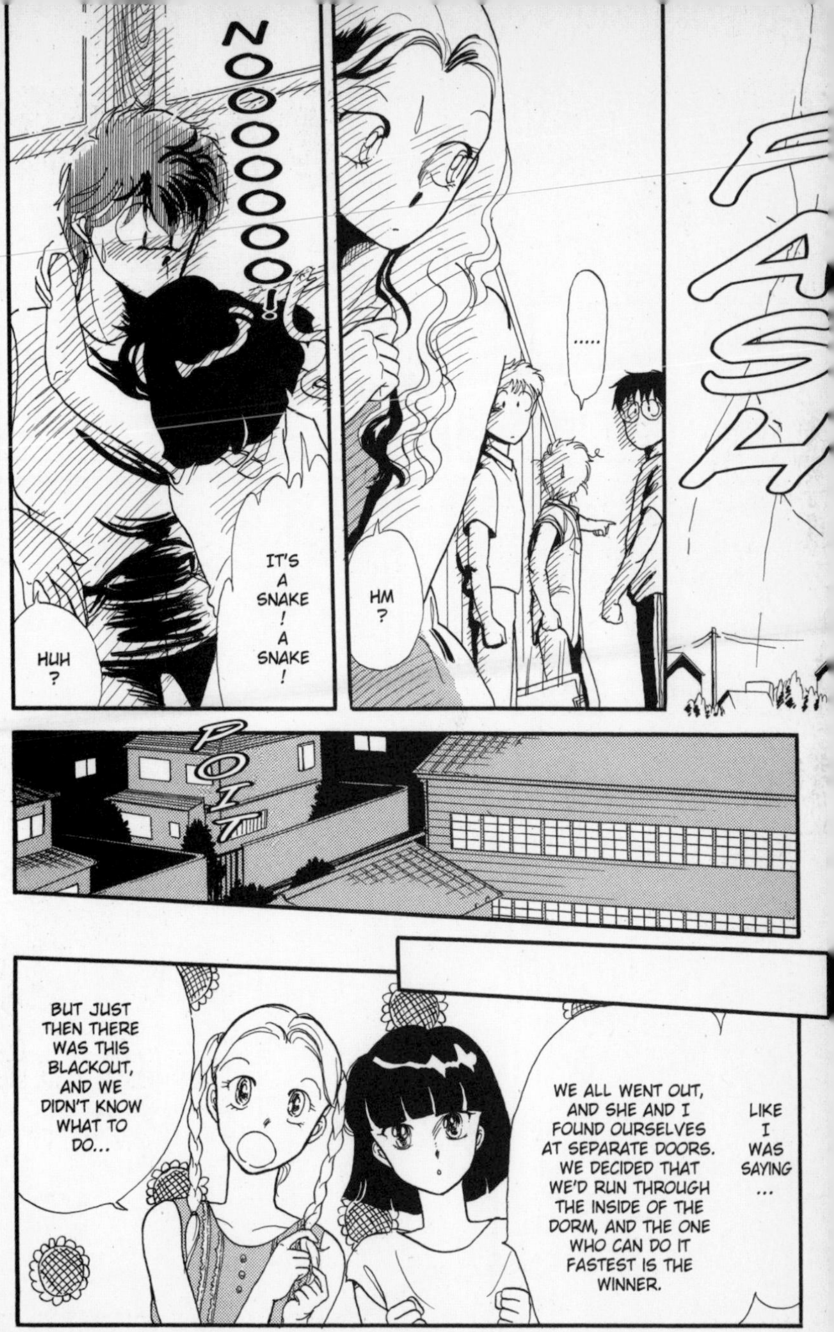
FASH
.....
HM?
NOOOOOO!
IT'S A SNAKE! A SNAKE!
HUH?
POIT
LIKE I WAS SAYING...
WE ALL WENT OUT, AND SHE AND I FOUND OURSELVES AT SEPARATE DOORS. WE DECIDED THAT WE'D RUN THROUGH THE INSIDE OF THE DORM, AND THE ONE WHO CAN DO IT FASTEST IS THE WINNER.
BUT JUST THEN THERE WAS THIS BLACKOUT, AND WE DIDN'T KNOW WHAT TO DO...

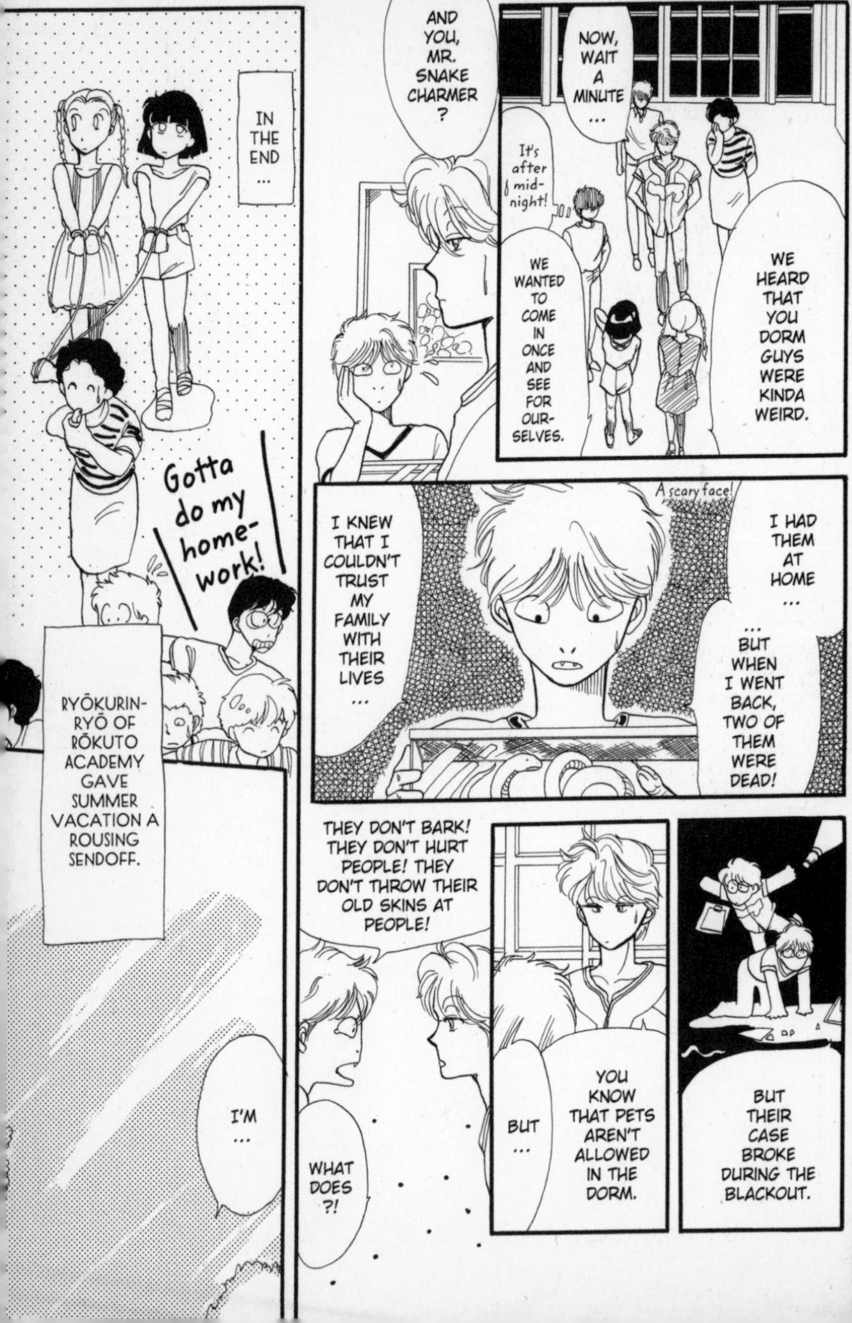
NOW, WAIT A MINUTE ...
It's after mid-night!
WE HEARD THAT YOU DORM GUYS WERE KINDA WEIRD.
WE WANTED TO COME IN ONCE AND SEE FOR OUR-SELVES.
AND YOU, MR. SNAKE CHARMER?
A scary face!
I HAD THEM AT HOME ...
... BUT WHEN I WENT BACK, TWO OF THEM WERE DEAD!
I KNEW THAT I COULDN'T TRUST MY FAMILY WITH THEIR LIVES ...
BUT THEIR CASE BROKE DURING THE BLACKOUT.
YOU KNOW THAT PETS AREN'T ALLOWED IN THE DORM.
BUT ...
THEY DON'T BARK! THEY DON'T HURT PEOPLE! THEY DON'T THROW THEIR OLD SKINS AT PEOPLE!
WHAT DOES ?!
I'M ...
IN THE END ...
Gotta do my home-work!
RYŌKURIN-RYŌ OF RŌKUTO ACADEMY GAVE SUMMER VACATION A ROUSING SENDOFF.

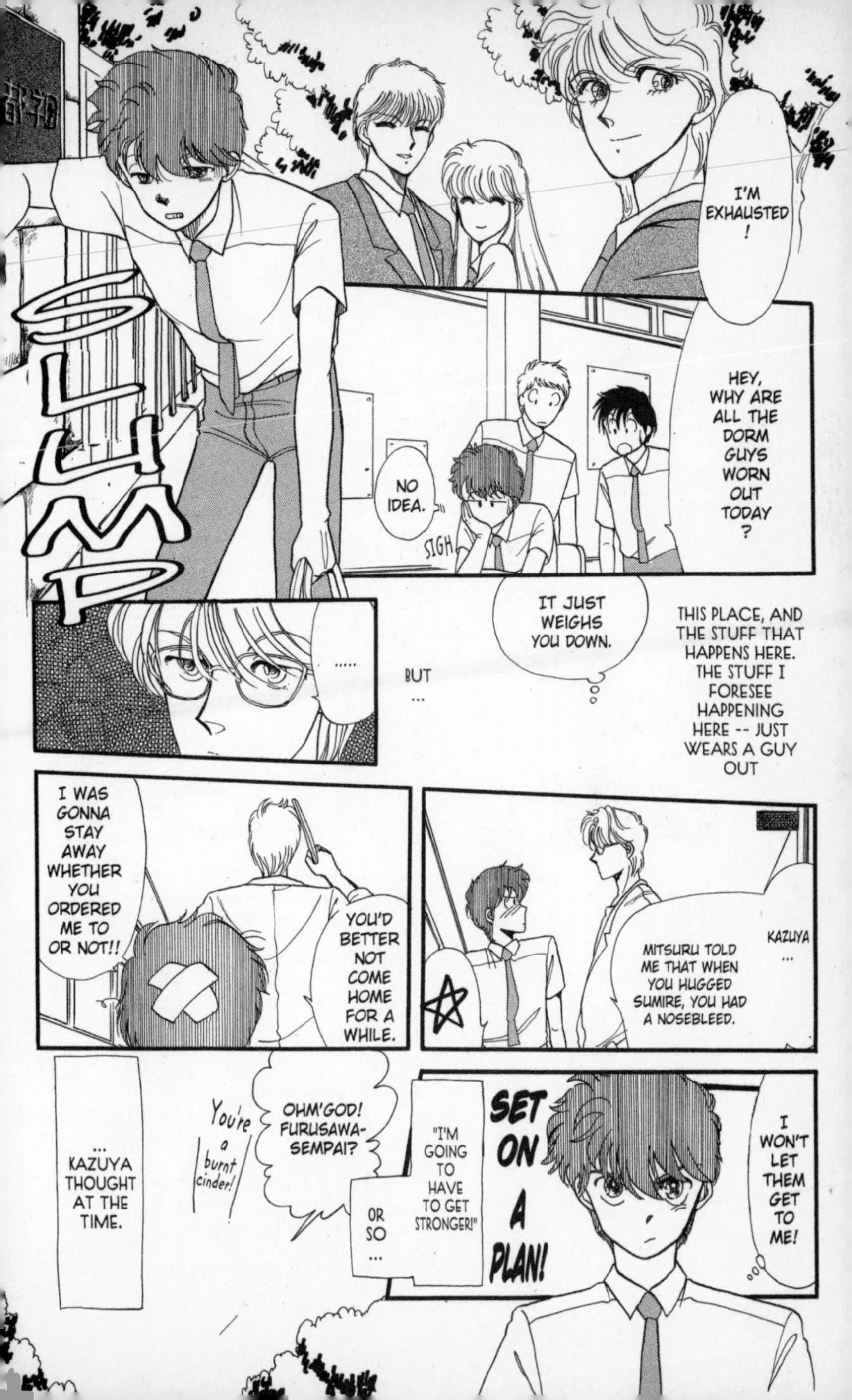
I'M EXHAUSTED!
SLUMP
HEY, WHY ARE ALL THE DORM GUYS WORN OUT TODAY?
NO IDEA.
SIGH
THIS PLACE, AND THE STUFF THAT HAPPENS HERE. THE STUFF I FORESEE HAPPENING HERE -- JUST WEARS A GUY OUT
IT JUST WEIGHS YOU DOWN.
BUT ...
.....
KAZUYA ...
MITSURU TOLD ME THAT WHEN YOU HUGGED SUMIRE, YOU HAD A NOSEBLEED.
YOU'D BETTER NOT COME HOME FOR A WHILE.
I WAS GONNA STAY AWAY WHETHER YOU ORDERED ME TO OR NOT!!
I WON'T LET THEM GET TO ME!
SET ON A PLAN!
"I'M GOING TO HAVE TO GET STRONGER!"
OR SO ...
OHM'GOD! FURUSAWA-SEMPAI?
You're a burnt cinder!
... KAZUYA THOUGHT AT THE TIME.

TILL WE MEET AGAIN AT GREENWOOD

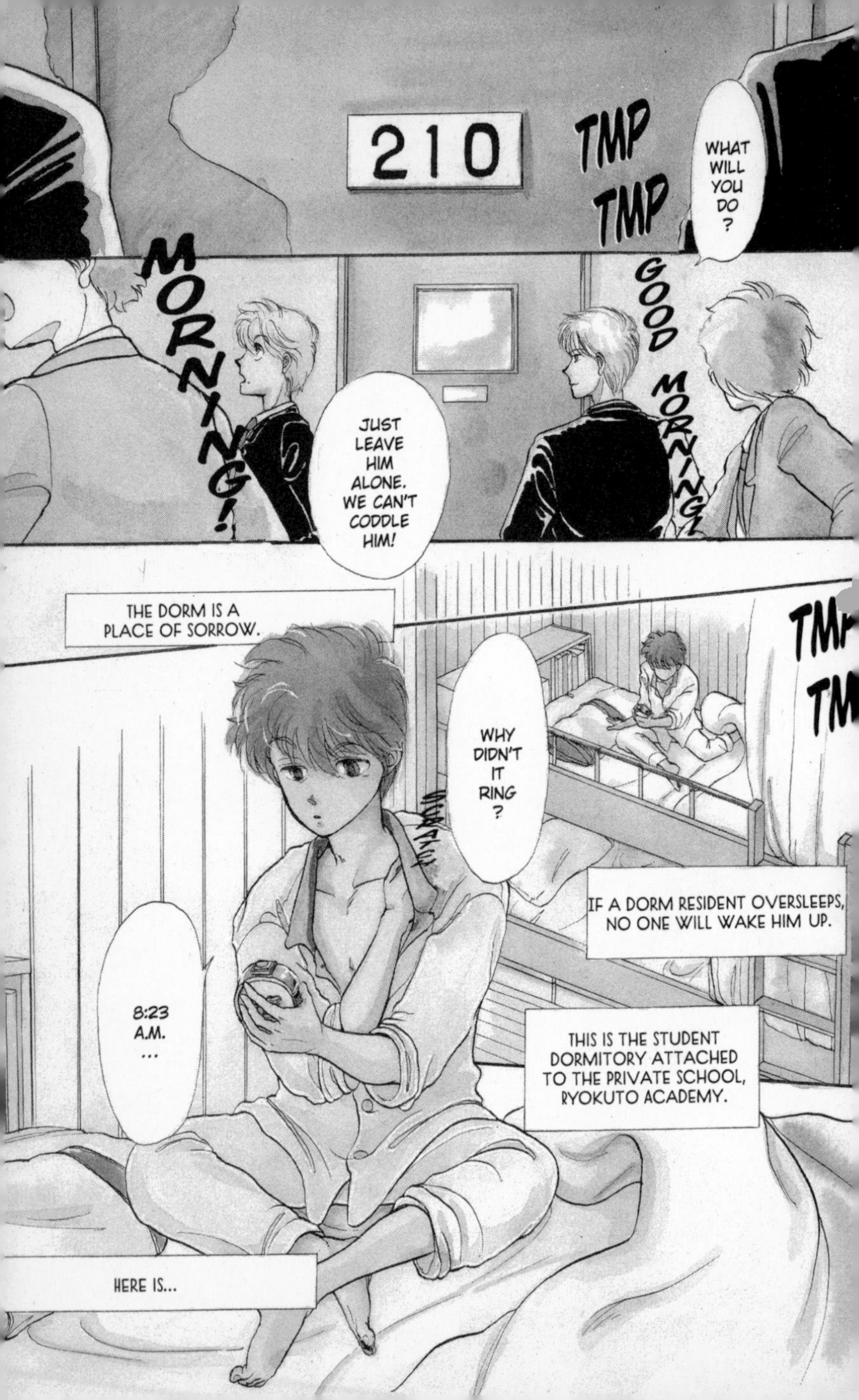
WHAT WILL YOU DO?
TMP TMP
210
GOOD MORNING
JUST LEAVE HIM ALONE. WE CAN'T CODDLE HIM!
MORNING!
TM TM
THE DORM IS A PLACE OF SORROW.
WHY DIDN'T IT RING?
IF A DORM RESIDENT OVERSLEEPS, NO ONE WILL WAKE HIM UP.
THIS IS THE STUDENT DORMITORY ATTACHED TO THE PRIVATE SCHOOL, RYOKUTO ACADEMY.
8:23 A.M. ...
HERE IS...

TILL WE MEET AGAIN AT GREENWOOD

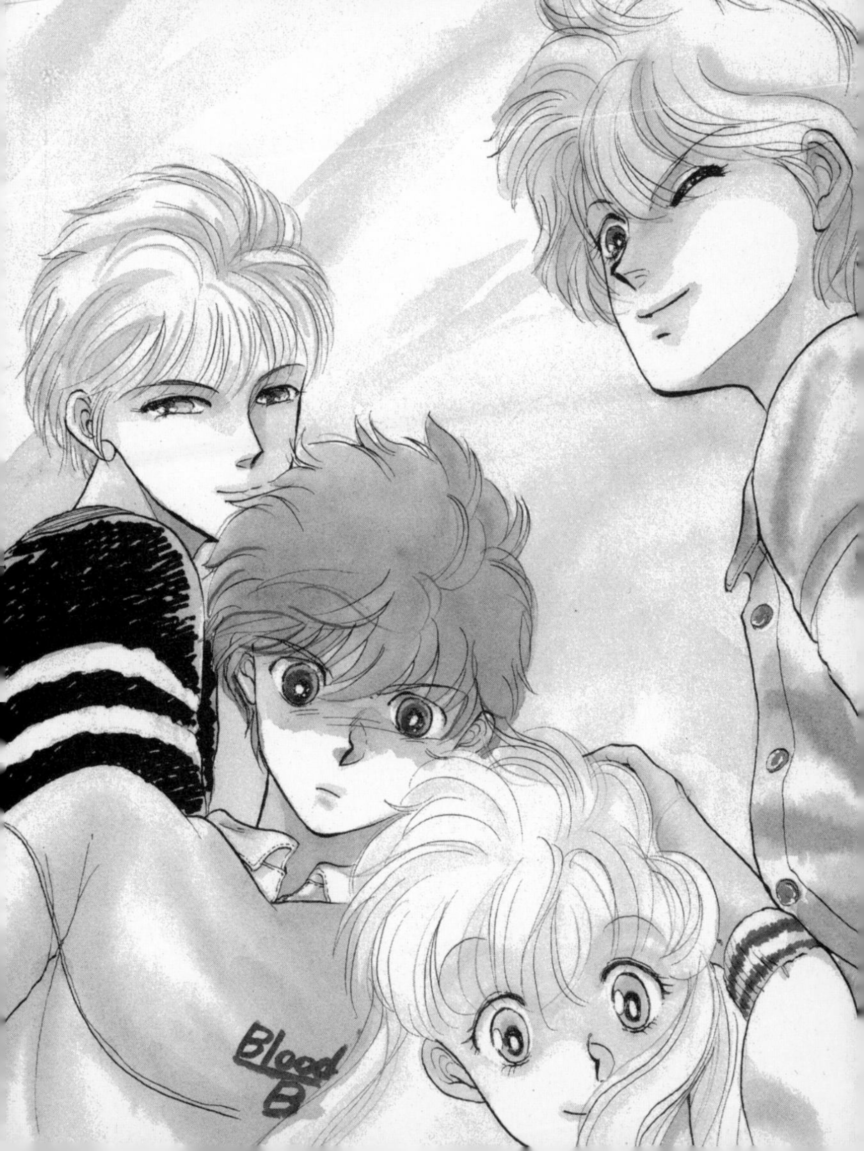
Blood
B

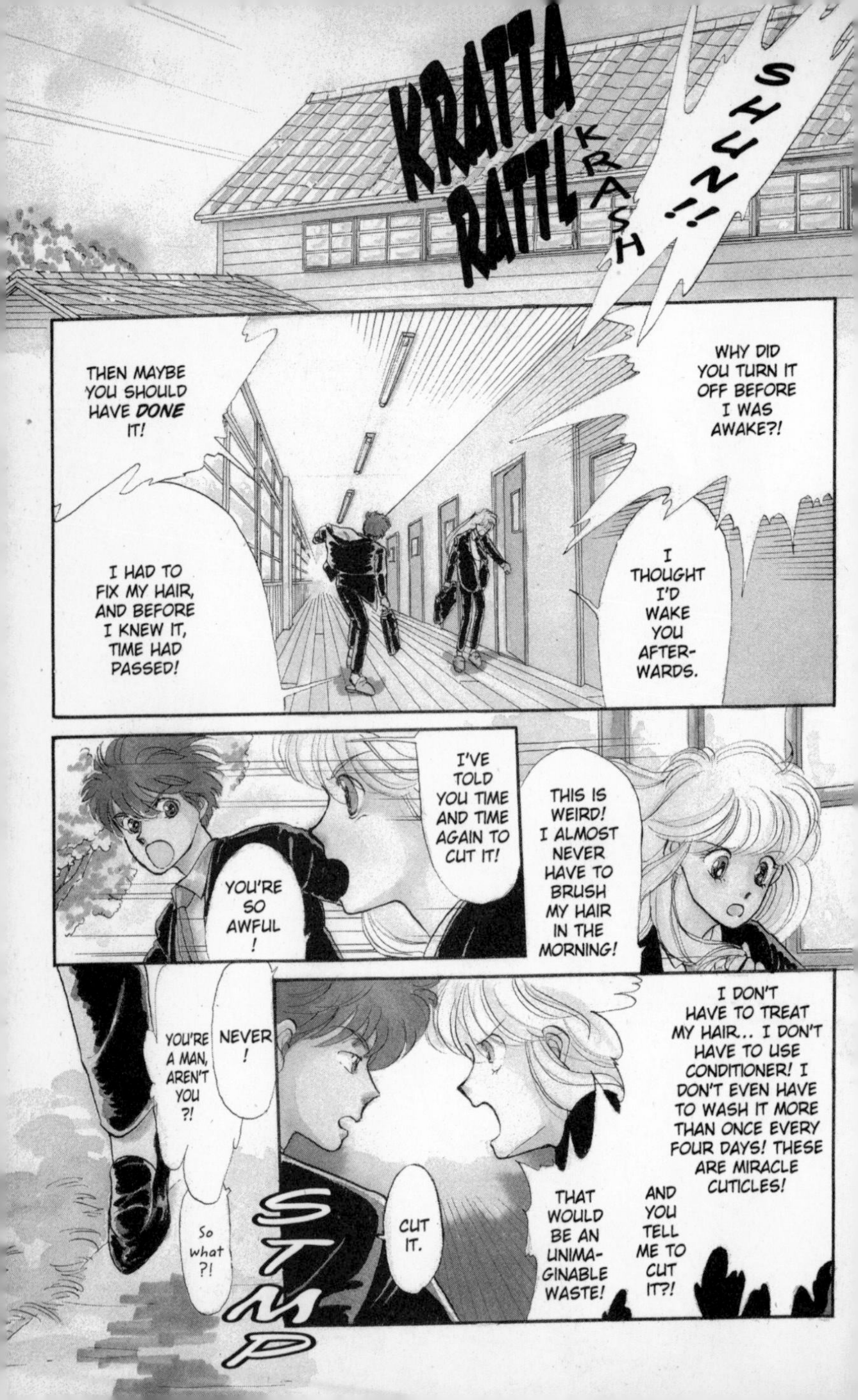

SHUN!!
KRASH
KRATTA RATTL
WHY DID YOU TURN IT OFF BEFORE I WAS AWAKE?!
THEN MAYBE YOU SHOULD HAVE *DONE* IT!
I THOUGHT I'D WAKE YOU AFTERWARDS.
I HAD TO FIX MY HAIR, AND BEFORE I KNEW IT, TIME HAD PASSED!
THIS IS WEIRD! I ALMOST NEVER HAVE TO BRUSH MY HAIR IN THE MORNING!
I'VE TOLD YOU TIME AND TIME AGAIN TO CUT IT!
YOU'RE SO AWFUL!
I DON'T HAVE TO TREAT MY HAIR... I DON'T HAVE TO USE CONDITIONER! I DON'T EVEN HAVE TO WASH IT MORE THAN ONCE EVERY FOUR DAYS! THESE ARE MIRACLE CUTICLES!
AND YOU TELL ME TO CUT IT?!
THAT WOULD BE AN UNIMAGINABLE WASTE!
CUT IT.
NEVER!
YOU'RE A MAN, AREN'T YOU?!
So what?!
STMP

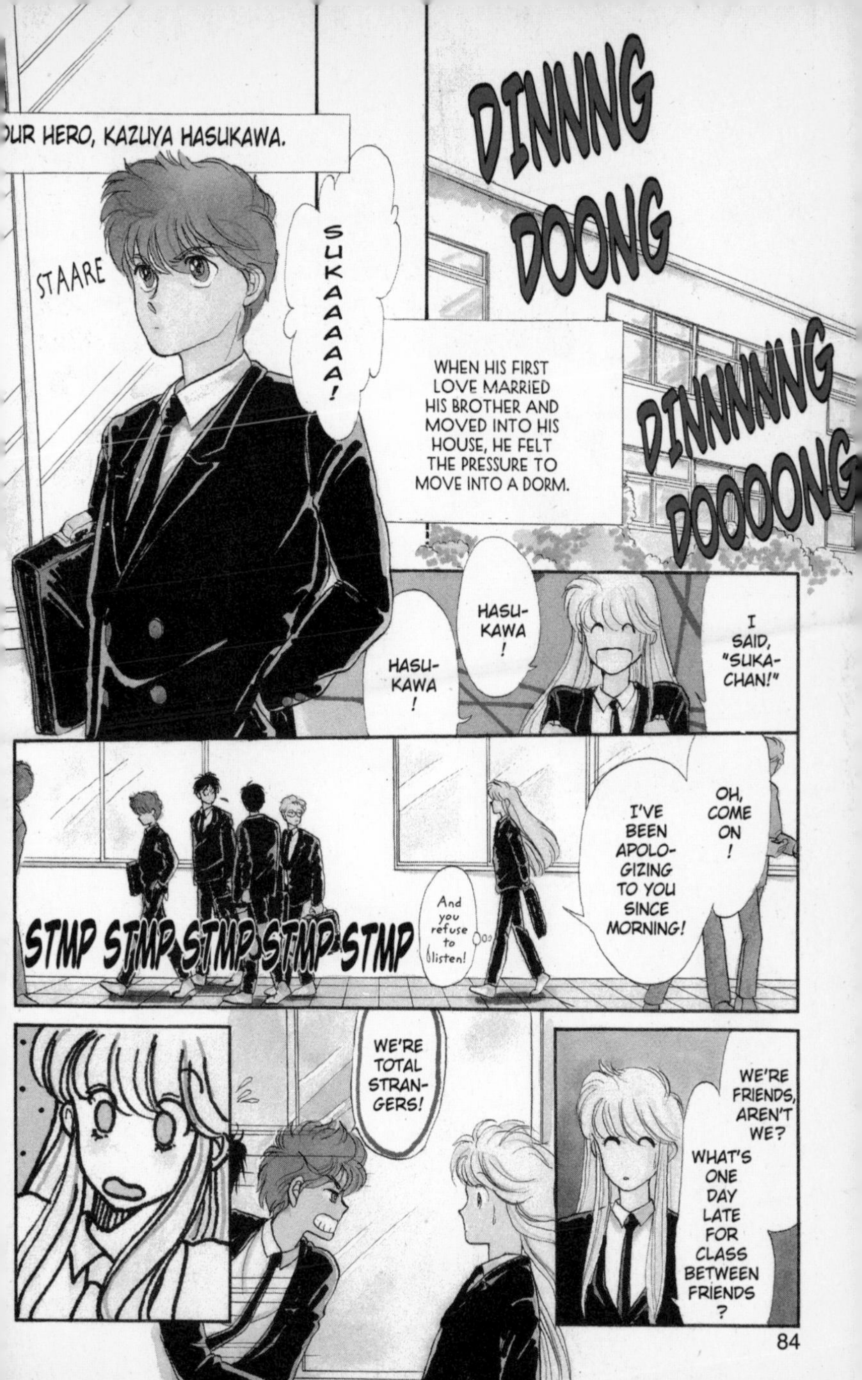
DINNNG DOONG
DINNNNG DOOOONG
WHEN HIS FIRST LOVE MARRIED HIS BROTHER AND MOVED INTO HIS HOUSE, HE FELT THE PRESSURE TO MOVE INTO A DORM.
I SAID, "SUKA-CHAN!"
HASU-KAWA!
HASU-KAWA!
UR HERO, KAZUYA HASUKAWA.
SUKAAAAAA!
STAARE
OH, COME ON!
I'VE BEEN APOLOGIZING TO YOU SINCE MORNING!
And you refuse to listen!
STMP STMP STMP STMP STMP
WE'RE FRIENDS, AREN'T WE?
WHAT'S ONE DAY LATE FOR CLASS BETWEEN FRIENDS?
WE'RE TOTAL STRANGERS!

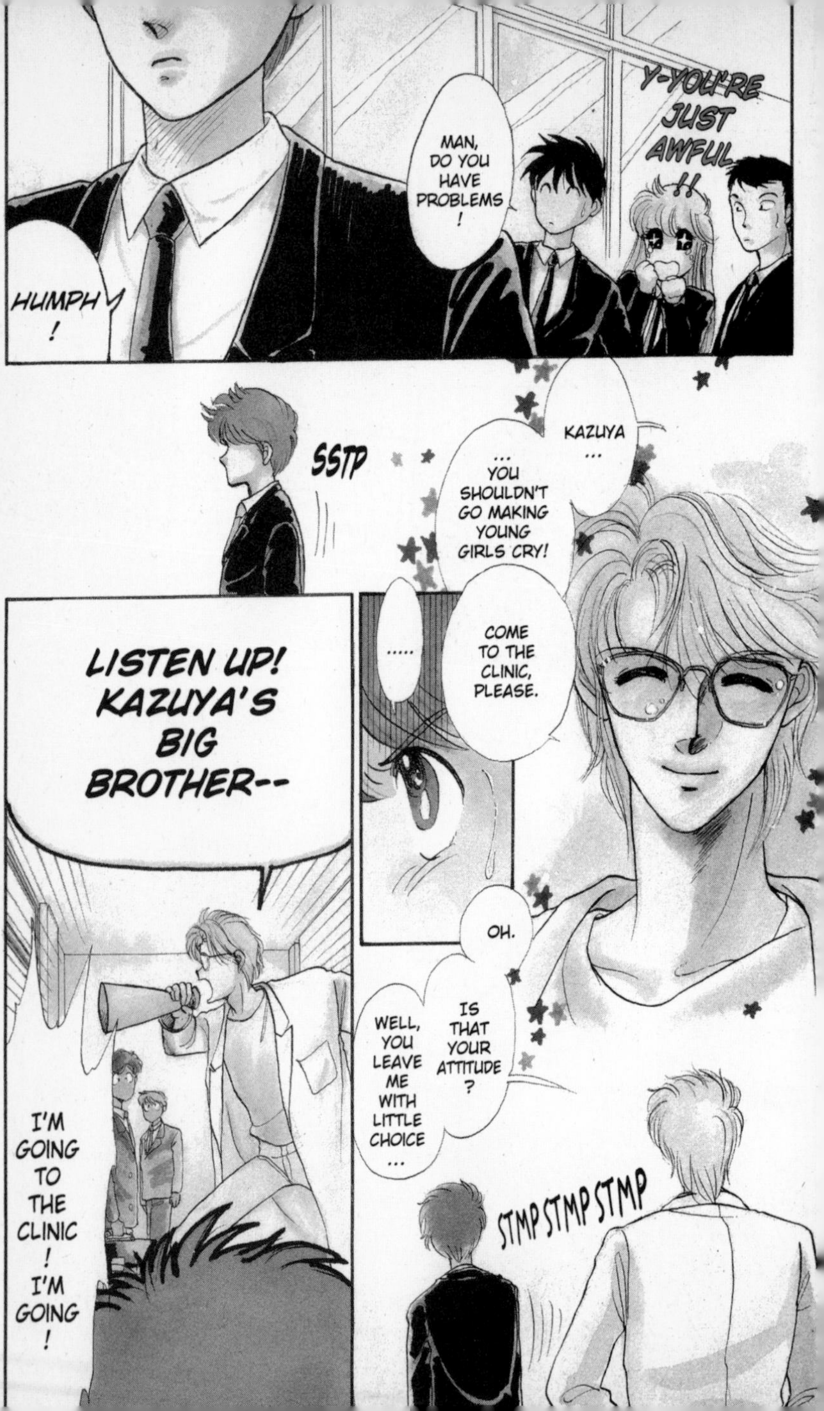

Y-YOU'RE JUST AWFUL!!
MAN, DO YOU HAVE PROBLEMS!
HUMPH!
SSTP
KAZUYA...
...YOU SHOULDN'T GO MAKING YOUNG GIRLS CRY!
COME TO THE CLINIC, PLEASE.
......
OH.
IS THAT YOUR ATTITUDE?
WELL, YOU LEAVE ME WITH LITTLE CHOICE...
STMP STMP STMP
LISTEN UP! KAZUYA'S BIG BROTHER--
I'M GOING TO THE CLINIC! I'M GOING!

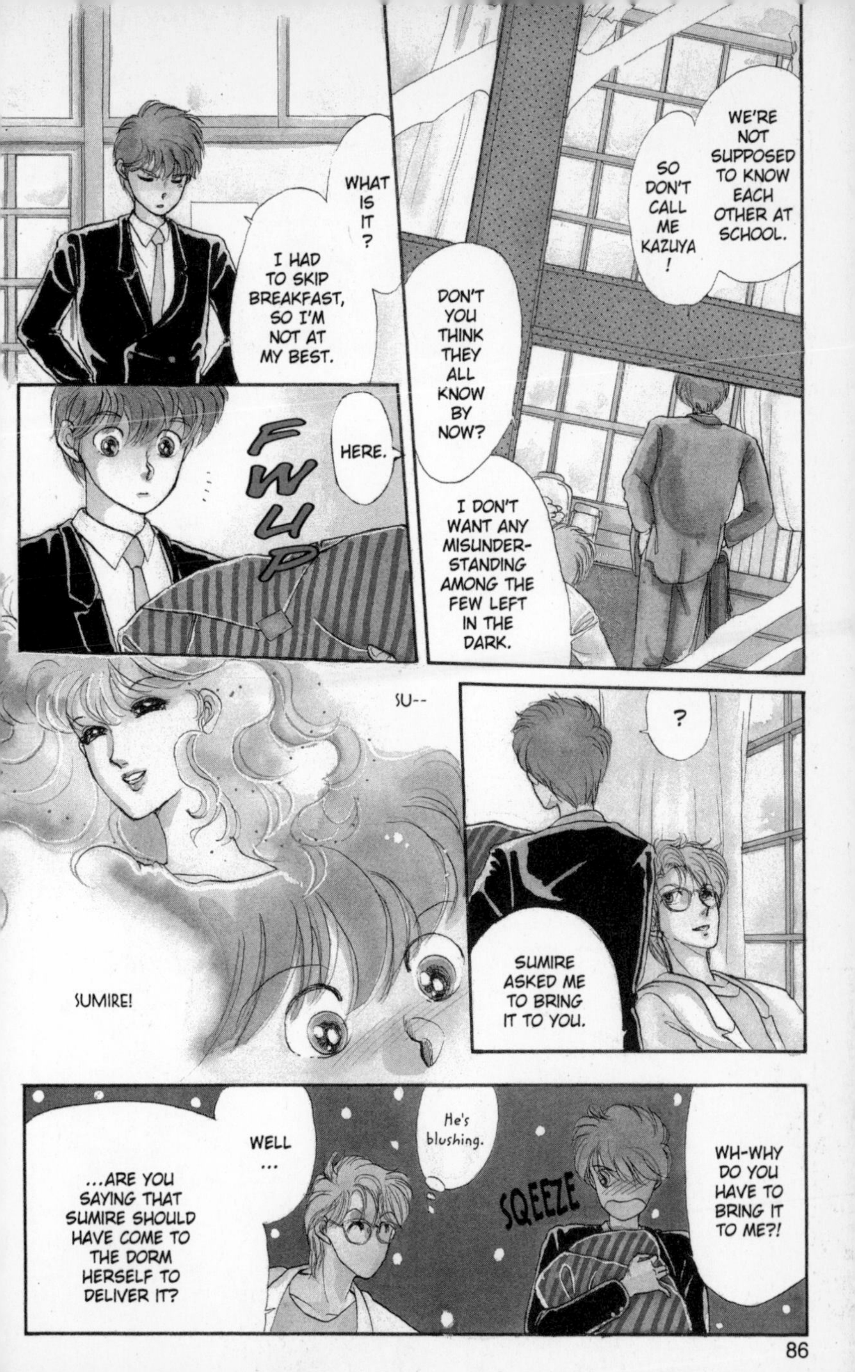
WE'RE NOT SUPPOSED TO KNOW EACH OTHER AT SCHOOL.
SO DON'T CALL ME KAZUYA!
DON'T YOU THINK THEY ALL KNOW BY NOW?
I DON'T WANT ANY MISUNDER-STANDING AMONG THE FEW LEFT IN THE DARK.
WHAT IS IT?
I HAD TO SKIP BREAKFAST, SO I'M NOT AT MY BEST.
HERE.
FWUP
?
SUMIRE ASKED ME TO BRING IT TO YOU.
SU--
SUMIRE!
WH-WHY DO YOU HAVE TO BRING IT TO ME?!
SQEEZE
He's blushing.
WELL...
...ARE YOU SAYING THAT SUMIRE SHOULD HAVE COME TO THE DORM HERSELF TO DELIVER IT?

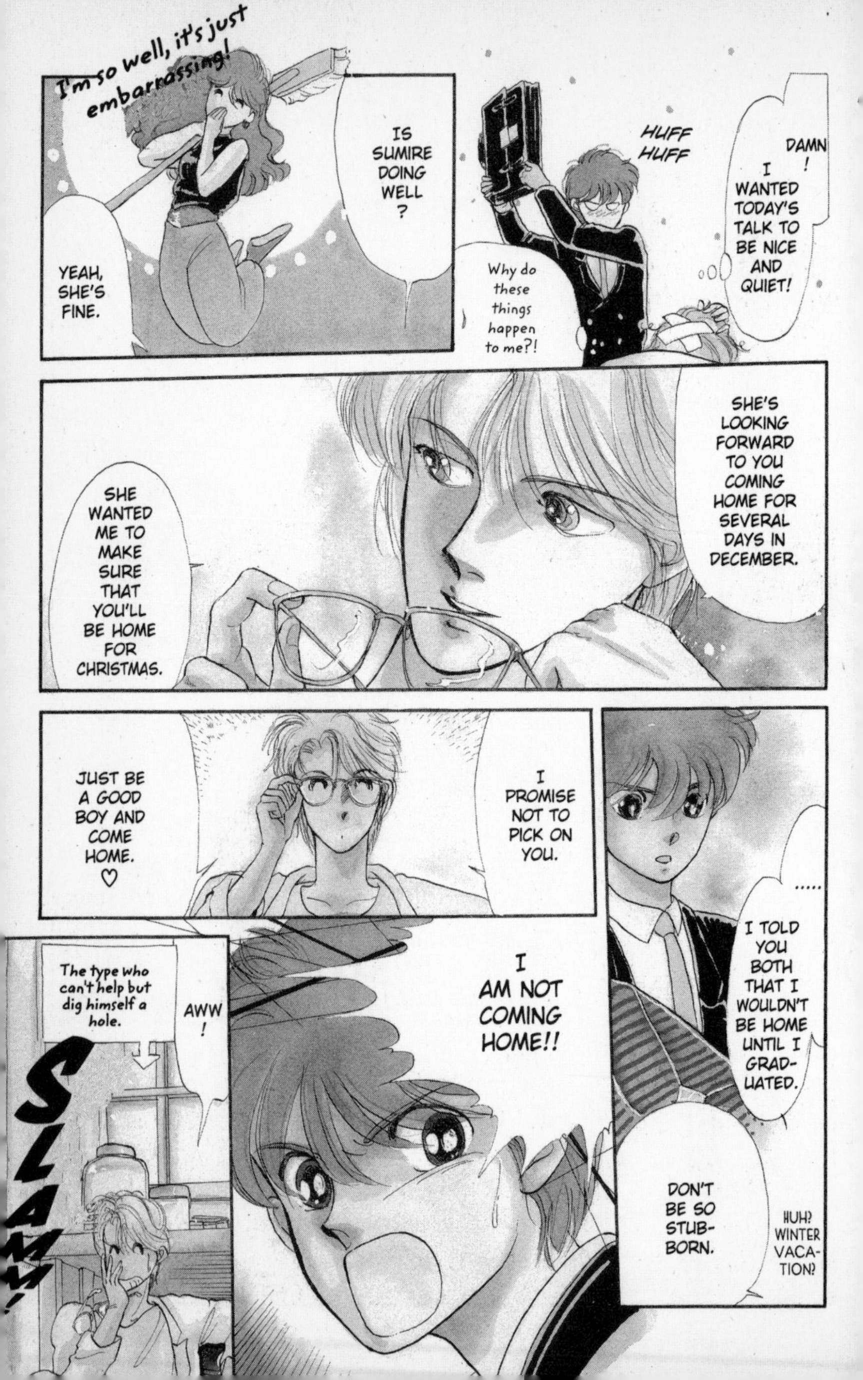
HUFF HUFF
DAMN! I WANTED TODAY'S TALK TO BE NICE AND QUIET!
Why do these things happen to me?!
IS SUMIRE DOING WELL?
I'm so well, it's just embarrassing!
YEAH, SHE'S FINE.
SHE'S LOOKING FORWARD TO YOU COMING HOME FOR SEVERAL DAYS IN DECEMBER.
SHE WANTED ME TO MAKE SURE THAT YOU'LL BE HOME FOR CHRISTMAS.
.....
I TOLD YOU BOTH THAT I WOULDN'T BE HOME UNTIL I GRAD-UATED.
HUH? WINTER VACA-TION?
DON'T BE SO STUB-BORN.
I PROMISE NOT TO PICK ON YOU.
JUST BE A GOOD BOY AND COME HOME. ♡
I AM NOT COMING HOME!!
AWW!
The type who can't help but dig himself a hole.
SLAM!

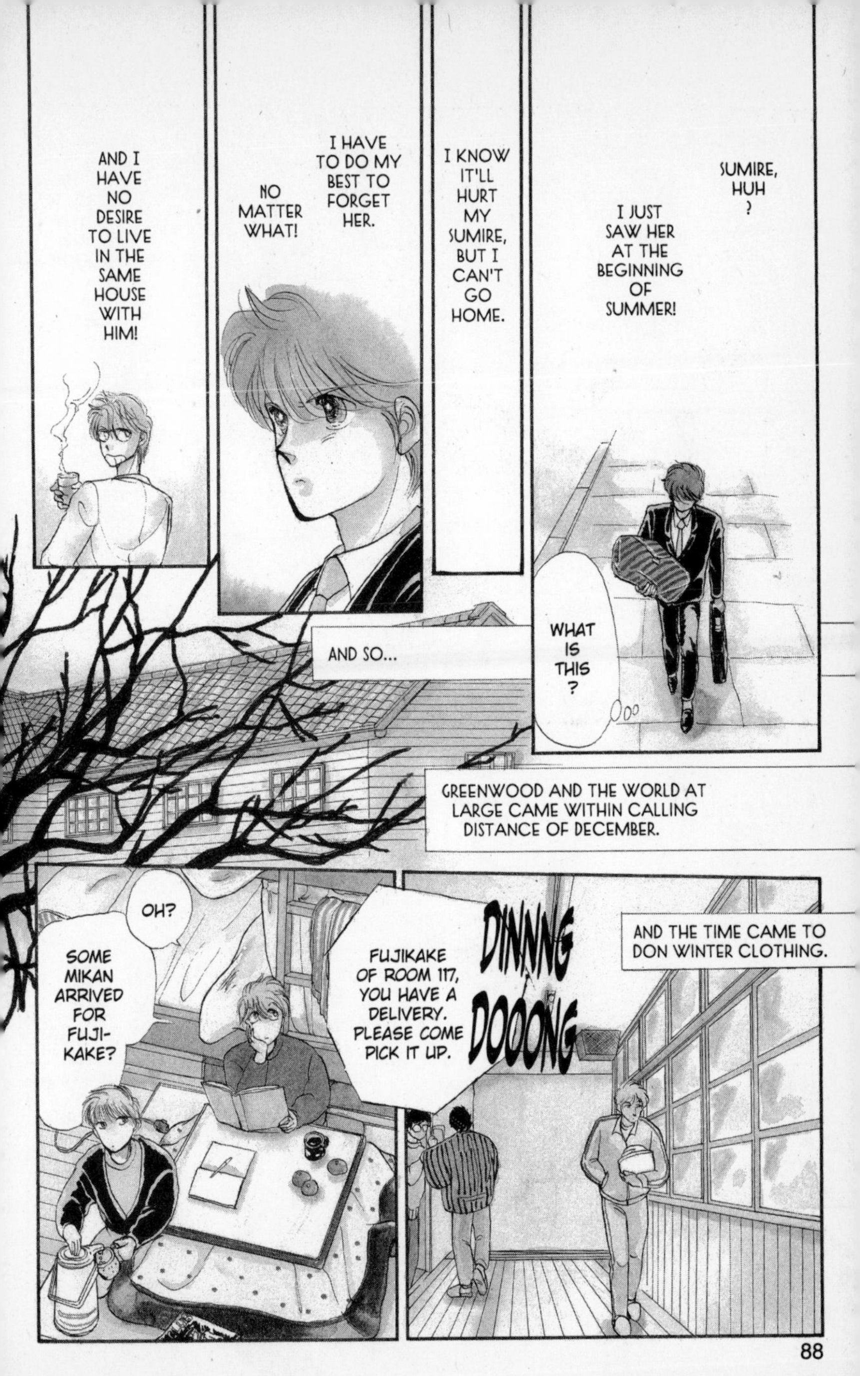
SUMIRE, HUH?
I JUST SAW HER AT THE BEGINNING OF SUMMER!
WHAT IS THIS?
I KNOW IT'LL HURT MY SUMIRE, BUT I CAN'T GO HOME.
I HAVE TO DO MY BEST TO FORGET HER.
NO MATTER WHAT!
AND I HAVE NO DESIRE TO LIVE IN THE SAME HOUSE WITH HIM!
AND SO...
GREENWOOD AND THE WORLD AT LARGE CAME WITHIN CALLING DISTANCE OF DECEMBER.
AND THE TIME CAME TO DON WINTER CLOTHING.
DINNNG
DOOONG
FUJIKAKE OF ROOM 117, YOU HAVE A DELIVERY. PLEASE COME PICK IT UP.
OH?
SOME MIKAN ARRIVED FOR FUJI-KAKE?

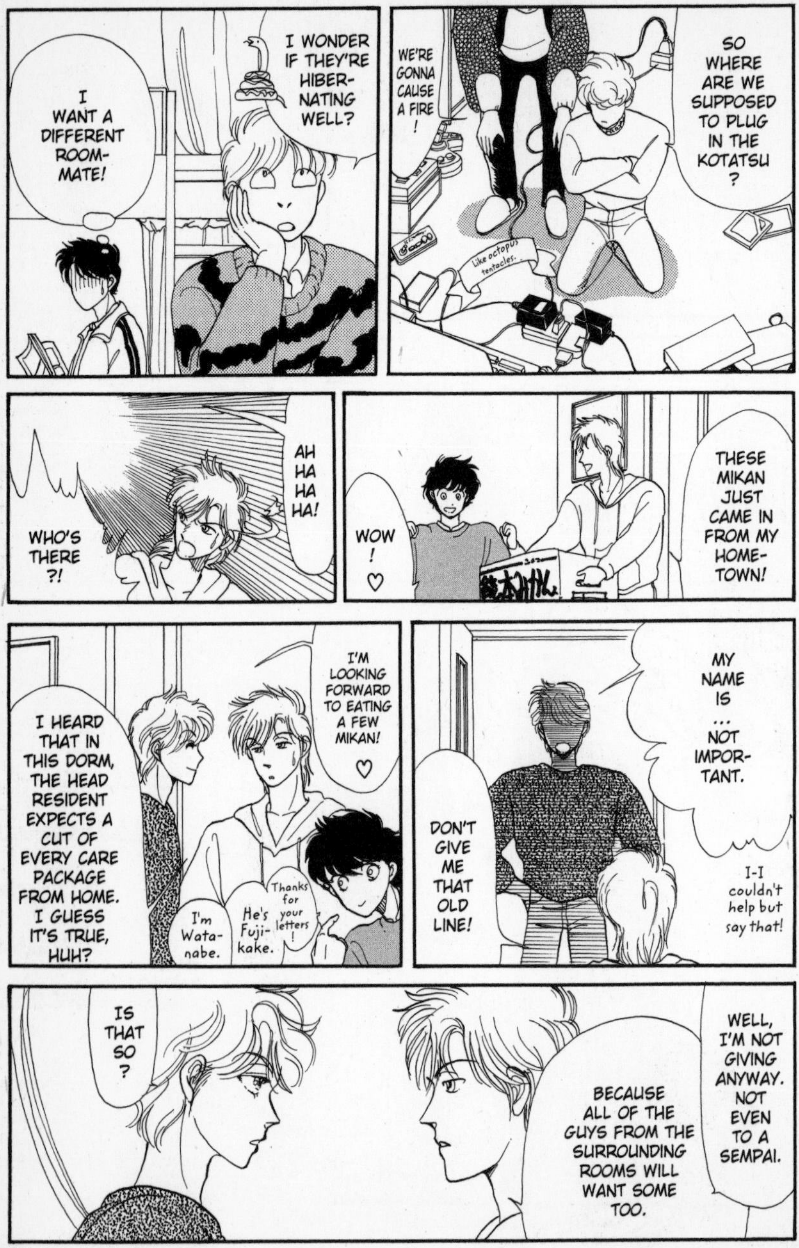
SO WHERE ARE WE SUPPOSED TO PLUG IN THE KOTATSU?
WE'RE GONNA CAUSE A FIRE!
Like octopus tentacles.
I WONDER IF THEY'RE HIBERNATING WELL?
I WANT A DIFFERENT ROOMMATE!
THESE MIKAN JUST CAME IN FROM MY HOMETOWN!
WOW! ♡
AH HA HA HA!
WHO'S THERE?!
MY NAME IS... NOT IMPORTANT.
I-I couldn't help but say that!
DON'T GIVE ME THAT OLD LINE!
I'M LOOKING FORWARD TO EATING A FEW MIKAN! ♡
I HEARD THAT IN THIS DORM, THE HEAD RESIDENT EXPECTS A CUT OF EVERY CARE PACKAGE FROM HOME. I GUESS IT'S TRUE, HUH?
Thanks for your letters!
He's Fujikake.
I'm Watanabe.
WELL, I'M NOT GIVING ANYWAY. NOT EVEN TO A SEMPAI.
BECAUSE ALL OF THE GUYS FROM THE SURROUNDING ROOMS WILL WANT SOME TOO.
IS THAT SO?

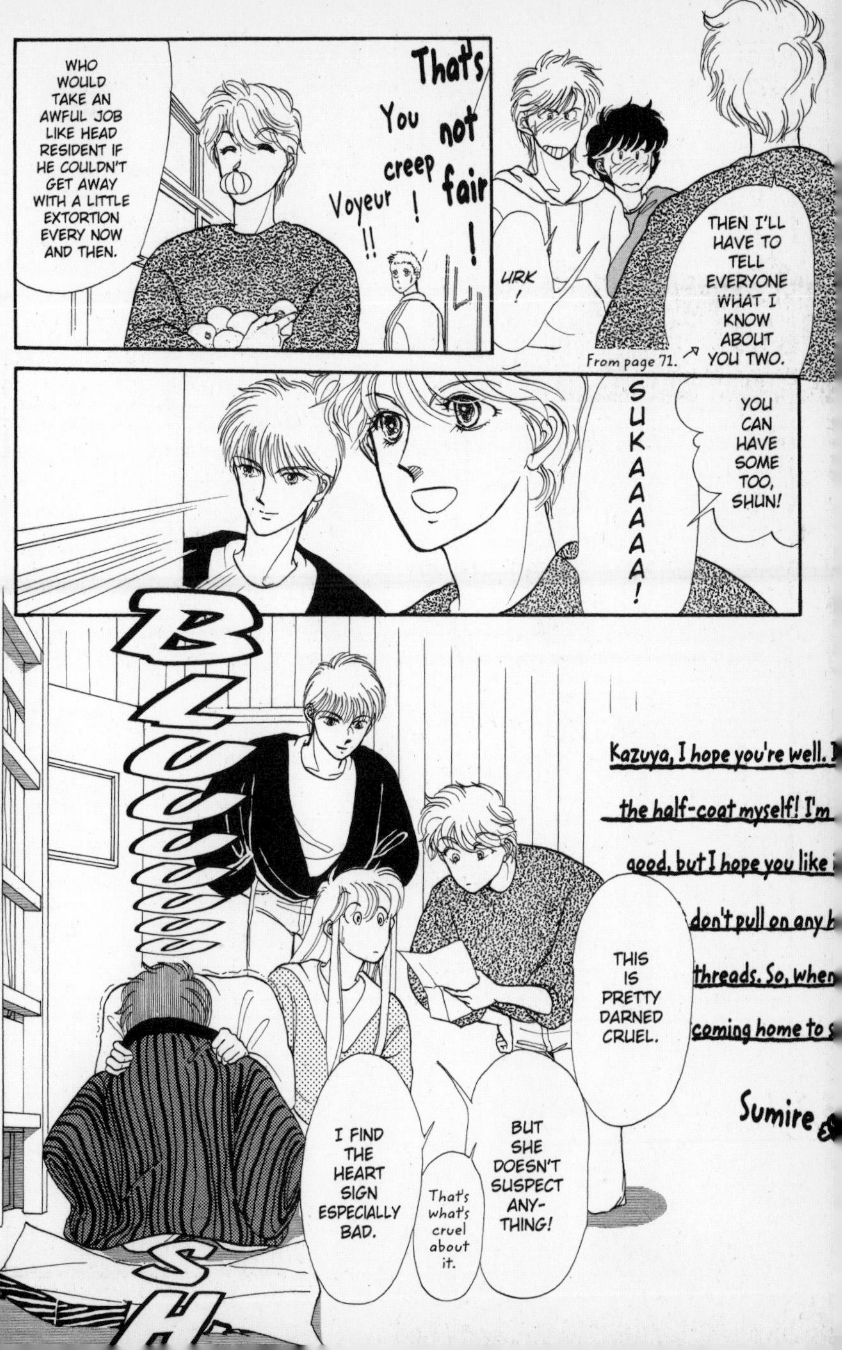

THEN I'LL HAVE TO TELL EVERYONE WHAT I KNOW ABOUT YOU TWO.
From page 71.
URK!
That's not fair!
You creep!
Voyeur!!
WHO WOULD TAKE AN AWFUL JOB LIKE HEAD RESIDENT IF HE COULDN'T GET AWAY WITH A LITTLE EXTORTION EVERY NOW AND THEN.
YOU CAN HAVE SOME TOO, SHUN!
SUKAAAAAA!
Kazuya, I hope you're well.
the half-coat myself! I'm
good, but I hope you like
don't pull on any
threads. So, when
coming home to
Sumire
THIS IS PRETTY DARNED CRUEL.
BUT SHE DOESN'T SUSPECT ANYTHING!
That's what's cruel about it.
I FIND THE HEART SIGN ESPECIALLY BAD.
BLUUUUUUSH

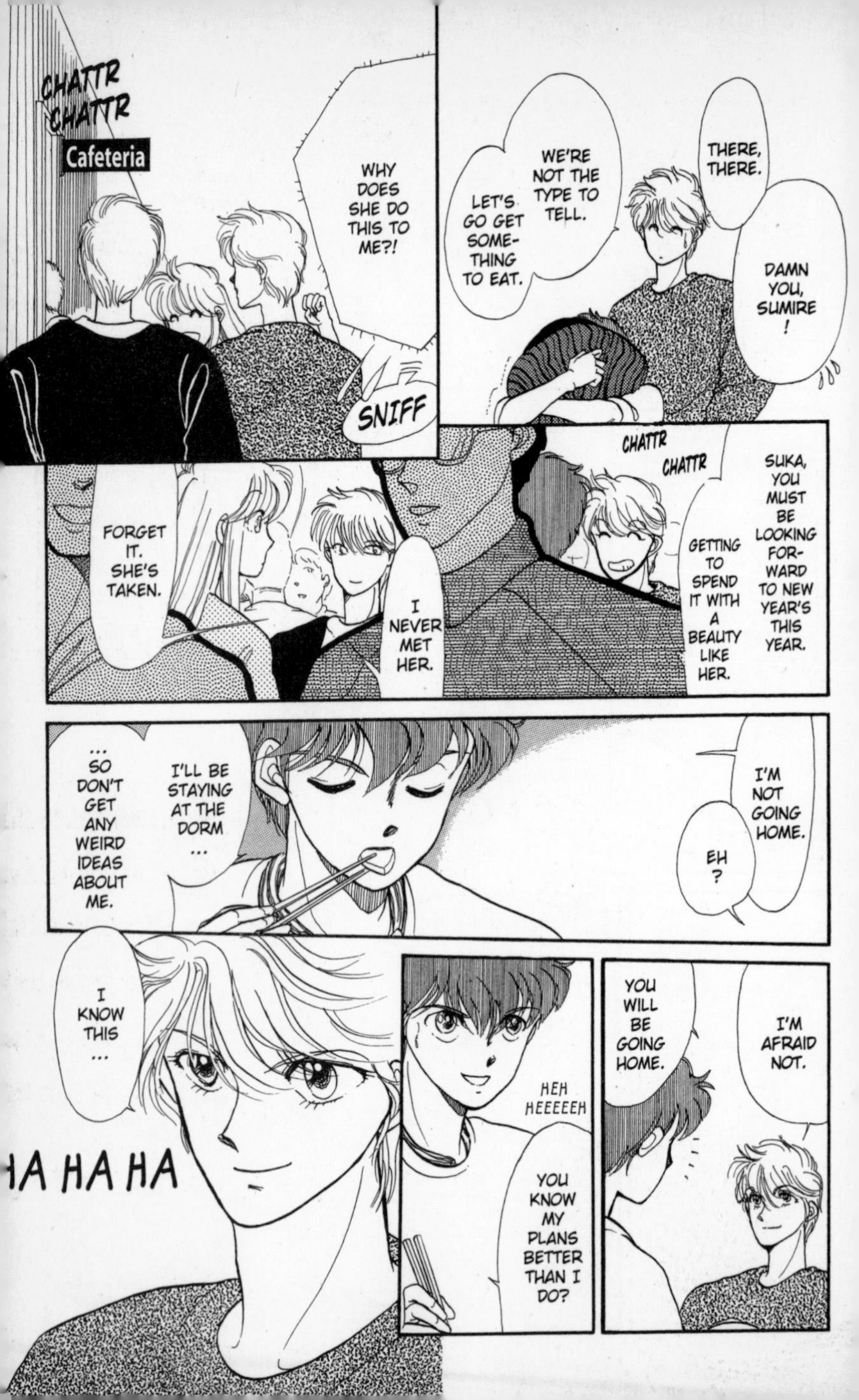
THERE, THERE.
DAMN YOU, SUMIRE!
WE'RE NOT THE TYPE TO TELL.
LET'S GO GET SOME-THING TO EAT.
CHATTR CHATTR
Cafeteria
WHY DOES SHE DO THIS TO ME?!
SNIFF
CHATTR CHATTR
SUKA, YOU MUST BE LOOKING FOR-WARD TO NEW YEAR'S THIS YEAR.
GETTING TO SPEND IT WITH A BEAUTY LIKE HER.
I NEVER MET HER.
FORGET IT. SHE'S TAKEN.
I'M NOT GOING HOME.
EH?
I'LL BE STAYING AT THE DORM...
...SO DON'T GET ANY WEIRD IDEAS ABOUT ME.
I'M AFRAID NOT.
YOU WILL BE GOING HOME.
HEH HEEEEEH
YOU KNOW MY PLANS BETTER THAN I DO?
I KNOW THIS...
HA HA HA

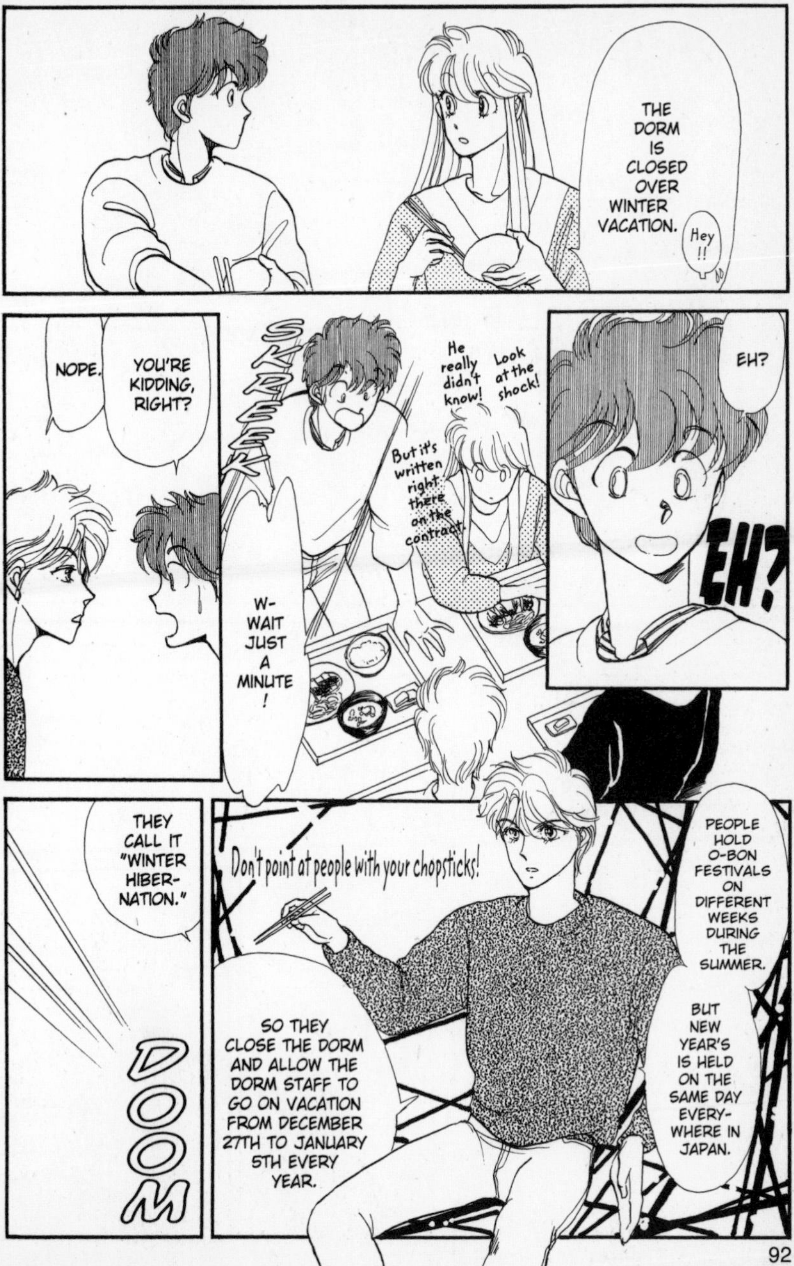
THE DORM IS CLOSED OVER WINTER VACATION.
Hey !!
EH?
EH?
Look at the shock!
He really didn't know!
But it's written right there on the contract.
SKREEEK
W-WAIT JUST A MINUTE!
YOU'RE KIDDING, RIGHT?
NOPE.
PEOPLE HOLD O-BON FESTIVALS ON DIFFERENT WEEKS DURING THE SUMMER.
BUT NEW YEAR'S IS HELD ON THE SAME DAY EVERYWHERE IN JAPAN.
Don't point at people with your chopsticks!
SO THEY CLOSE THE DORM AND ALLOW THE DORM STAFF TO GO ON VACATION FROM DECEMBER 27TH TO JANUARY 5TH EVERY YEAR.
THEY CALL IT "WINTER HIBERNATION."
DOOM

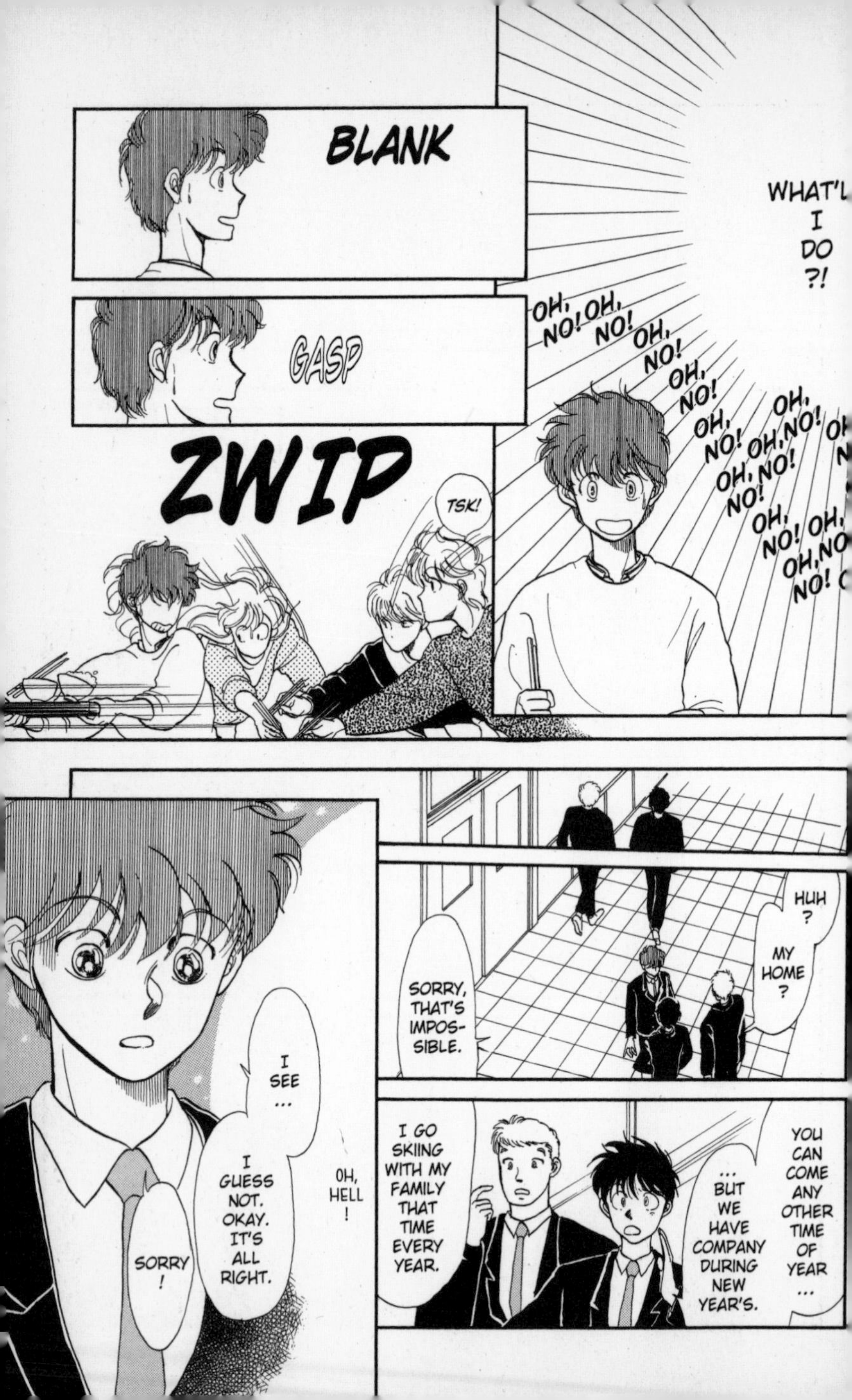
WHAT'L I DO ?!
OH, NO! OH, NO! OH, NO! OH, NO! OH, NO! OH, NO! OH, NO! OH, NO! OH, NO! OH, OH, NO!
BLANK
GASP
ZWIP
TSK!
HUH ?
MY HOME ?
SORRY, THAT'S IMPOSSIBLE.
YOU CAN COME ANY OTHER TIME OF YEAR ...
... BUT WE HAVE COMPANY DURING NEW YEAR'S.
I GO SKIING WITH MY FAMILY THAT TIME EVERY YEAR.
I SEE ...
I GUESS NOT. OKAY. IT'S ALL RIGHT.
OH, HELL !
SORRY !

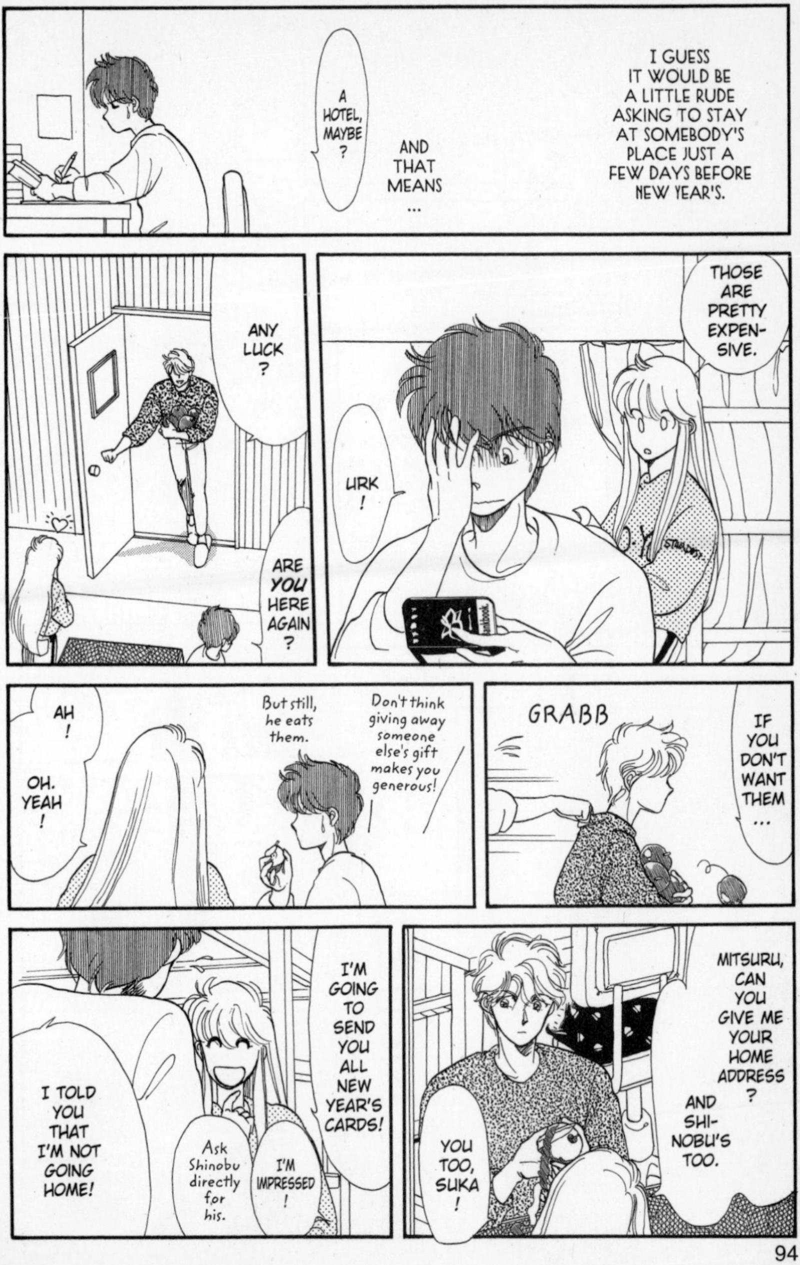
I GUESS IT WOULD BE A LITTLE RUDE ASKING TO STAY AT SOMEBODY'S PLACE JUST A FEW DAYS BEFORE NEW YEAR'S.
AND THAT MEANS...
A HOTEL, MAYBE?
THOSE ARE PRETTY EXPEN-SIVE.
URK!
ANY LUCK?
ARE *YOU* HERE AGAIN?
IF YOU DON'T WANT THEM...
GRABB
Don't think giving away someone else's gift makes you generous!
But still, he eats them.
AH!
OH. YEAH!
MITSURU, CAN YOU GIVE ME YOUR HOME ADDRESS?
AND SHI-NOBU'S TOO.
YOU TOO, SUKA!
I'M GOING TO SEND YOU ALL NEW YEAR'S CARDS!
I'M IMPRESSED!
Ask Shinobu directly for his.
I TOLD YOU THAT I'M NOT GOING HOME!

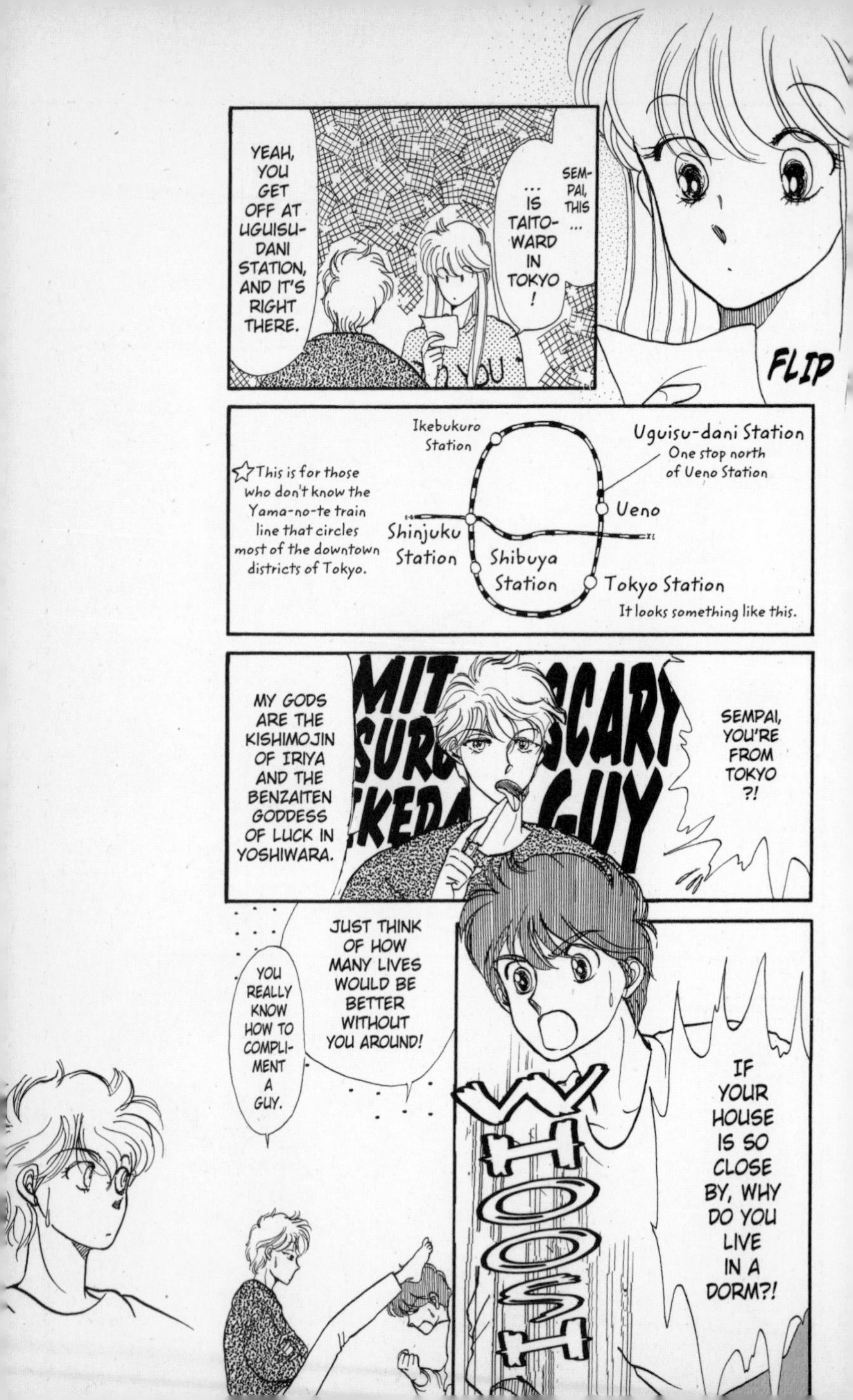
FLIP
SEMPAI, THIS ...
... IS TAITO-WARD IN TOKYO!
YEAH, YOU GET OFF AT UGUISU-DANI STATION, AND IT'S RIGHT THERE.
Uguisu-dani Station
One stop north of Ueno Station
Ikebukuro Station
This is for those who don't know the Yama-no-te train line that circles most of the downtown districts of Tokyo.
Ueno
Shinjuku Station
Shibuya Station
Tokyo Station
It looks something like this.
SEMPAI, YOU'RE FROM TOKYO?!
SCARY GUY
MY GODS ARE THE KISHIMOJIN OF IRIYA AND THE BENZAITEN GODDESS OF LUCK IN YOSHIWARA.
IF YOUR HOUSE IS SO CLOSE BY, WHY DO YOU LIVE IN A DORM?!
WHOOSH
JUST THINK OF HOW MANY LIVES WOULD BE BETTER WITHOUT YOU AROUND!
YOU REALLY KNOW HOW TO COMPLIMENT A GUY.

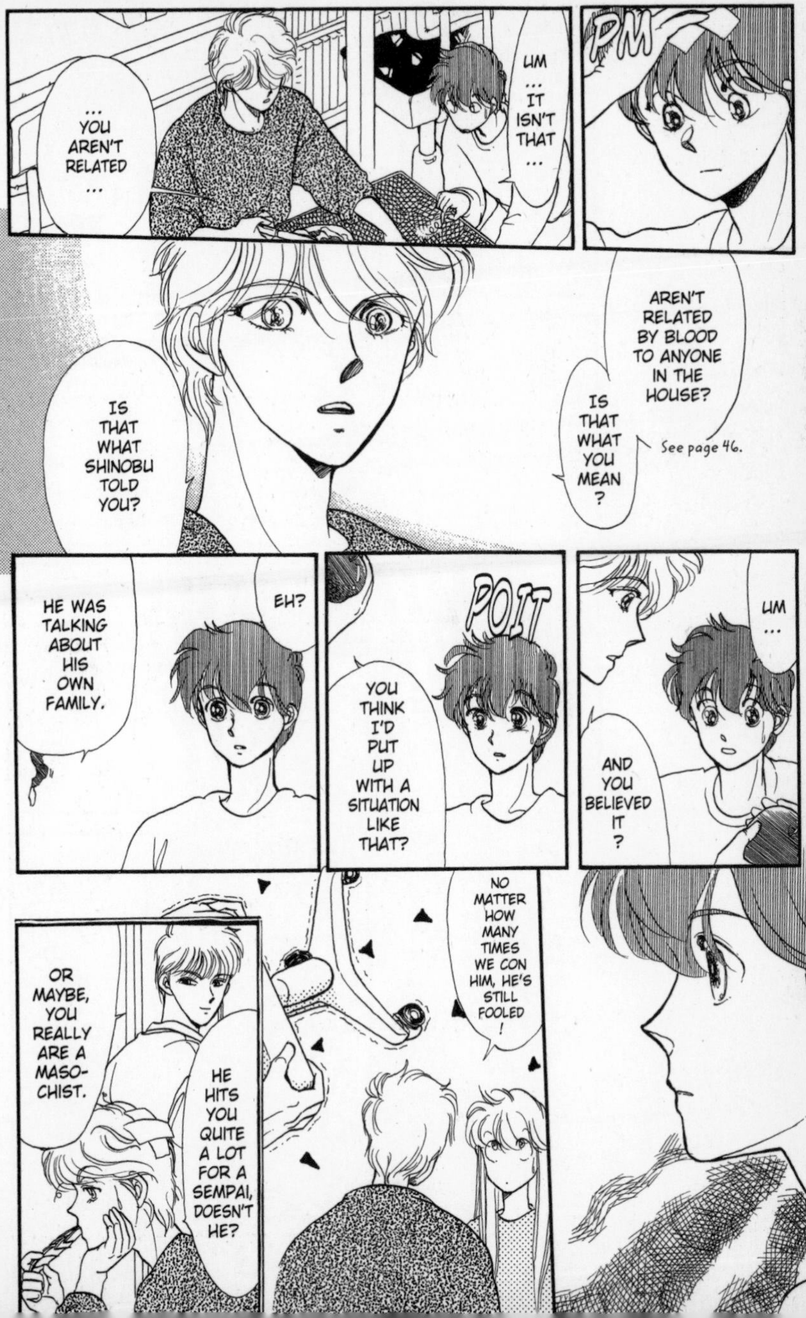
PM
UM ... IT ISN'T THAT ...
... YOU AREN'T RELATED ...
AREN'T RELATED BY BLOOD TO ANYONE IN THE HOUSE?
IS THAT WHAT YOU MEAN?
See page 46.
IS THAT WHAT SHINOBU TOLD YOU?
UM ...
AND YOU BELIEVED IT?
POIT
YOU THINK I'D PUT UP WITH A SITUATION LIKE THAT?
EH?
HE WAS TALKING ABOUT HIS OWN FAMILY.
NO MATTER HOW MANY TIMES WE CON HIM, HE'S STILL FOOLED!
HE HITS YOU QUITE A LOT FOR A SEMPAI, DOESN'T HE?
OR MAYBE, YOU REALLY ARE A MASOCHIST.

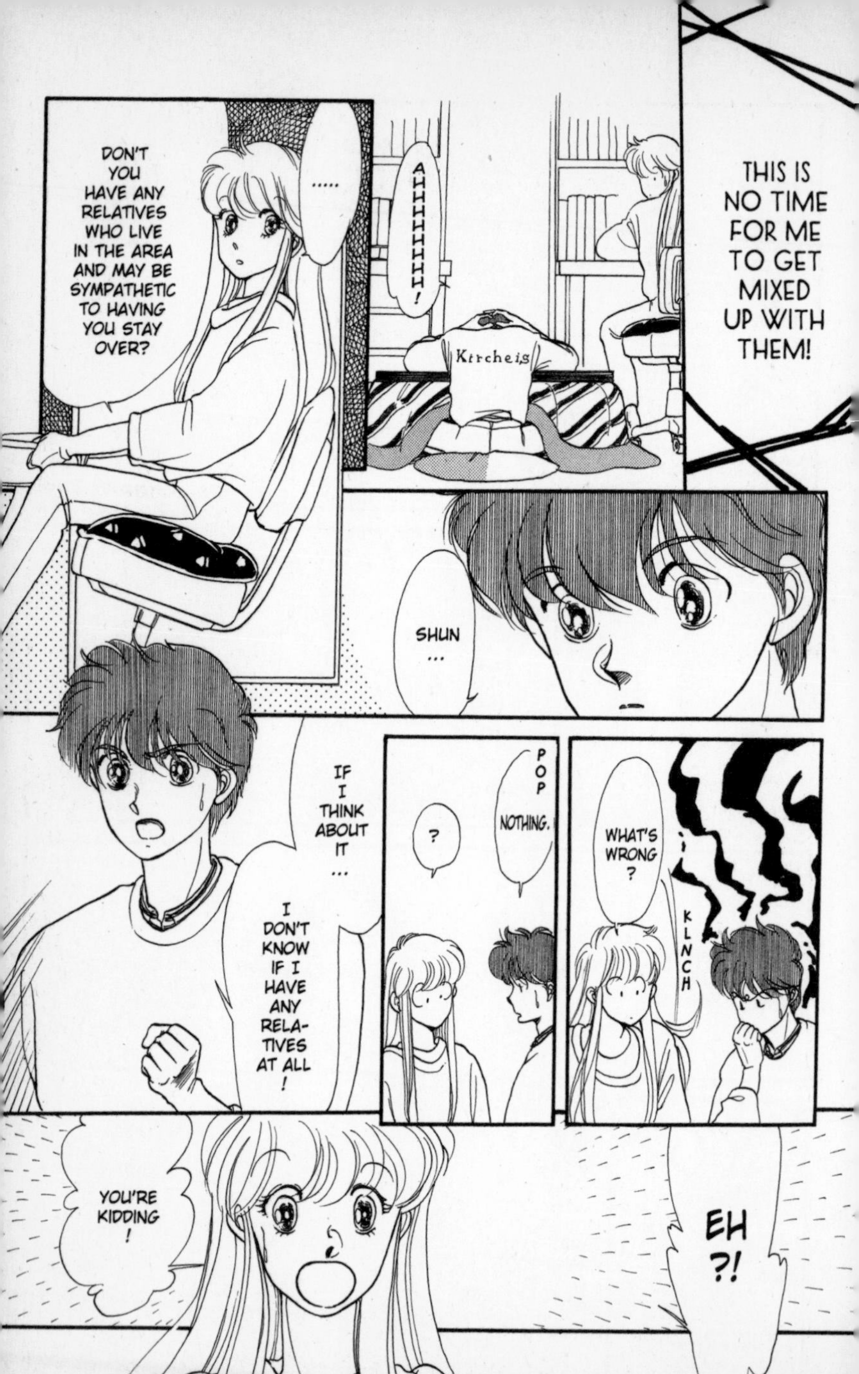
THIS IS NO TIME FOR ME TO GET MIXED UP WITH THEM!
AHHHHHHH!
Kircheis
SHUN ...
.....
DON'T YOU HAVE ANY RELATIVES WHO LIVE IN THE AREA AND MAY BE SYMPATHETIC TO HAVING YOU STAY OVER?
WHAT'S WRONG?
KLNCH
POP
NOTHING.
?
IF I THINK ABOUT IT ...
I DON'T KNOW IF I HAVE ANY RELA-TIVES AT ALL!
EH?!
YOU'RE KIDDING!

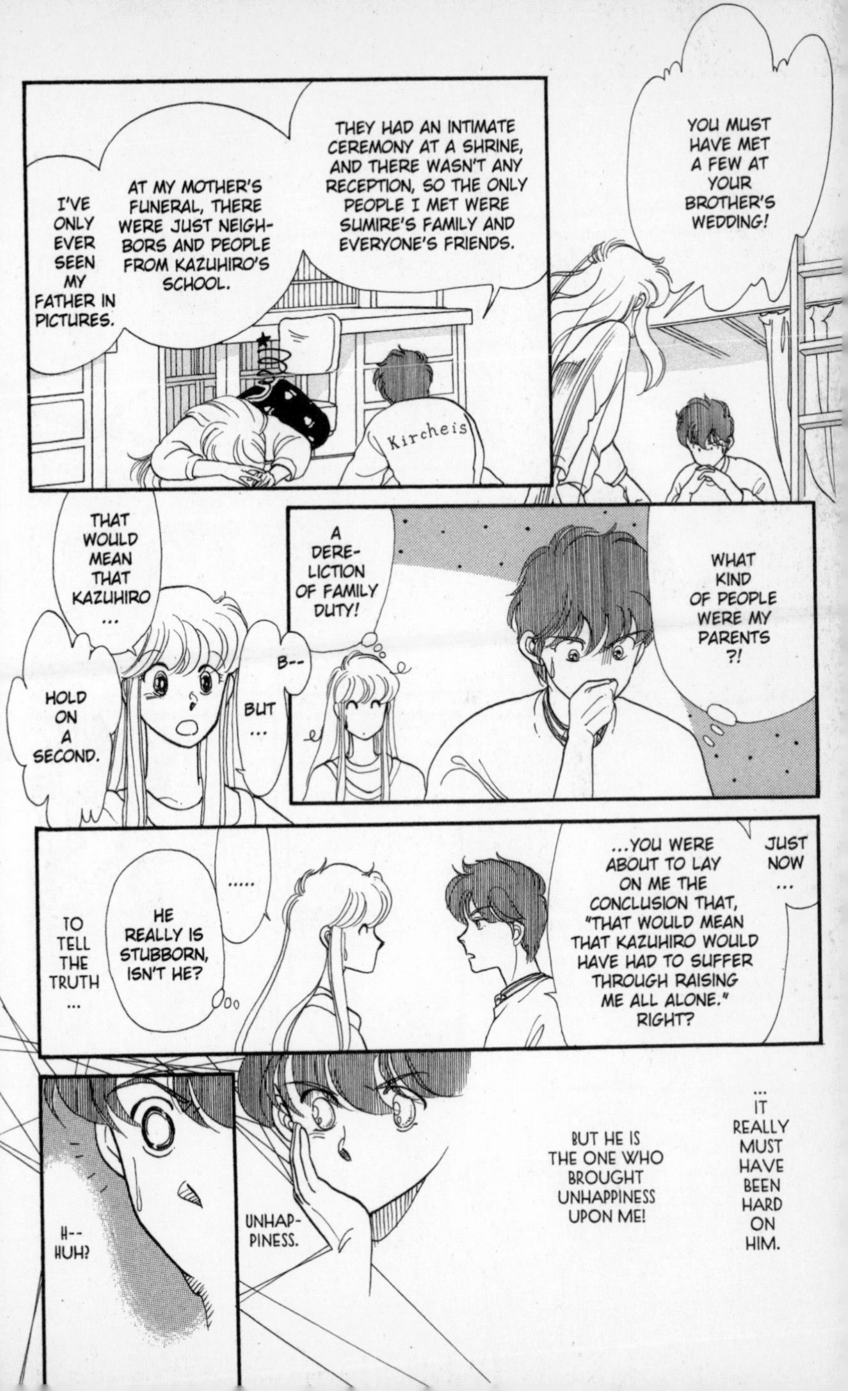
YOU MUST HAVE MET A FEW AT YOUR BROTHER'S WEDDING!
THEY HAD AN INTIMATE CEREMONY AT A SHRINE, AND THERE WASN'T ANY RECEPTION, SO THE ONLY PEOPLE I MET WERE SUMIRE'S FAMILY AND EVERYONE'S FRIENDS.
AT MY MOTHER'S FUNERAL, THERE WERE JUST NEIGH-BORS AND PEOPLE FROM KAZUHIRO'S SCHOOL.
I'VE ONLY EVER SEEN MY FATHER IN PICTURES.
Kircheis
WHAT KIND OF PEOPLE WERE MY PARENTS?!
A DERE-LICTION OF FAMILY DUTY!
THAT WOULD MEAN THAT KAZUHIRO...
B-- BUT...
HOLD ON A SECOND.
JUST NOW...
...YOU WERE ABOUT TO LAY ON ME THE CONCLUSION THAT, "THAT WOULD MEAN THAT KAZUHIRO WOULD HAVE HAD TO SUFFER THROUGH RAISING ME ALL ALONE." RIGHT?
......
HE REALLY IS STUBBORN, ISN'T HE?
TO TELL THE TRUTH...
... IT REALLY MUST HAVE BEEN HARD ON HIM.
BUT HE IS THE ONE WHO BROUGHT UNHAPPINESS UPON ME!
UNHAP-PINESS.
H-- HUH?

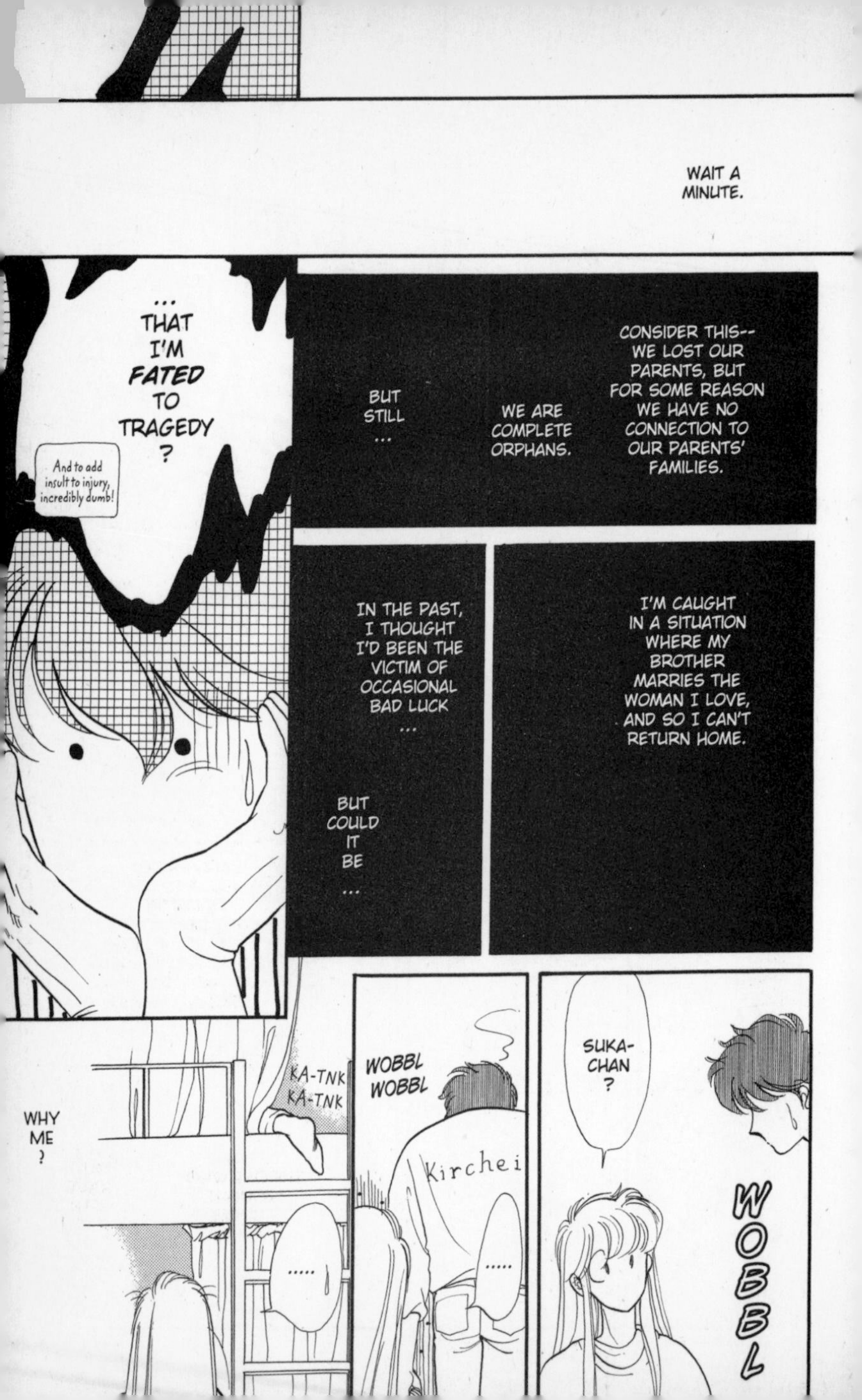
WAIT A MINUTE.
CONSIDER THIS-- WE LOST OUR PARENTS, BUT FOR SOME REASON WE HAVE NO CONNECTION TO OUR PARENTS' FAMILIES.
WE ARE COMPLETE ORPHANS.
BUT STILL ...
I'M CAUGHT IN A SITUATION WHERE MY BROTHER MARRIES THE WOMAN I LOVE, AND SO I CAN'T RETURN HOME.
IN THE PAST, I THOUGHT I'D BEEN THE VICTIM OF OCCASIONAL BAD LUCK ...
BUT COULD IT BE ...
... THAT I'M FATED TO TRAGEDY?
And to add insult to injury, incredibly dumb!
SUKA-CHAN?
WOBBL
WOBBL WOBBL
Kirchei
.....
KA-TNK KA-TNK
.....
WHY ME?

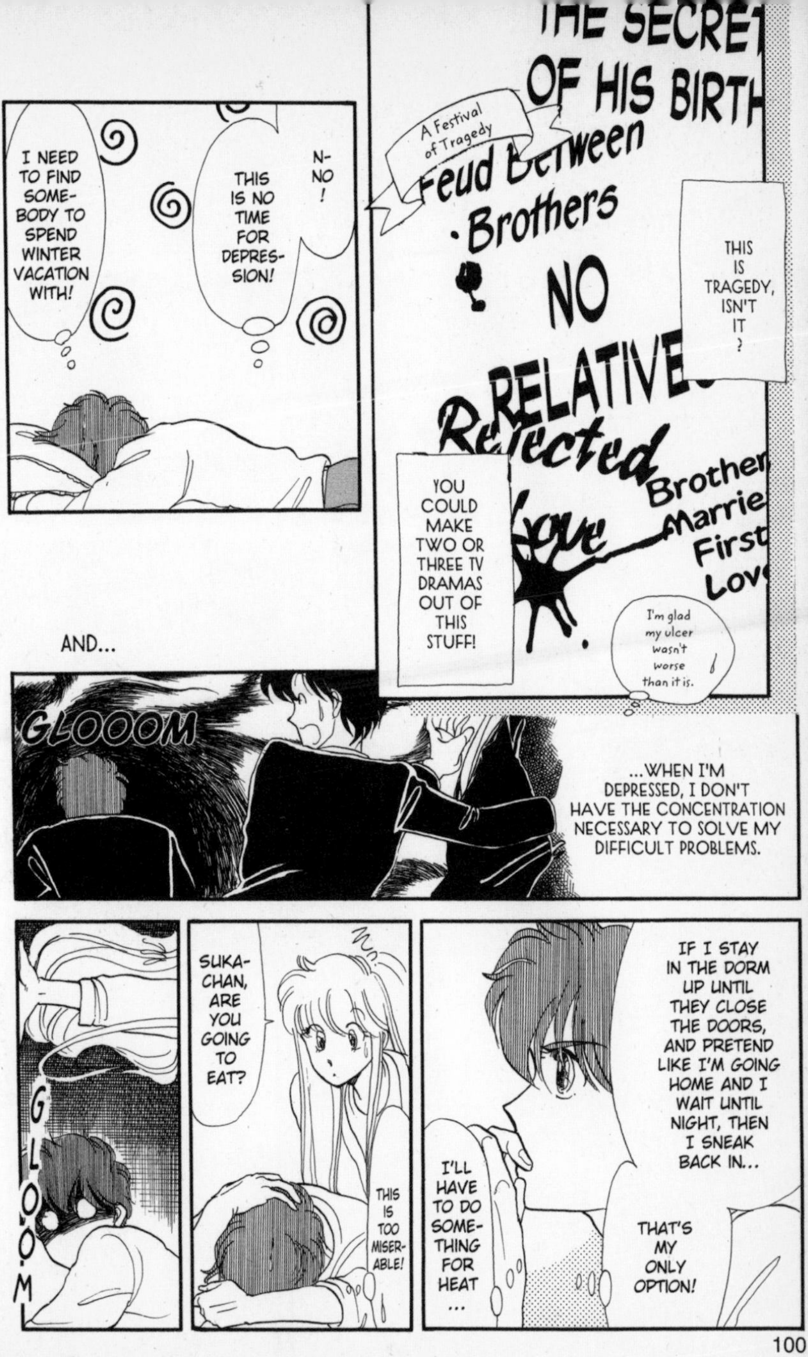
HE SECRET OF HIS BIRTH
A Festival of Tragedy
Feud Between Brothers
NO RELATIVE
Rejected Love
Brother Marrie First Lov
THIS IS TRAGEDY, ISN'T IT?
YOU COULD MAKE TWO OR THREE TV DRAMAS OUT OF THIS STUFF!
I'm glad my ulcer wasn't worse than it is.
N-NO!
THIS IS NO TIME FOR DEPRESSION!
I NEED TO FIND SOMEBODY TO SPEND WINTER VACATION WITH!
AND...
...WHEN I'M DEPRESSED, I DON'T HAVE THE CONCENTRATION NECESSARY TO SOLVE MY DIFFICULT PROBLEMS.
GLOOOM
IF I STAY IN THE DORM UP UNTIL THEY CLOSE THE DOORS, AND PRETEND LIKE I'M GOING HOME AND I WAIT UNTIL NIGHT, THEN I SNEAK BACK IN...
THAT'S MY ONLY OPTION!
I'LL HAVE TO DO SOMETHING FOR HEAT...
SUKA-CHAN, ARE YOU GOING TO EAT?
THIS IS TOO MISERABLE!
GLOOOM

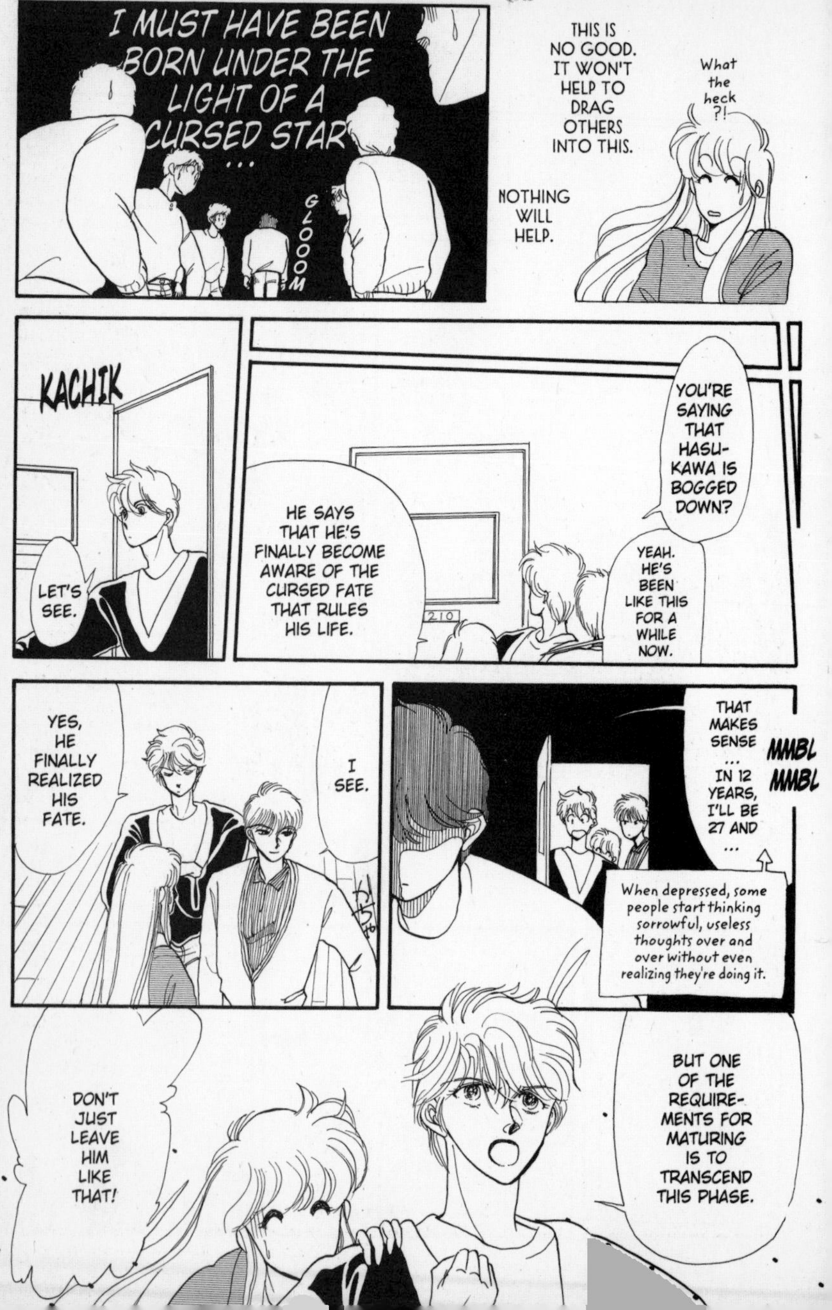
THIS IS NO GOOD. IT WON'T HELP TO DRAG OTHERS INTO THIS.
What the heck ?!
NOTHING WILL HELP.
I MUST HAVE BEEN BORN UNDER THE LIGHT OF A CURSED STAR ...
GLOOOM
YOU'RE SAYING THAT HASU-KAWA IS BOGGED DOWN?
YEAH. HE'S BEEN LIKE THIS FOR A WHILE NOW.
HE SAYS THAT HE'S FINALLY BECOME AWARE OF THE CURSED FATE THAT RULES HIS LIFE.
KACHIK
LET'S SEE.
THAT MAKES SENSE ... IN 12 YEARS, I'LL BE 27 AND ...
MMBL MMBL
When depressed, some people start thinking sorrowful, useless thoughts over and over without even realizing they're doing it.
I SEE.
YES, HE FINALLY REALIZED HIS FATE.
BUT ONE OF THE REQUIREMENTS FOR MATURING IS TO TRANSCEND THIS PHASE.
DON'T JUST LEAVE HIM LIKE THAT!

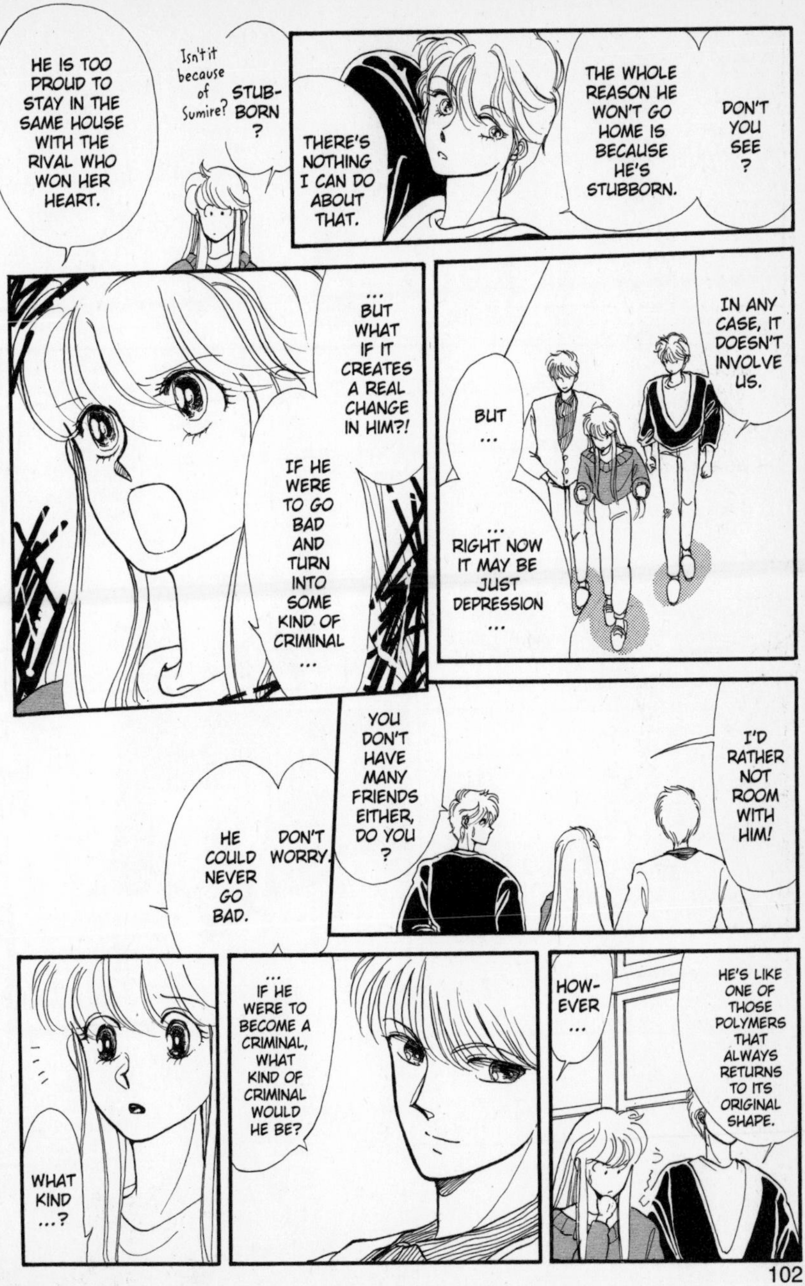
DON'T YOU SEE?
THE WHOLE REASON HE WON'T GO HOME IS BECAUSE HE'S STUBBORN.
THERE'S NOTHING I CAN DO ABOUT THAT.
STUB-BORN?
Isn't it because of Sumire?
HE IS TOO PROUD TO STAY IN THE SAME HOUSE WITH THE RIVAL WHO WON HER HEART.
IN ANY CASE, IT DOESN'T INVOLVE US?
BUT ...
... RIGHT NOW IT MAY BE JUST DEPRESSION ...
... BUT WHAT IF IT CREATES A REAL CHANGE IN HIM?!
IF HE WERE TO GO BAD AND TURN INTO SOME KIND OF CRIMINAL ...
I'D RATHER NOT ROOM WITH HIM!
YOU DON'T HAVE MANY FRIENDS EITHER, DO YOU?
DON'T WORRY.
HE COULD NEVER GO BAD.
HE'S LIKE ONE OF THOSE POLYMERS THAT ALWAYS RETURNS TO ITS ORIGINAL SHAPE.
HOW-EVER ...
... IF HE WERE TO BECOME A CRIMINAL, WHAT KIND OF CRIMINAL WOULD HE BE?
WHAT KIND ...?

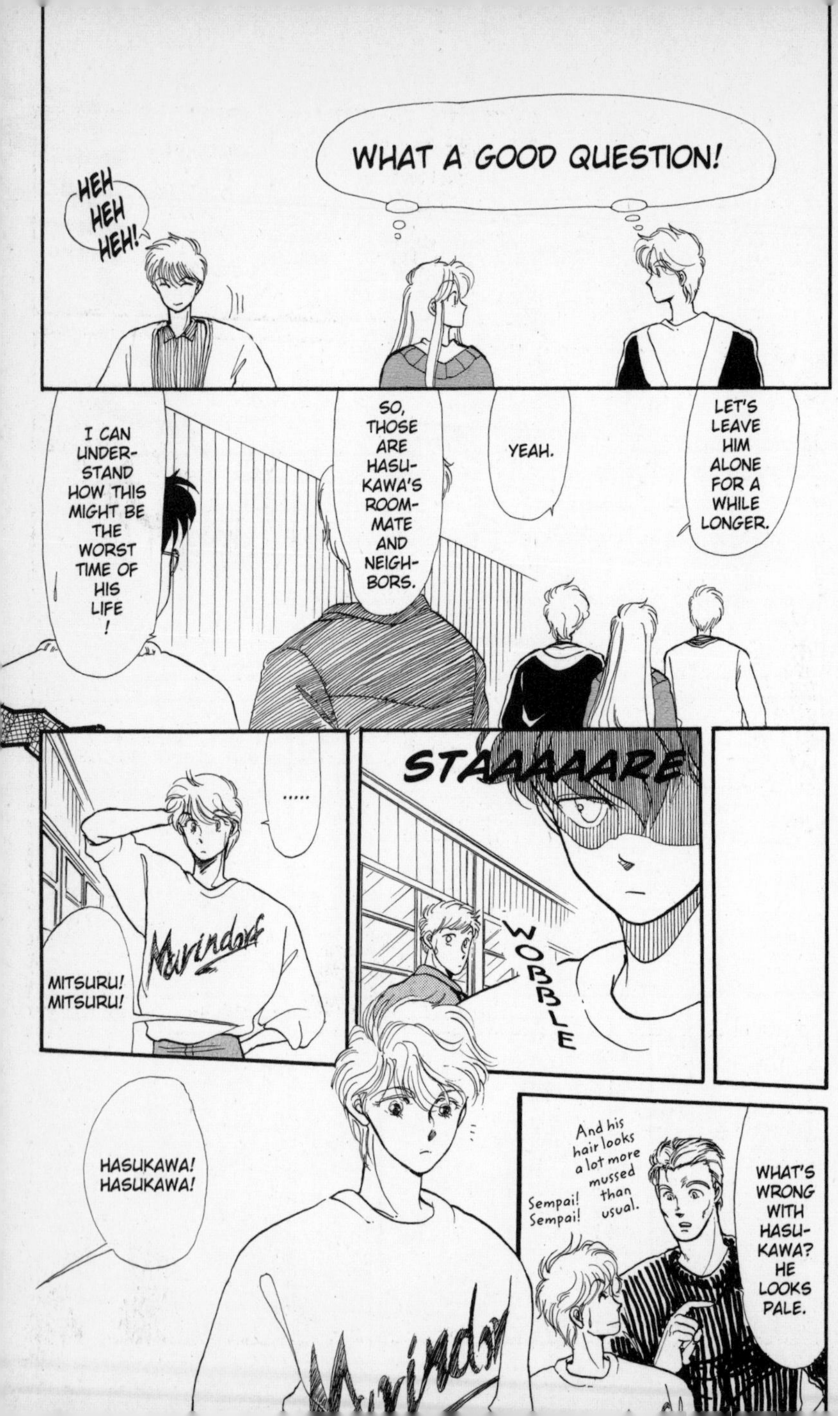

WHAT A GOOD QUESTION!
HEH HEH HEH!
LET'S LEAVE HIM ALONE FOR A WHILE LONGER.
YEAH.
SO, THOSE ARE HASUKAWA'S ROOMMATE AND NEIGHBORS.
I CAN UNDERSTAND HOW THIS MIGHT BE THE WORST TIME OF HIS LIFE!
STAAAAAARE
WOBBLE
.....
MITSURU! MITSURU!
WHAT'S WRONG WITH HASUKAWA? HE LOOKS PALE.
And his hair looks a lot more mussed than usual.
Sempai! Sempai!
HASUKAWA! HASUKAWA!

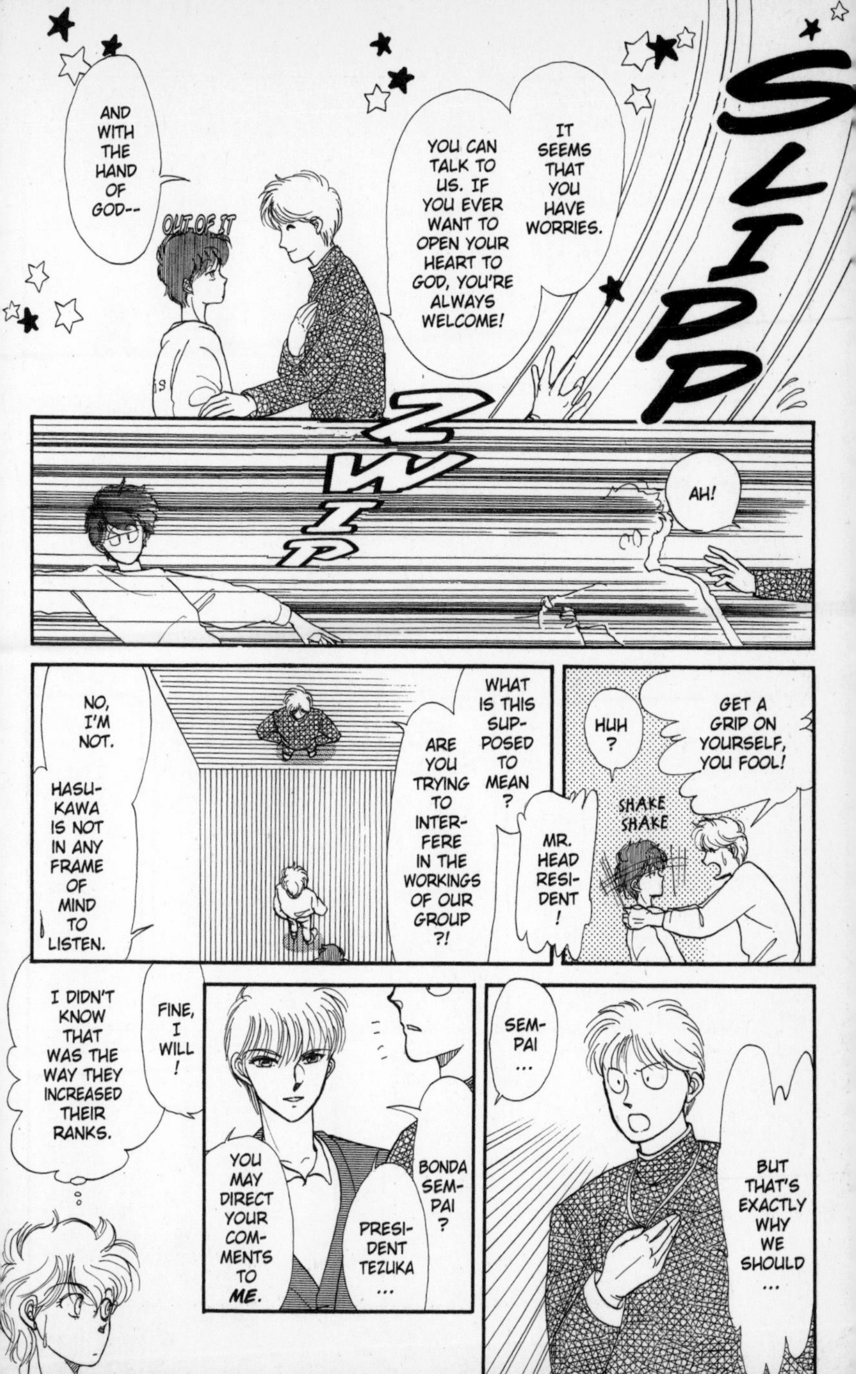
SLIPP
IT SEEMS THAT YOU HAVE WORRIES.
YOU CAN TALK TO US. IF YOU EVER WANT TO OPEN YOUR HEART TO GOD, YOU'RE ALWAYS WELCOME!
OUT OF IT
AND WITH THE HAND OF GOD--
AH!
ZWIP
GET A GRIP ON YOURSELF, YOU FOOL!
HUH?
SHAKE SHAKE
MR. HEAD RESIDENT!
WHAT IS THIS SUPPOSED TO MEAN?
ARE YOU TRYING TO INTERFERE IN THE WORKINGS OF OUR GROUP?!
NO, I'M NOT.
HASUKAWA IS NOT IN ANY FRAME OF MIND TO LISTEN.
SEMPAI...
BUT THAT'S EXACTLY WHY WE SHOULD...
BONDA SEMPAI?
PRESIDENT TEZUKA...
YOU MAY DIRECT YOUR COMMENTS TO ME.
FINE, I WILL!
I DIDN'T KNOW THAT WAS THE WAY THEY INCREASED THEIR RANKS.

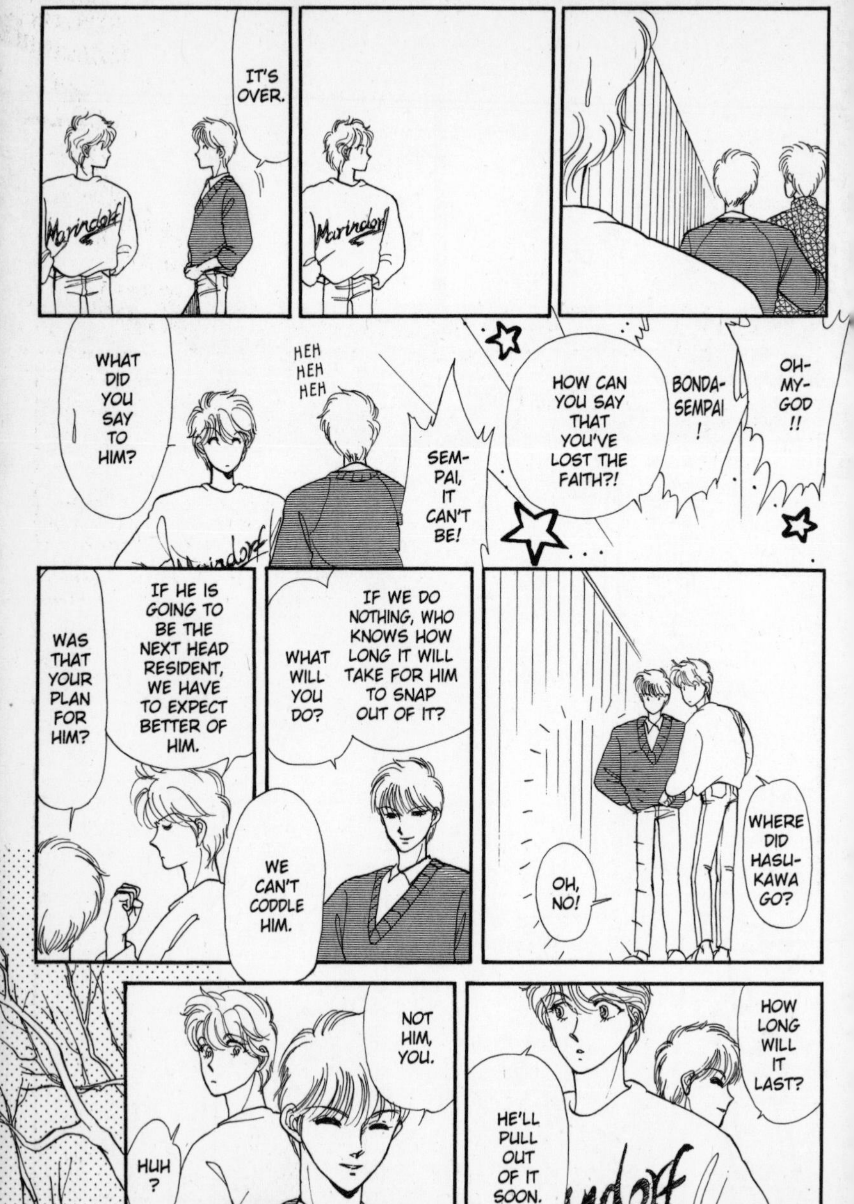
IT'S OVER.
OH-MY-GOD!!
BONDA-SEMPAI!
HOW CAN YOU SAY THAT YOU'VE LOST THE FAITH?!
SEMPAI, IT CAN'T BE!
HEH HEH HEH
WHAT DID YOU SAY TO HIM?
WHERE DID HASUKAWA GO?
OH, NO!
IF WE DO NOTHING, WHO KNOWS HOW LONG IT WILL TAKE FOR HIM TO SNAP OUT OF IT?
WHAT WILL YOU DO?
IF HE IS GOING TO BE THE NEXT HEAD RESIDENT, WE HAVE TO EXPECT BETTER OF HIM.
WAS THAT YOUR PLAN FOR HIM?
WE CAN'T CODDLE HIM.
HOW LONG WILL IT LAST?
HE'LL PULL OUT OF IT SOON.
NOT HIM, YOU.
HUH?

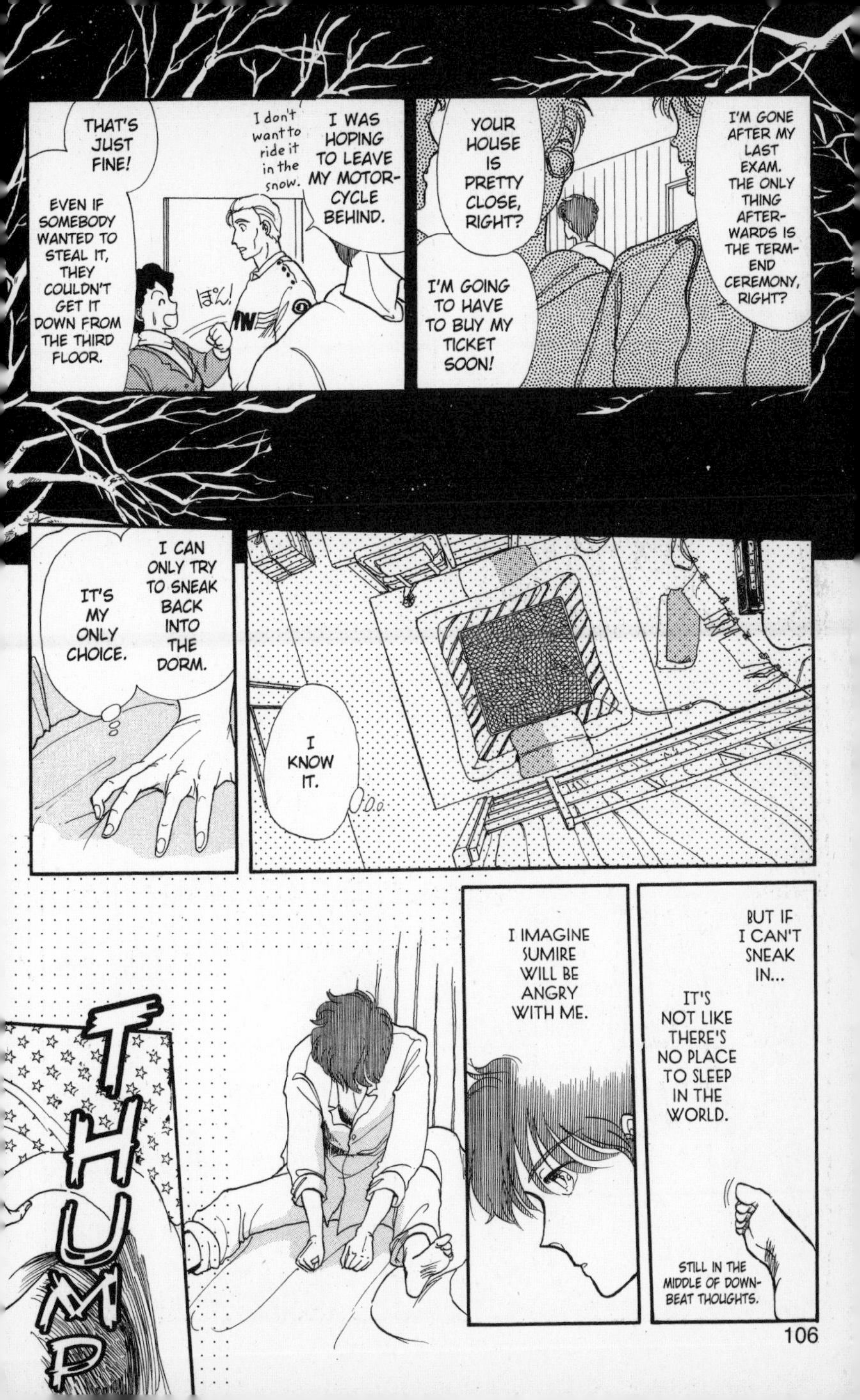
I'M GONE AFTER MY LAST EXAM. THE ONLY THING AFTER-WARDS IS THE TERM-END CEREMONY, RIGHT?
YOUR HOUSE IS PRETTY CLOSE, RIGHT?
I'M GOING TO HAVE TO BUY MY TICKET SOON!
I WAS HOPING TO LEAVE MY MOTOR-CYCLE BEHIND.
I don't want to ride it in the snow.
THAT'S JUST FINE!
EVEN IF SOMEBODY WANTED TO STEAL IT, THEY COULDN'T GET IT DOWN FROM THE THIRD FLOOR.
ぽん!
I KNOW IT.
I CAN ONLY TRY TO SNEAK BACK INTO THE DORM.
IT'S MY ONLY CHOICE.
BUT IF I CAN'T SNEAK IN...
IT'S NOT LIKE THERE'S NO PLACE TO SLEEP IN THE WORLD.
STILL IN THE MIDDLE OF DOWN-BEAT THOUGHTS.
I IMAGINE SUMIRE WILL BE ANGRY WITH ME.
THUMP

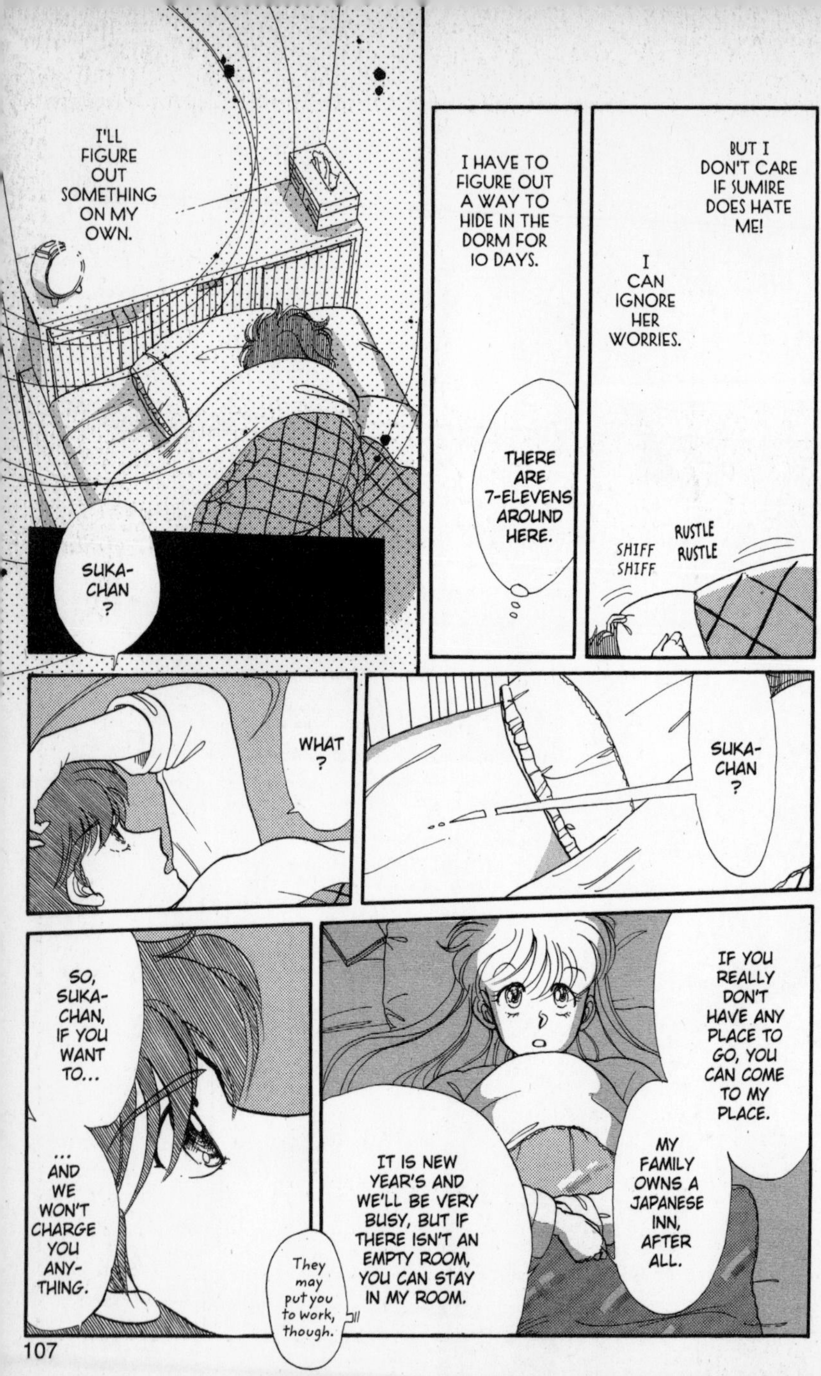

BUT I DON'T CARE IF SUMIRE DOES HATE ME!
I CAN IGNORE HER WORRIES.
RUSTLE RUSTLE
SHIFF SHIFF
I HAVE TO FIGURE OUT A WAY TO HIDE IN THE DORM FOR 10 DAYS.
THERE ARE 7-ELEVENS AROUND HERE.
I'LL FIGURE OUT SOMETHING ON MY OWN.
SUKA-CHAN?
SUKA-CHAN?
WHAT?
IF YOU REALLY DON'T HAVE ANY PLACE TO GO, YOU CAN COME TO MY PLACE.
MY FAMILY OWNS A JAPANESE INN, AFTER ALL.
IT IS NEW YEAR'S AND WE'LL BE VERY BUSY, BUT IF THERE ISN'T AN EMPTY ROOM, YOU CAN STAY IN MY ROOM.
They may put you to work, though.
SO, SUKA-CHAN, IF YOU WANT TO...
... AND WE WON'T CHARGE YOU ANYTHING.

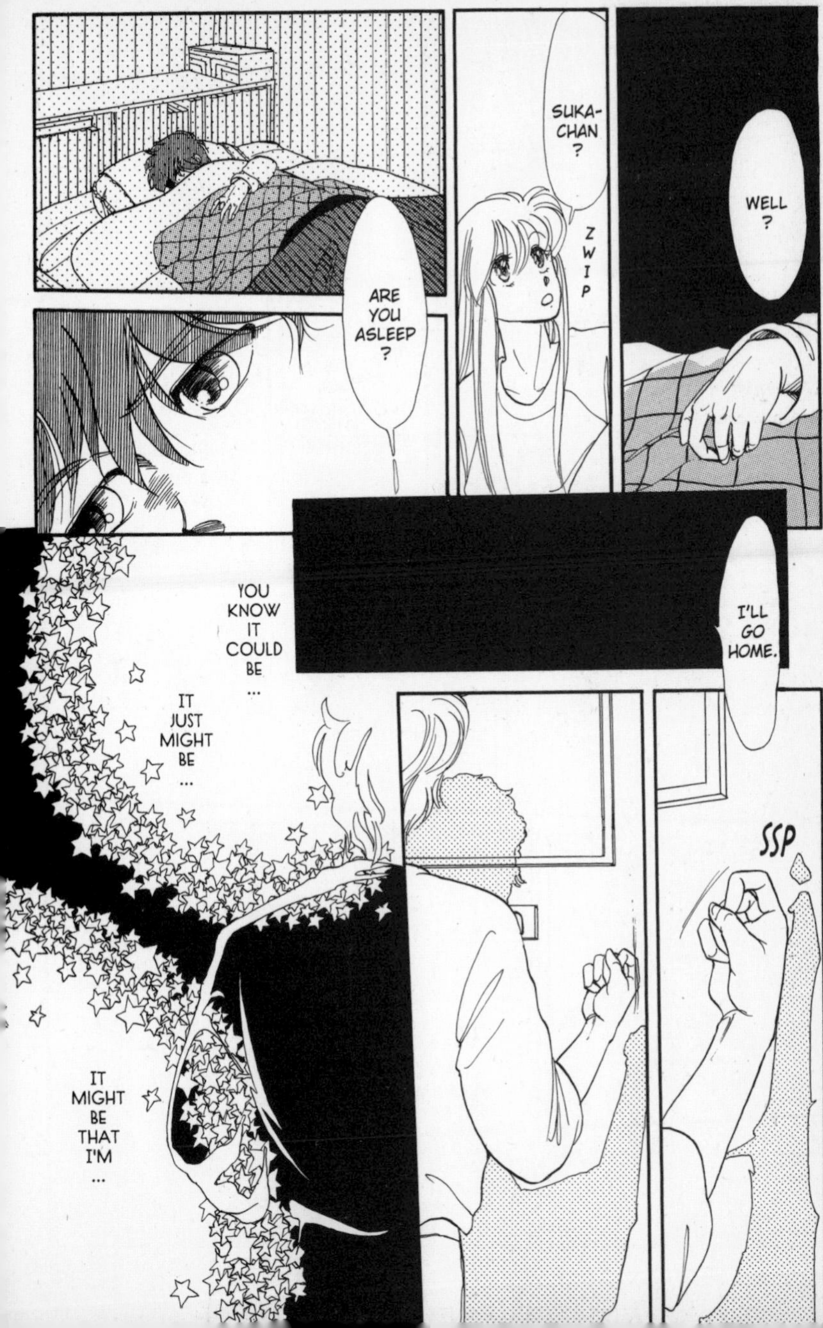
WELL?
SUKA-CHAN?
ZWIP
ARE YOU ASLEEP?
I'LL GO HOME.
SSP
YOU KNOW IT COULD BE...
IT JUST MIGHT BE...
IT MIGHT BE THAT I'M...

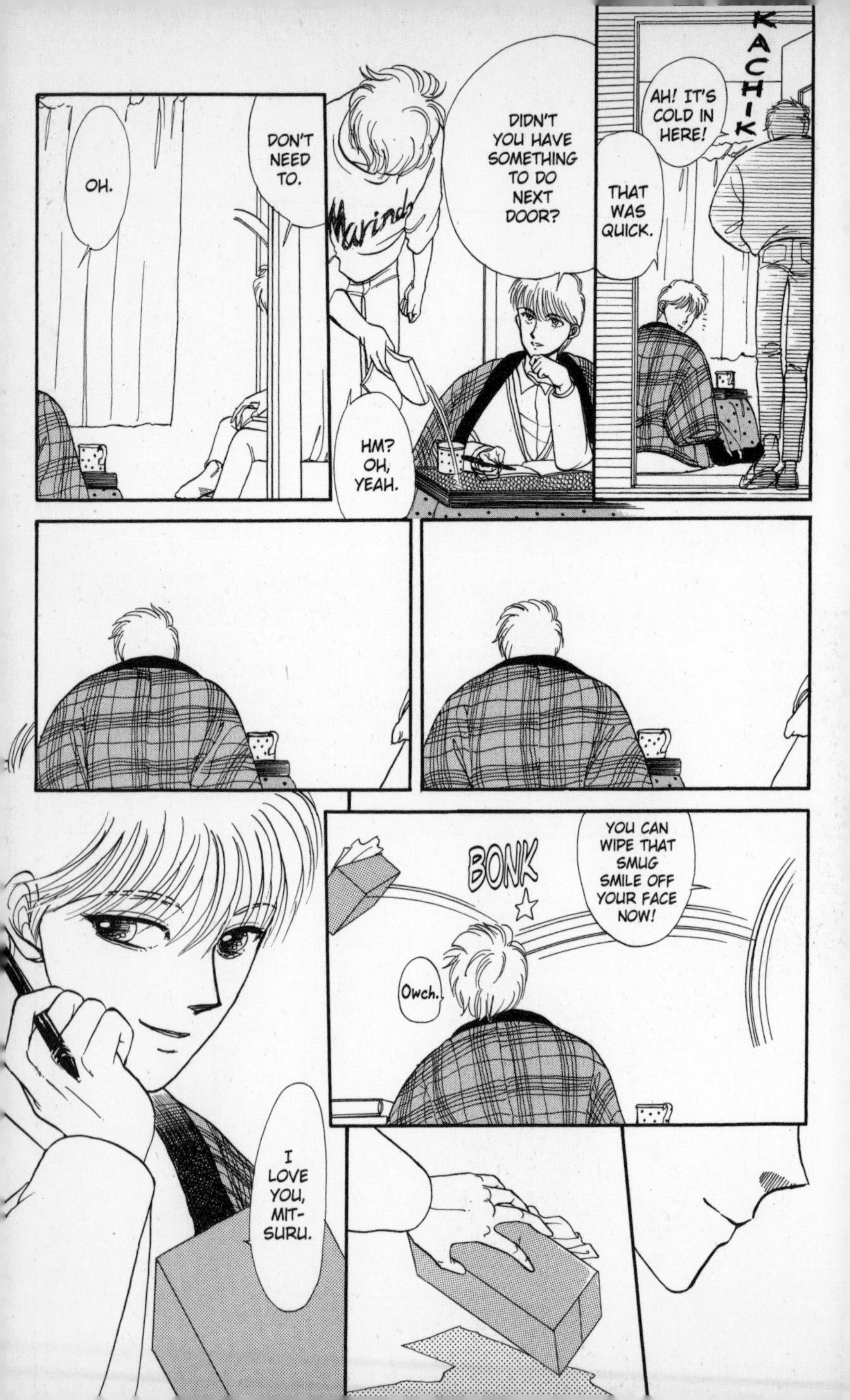
KACHIK
AH! IT'S COLD IN HERE!
THAT WAS QUICK.
DIDN'T YOU HAVE SOMETHING TO DO NEXT DOOR?
HM? OH, YEAH.
DON'T NEED TO.
OH.
YOU CAN WIPE THAT SMUG SMILE OFF YOUR FACE NOW!
BONK
Owch..
I LOVE YOU, MIT-SURU.

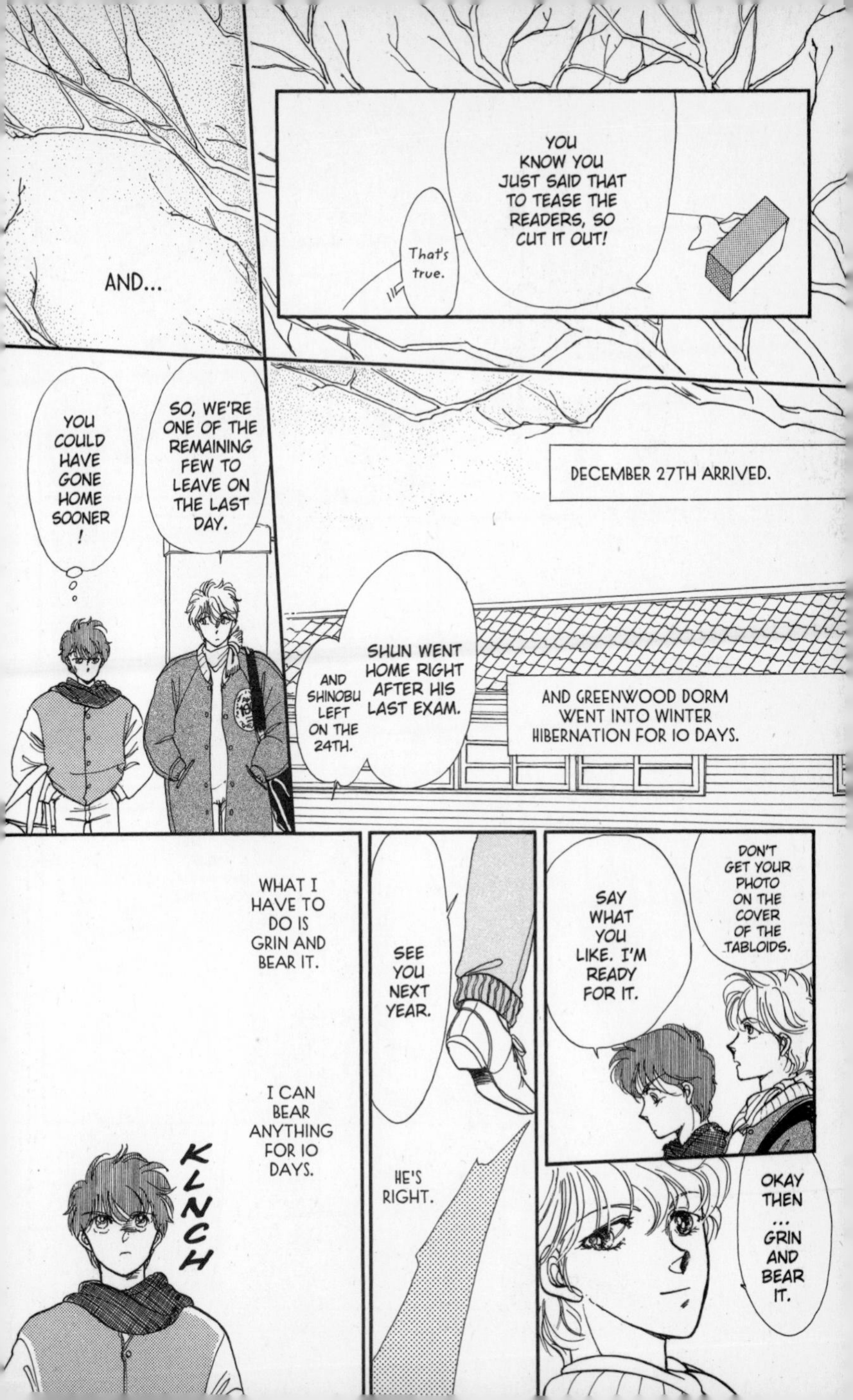
YOU KNOW YOU JUST SAID THAT TO TEASE THE READERS, SO CUT IT OUT!
That's true.
AND...
DECEMBER 27TH ARRIVED.
AND GREENWOOD DORM WENT INTO WINTER HIBERNATION FOR 10 DAYS.
SHUN WENT HOME RIGHT AFTER HIS LAST EXAM.
AND SHINOBU LEFT ON THE 24TH.
SO, WE'RE ONE OF THE REMAINING FEW TO LEAVE ON THE LAST DAY.
YOU COULD HAVE GONE HOME SOONER!
DON'T GET YOUR PHOTO ON THE COVER OF THE TABLOIDS.
SAY WHAT YOU LIKE. I'M READY FOR IT.
OKAY THEN ... GRIN AND BEAR IT.
SEE YOU NEXT YEAR.
HE'S RIGHT.
WHAT I HAVE TO DO IS GRIN AND BEAR IT.
I CAN BEAR ANYTHING FOR 10 DAYS.
KLNCH

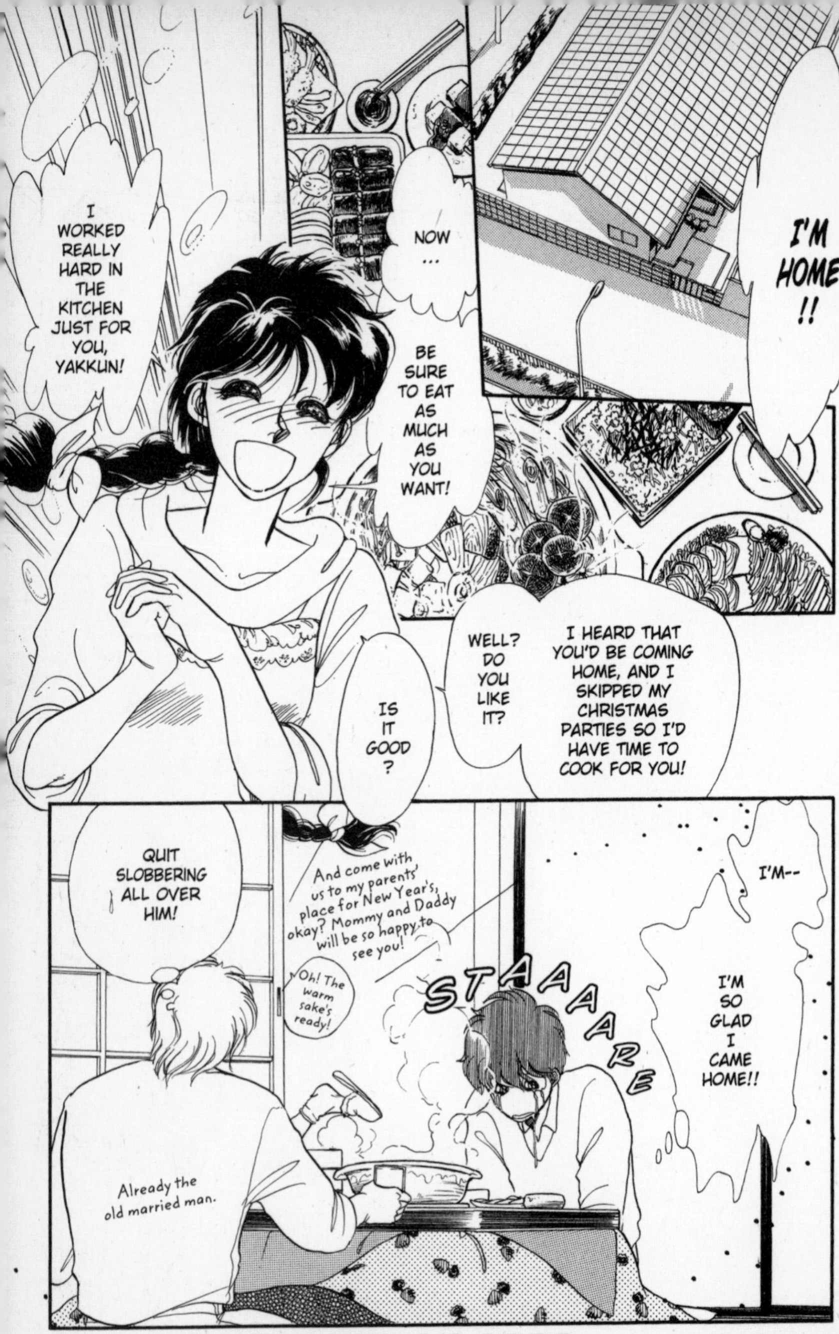
I'M HOME!!
NOW ...
BE SURE TO EAT AS MUCH AS YOU WANT!
I WORKED REALLY HARD IN THE KITCHEN JUST FOR YOU, YAKKUN!
I HEARD THAT YOU'D BE COMING HOME, AND I SKIPPED MY CHRISTMAS PARTIES SO I'D HAVE TIME TO COOK FOR YOU!
WELL? DO YOU LIKE IT?
IS IT GOOD?
I'M--
I'M SO GLAD I CAME HOME!!
STAAAAARE
And come with us to my parents' place for New Year's, okay? Mommy and Daddy will be so happy to see you!
Oh! The warm sake's ready!
QUIT SLOBBERING ALL OVER HIM!
Already the old married man.

TILL WE MEET AGAIN AT GREENWOOD: THE END

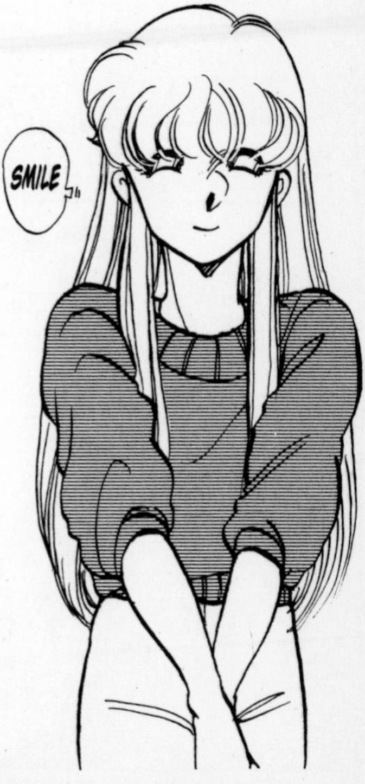
SMILE

LIVE
OFF
GREENWOOD

LIVE OFF
GREENWOOD

M·I·E·K·O·N·I·T·T·A

Shibuya
Center fo

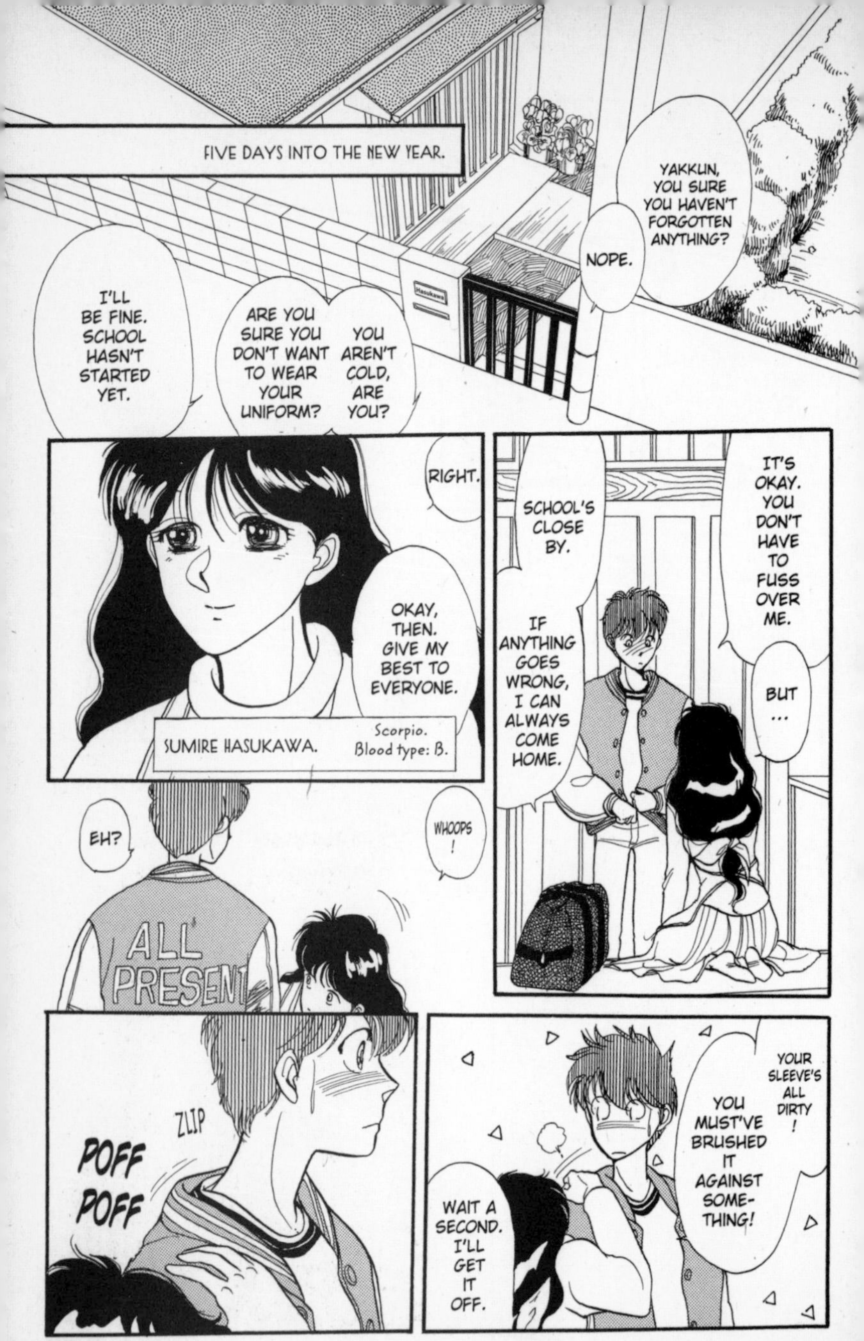

FIVE DAYS INTO THE NEW YEAR.
YAKKUN, YOU SURE YOU HAVEN'T FORGOTTEN ANYTHING?
NOPE.
Hasukawa
YOU AREN'T COLD, ARE YOU?
ARE YOU SURE YOU DON'T WANT TO WEAR YOUR UNIFORM?
I'LL BE FINE. SCHOOL HASN'T STARTED YET.
IT'S OKAY. YOU DON'T HAVE TO FUSS OVER ME.
SCHOOL'S CLOSE BY.
BUT...
IF ANYTHING GOES WRONG, I CAN ALWAYS COME HOME.
RIGHT.
OKAY, THEN. GIVE MY BEST TO EVERYONE.
SUMIRE HASUKAWA. Scorpio. Blood type: B.
WHOOPS!
EH?
ALL PRESENT
YOUR SLEEVE'S ALL DIRTY!
YOU MUST'VE BRUSHED IT AGAINST SOME-THING!
WAIT A SECOND. I'LL GET IT OFF.
ZLIP
POFF POFF

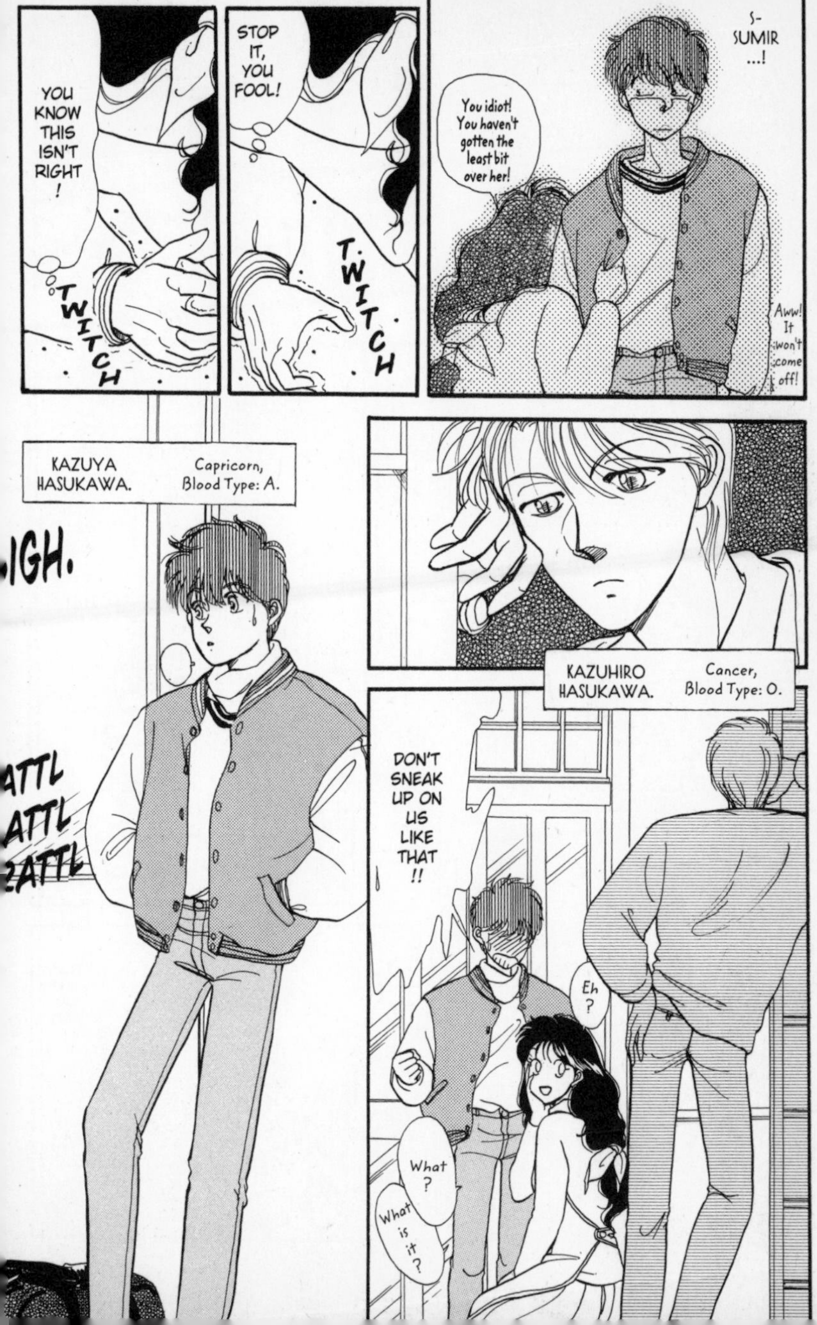
S-SUMIR...!
You idiot! You haven't gotten the least bit over her!
Aww! It won't come off!
STOP IT, YOU FOOL!
TWITCH
YOU KNOW THIS ISN'T RIGHT!
TWITCH
KAZUHIRO HASUKAWA. Cancer, Blood Type: O.
DON'T SNEAK UP ON US LIKE THAT!!
Eh?
What?
What is it?
KAZUYA HASUKAWA. Capricorn, Blood Type: A.

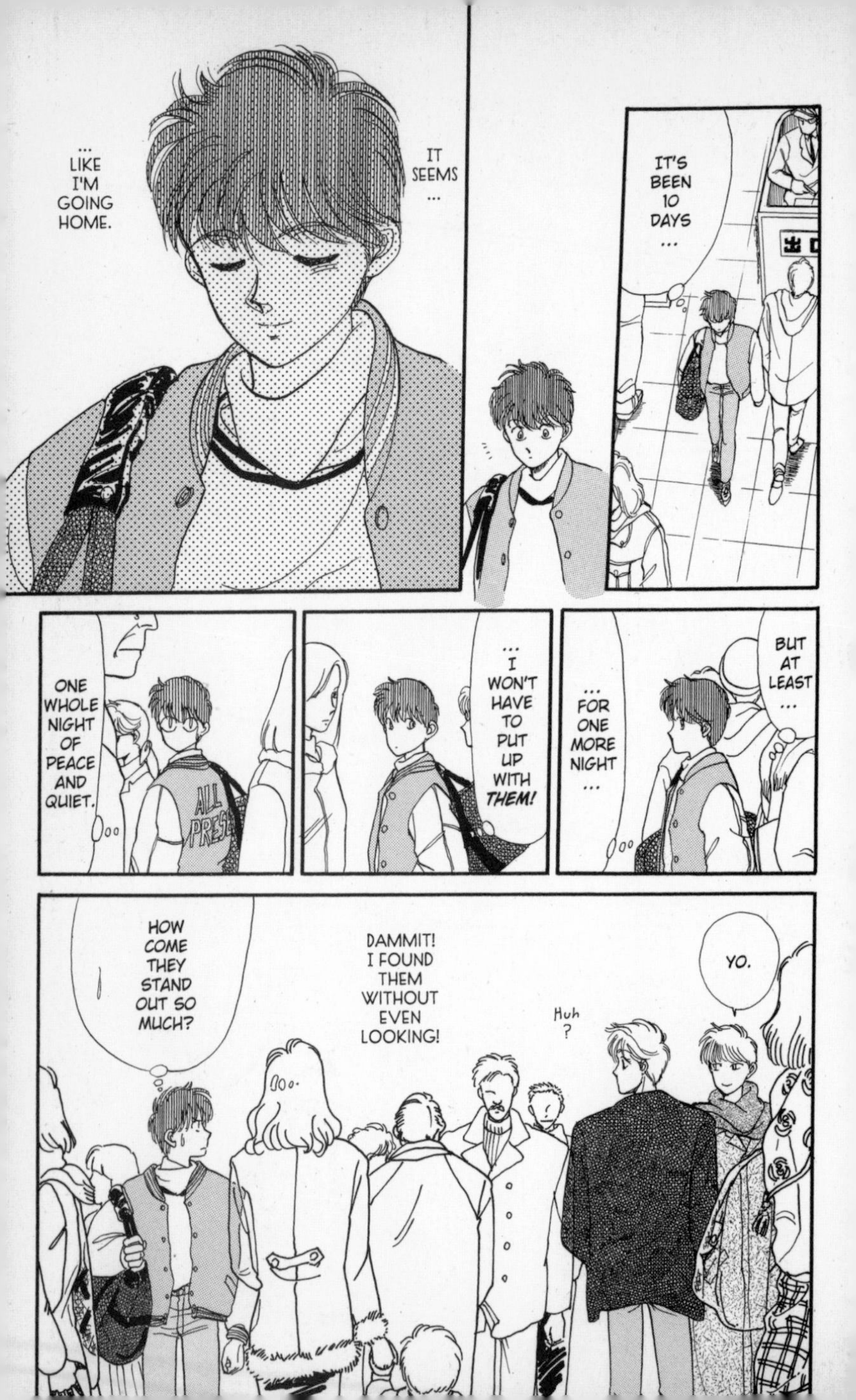
IT'S BEEN 10 DAYS ...
IT SEEMS ...
... LIKE I'M GOING HOME.
BUT AT LEAST ...
... FOR ONE MORE NIGHT ...
... I WON'T HAVE TO PUT UP WITH *THEM!*
ONE WHOLE NIGHT OF PEACE AND QUIET.
YO.
Huh ?
DAMMIT! I FOUND THEM WITHOUT EVEN LOOKING!
HOW COME THEY STAND OUT SO MUCH?

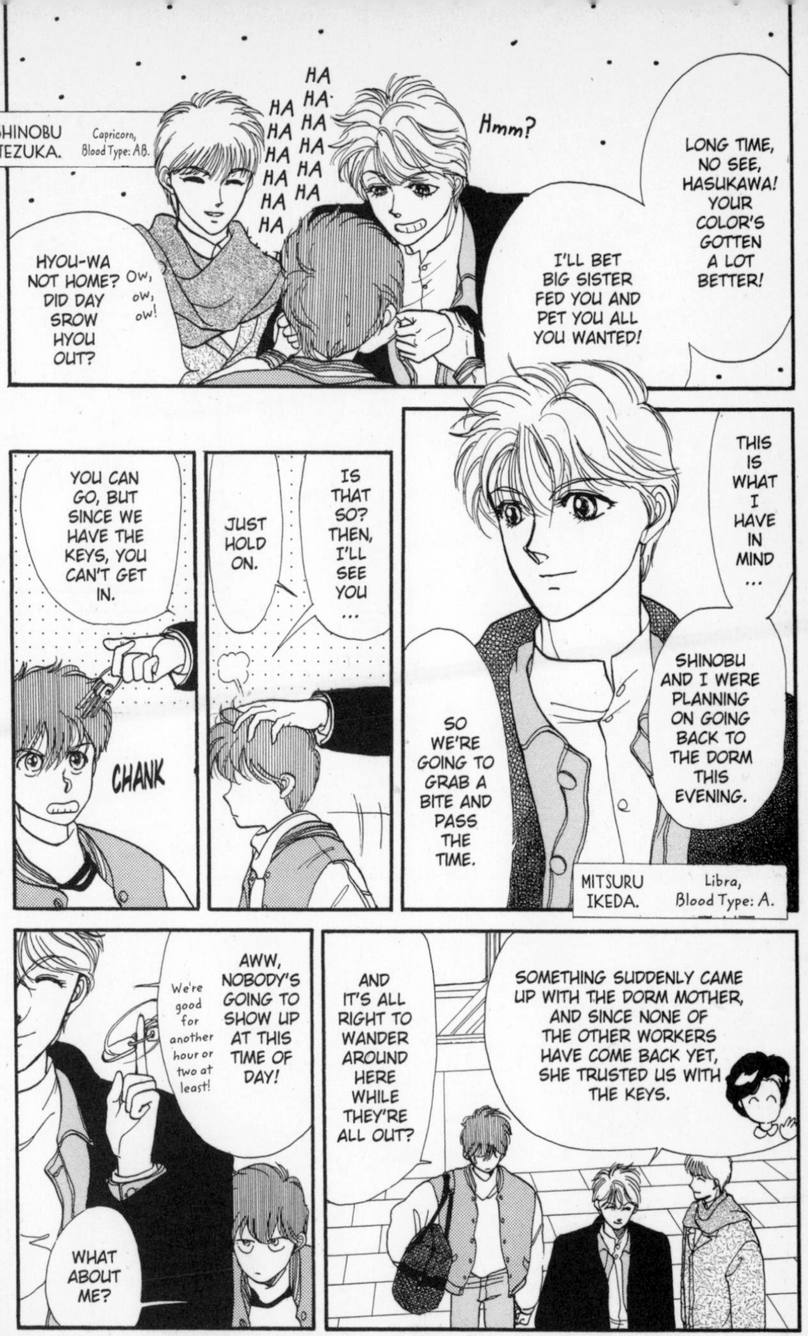
LONG TIME, NO SEE, HASUKAWA! YOUR COLOR'S GOTTEN A LOT BETTER!
Hmm?
I'LL BET BIG SISTER FED YOU AND PET YOU ALL YOU WANTED!
HA HA HA HA HA HA HA HA HA HA HA HA
SHINOBU TEZUKA. Capricorn, Blood Type: AB.
HYOU-WA NOT HOME? DID DAY SROW HYOU OUT?
Ow, ow, ow!
THIS IS WHAT I HAVE IN MIND ...
SHINOBU AND I WERE PLANNING ON GOING BACK TO THE DORM THIS EVENING.
SO WE'RE GOING TO GRAB A BITE AND PASS THE TIME.
MITSURU IKEDA. Libra, Blood Type: A.
IS THAT SO? THEN, I'LL SEE YOU ...
JUST HOLD ON.
YOU CAN GO, BUT SINCE WE HAVE THE KEYS, YOU CAN'T GET IN.
CHANK
SOMETHING SUDDENLY CAME UP WITH THE DORM MOTHER, AND SINCE NONE OF THE OTHER WORKERS HAVE COME BACK YET, SHE TRUSTED US WITH THE KEYS.
AND IT'S ALL RIGHT TO WANDER AROUND HERE WHILE THEY'RE ALL OUT?
AWW, NOBODY'S GOING TO SHOW UP AT THIS TIME OF DAY!
We're good for another hour or two at least!
WHAT ABOUT ME?

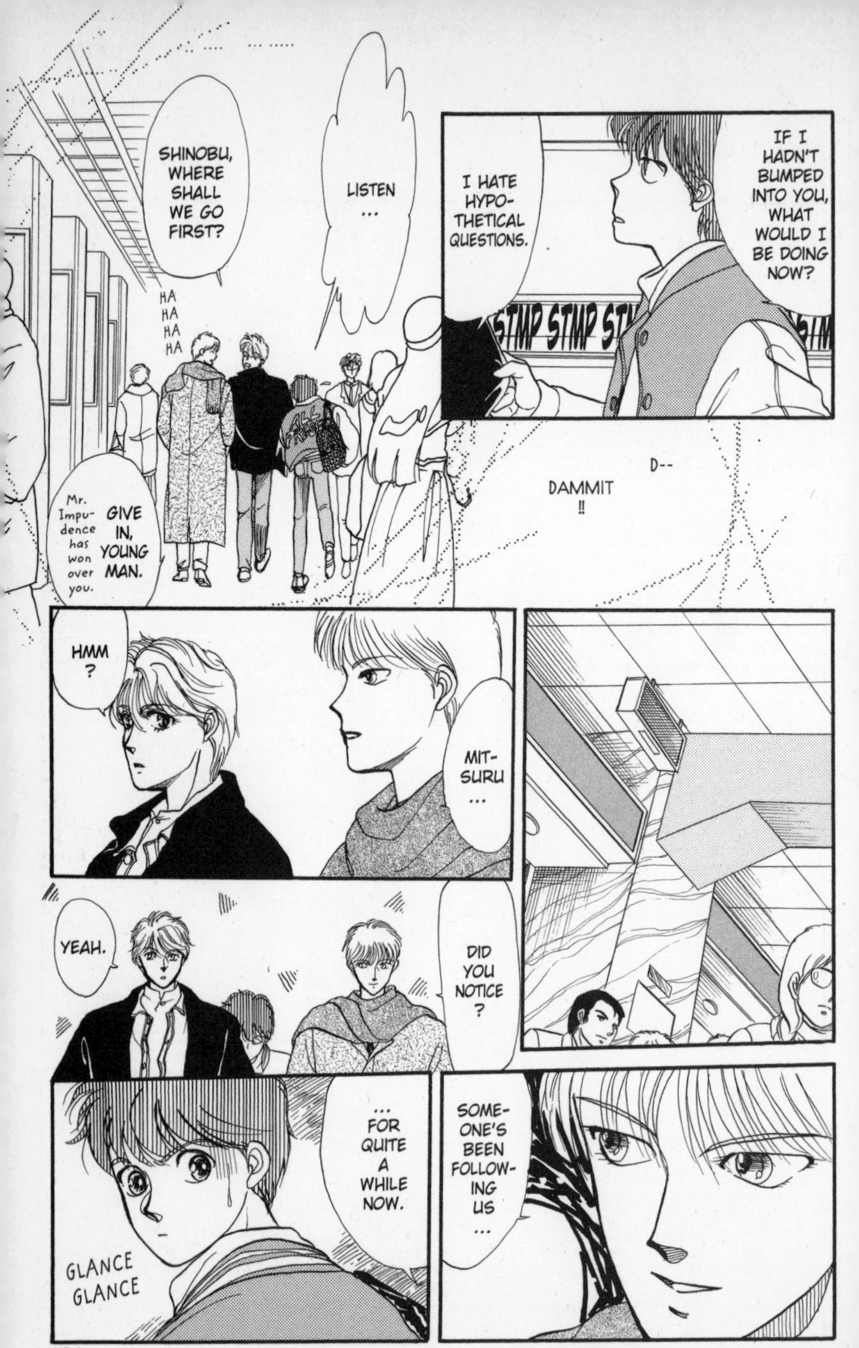
IF I HADN'T BUMPED INTO YOU, WHAT WOULD I BE DOING NOW?
I HATE HYPO-THETICAL QUESTIONS.
STMP STMP STMP
LISTEN ...
SHINOBU, WHERE SHALL WE GO FIRST?
HA HA HA HA
D--
DAMMIT !!
GIVE IN, YOUNG MAN.
Mr. Impudence has won over you.
MIT-SURU ...
HMM ?
DID YOU NOTICE ?
YEAH.
SOME-ONE'S BEEN FOLLOW-ING US ...
... FOR QUITE A WHILE NOW.
GLANCE GLANCE

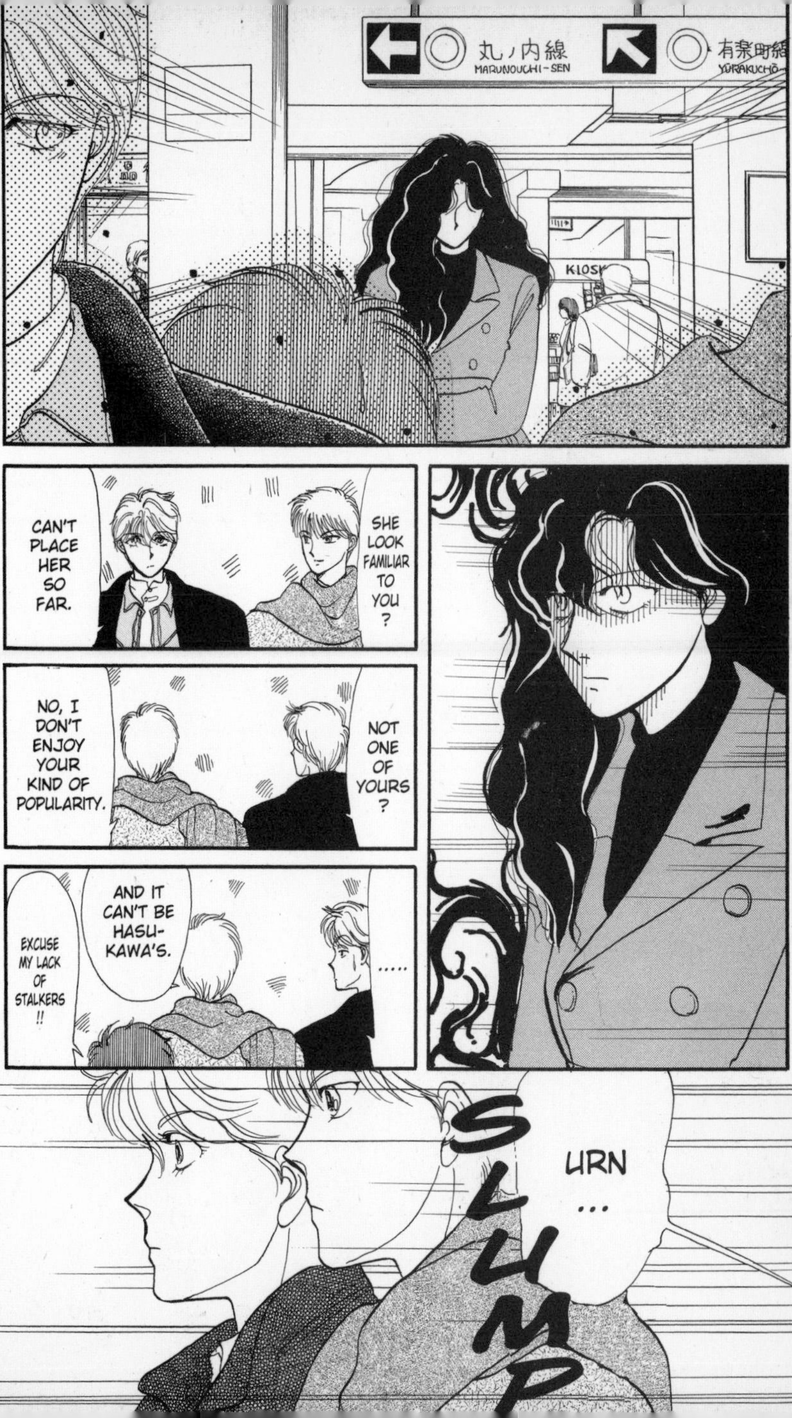
丸ノ内線
MARUNOUCHI-SEN
SHE LOOK FAMILIAR TO YOU?
CAN'T PLACE HER SO FAR.
NOT ONE OF YOURS?
NO, I DON'T ENJOY YOUR KIND OF POPULARITY.
.....
AND IT CAN'T BE HASU-KAWA'S.
EXCUSE MY LACK OF STALKERS!!
URN ...
SLUMP

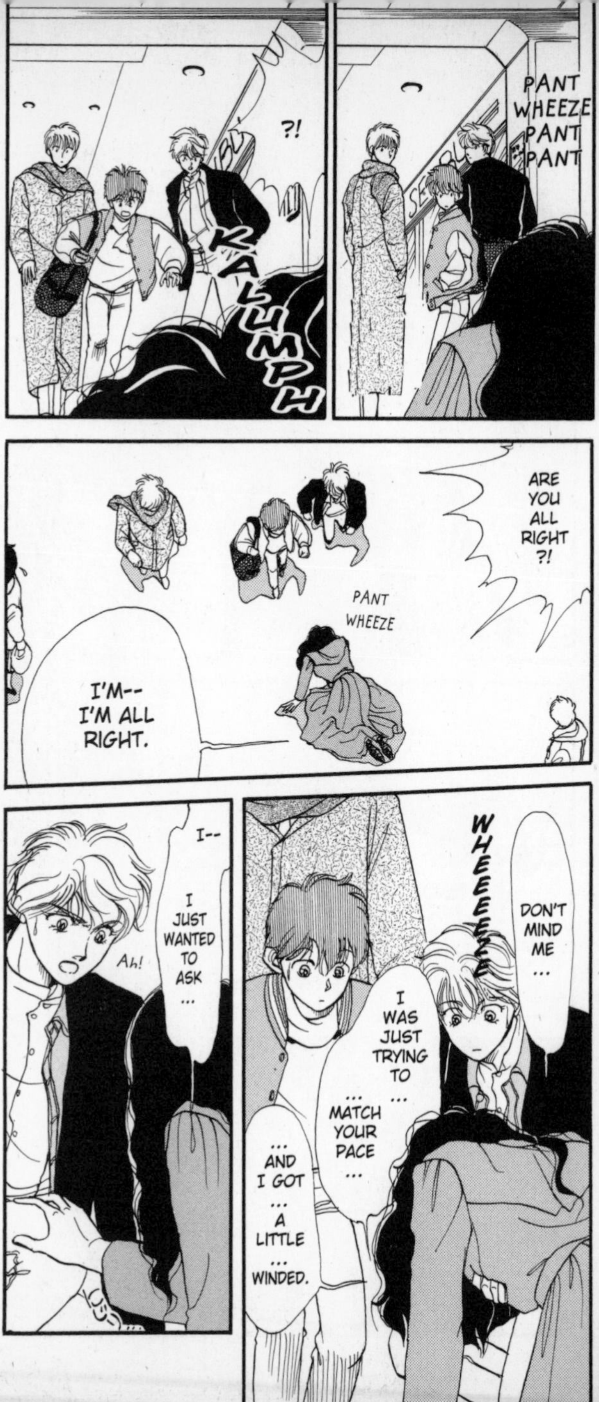
PANT WHEEZE PANT PANT
?!
KALUMPH
ARE YOU ALL RIGHT?!
PANT WHEEZE
I'M-- I'M ALL RIGHT.
WHEEEEEZE
DON'T MIND ME ...
I WAS JUST TRYING TO ...
... MATCH YOUR PACE ...
... AND I GOT ... A LITTLE ... WINDED.
I--
I JUST WANTED TO ASK ...
Ah!
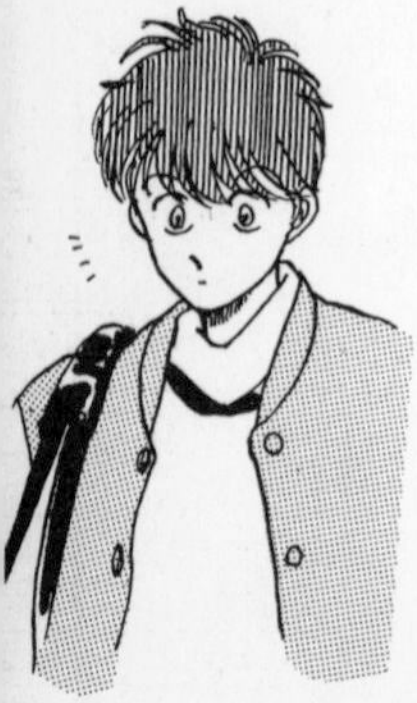

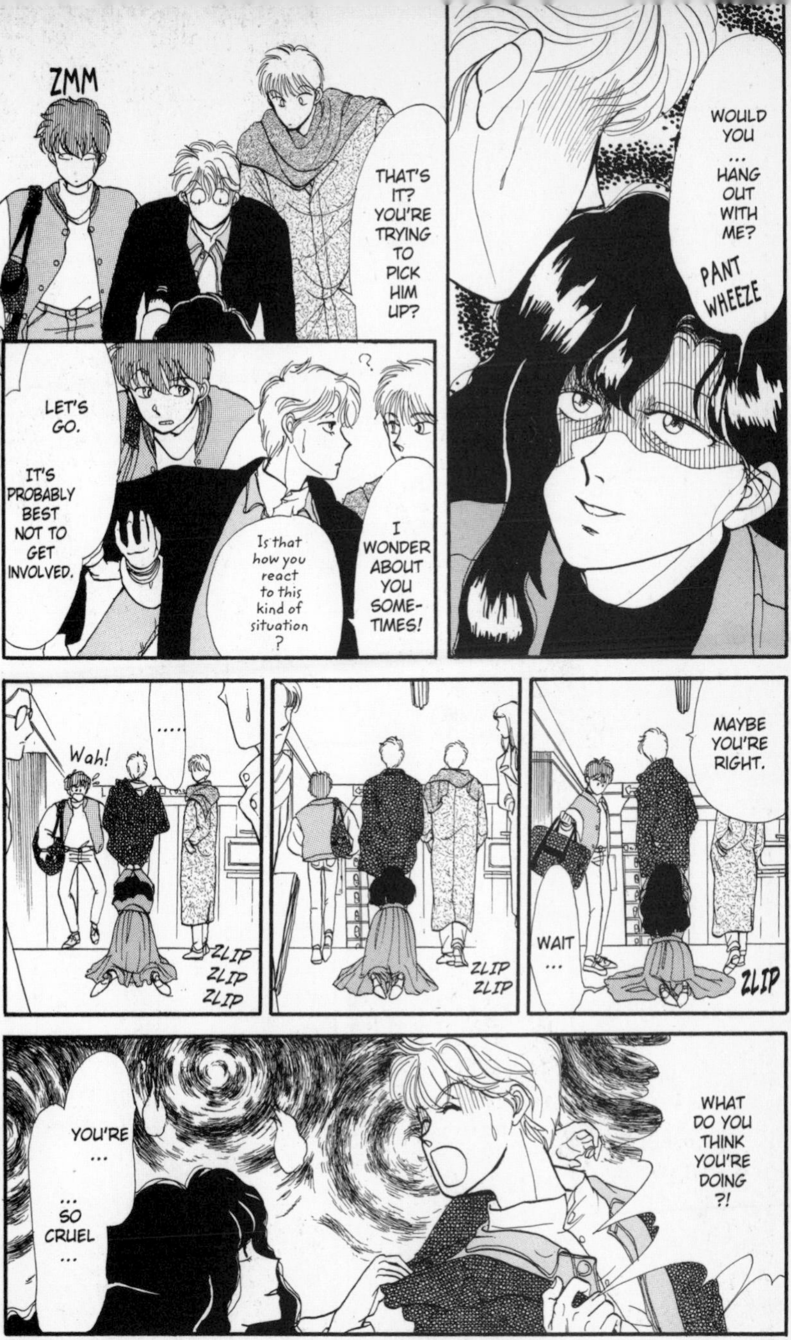
WOULD YOU ... HANG OUT WITH ME?
PANT WHEEZE
ZMM
THAT'S IT? YOU'RE TRYING TO PICK HIM UP?
?
I WONDER ABOUT YOU SOME-TIMES!
Is that how you react to this kind of situation?
LET'S GO.
IT'S PROBABLY BEST NOT TO GET INVOLVED.
MAYBE YOU'RE RIGHT.
WAIT ...
ZLIP
ZLIP ZLIP
.....
Wah!
ZLIP ZLIP ZLIP
WHAT DO YOU THINK YOU'RE DOING ?!
YOU'RE ...
... SO CRUEL ...

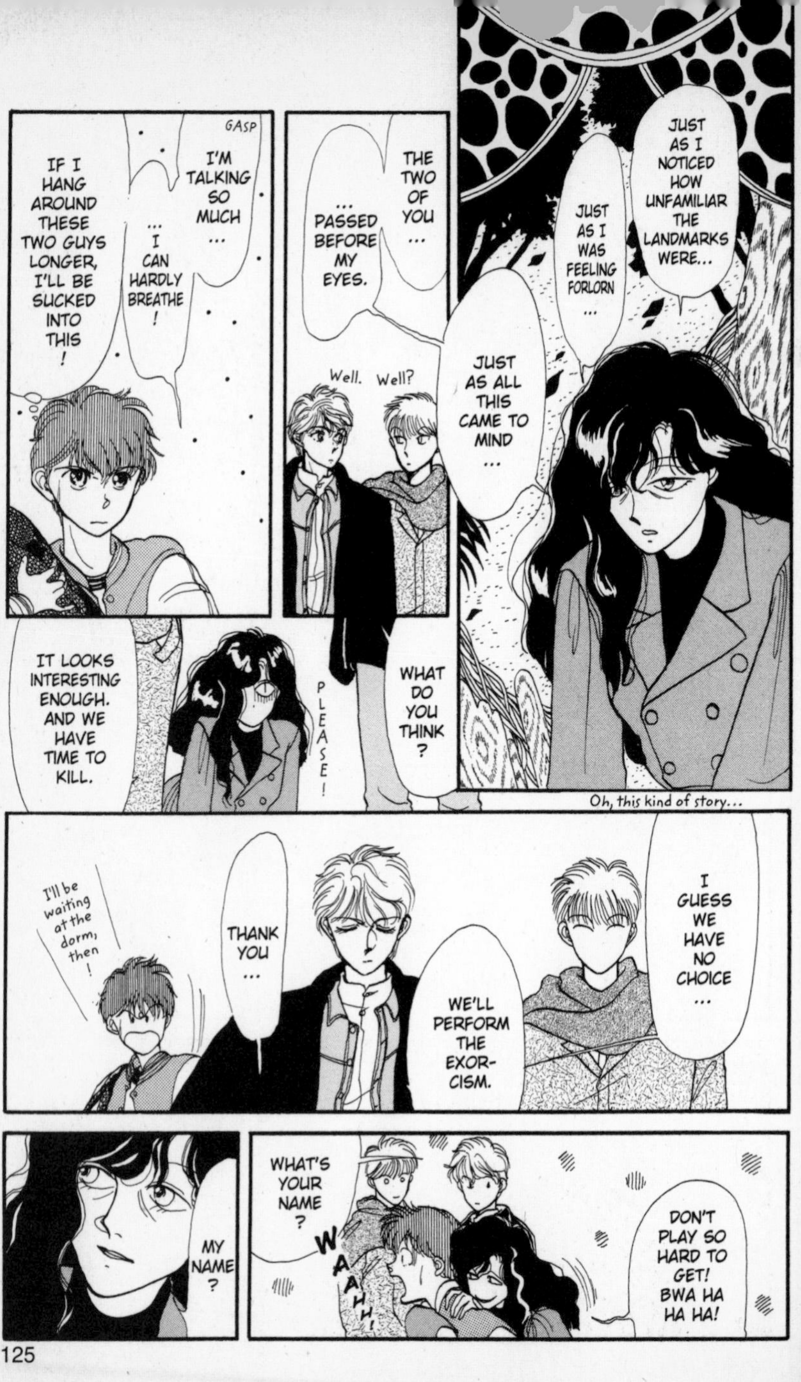
JUST AS I NOTICED HOW UNFAMILIAR THE LANDMARKS WERE...
JUST AS I WAS FEELING FORLORN...
JUST AS ALL THIS CAME TO MIND...
THE TWO OF YOU...
...PASSED BEFORE MY EYES.
Well. Well?
GASP
I'M TALKING SO MUCH...
...I CAN HARDLY BREATHE!
IF I HANG AROUND THESE TWO GUYS LONGER, I'LL BE SUCKED INTO THIS!
WHAT DO YOU THINK?
PLEASE!
IT LOOKS INTERESTING ENOUGH. AND WE HAVE TIME TO KILL.
Oh, this kind of story...
I GUESS WE HAVE NO CHOICE...
WE'LL PERFORM THE EXORCISM.
THANK YOU...
I'll be waiting at the dorm, then!
DON'T PLAY SO HARD TO GET! BWA HA HA HA!
WAAHH!
WHAT'S YOUR NAME?
MY NAME?

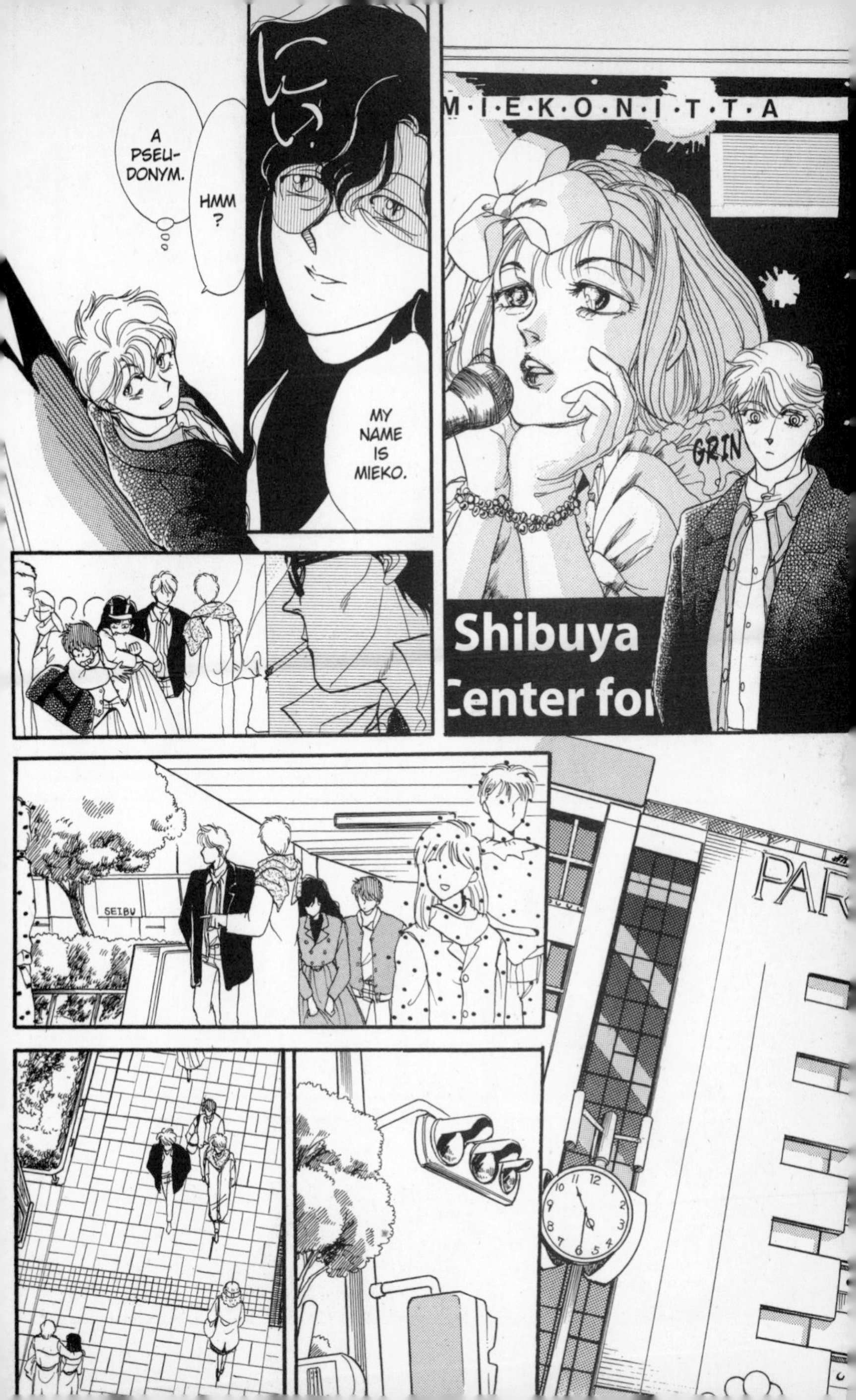
M·I·E·K·O·N·I·T·T·A
GRIN
Shibuya
Center for
MY NAME IS MIEKO.
HMM?
A PSEUDONYM.
PAR
SEIBU

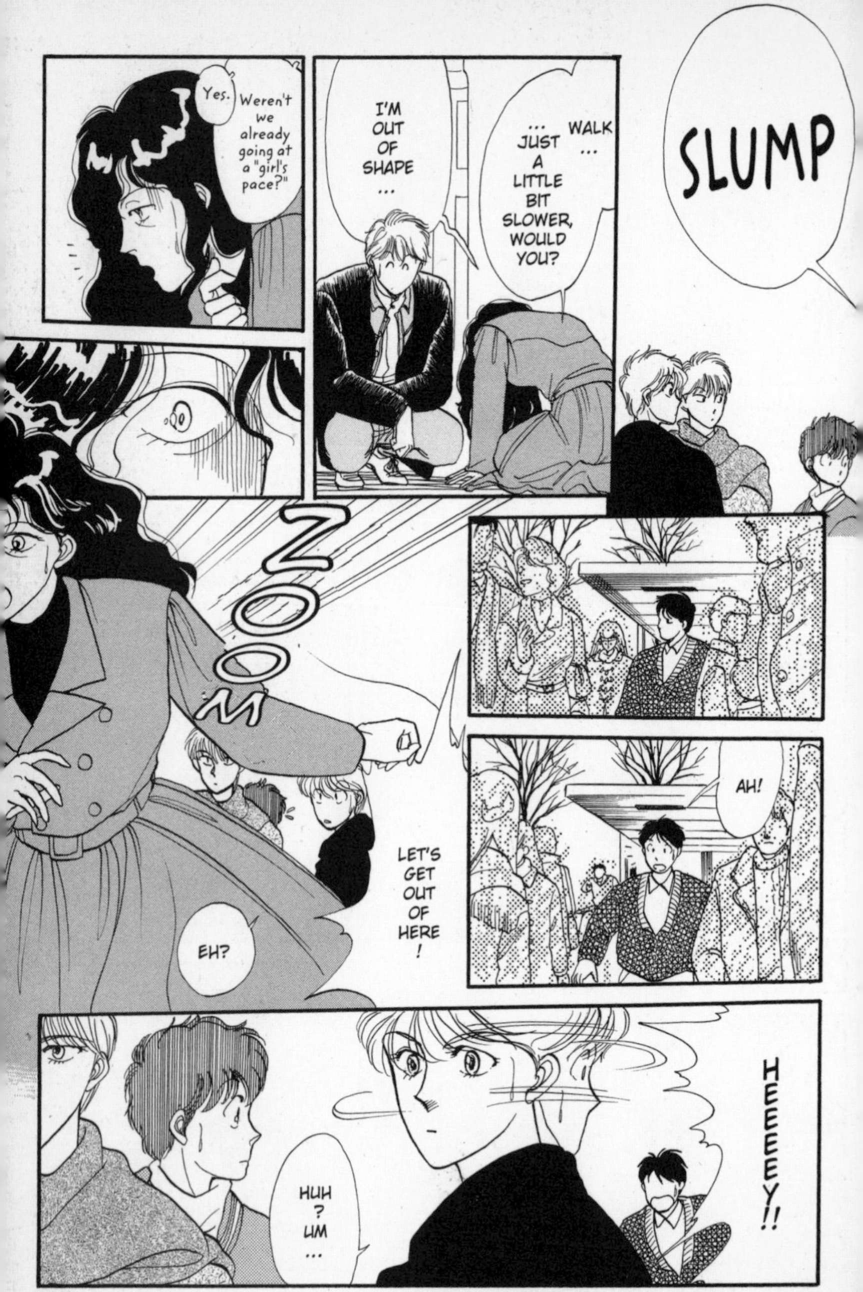
SLUMP
WALK ... ... JUST A LITTLE BIT SLOWER, WOULD YOU?
I'M OUT OF SHAPE ...
Yes.
Weren't we already going at a "girl's pace?"
AH!
ZOOM
LET'S GET OUT OF HERE!
EH?
HEEEEEY!!
HUH? UM ...

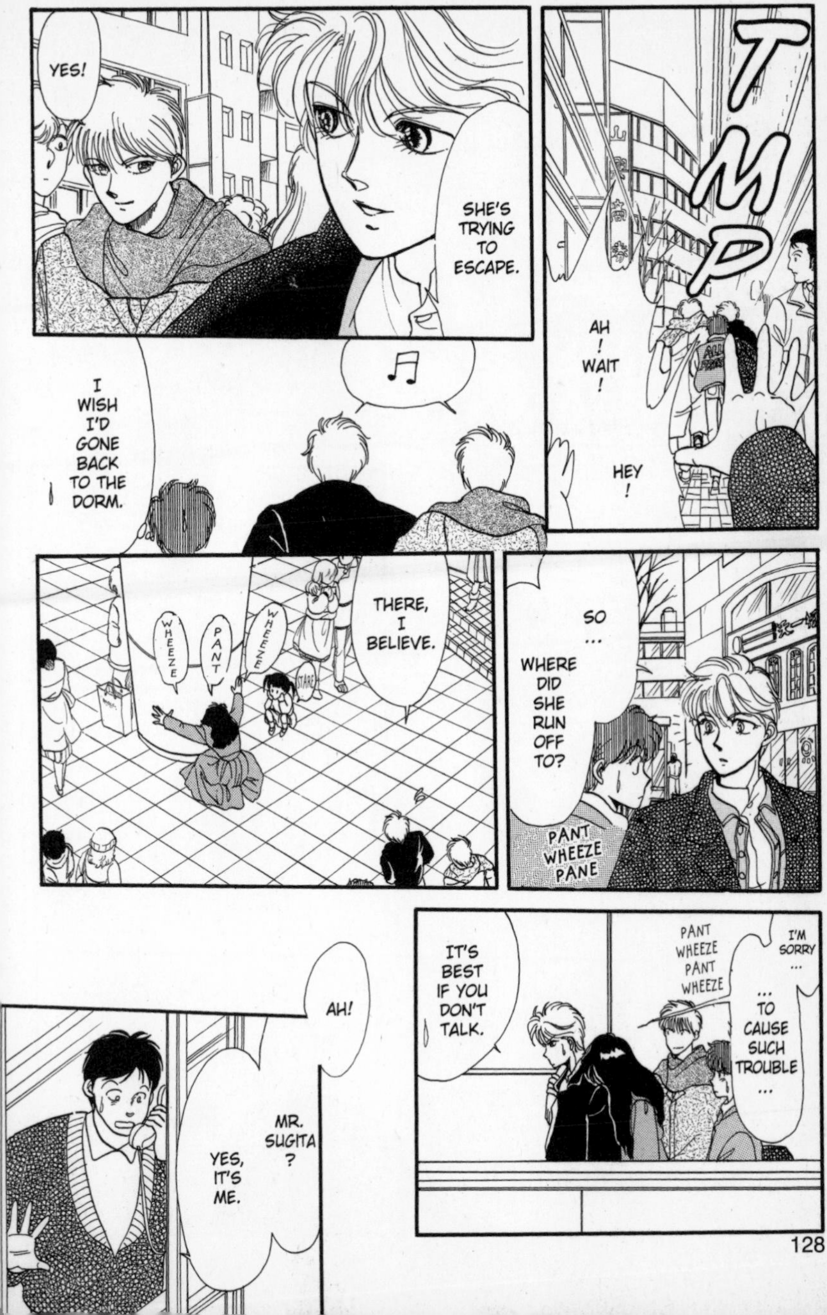
TMP
AH! WAIT!
HEY!
SHE'S TRYING TO ESCAPE.
YES!
♫
I WISH I'D GONE BACK TO THE DORM.
SO...
WHERE DID SHE RUN OFF TO?
PANT WHEEZE PANE
THERE, I BELIEVE.
WHEEZE
PANT
WHEEZE
STARE
I'M SORRY...
...TO CAUSE SUCH TROUBLE...
PANT WHEEZE PANT WHEEZE
IT'S BEST IF YOU DON'T TALK.
AH!
MR. SUGITA?
YES, IT'S ME.

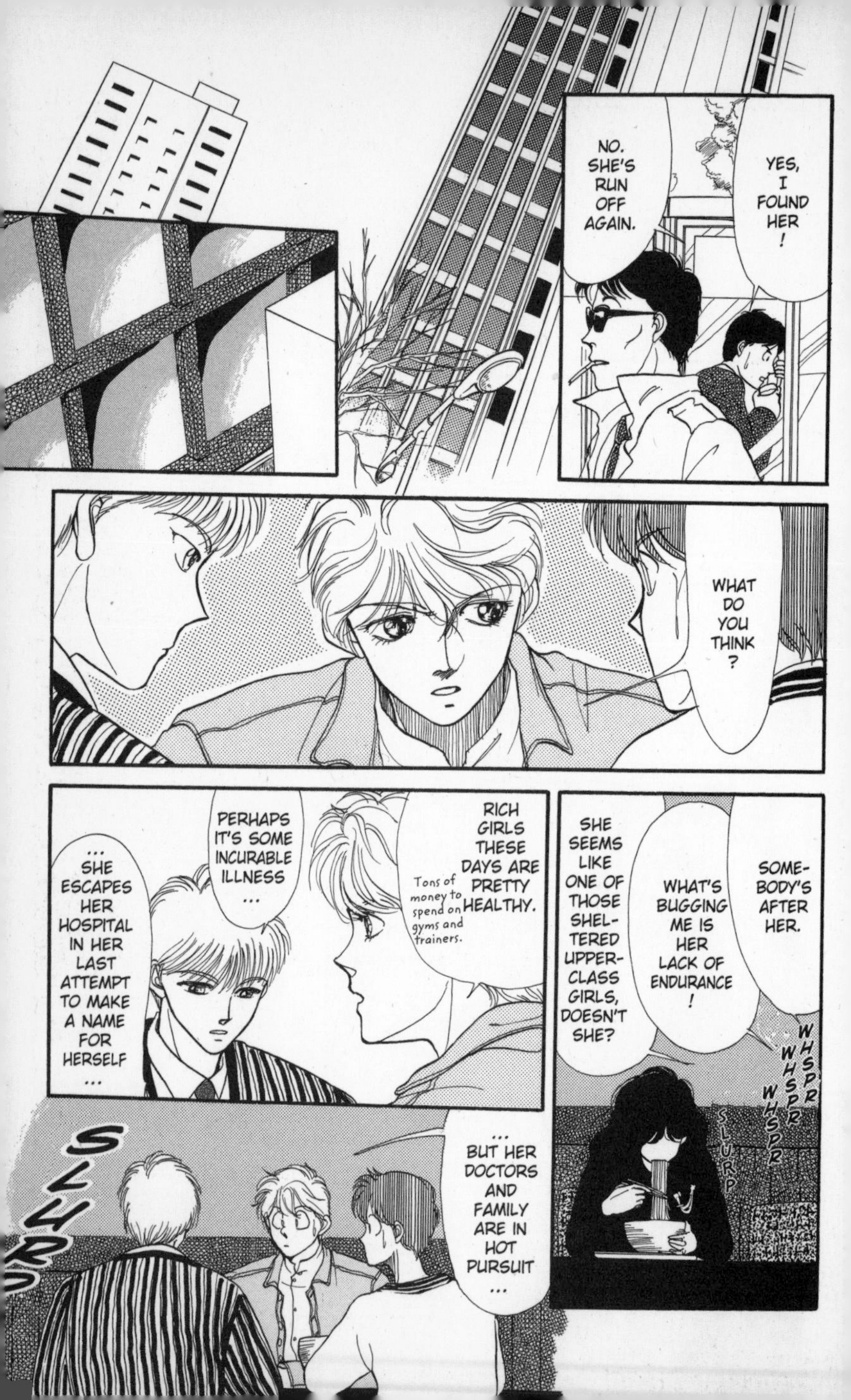
YES, I FOUND HER!
NO. SHE'S RUN OFF AGAIN.
WHAT DO YOU THINK?
SOMEBODY'S AFTER HER.
WHAT'S BUGGING ME IS HER LACK OF ENDURANCE!
SHE SEEMS LIKE ONE OF THOSE SHELTERED UPPER-CLASS GIRLS, DOESN'T SHE?
WHSPR
WHSPR
WHSPR
SLURP
RICH GIRLS THESE DAYS ARE PRETTY HEALTHY.
Tons of money to spend on gyms and trainers.
PERHAPS IT'S SOME INCURABLE ILLNESS ...
... SHE ESCAPES HER HOSPITAL IN HER LAST ATTEMPT TO MAKE A NAME FOR HERSELF ...
... BUT HER DOCTORS AND FAMILY ARE IN HOT PURSUIT ...
SLURP

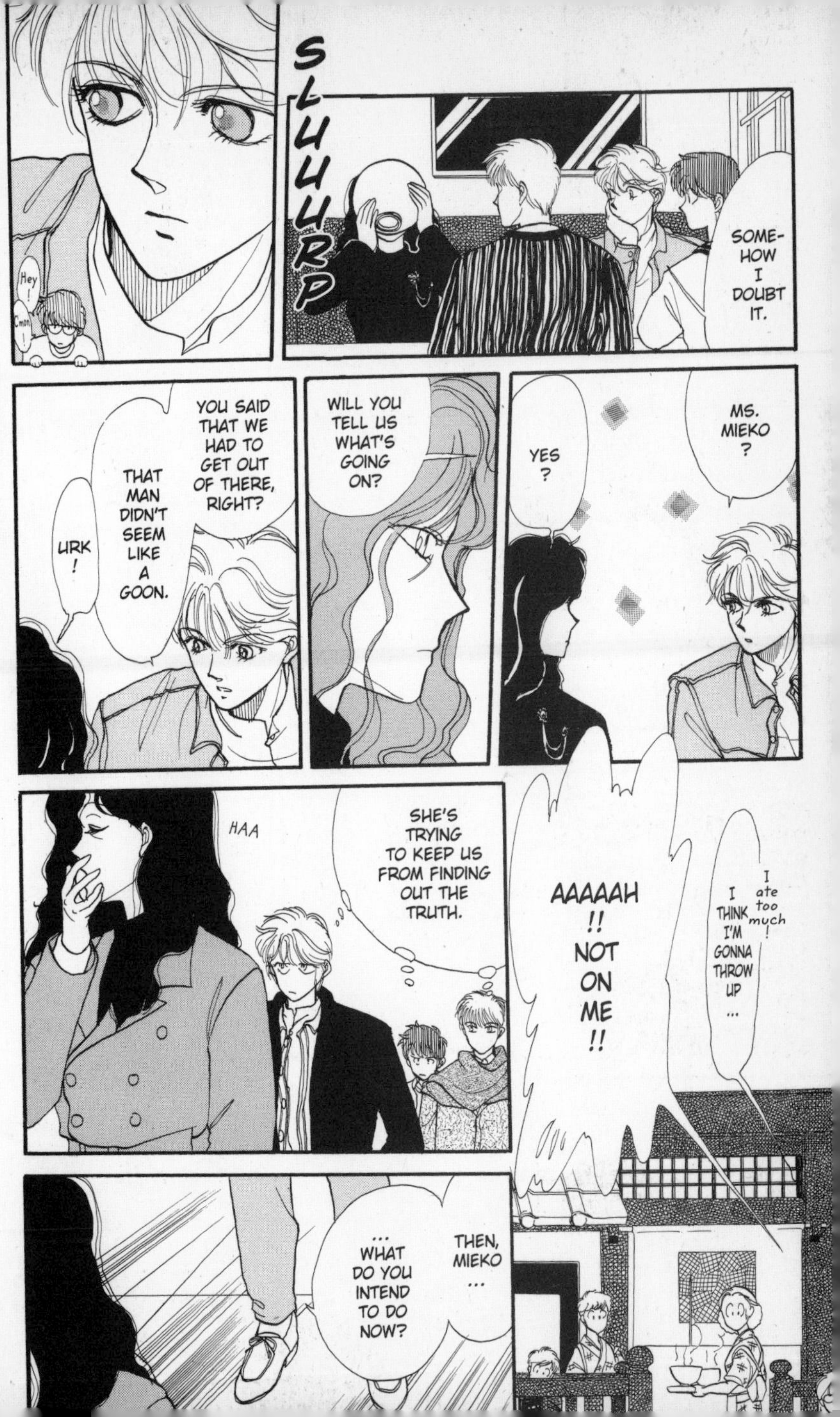
SOME-HOW I DOUBT IT.
SLUUURP
Hey!
C'mon!
MS. MIEKO?
YES?
WILL YOU TELL US WHAT'S GOING ON?
YOU SAID THAT WE HAD TO GET OUT OF THERE, RIGHT?
THAT MAN DIDN'T SEEM LIKE A GOON.
URK!
I ate too much!
I THINK I'M GONNA THROW UP...
AAAAAH!! NOT ON ME!!
SHE'S TRYING TO KEEP US FROM FINDING OUT THE TRUTH.
HAA
THEN, MIEKO...
...WHAT DO YOU INTEND TO DO NOW?

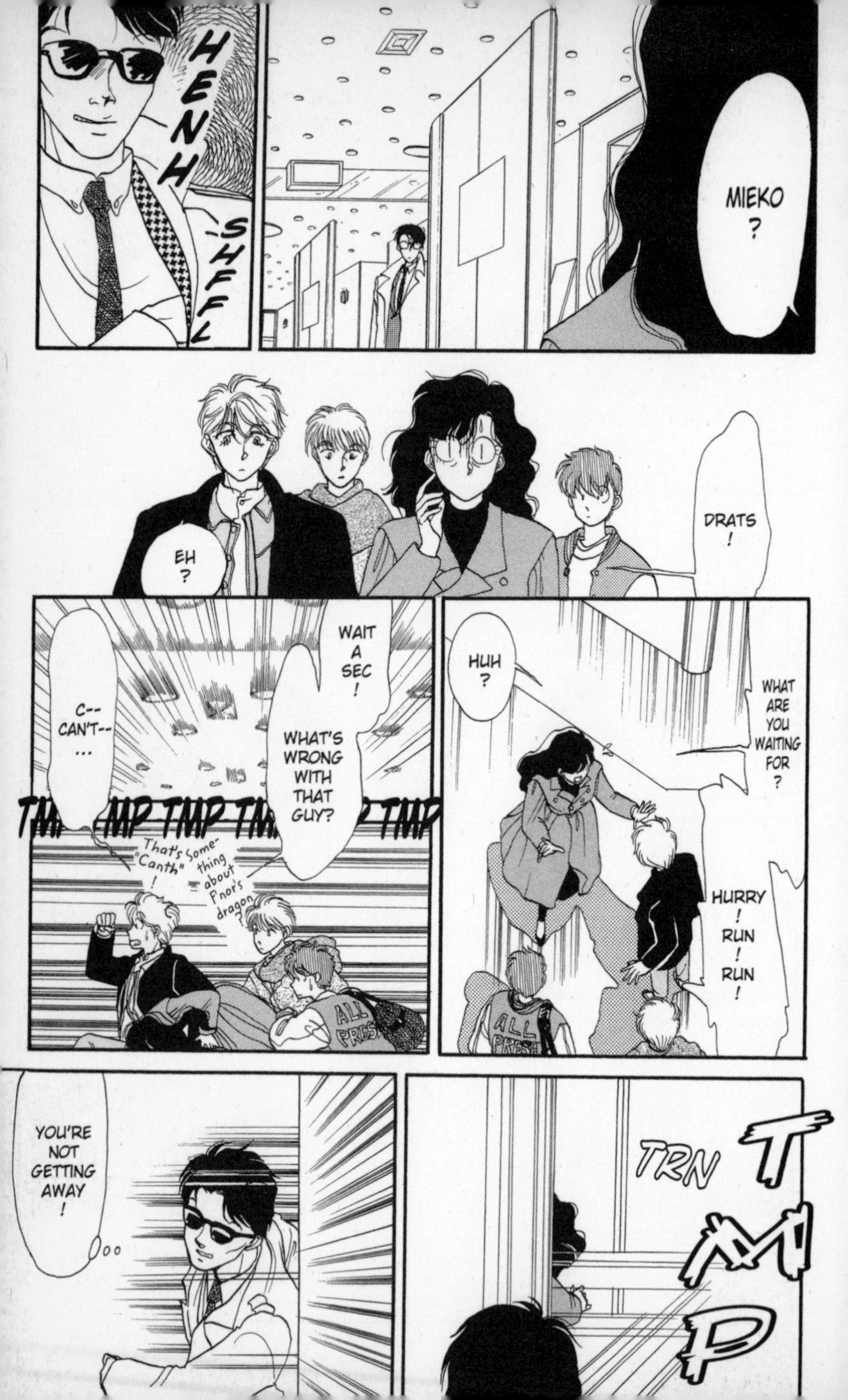

MIEKO ?
HENH
SHFFL
DRATS !
EH ?
WHAT ARE YOU WAITING FOR ?
HUH ?
HURRY ! RUN ! RUN !
WAIT A SEC !
WHAT'S WRONG WITH THAT GUY?
C-- CAN'T-- ...
TMP TMP
Something about F'nor's dragon ?
That's "Canth" !
TMP
TRN
YOU'RE NOT GETTING AWAY !

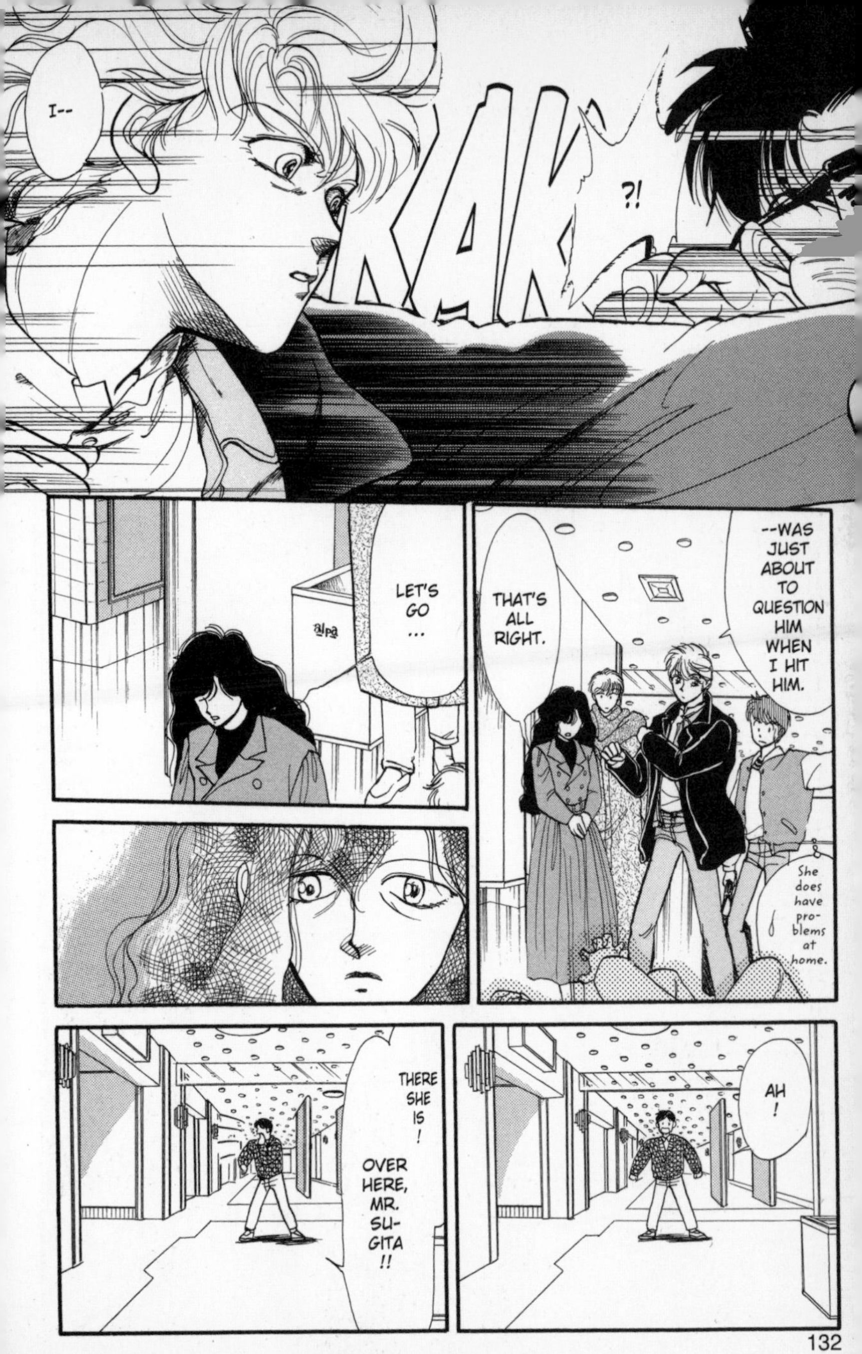
?!
KAK
I--
--WAS JUST ABOUT TO QUESTION HIM WHEN I HIT HIM.
THAT'S ALL RIGHT.
She does have pro-blems at home.
LET'S GO ...
AH!
THERE SHE IS!
OVER HERE, MR. SU-GITA!!

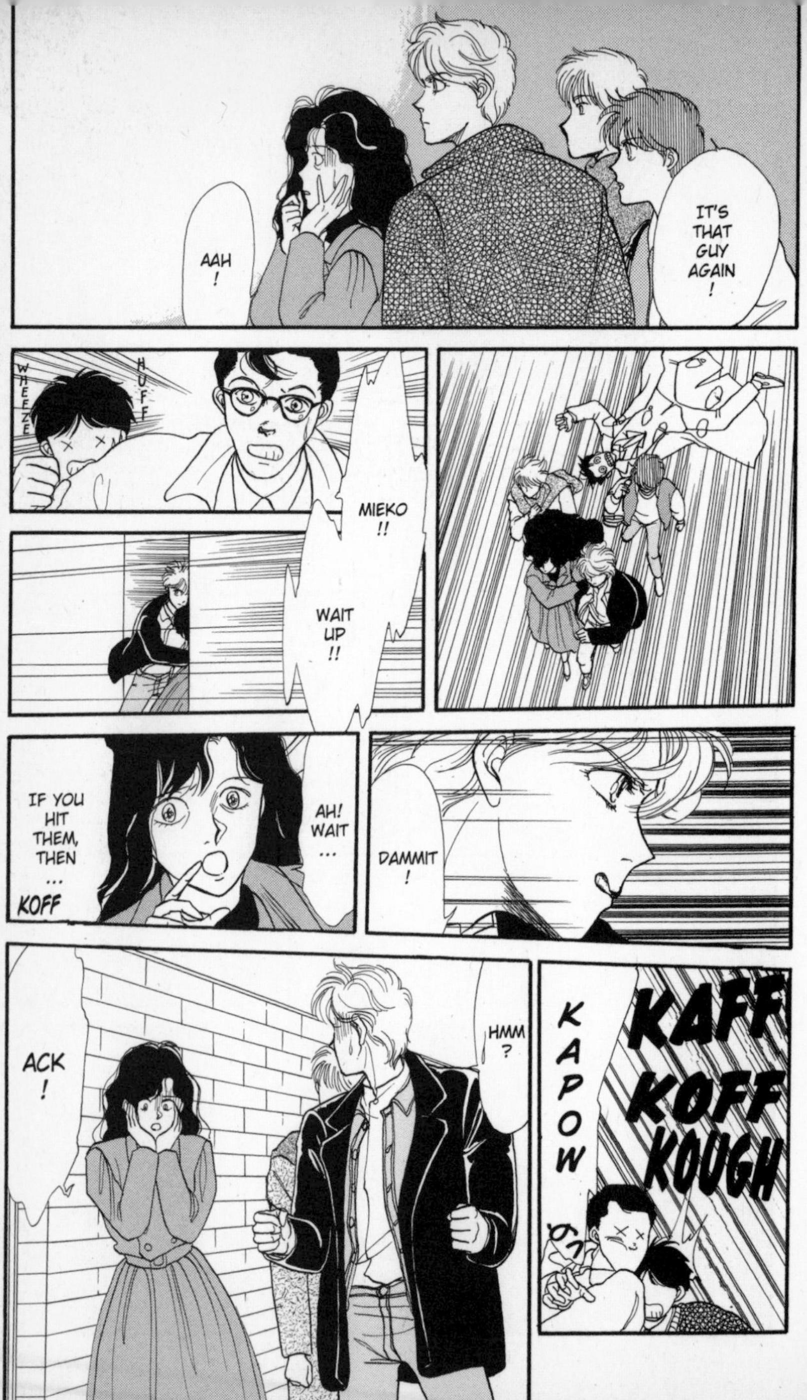
IT'S THAT GUY AGAIN!
AAH!
HUFF
WHEEZE
MIEKO!!
WAIT UP!!
DAMMIT!
AH! WAIT...
IF YOU HIT THEM, THEN...
KOFF
KAFF KOFF KOUGH
KAPOW
HMM?
ACK!

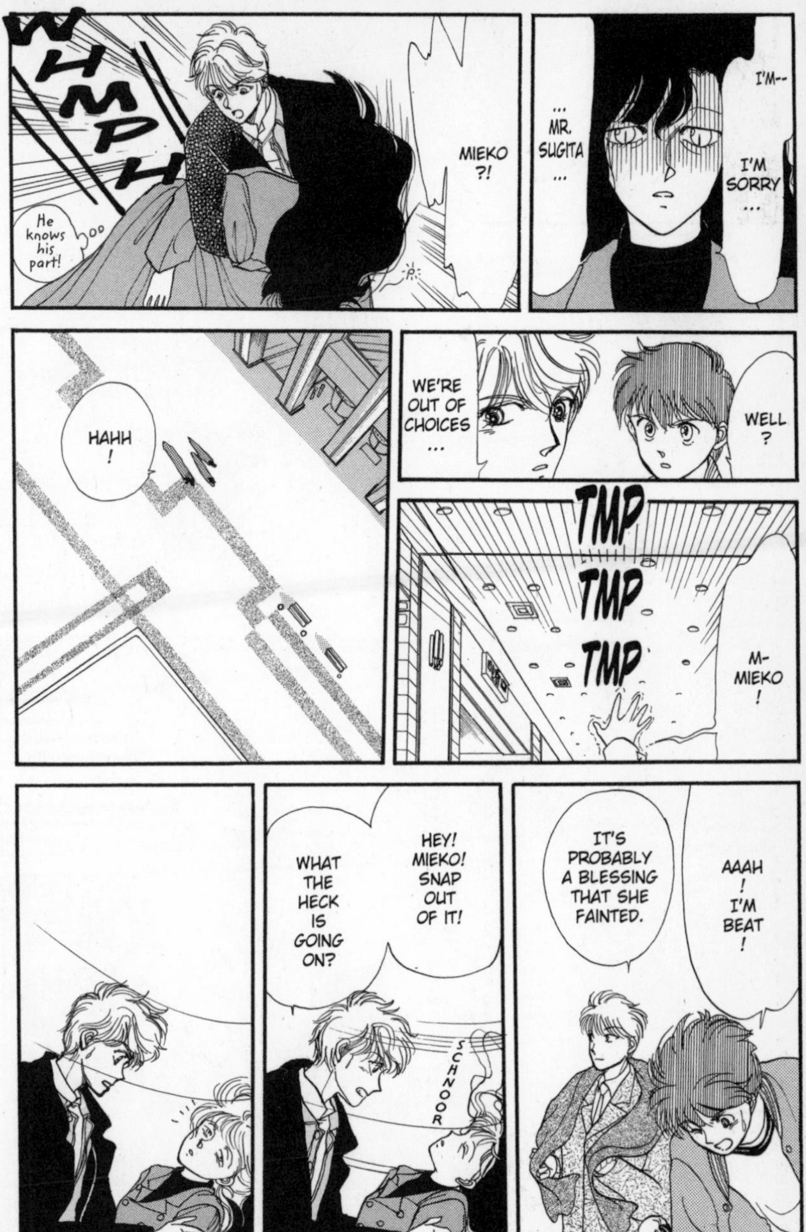
I'M--
I'M SORRY ...
... MR. SUGITA ...
WHMPH
MIEKO ?!
He knows his part!
WELL ?
WE'RE OUT OF CHOICES ...
TMP TMP TMP
M-MIEKO !
HAHH !
AAAH ! I'M BEAT !
IT'S PROBABLY A BLESSING THAT SHE FAINTED.
HEY! MIEKO! SNAP OUT OF IT!
WHAT THE HECK IS GOING ON?
SCHNOOR

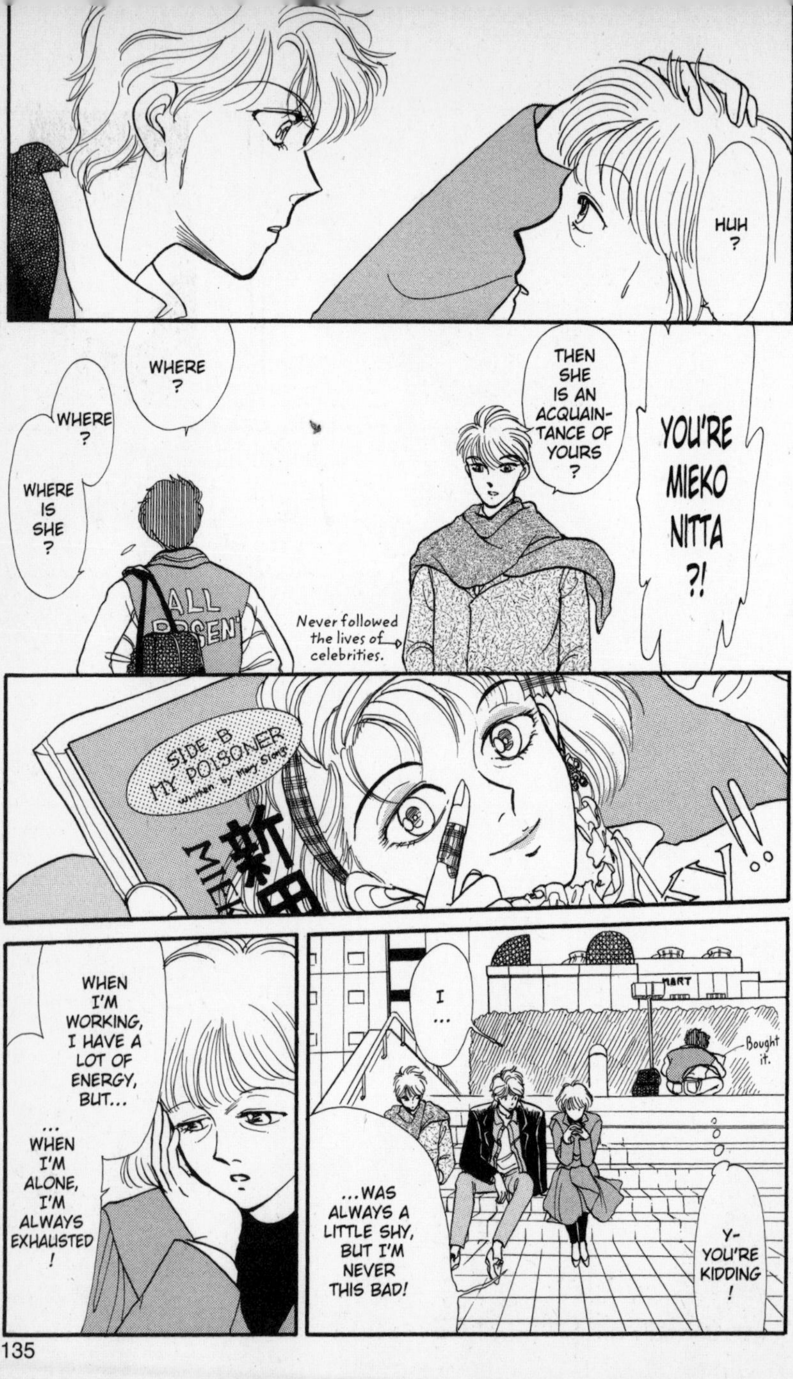
HUH ?
YOU'RE MIEKO NITTA ?!
THEN SHE IS AN ACQUAINTANCE OF YOURS ?
Never followed the lives of celebrities.
WHERE ?
WHERE ?
WHERE IS SHE ?
SIDE-B MY POISONER
I ...
Bought it.
Y-YOU'RE KIDDING !
...WAS ALWAYS A LITTLE SHY, BUT I'M NEVER THIS BAD!
WHEN I'M WORKING, I HAVE A LOT OF ENERGY, BUT...
... WHEN I'M ALONE, I'M ALWAYS EXHAUSTED !

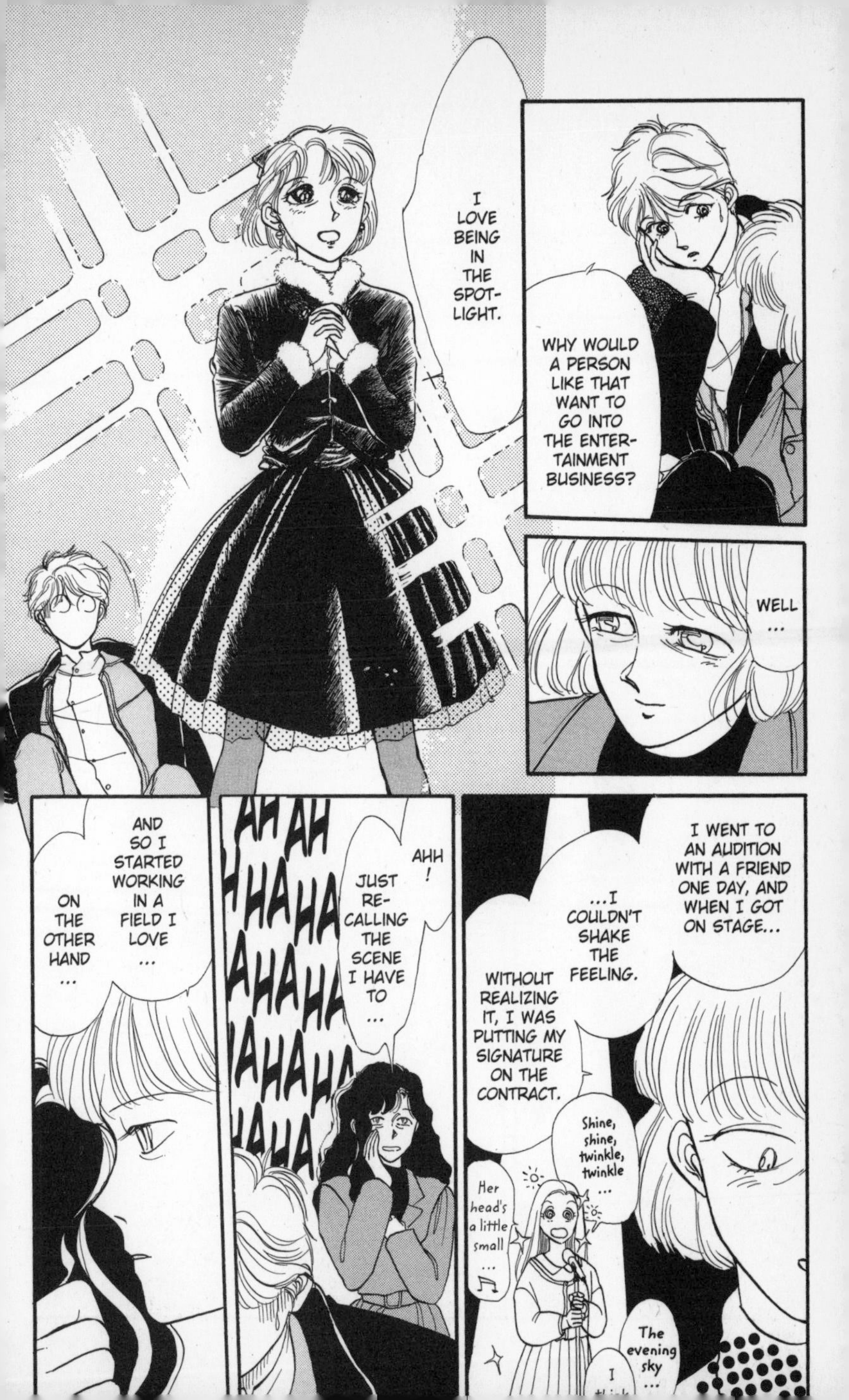
WHY WOULD A PERSON LIKE THAT WANT TO GO INTO THE ENTER-TAINMENT BUSINESS?
WELL ...
I LOVE BEING IN THE SPOT-LIGHT.
I WENT TO AN AUDITION WITH A FRIEND ONE DAY, AND WHEN I GOT ON STAGE...
...I COULDN'T SHAKE THE FEELING.
WITHOUT REALIZING IT, I WAS PUTTING MY SIGNATURE ON THE CONTRACT.
Shine, shine, twinkle, twinkle ...
Her head's a little small ...
The evening sky ...
AHH!
JUST RE-CALLING THE SCENE I HAVE TO ...
AH AH HAHAHAHAHAHA
AND SO I STARTED WORKING IN A FIELD I LOVE ...
ON THE OTHER HAND ...

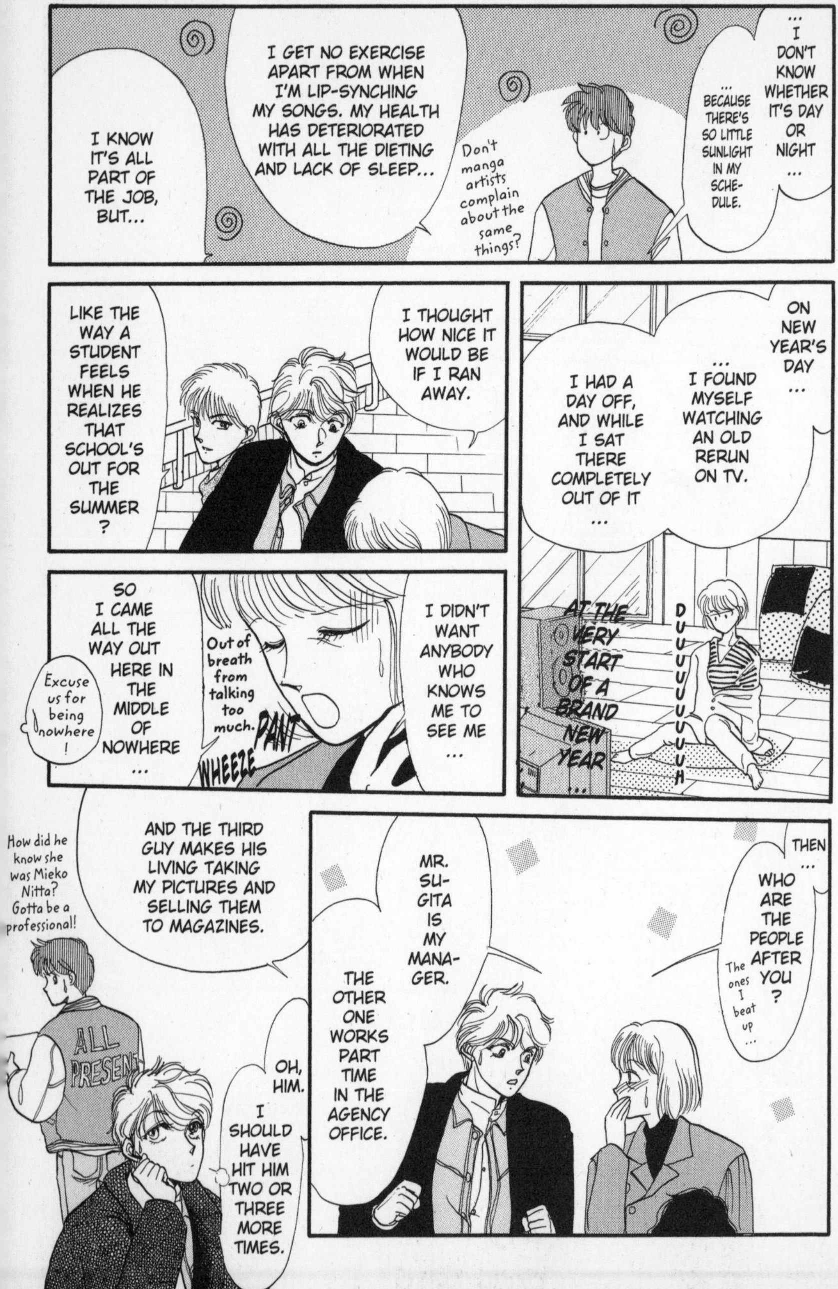
... I DON'T KNOW WHETHER IT'S DAY OR NIGHT ...
... BECAUSE THERE'S SO LITTLE SUNLIGHT IN MY SCHEDULE.
Don't manga artists complain about the same things?
I GET NO EXERCISE APART FROM WHEN I'M LIP-SYNCHING MY SONGS. MY HEALTH HAS DETERIORATED WITH ALL THE DIETING AND LACK OF SLEEP...
I KNOW IT'S ALL PART OF THE JOB, BUT...
ON NEW YEAR'S DAY ...
... I FOUND MYSELF WATCHING AN OLD RERUN ON TV.
I HAD A DAY OFF, AND WHILE I SAT THERE COMPLETELY OUT OF IT ...
DUUUUUUUUUUH
AT THE VERY START OF A BRAND NEW YEAR ...
I THOUGHT HOW NICE IT WOULD BE IF I RAN AWAY.
LIKE THE WAY A STUDENT FEELS WHEN HE REALIZES THAT SCHOOL'S OUT FOR THE SUMMER ?
I DIDN'T WANT ANYBODY WHO KNOWS ME TO SEE ME ...
Out of breath from talking too much.
PANT
WHEEZE
SO I CAME ALL THE WAY OUT HERE IN THE MIDDLE OF NOWHERE ...
Excuse us for being nowhere!
THEN ... WHO ARE THE PEOPLE AFTER YOU ?
The ones I beat up ...
MR. SUGITA IS MY MANAGER.
THE OTHER ONE WORKS PART TIME IN THE AGENCY OFFICE.
AND THE THIRD GUY MAKES HIS LIVING TAKING MY PICTURES AND SELLING THEM TO MAGAZINES.
How did he know she was Mieko Nitta? Gotta be a professional!
ALL PRESENT
OH, HIM.
I SHOULD HAVE HIT HIM TWO OR THREE MORE TIMES.

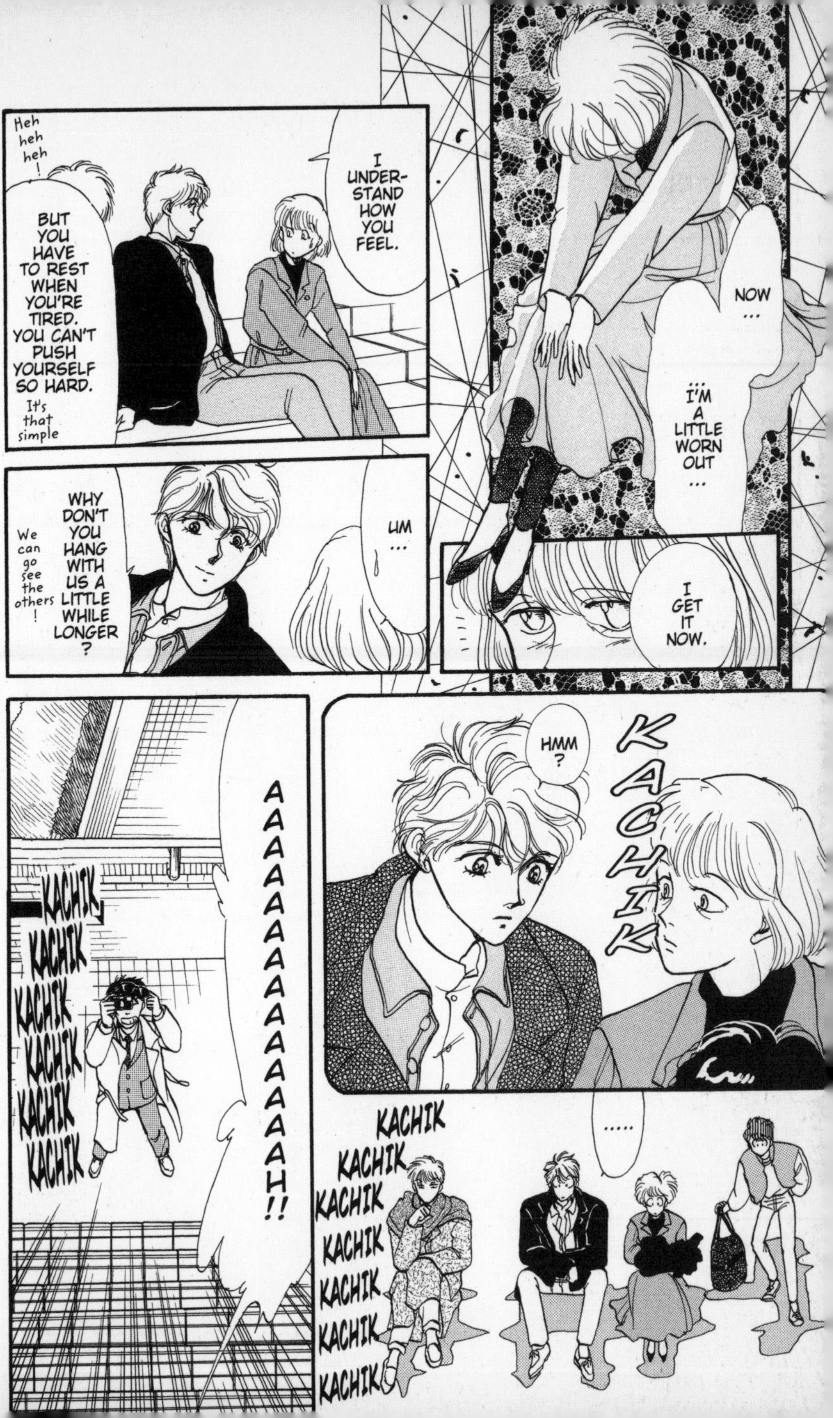
NOW ...
... I'M A LITTLE WORN OUT ...
I GET IT NOW.
I UNDERSTAND HOW YOU FEEL.
BUT YOU HAVE TO REST WHEN YOU'RE TIRED. YOU CAN'T PUSH YOURSELF SO HARD.
Heh heh heh!
It's that simple
UM ...
WHY DON'T YOU HANG WITH US A LITTLE WHILE LONGER?
We can go see the others!
HMM?
KACHIK
AAAAAAAAAAAAAAAAAH!!
KACHIK KACHIK KACHIK KACHIK KACHIK KACHIK
.....
KACHIK KACHIK KACHIK KACHIK KACHIK KACHIK KACHIK

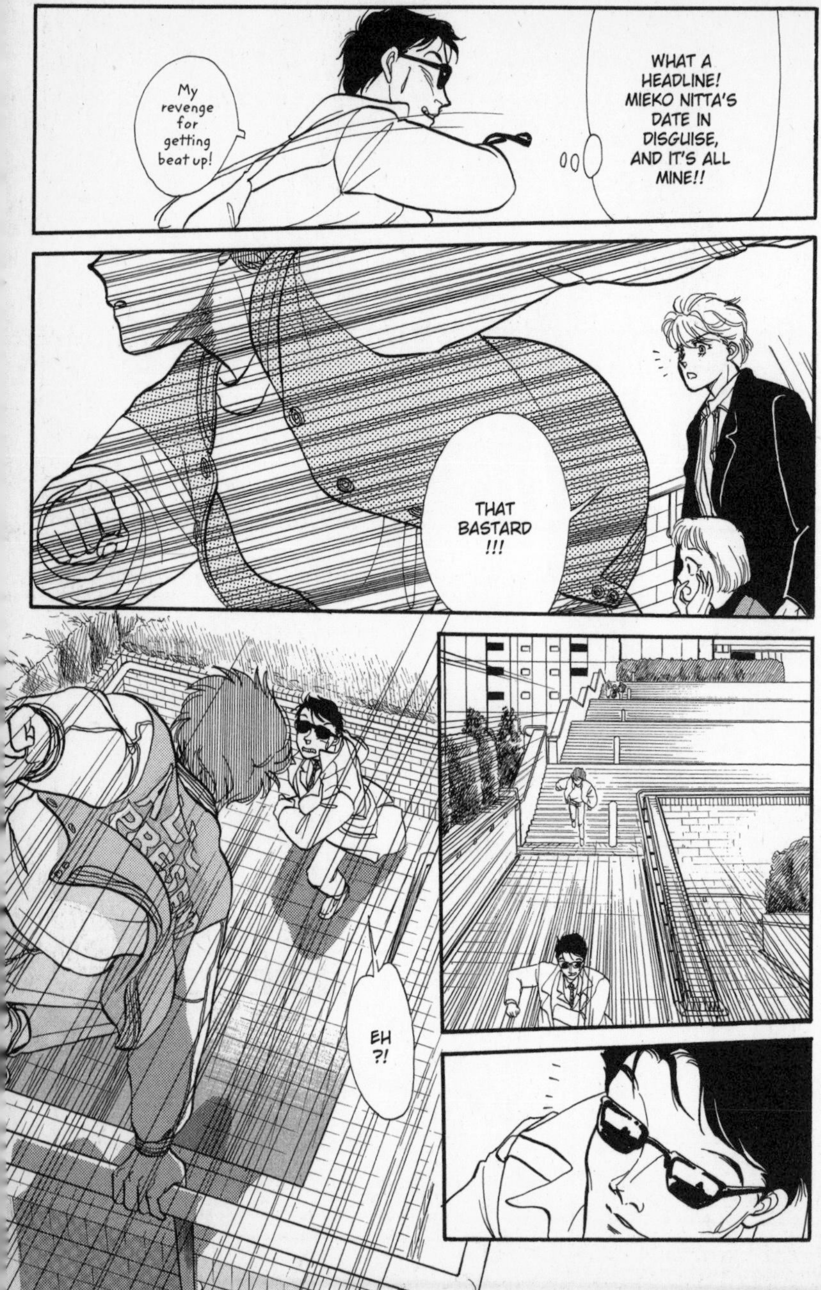
WHAT A HEADLINE! MIEKO NITTA'S DATE IN DISGUISE, AND IT'S ALL MINE!!
My revenge for getting beat up!
THAT BASTARD !!!
EH ?!

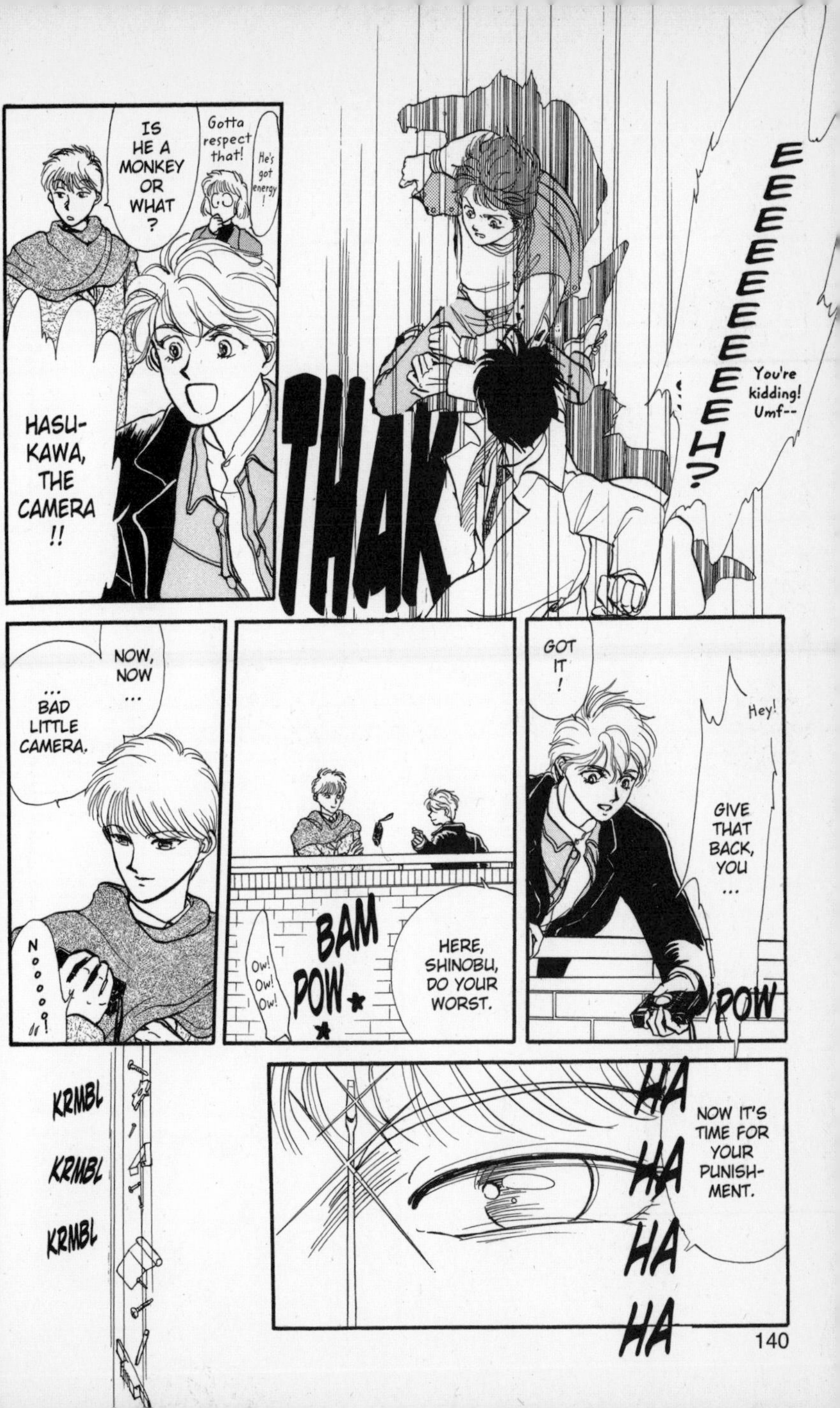

THAK
EEEEEEEEEEEH?
You're kidding! Umf--
He's got energy!
Gotta respect that!
IS HE A MONKEY OR WHAT?
HASU-KAWA, THE CAMERA!!
Hey!
GOT IT!
GIVE THAT BACK, YOU ...
POW
HERE, SHINOBU, DO YOUR WORST.
BAM
POW
Ow! Ow! Ow!
NOW, NOW ... BAD LITTLE CAMERA.
Noooooo!
HA HA HA HA HA
NOW IT'S TIME FOR YOUR PUNISH-MENT.
KRMBL
KRMBL
KRMBL

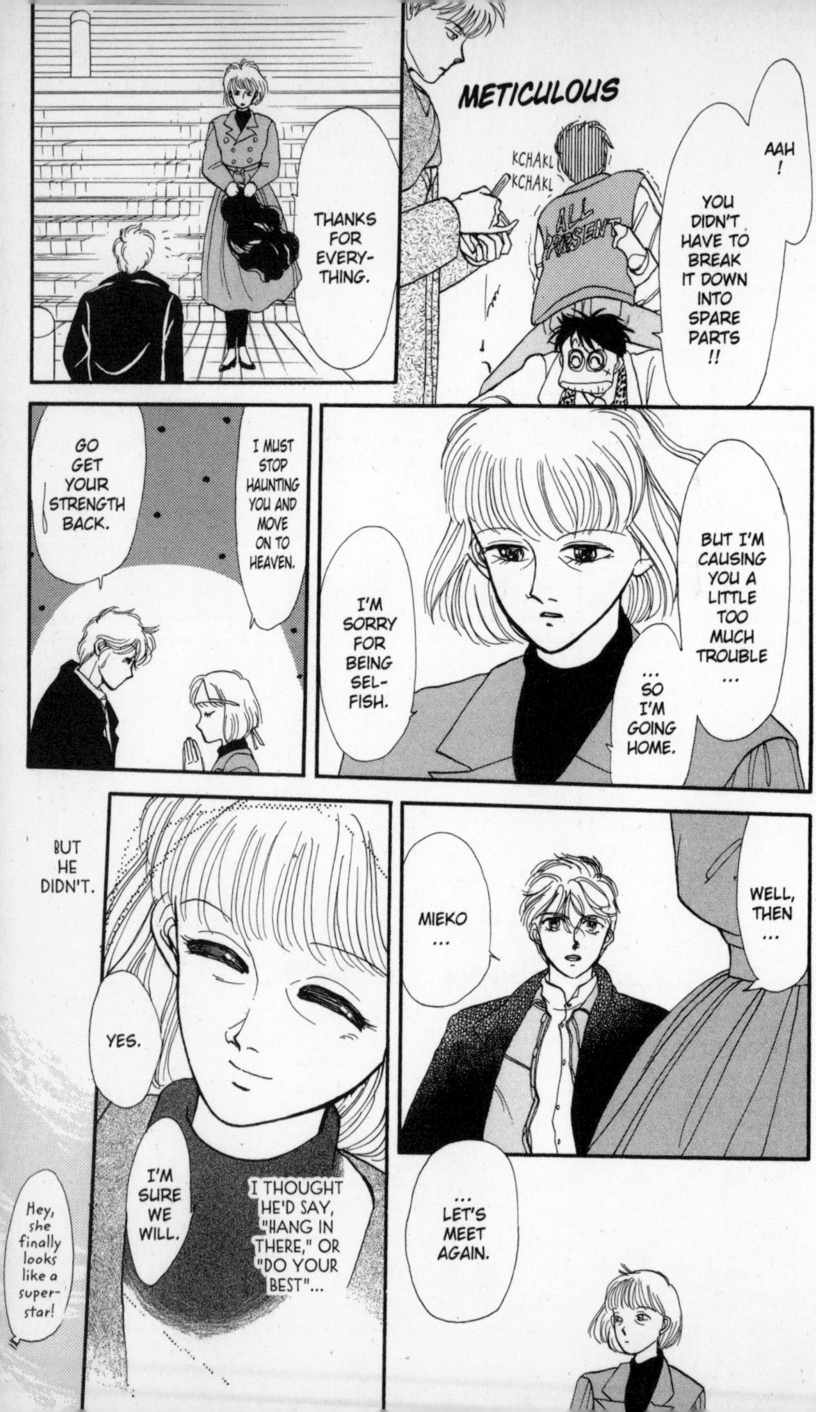
AAH! YOU DIDN'T HAVE TO BREAK IT DOWN INTO SPARE PARTS!!
METICULOUS
KCHAKL KCHAKL
THANKS FOR EVERY-THING.
BUT I'M CAUSING YOU A LITTLE TOO MUCH TROUBLE...
...SO I'M GOING HOME.
I'M SORRY FOR BEING SEL-FISH.
I MUST STOP HAUNTING YOU AND MOVE ON TO HEAVEN.
GO GET YOUR STRENGTH BACK.
WELL, THEN...
MIEKO...
...LET'S MEET AGAIN.
YES.
I'M SURE WE WILL.
I THOUGHT HE'D SAY, "HANG IN THERE," OR "DO YOUR BEST"...
BUT HE DIDN'T.
Hey, she finally looks like a super-star!

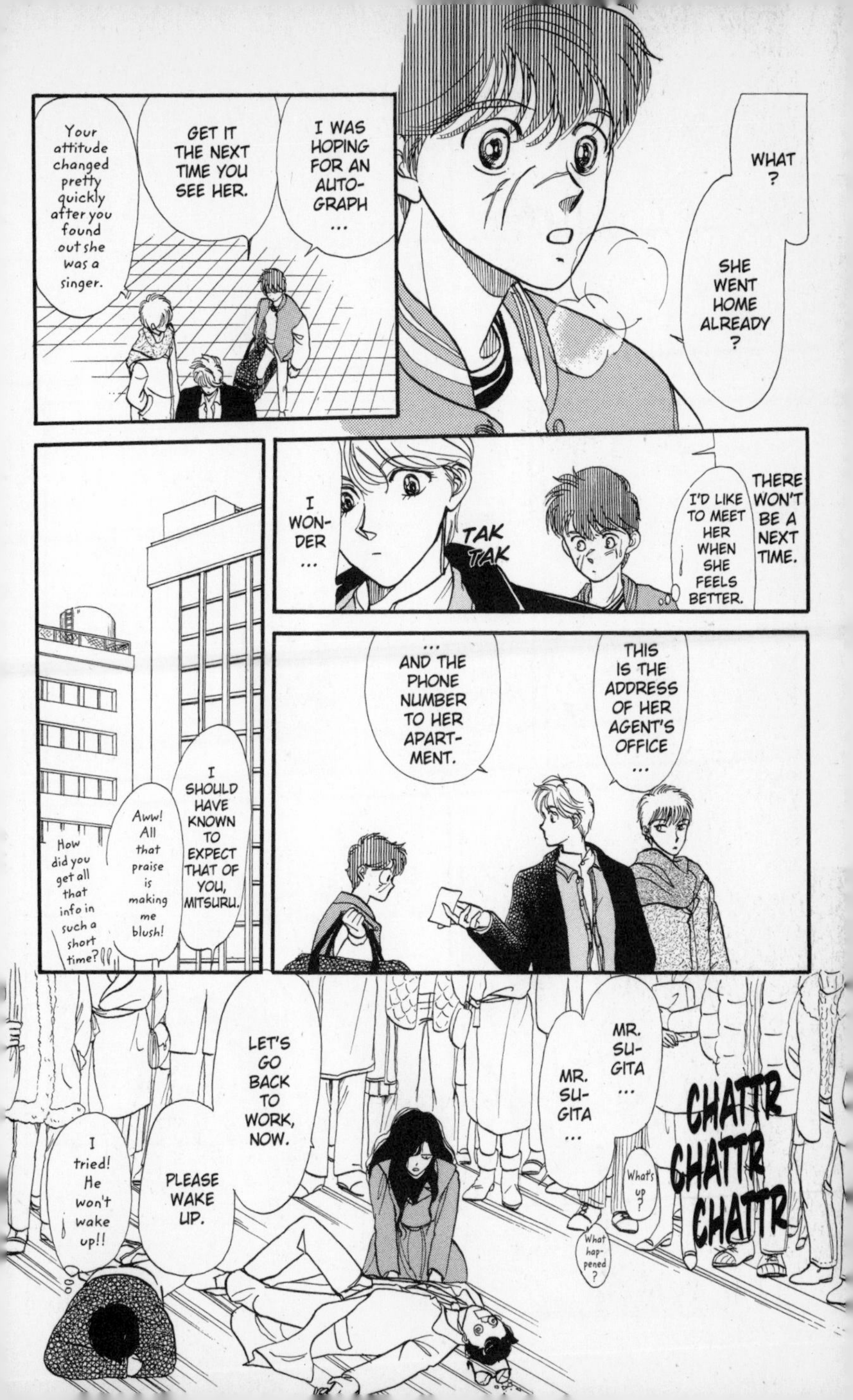
WHAT?
SHE WENT HOME ALREADY?
I WAS HOPING FOR AN AUTO-GRAPH ...
GET IT THE NEXT TIME YOU SEE HER.
Your attitude changed pretty quickly after you found out she was a singer.
THERE WON'T BE A NEXT TIME.
I'D LIKE TO MEET HER WHEN SHE FEELS BETTER.
TAK TAK
I WONDER ...
THIS IS THE ADDRESS OF HER AGENT'S OFFICE ...
... AND THE PHONE NUMBER TO HER APARTMENT.
I SHOULD HAVE KNOWN TO EXPECT THAT OF YOU, MITSURU.
Aww! All that praise is making me blush!
How did you get all that info in such a short time?
MR. SUGITA ...
MR. SUGITA ...
CHATTR CHATTR CHATTR
What's up?
What happened?
LET'S GO BACK TO WORK, NOW.
PLEASE WAKE UP.
I tried! He won't wake up!!

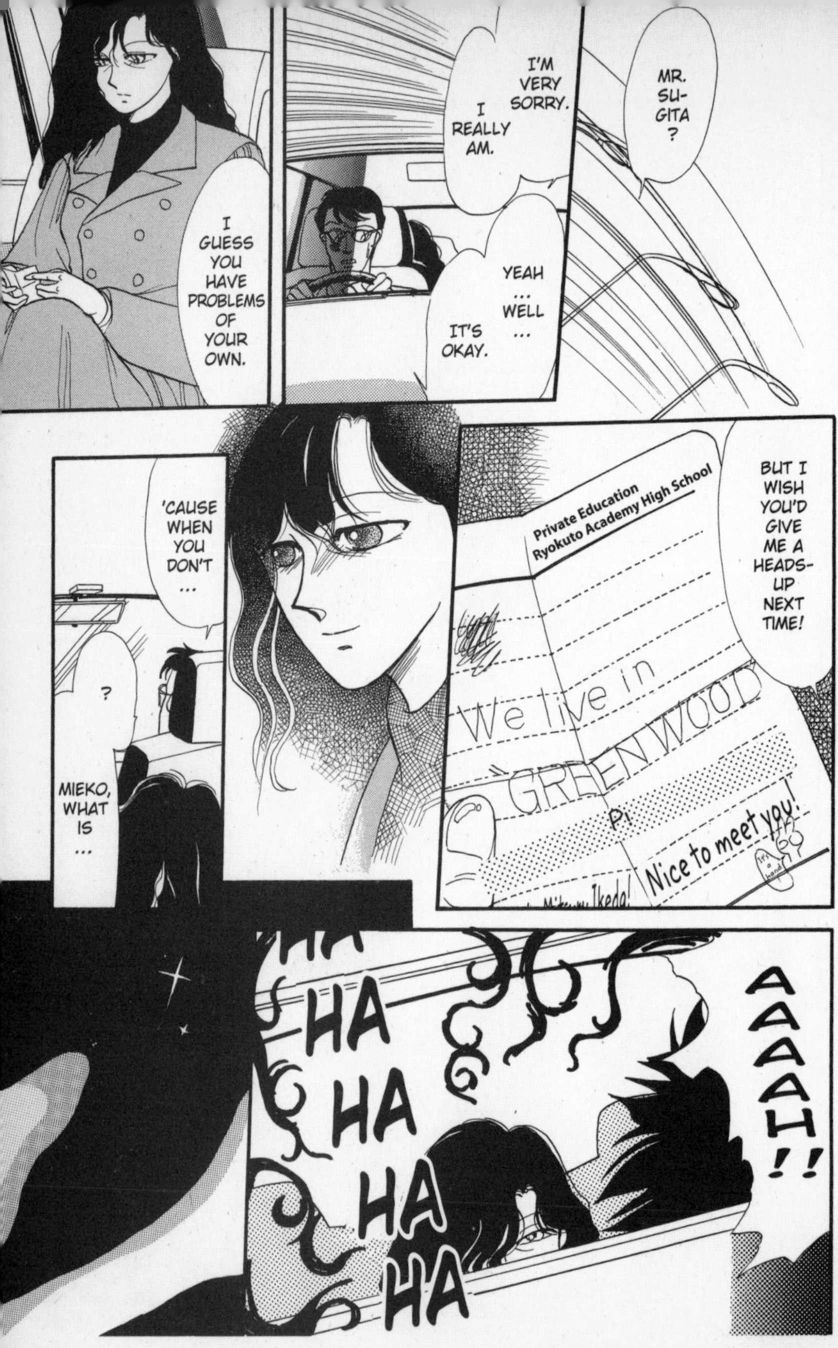
MR. SU-GITA?
I'M VERY SORRY.
I REALLY AM.
YEAH ... WELL ...
IT'S OKAY.
I GUESS YOU HAVE PROBLEMS OF YOUR OWN.
BUT I WISH YOU'D GIVE ME A HEADS-UP NEXT TIME!
Private Education
Ryokuto Academy High School
We live in
GREENWOOD
Pi
Nice to meet you!
'CAUSE WHEN YOU DON'T ...
?
MIEKO, WHAT IS ...
AAAAH!!
HA HA HA HA HA

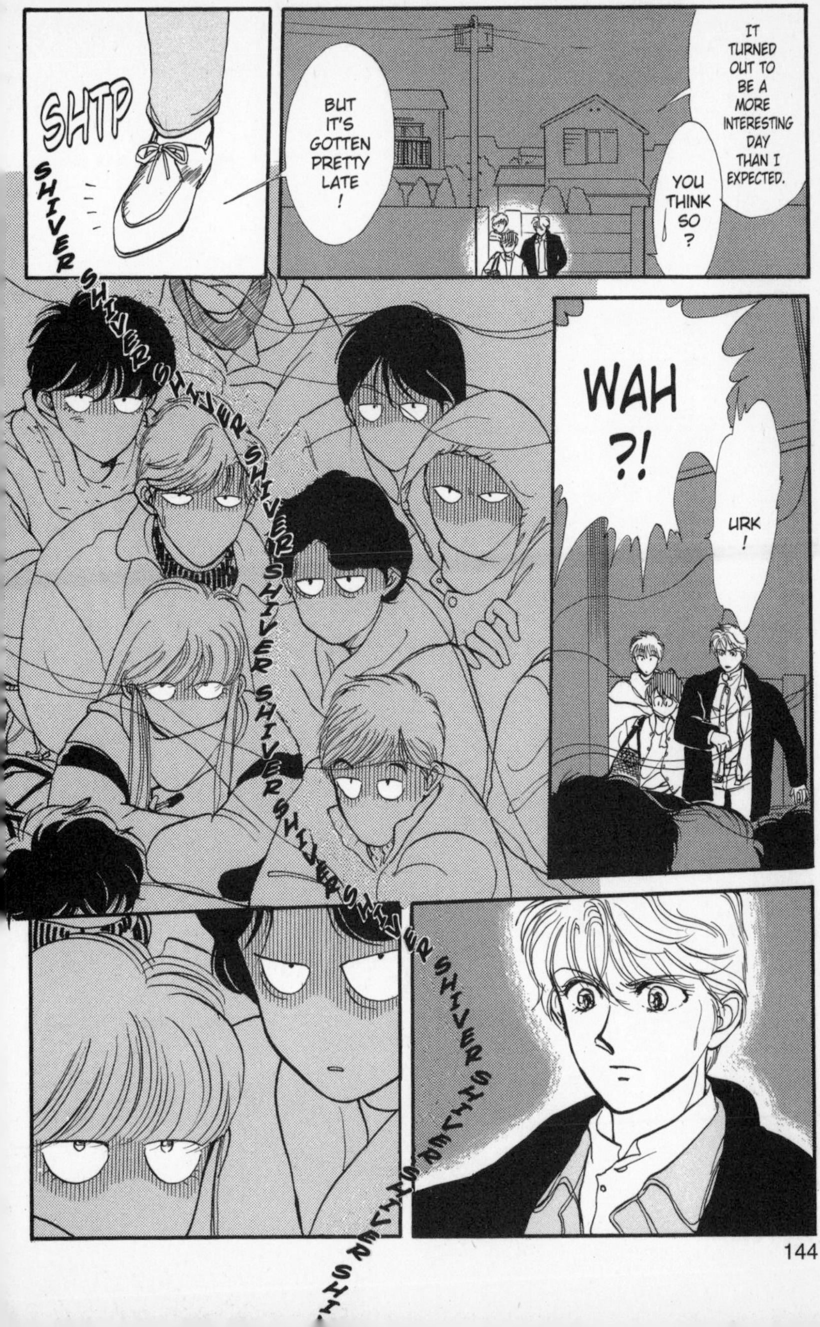
IT TURNED OUT TO BE A MORE INTERESTING DAY THAN I EXPECTED.
YOU THINK SO?
BUT IT'S GOTTEN PRETTY LATE!
SHTP
SHIVER
WAH?!
URK!
SHIVER SHIVER SHIVER SHIVER SHIVER SHIVER SHIVER
SHIVER SHIVER SHI...

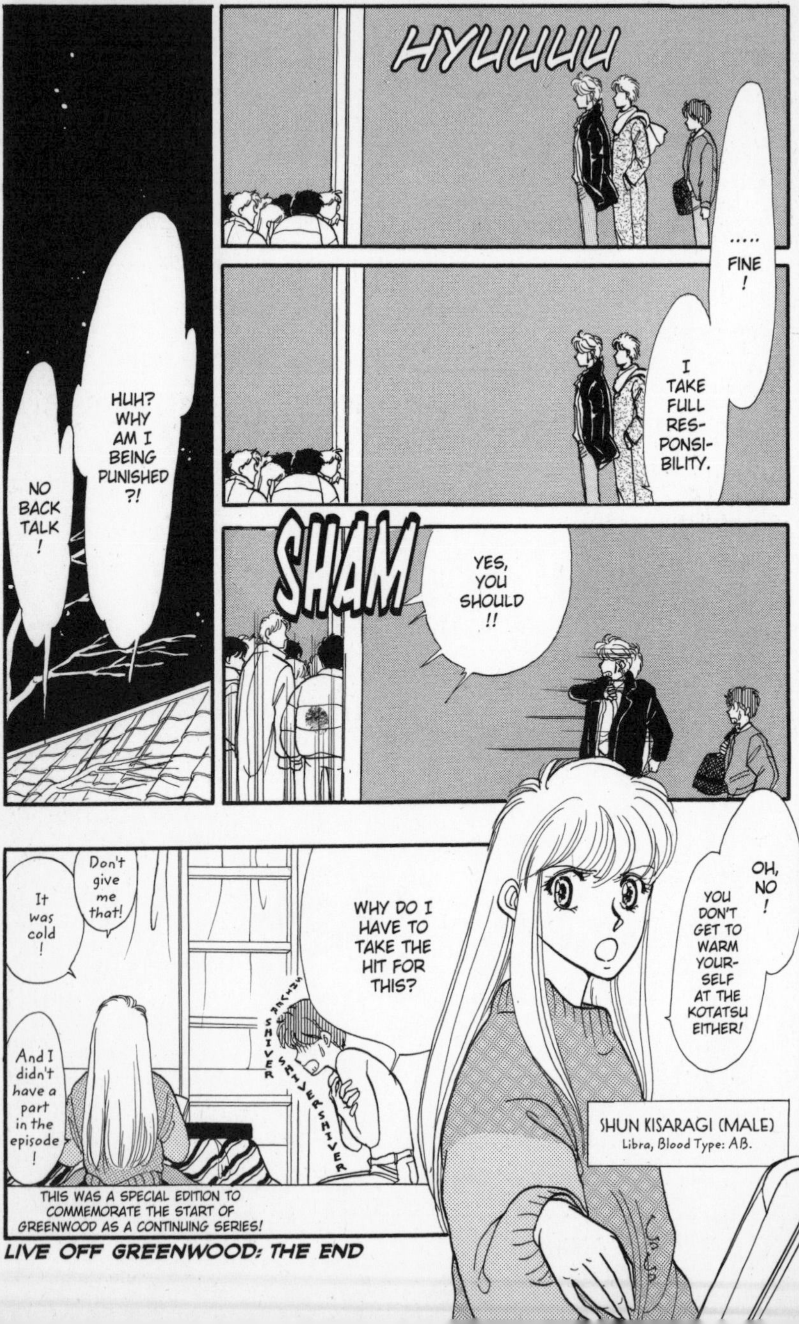
HYUUUU
..... FINE!
I TAKE FULL RESPONSIBILITY.
SHAM
YES, YOU SHOULD!!
HUH? WHY AM I BEING PUNISHED?!
NO BACK TALK!
OH, NO! YOU DON'T GET TO WARM YOURSELF AT THE KOTATSU EITHER!
SHUN KISARAGI (MALE)
Libra, Blood Type: AB.
WHY DO I HAVE TO TAKE THE HIT FOR THIS?
SHIVER SHIVERSHIVER
Don't give me that!
It was cold!
And I didn't have a part in the episode!
THIS WAS A SPECIAL EDITION TO COMMEMORATE THE START OF GREENWOOD AS A CONTINUING SERIES!
LIVE OFF GREENWOOD: THE END

IT'S
ALL
LOVE'S
FAULT

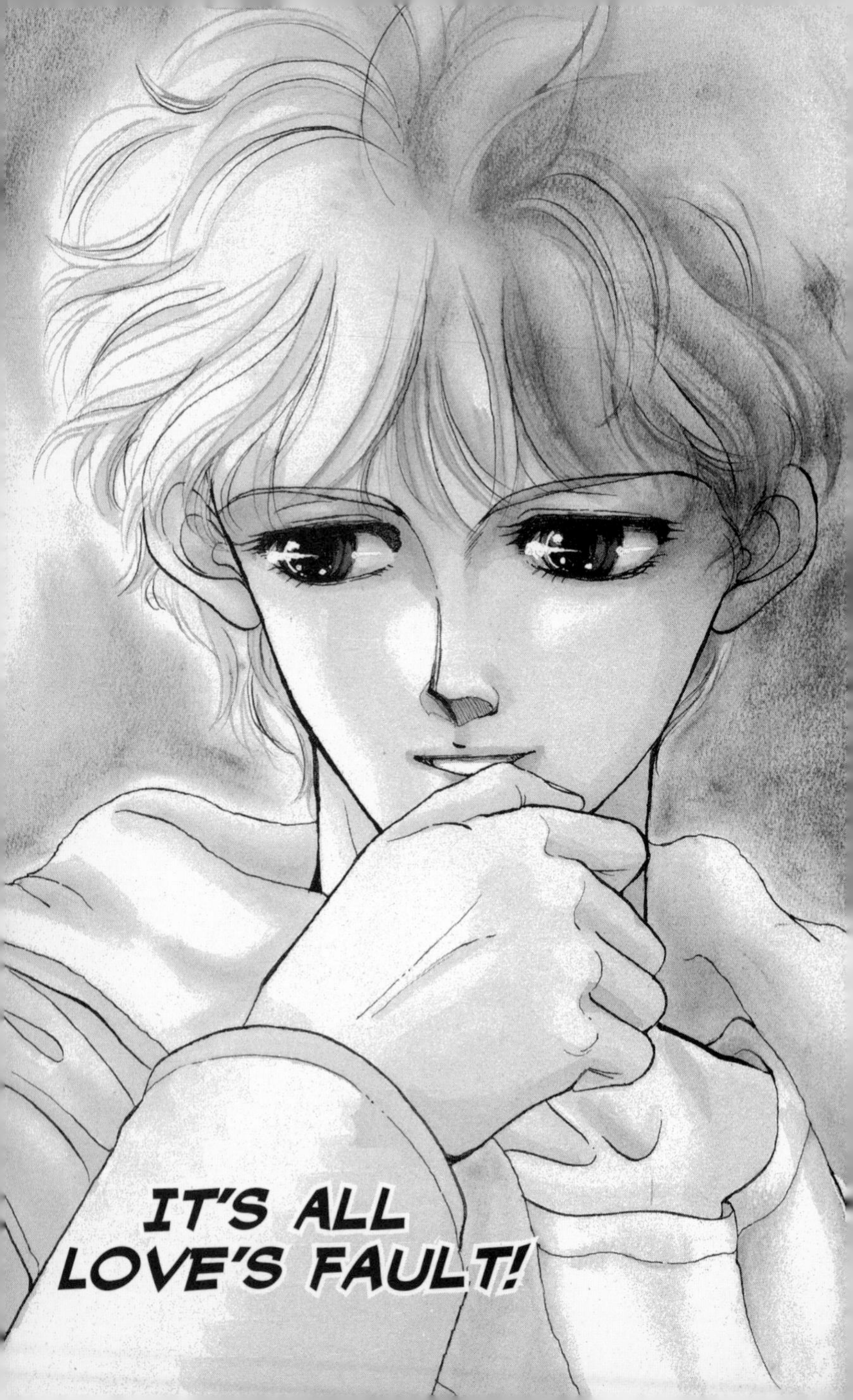
IT'S ALL
LOVE'S FAULT!

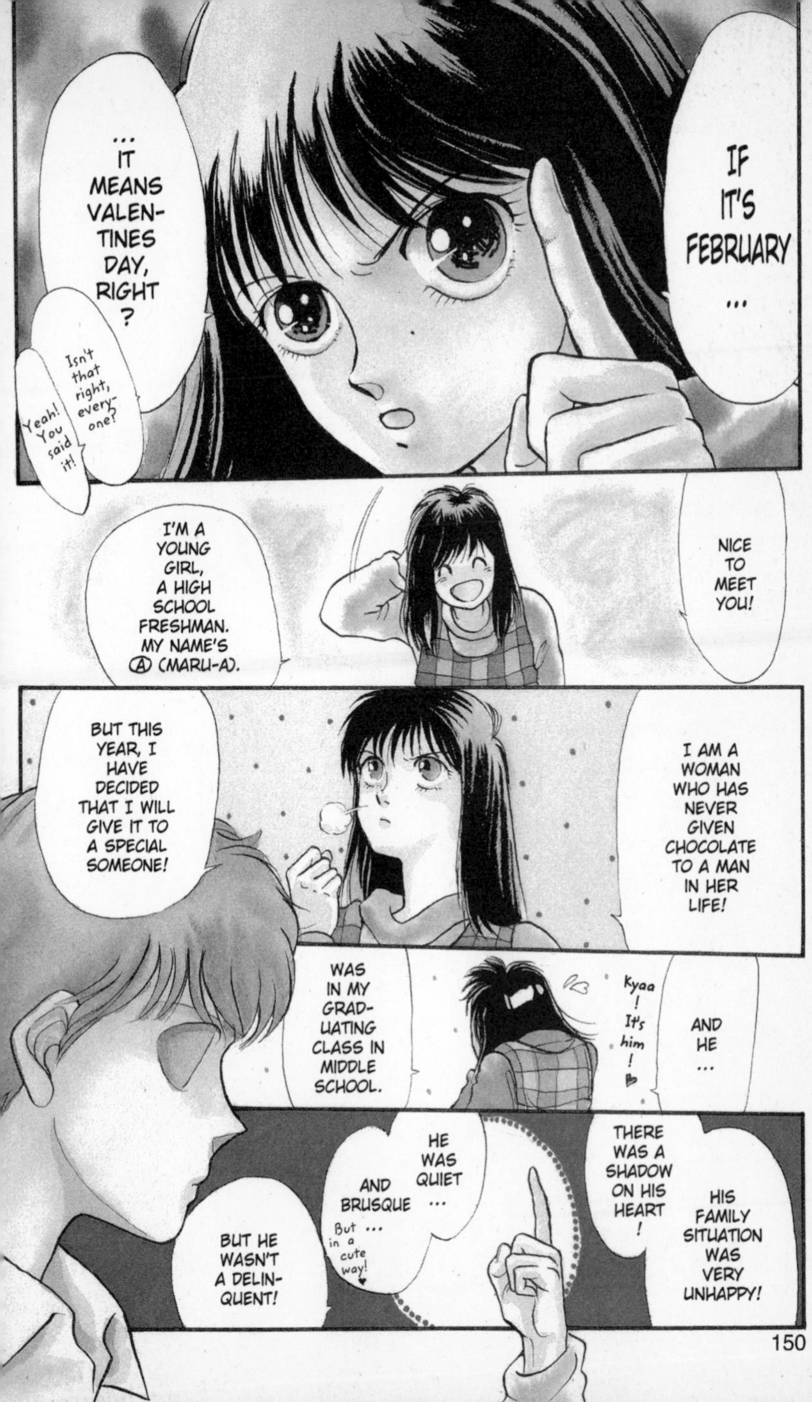
IF IT'S FEBRUARY ...
... IT MEANS VALEN-TINES DAY, RIGHT ?
Isn't that right, every-one?
Yeah! You said it!
NICE TO MEET YOU!
I'M A YOUNG GIRL, A HIGH SCHOOL FRESHMAN. MY NAME'S Ⓐ (MARU-A).
I AM A WOMAN WHO HAS NEVER GIVEN CHOCOLATE TO A MAN IN HER LIFE!
BUT THIS YEAR, I HAVE DECIDED THAT I WILL GIVE IT TO A SPECIAL SOMEONE!
AND HE ...
Kyaa! It's him!
WAS IN MY GRAD-UATING CLASS IN MIDDLE SCHOOL.
HIS FAMILY SITUATION WAS VERY UNHAPPY!
THERE WAS A SHADOW ON HIS HEART!
HE WAS QUIET ...
AND BRUSQUE
But ... in a cute way!
BUT HE WASN'T A DELIN-QUENT!

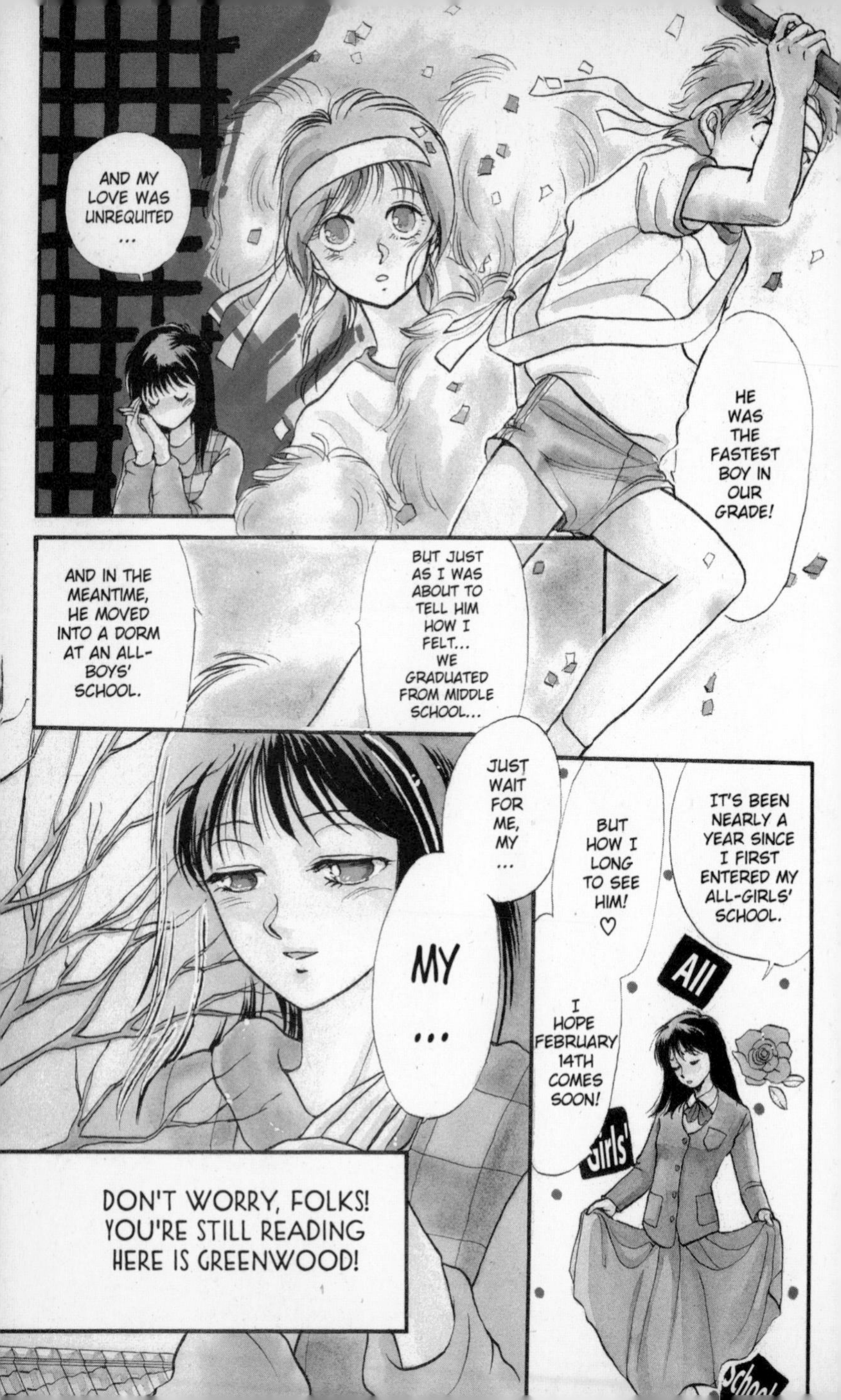
HE WAS THE FASTEST BOY IN OUR GRADE!
AND MY LOVE WAS UNREQUITED ...
BUT JUST AS I WAS ABOUT TO TELL HIM HOW I FELT... WE GRADUATED FROM MIDDLE SCHOOL...
AND IN THE MEANTIME, HE MOVED INTO A DORM AT AN ALL-BOYS' SCHOOL.
IT'S BEEN NEARLY A YEAR SINCE I FIRST ENTERED MY ALL-GIRLS' SCHOOL.
BUT HOW I LONG TO SEE HIM! ♡
I HOPE FEBRUARY 14TH COMES SOON!
All
Girls'
JUST WAIT FOR ME, MY ...
MY ...
DON'T WORRY, FOLKS! YOU'RE STILL READING HERE IS GREENWOOD!

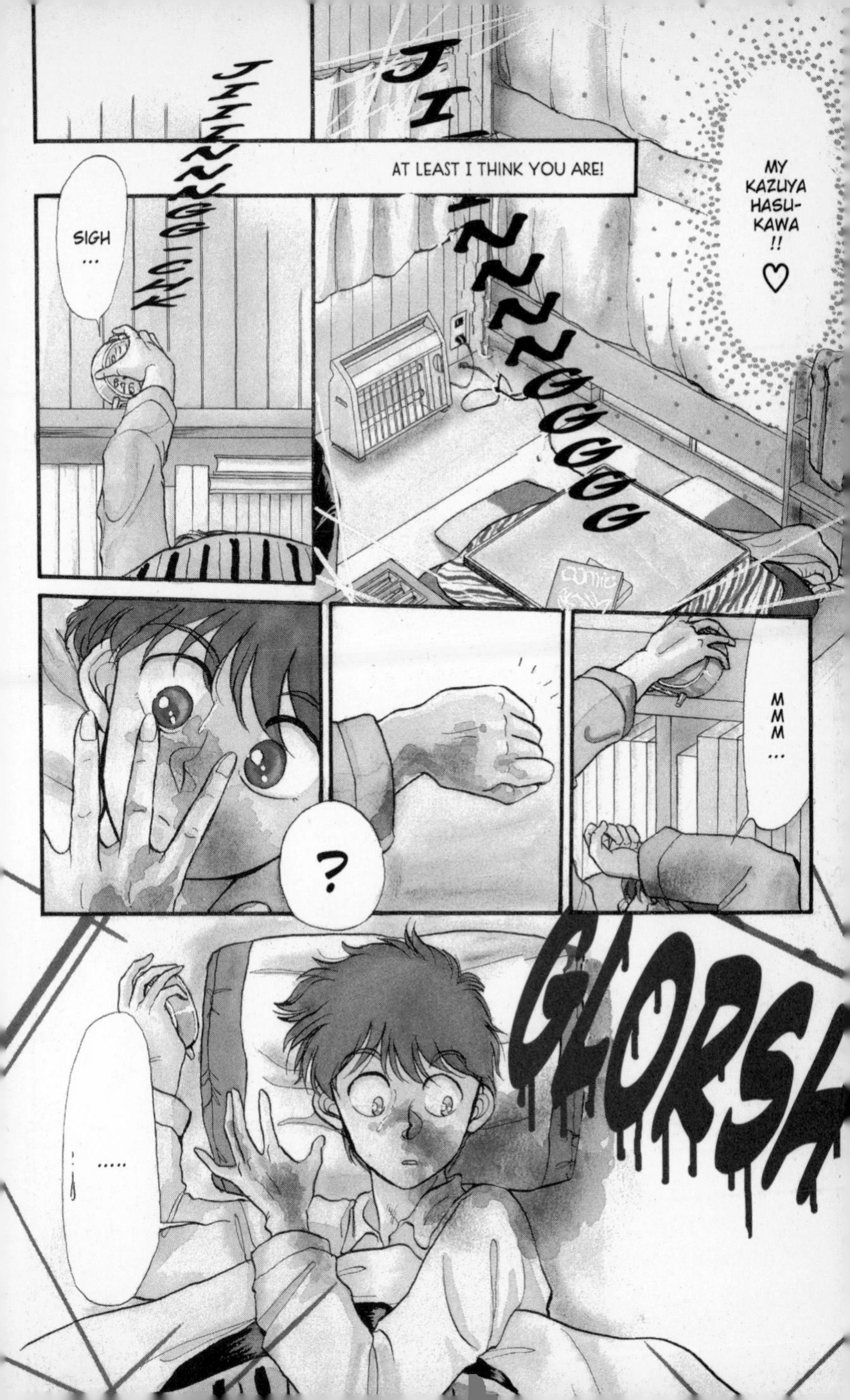
MY KAZUYA HASU-KAWA!! ♡
AT LEAST I THINK YOU ARE!
JI-INNNNGGGGGG
JIIINNNGG-GNN
SIGH ...
MMM ...
?
GLORSH
.....

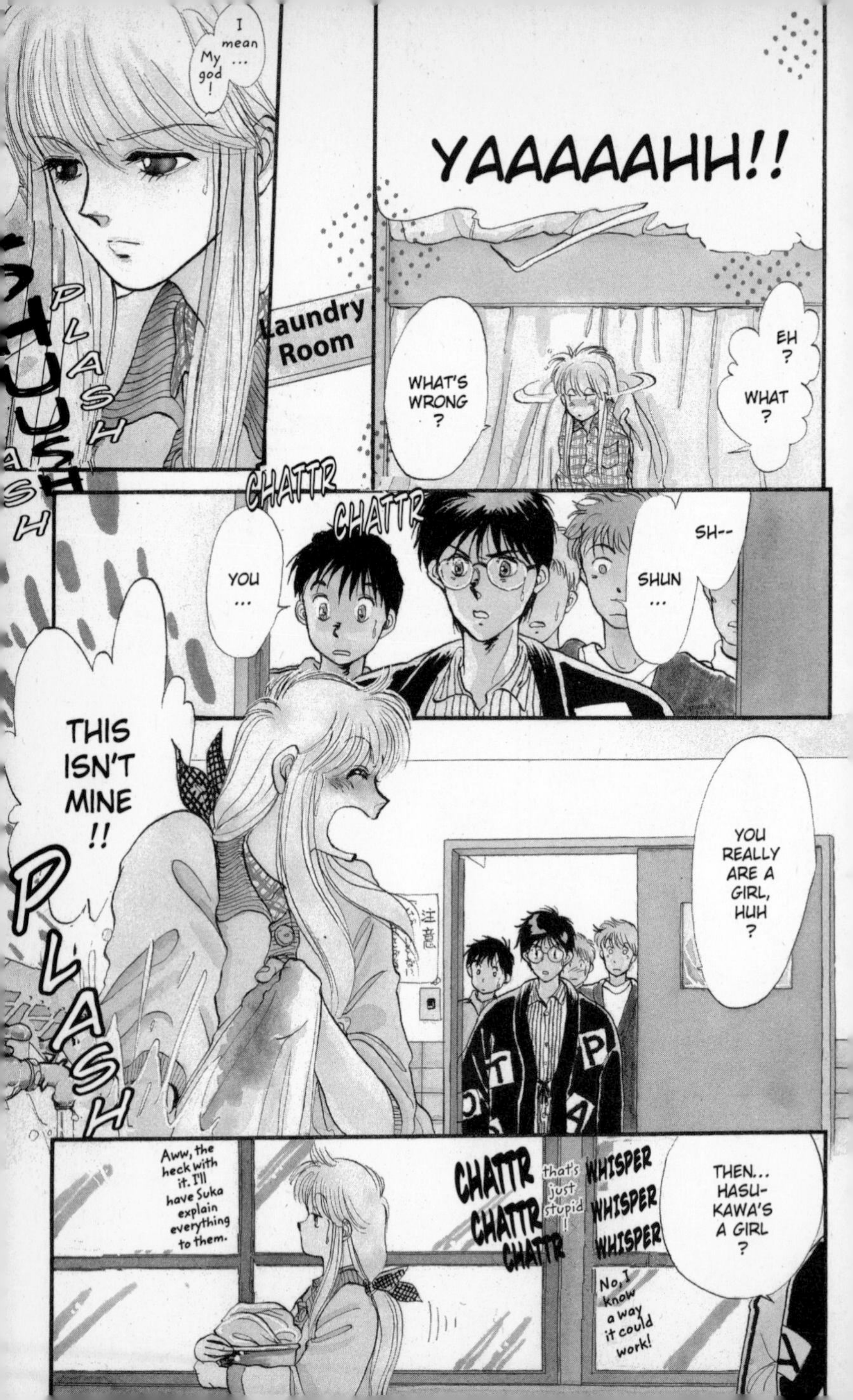
YAAAAAHH!!
WHAT'S WRONG?
EH? WHAT?
I mean... My god!
Laundry Room
PLASH
SH-- SHUN...
YOU...
CHATTR
CHATTR
YOU REALLY ARE A GIRL, HUH?
THIS ISN'T MINE!!
PLASH
THEN... HASU-KAWA'S A GIRL?
No, I know a way it could work!
WHISPER WHISPER WHISPER
that's just stupid!
CHATTR CHATTR CHATTR
Aww, the heck with it. I'll have Suka explain everything to them.

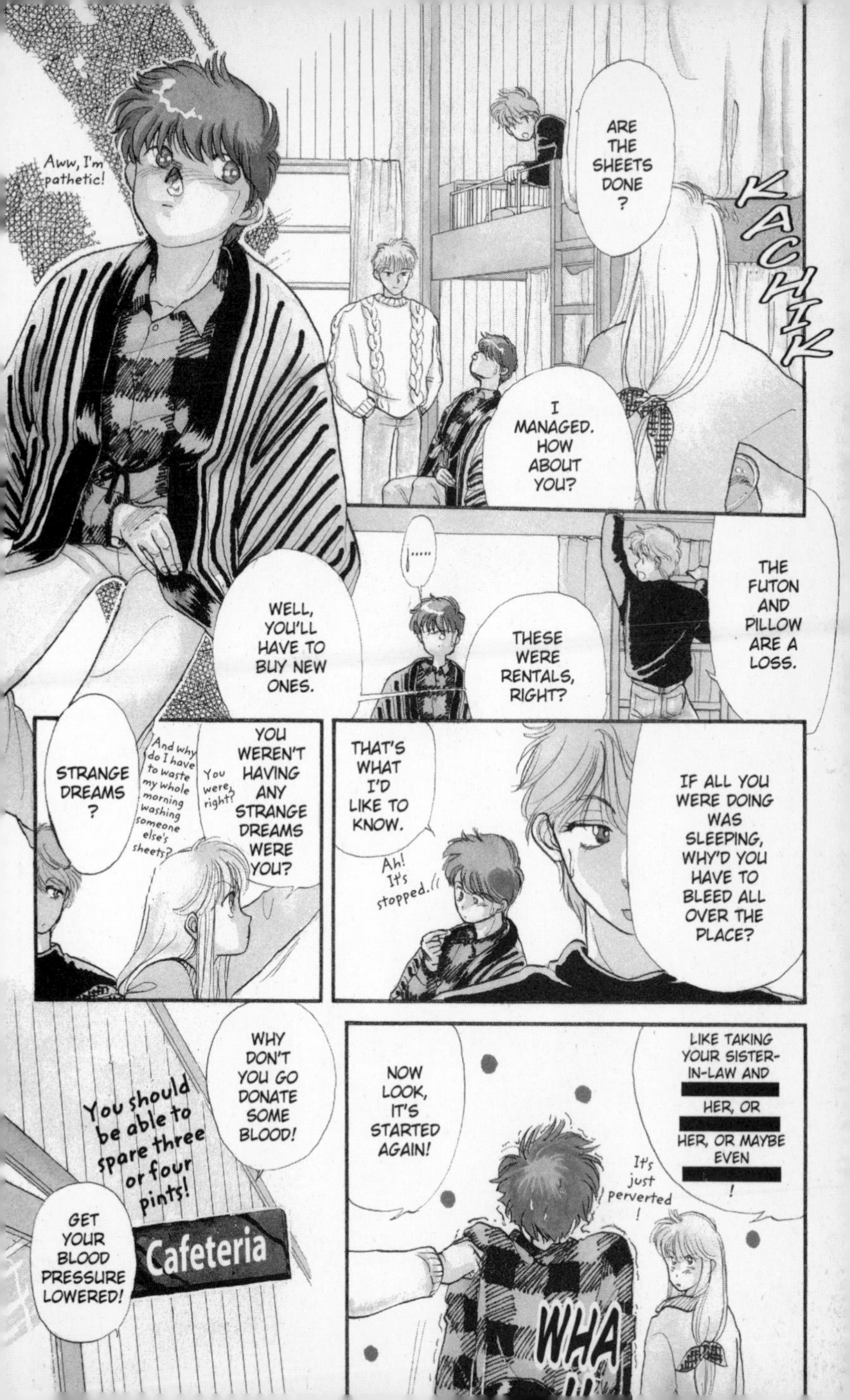
ARE THE SHEETS DONE ?
KACHIK
I MANAGED. HOW ABOUT YOU?
THE FUTON AND PILLOW ARE A LOSS.
THESE WERE RENTALS, RIGHT?
......
WELL, YOU'LL HAVE TO BUY NEW ONES.
Aww, I'm pathetic!
IF ALL YOU WERE DOING WAS SLEEPING, WHY'D YOU HAVE TO BLEED ALL OVER THE PLACE?
Ah! It's stopped.
THAT'S WHAT I'D LIKE TO KNOW.
YOU WEREN'T HAVING ANY STRANGE DREAMS WERE YOU?
You were, right?
And why do I have to waste my whole morning washing someone else's sheets?
STRANGE DREAMS ?
LIKE TAKING YOUR SISTER-IN-LAW AND [redacted] HER, OR [redacted] HER, OR MAYBE EVEN [redacted] !
It's just perverted !
NOW LOOK, IT'S STARTED AGAIN!
WHA
WHY DON'T YOU GO DONATE SOME BLOOD!
You should be able to spare three or four pints!
Cafeteria
GET YOUR BLOOD PRESSURE LOWERED!

The series of full names, star signs, and blood types, continued for your enjoyment. -- NASU

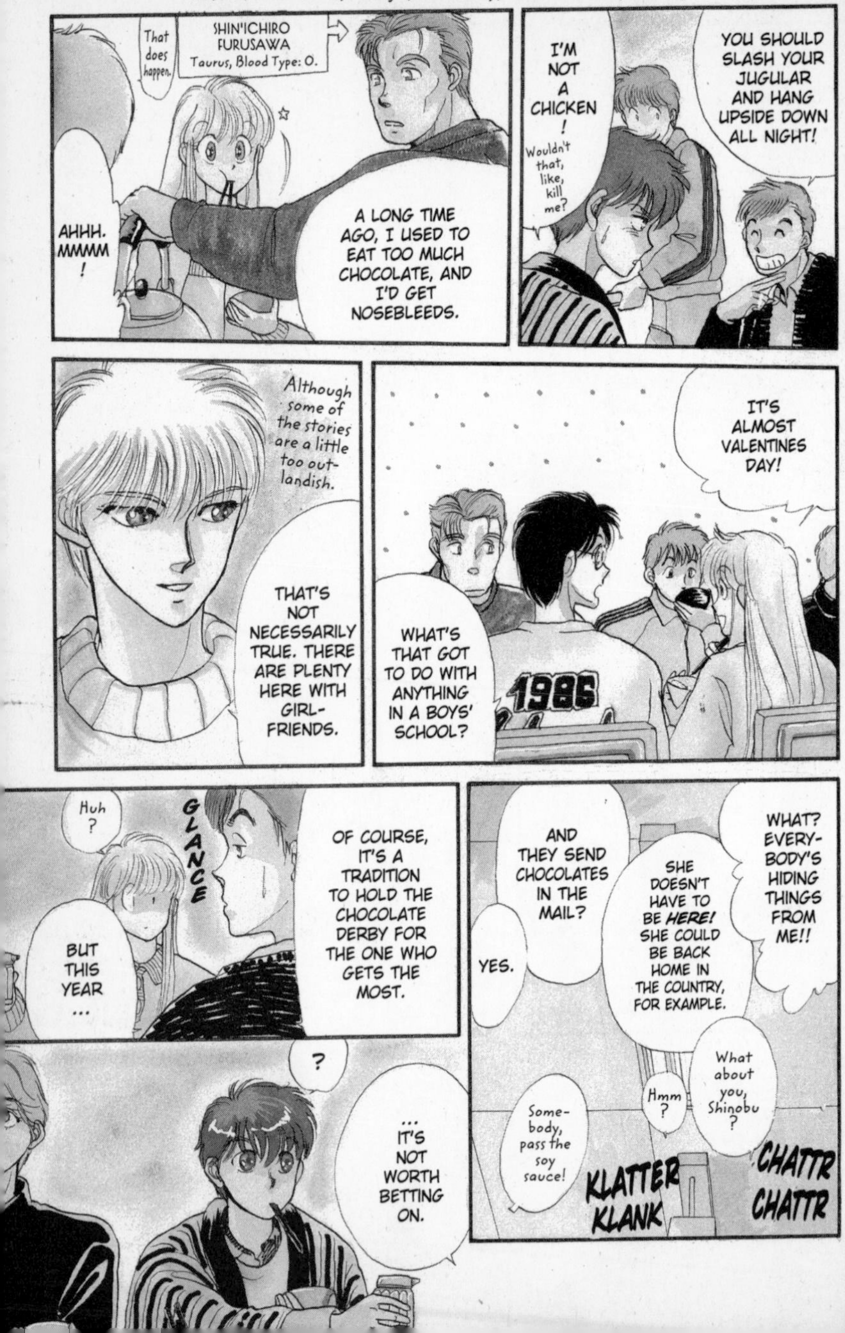
YOU SHOULD SLASH YOUR JUGULAR AND HANG UPSIDE DOWN ALL NIGHT!
I'M NOT A CHICKEN!
Wouldn't that, like, kill me?
SHIN'ICHIRO FURUSAWA Taurus, Blood Type: O.
That does happen.
A LONG TIME AGO, I USED TO EAT TOO MUCH CHOCOLATE, AND I'D GET NOSEBLEEDS.
AHHH. MMMM!
IT'S ALMOST VALENTINES DAY!
WHAT'S THAT GOT TO DO WITH ANYTHING IN A BOYS' SCHOOL?
1986
Although some of the stories are a little too out-landish.
THAT'S NOT NECESSARILY TRUE. THERE ARE PLENTY HERE WITH GIRL-FRIENDS.
WHAT? EVERY-BODY'S HIDING THINGS FROM ME!!
AND THEY SEND CHOCOLATES IN THE MAIL?
YES.
SHE DOESN'T HAVE TO BE HERE! SHE COULD BE BACK HOME IN THE COUNTRY, FOR EXAMPLE.
What about you, Shinobu?
CHATTR CHATTR
Hmm?
Some-body, pass the soy sauce!
KLATTER KLANK
OF COURSE, IT'S A TRADITION TO HOLD THE CHOCOLATE DERBY FOR THE ONE WHO GETS THE MOST.
GLANCE
Huh?
BUT THIS YEAR...
?
... IT'S NOT WORTH BETTING ON.

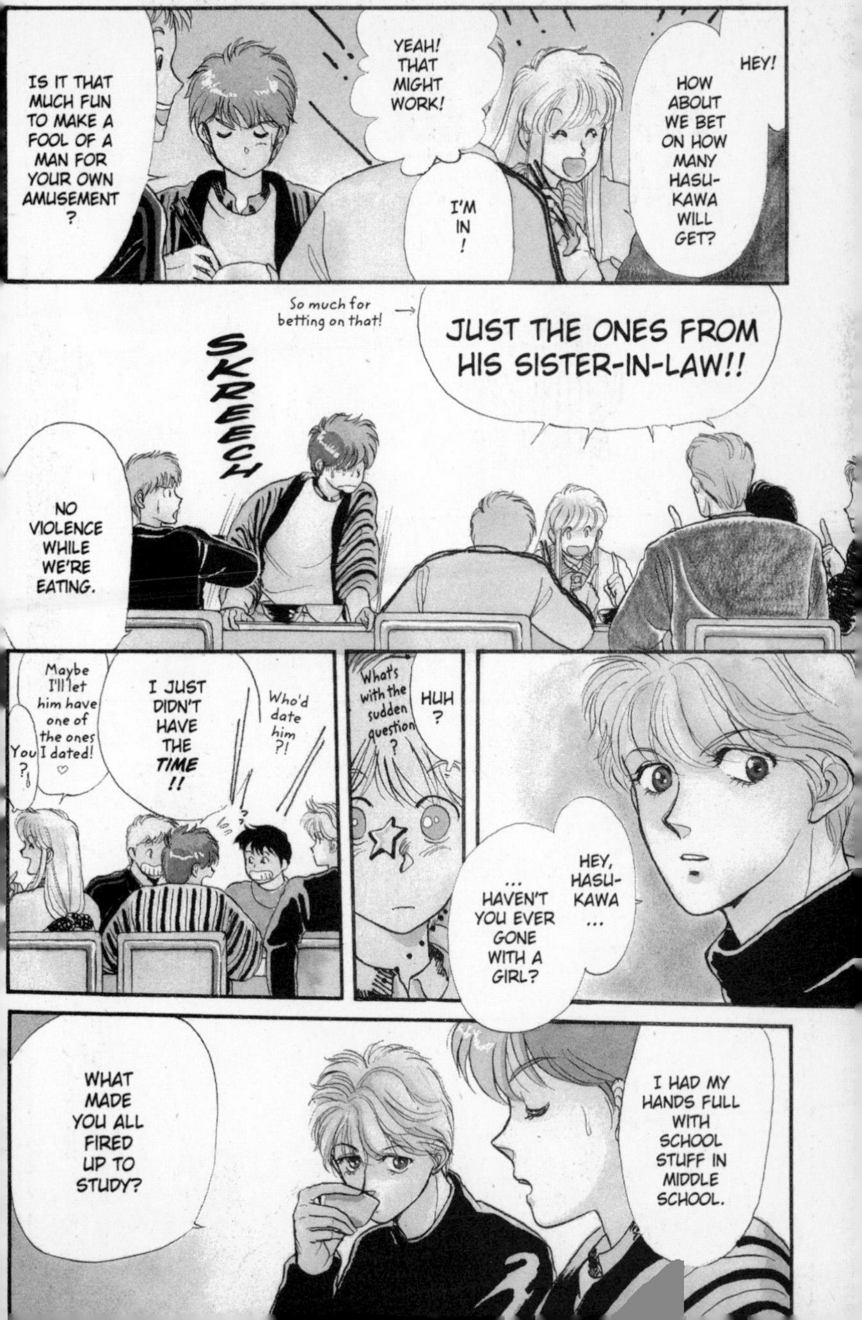
HEY!
HOW ABOUT WE BET ON HOW MANY HASU-KAWA WILL GET?
I'M IN!
YEAH! THAT MIGHT WORK!
IS IT THAT MUCH FUN TO MAKE A FOOL OF A MAN FOR YOUR OWN AMUSEMENT?
JUST THE ONES FROM HIS SISTER-IN-LAW!!
So much for betting on that!
SKREECH
NO VIOLENCE WHILE WE'RE EATING.
HEY, HASU-KAWA...
... HAVEN'T YOU EVER GONE WITH A GIRL?
HUH?
What's with the sudden question?
I JUST DIDN'T HAVE THE TIME!!
Who'd date him?!
Maybe I'll let him have one of the ones I dated! ♡
You?!
I HAD MY HANDS FULL WITH SCHOOL STUFF IN MIDDLE SCHOOL.
WHAT MADE YOU ALL FIRED UP TO STUDY?

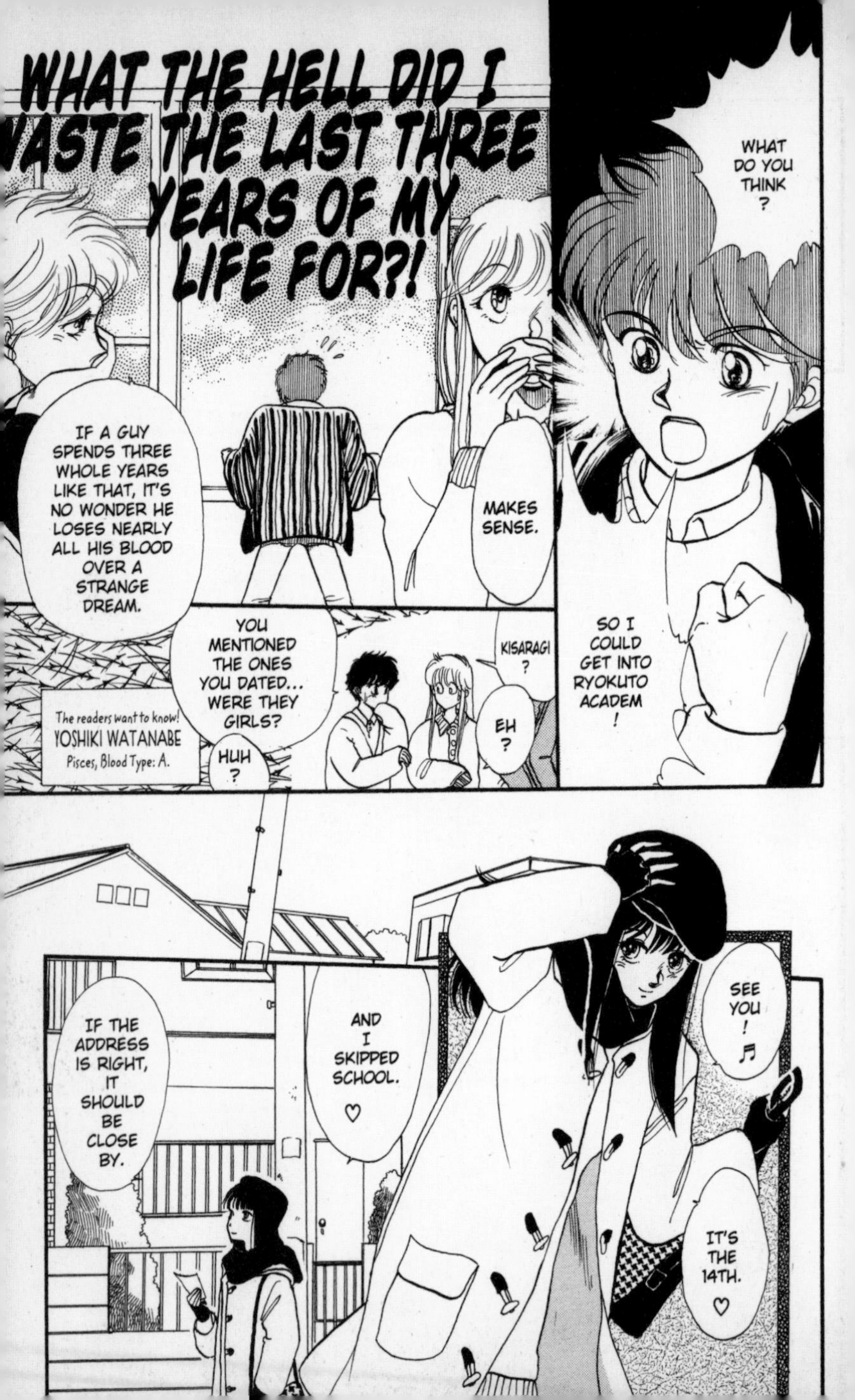

WHAT DO YOU THINK?
SO I COULD GET INTO RYOKUTO ACADEM!
WHAT THE HELL DID I WASTE THE LAST THREE YEARS OF MY LIFE FOR?!
MAKES SENSE.
IF A GUY SPENDS THREE WHOLE YEARS LIKE THAT, IT'S NO WONDER HE LOSES NEARLY ALL HIS BLOOD OVER A STRANGE DREAM.
KISARAGI?
EH?
YOU MENTIONED THE ONES YOU DATED... WERE THEY GIRLS?
HUH?
The readers want to know!
YOSHIKI WATANABE
Pisces, Blood Type: A.
SEE YOU! ♬
IT'S THE 14TH. ♡
AND I SKIPPED SCHOOL. ♡
IF THE ADDRESS IS RIGHT, IT SHOULD BE CLOSE BY.

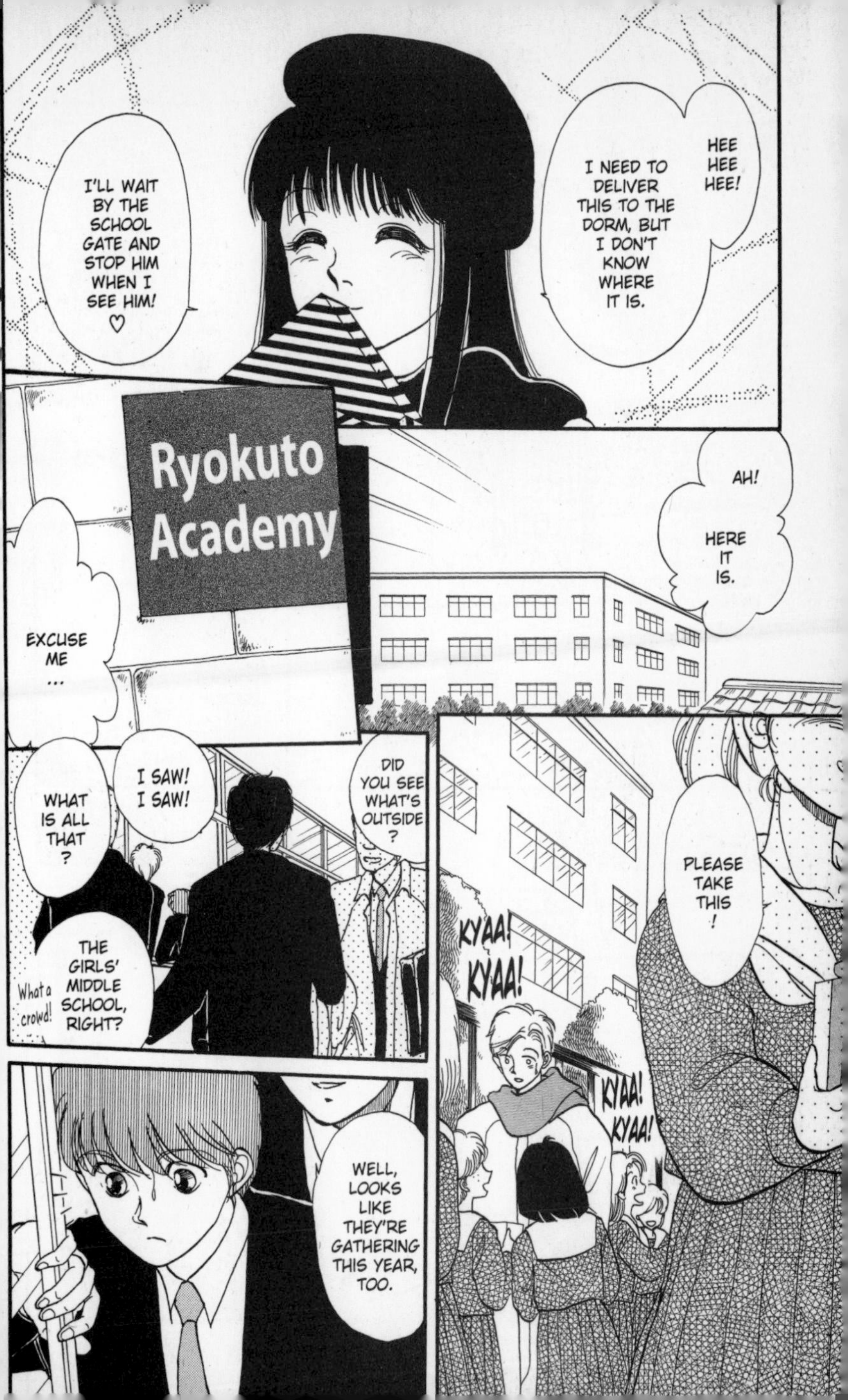
HEE HEE HEE!
I NEED TO DELIVER THIS TO THE DORM, BUT I DON'T KNOW WHERE IT IS.
I'LL WAIT BY THE SCHOOL GATE AND STOP HIM WHEN I SEE HIM! ♡
AH! HERE IT IS.
Ryokuto Academy
EXCUSE ME ...
PLEASE TAKE THIS!
KYAA! KYAA!
KYAA! KYAA!
DID YOU SEE WHAT'S OUTSIDE?
I SAW! I SAW!
WHAT IS ALL THAT?
THE GIRLS' MIDDLE SCHOOL, RIGHT?
What a crowd!
WELL, LOOKS LIKE THEY'RE GATHERING THIS YEAR, TOO.

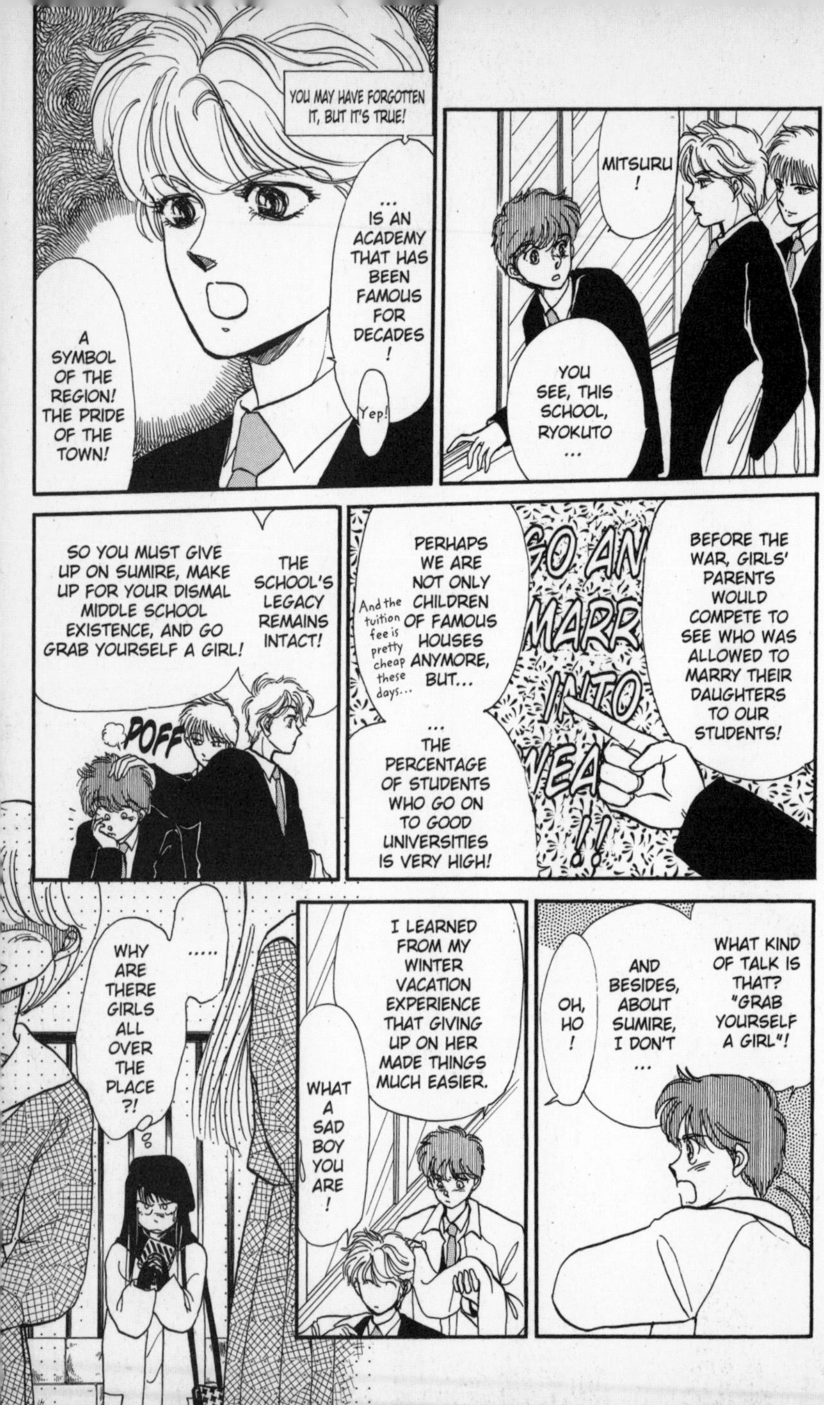
MITSURU!
YOU SEE, THIS SCHOOL, RYOKUTO...
YOU MAY HAVE FORGOTTEN IT, BUT IT'S TRUE!
... IS AN ACADEMY THAT HAS BEEN FAMOUS FOR DECADES!
Yep!
A SYMBOL OF THE REGION! THE PRIDE OF THE TOWN!
BEFORE THE WAR, GIRLS' PARENTS WOULD COMPETE TO SEE WHO WAS ALLOWED TO MARRY THEIR DAUGHTERS TO OUR STUDENTS!
PERHAPS WE ARE NOT ONLY CHILDREN OF FAMOUS HOUSES ANYMORE, BUT...
And the tuition fee is pretty cheap these days...
... THE PERCENTAGE OF STUDENTS WHO GO ON TO GOOD UNIVERSITIES IS VERY HIGH!
THE SCHOOL'S LEGACY REMAINS INTACT!
SO YOU MUST GIVE UP ON SUMIRE, MAKE UP FOR YOUR DISMAL MIDDLE SCHOOL EXISTENCE, AND GO GRAB YOURSELF A GIRL!
POFF
WHAT KIND OF TALK IS THAT? "GRAB YOURSELF A GIRL"!
AND BESIDES, ABOUT SUMIRE, I DON'T ...
OH, HO!
I LEARNED FROM MY WINTER VACATION EXPERIENCE THAT GIVING UP ON HER MADE THINGS MUCH EASIER.
WHAT A SAD BOY YOU ARE!
.....
WHY ARE THERE GIRLS ALL OVER THE PLACE?!

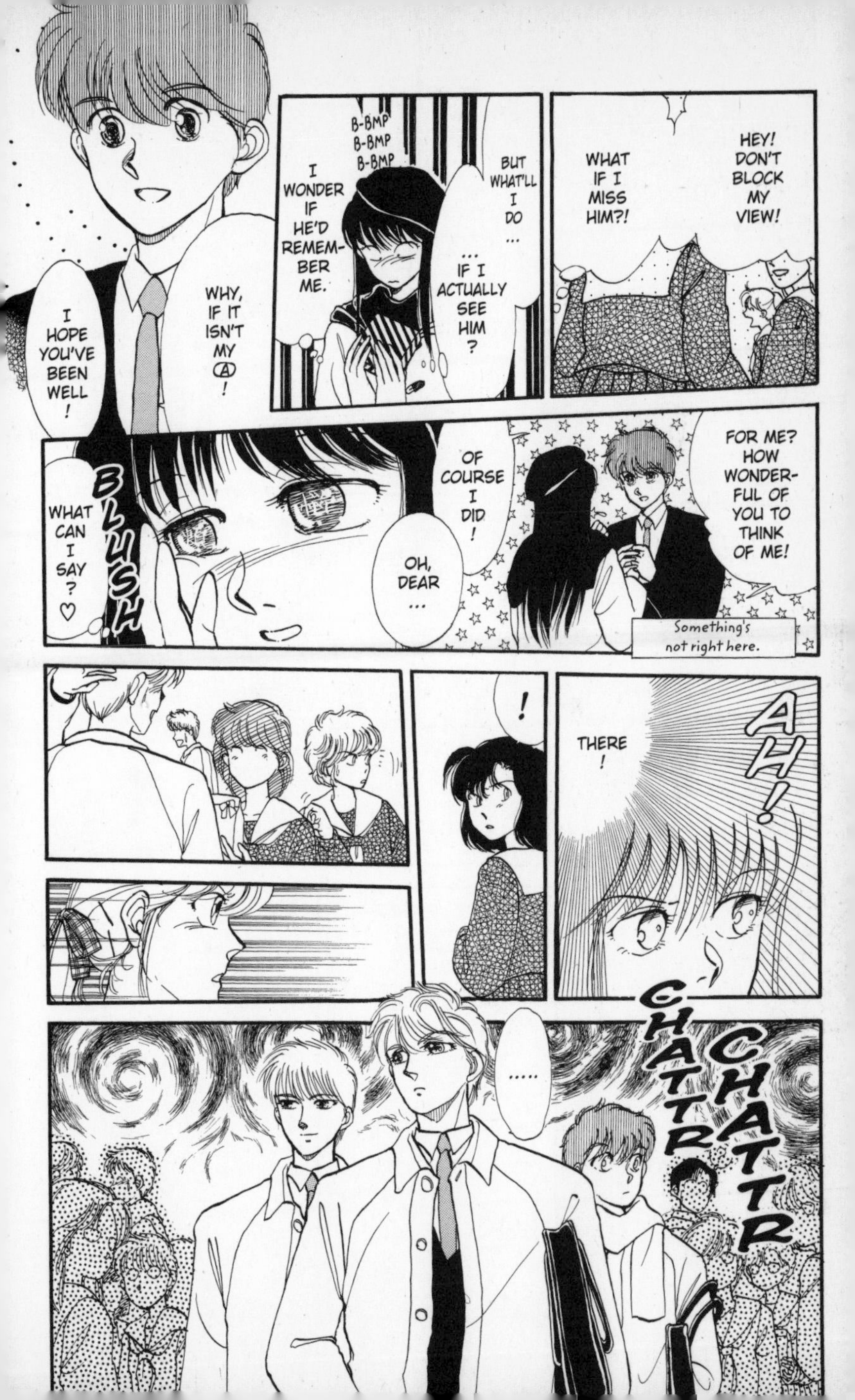
HEY! DON'T BLOCK MY VIEW!
WHAT IF I MISS HIM?!
B-BMP B-BMP B-BMP
BUT WHAT'LL I DO ...
... IF I ACTUALLY SEE HIM ?
I WONDER IF HE'D REMEMBER ME.
WHY, IF IT ISN'T MY Ⓐ!
I HOPE YOU'VE BEEN WELL!
FOR ME? HOW WONDERFUL OF YOU TO THINK OF ME!
OF COURSE I DID!
OH, DEAR ...
Something's not right here.
BLUSH
WHAT CAN I SAY? ♡
AH!
THERE!
!
CHATTR CHATTR
......

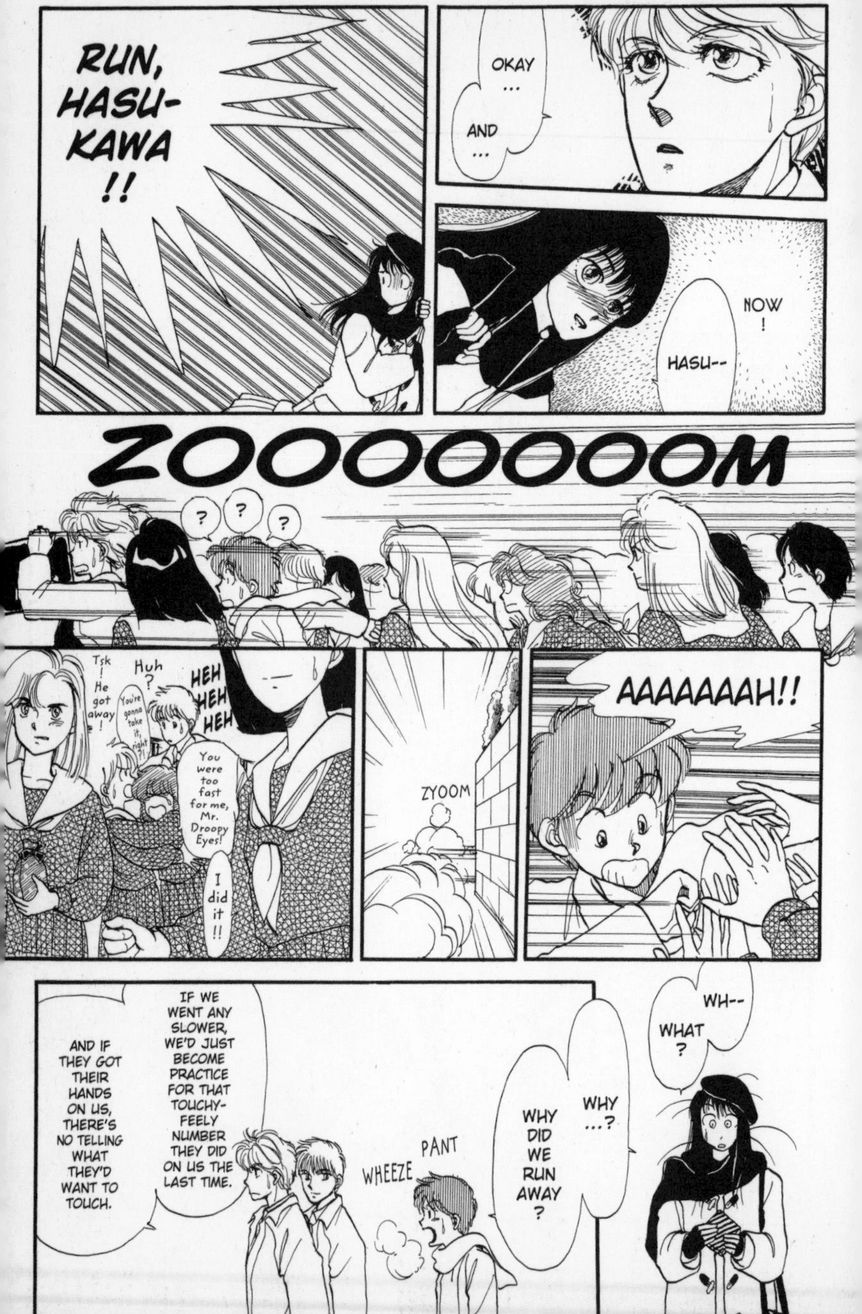
OKAY ... AND ...
NOW! HASU--
RUN, HASU-KAWA!!
ZOOOOOOOM
? ? ?
AAAAAAH!!
ZYOOM
HEH HEH HEH
You were too fast for me, Mr. Droopy Eyes!
I did it!!
Huh?
You're gonna take it, right?!
Tsk! He got away!
WH-- WHAT?
WHY ...?
WHY DID WE RUN AWAY?
PANT
WHEEZE
IF WE WENT ANY SLOWER, WE'D JUST BECOME PRACTICE FOR THAT TOUCHY-FEELY NUMBER THEY DID ON US THE LAST TIME.
AND IF THEY GOT THEIR HANDS ON US, THERE'S NO TELLING WHAT THEY'D WANT TO TOUCH.

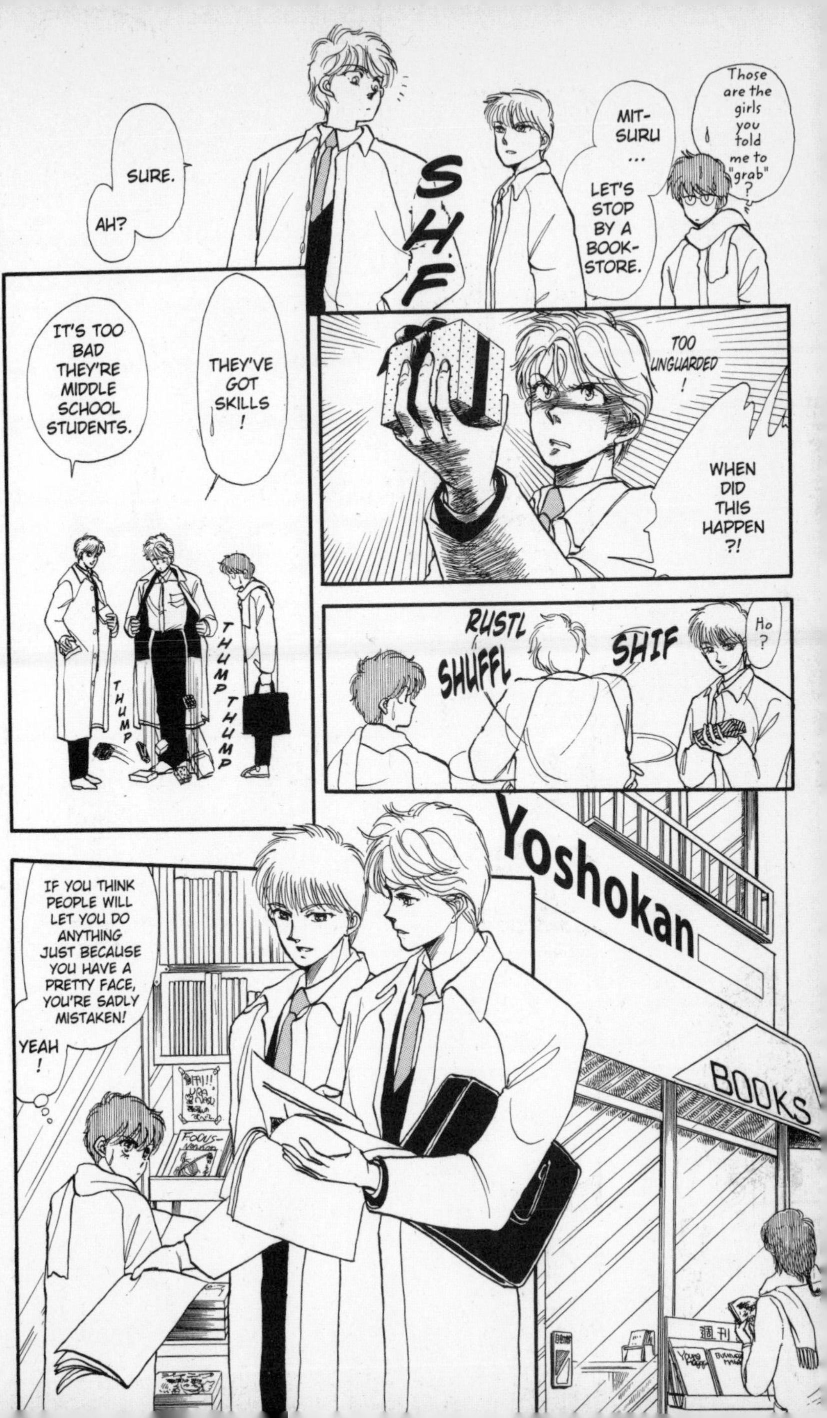

Those are the girls you told me to "grab"?
MIT-SURU ... LET'S STOP BY A BOOK-STORE.
SHF
SURE.
AH?
TOO UNGUARDED!
WHEN DID THIS HAPPEN?!
Ho?
SHIF
SHUFFL
RUSTL
THEY'VE GOT SKILLS!
IT'S TOO BAD THEY'RE MIDDLE SCHOOL STUDENTS.
THUMP
THUMP
THUMP
Yoshokan
BOOKS
IF YOU THINK PEOPLE WILL LET YOU DO ANYTHING JUST BECAUSE YOU HAVE A PRETTY FACE, YOU'RE SADLY MISTAKEN!
YEAH!

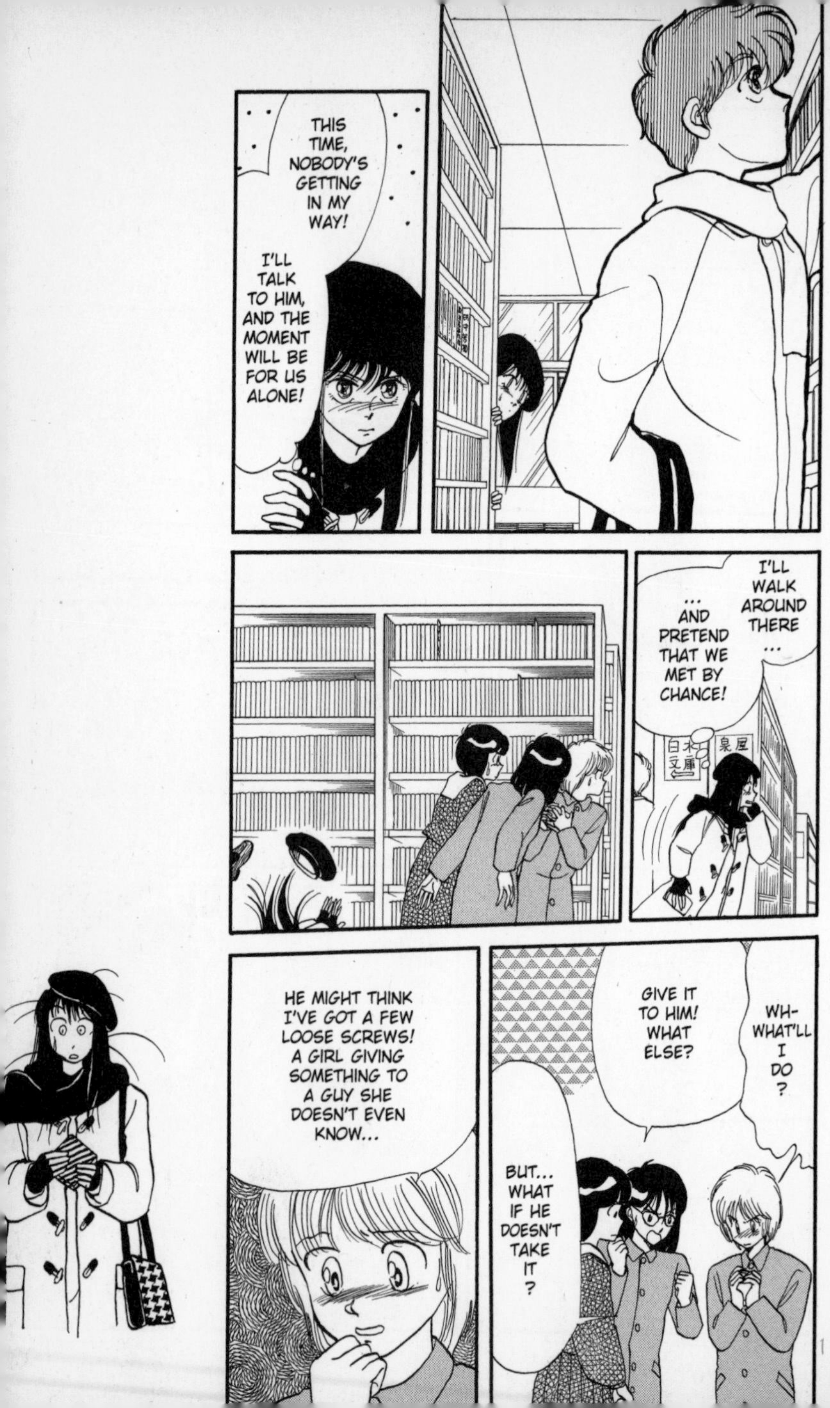
THIS TIME, NOBODY'S GETTING IN MY WAY!
I'LL TALK TO HIM, AND THE MOMENT WILL BE FOR US ALONE!
I'LL WALK AROUND THERE...
...AND PRETEND THAT WE MET BY CHANCE!
WH-WHAT'LL I DO?
GIVE IT TO HIM! WHAT ELSE?
BUT... WHAT IF HE DOESN'T TAKE IT?
HE MIGHT THINK I'VE GOT A FEW LOOSE SCREWS! A GIRL GIVING SOMETHING TO A GUY SHE DOESN'T EVEN KNOW...

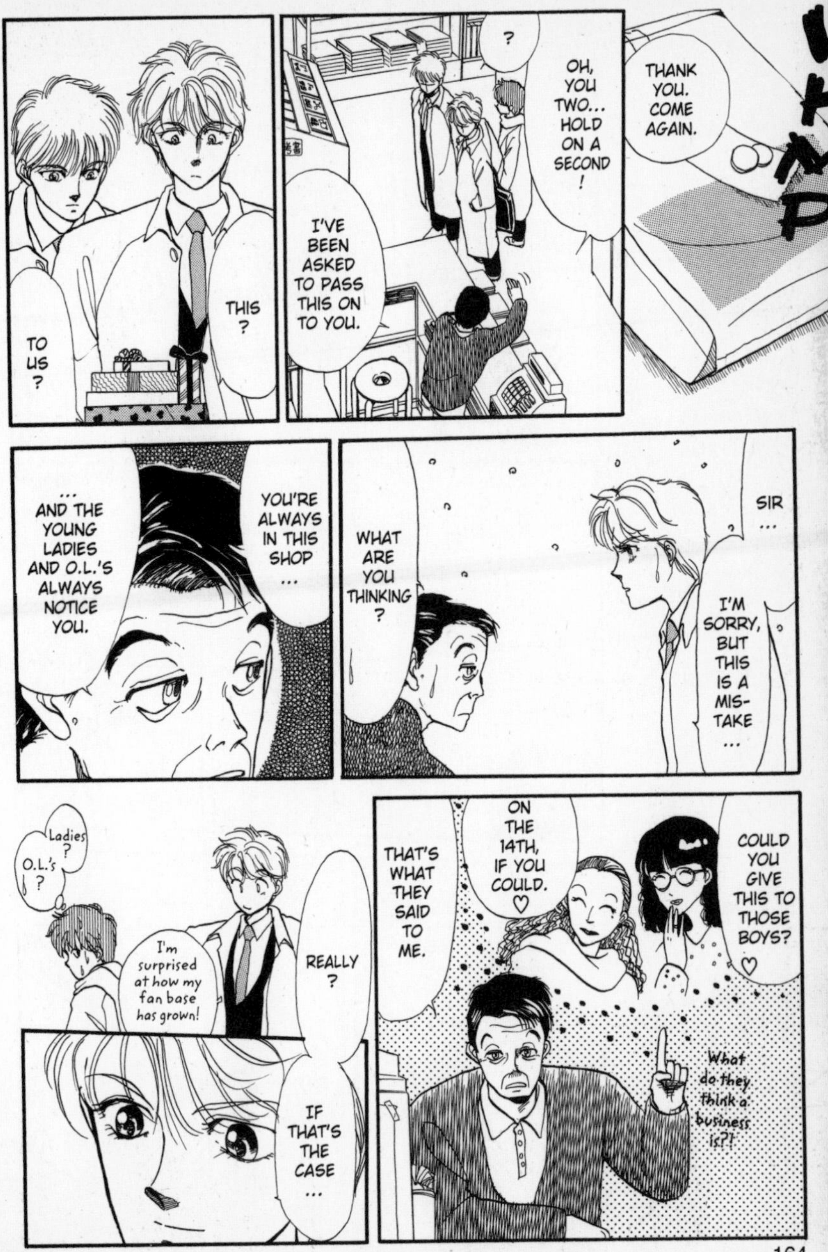
THANK YOU. COME AGAIN.
?
OH, YOU TWO... HOLD ON A SECOND!
I'VE BEEN ASKED TO PASS THIS ON TO YOU.
THIS?
TO US?
SIR...
I'M SORRY, BUT THIS IS A MISTAKE...
WHAT ARE YOU THINKING?
YOU'RE ALWAYS IN THIS SHOP...
...AND THE YOUNG LADIES AND O.L.'S ALWAYS NOTICE YOU.
COULD YOU GIVE THIS TO THOSE BOYS? ♡
ON THE 14TH, IF YOU COULD. ♡
THAT'S WHAT THEY SAID TO ME.
What do they think a business is?!
REALLY?
I'm surprised at how my fan base has grown!
Ladies? O.L.'s?
IF THAT'S THE CASE...

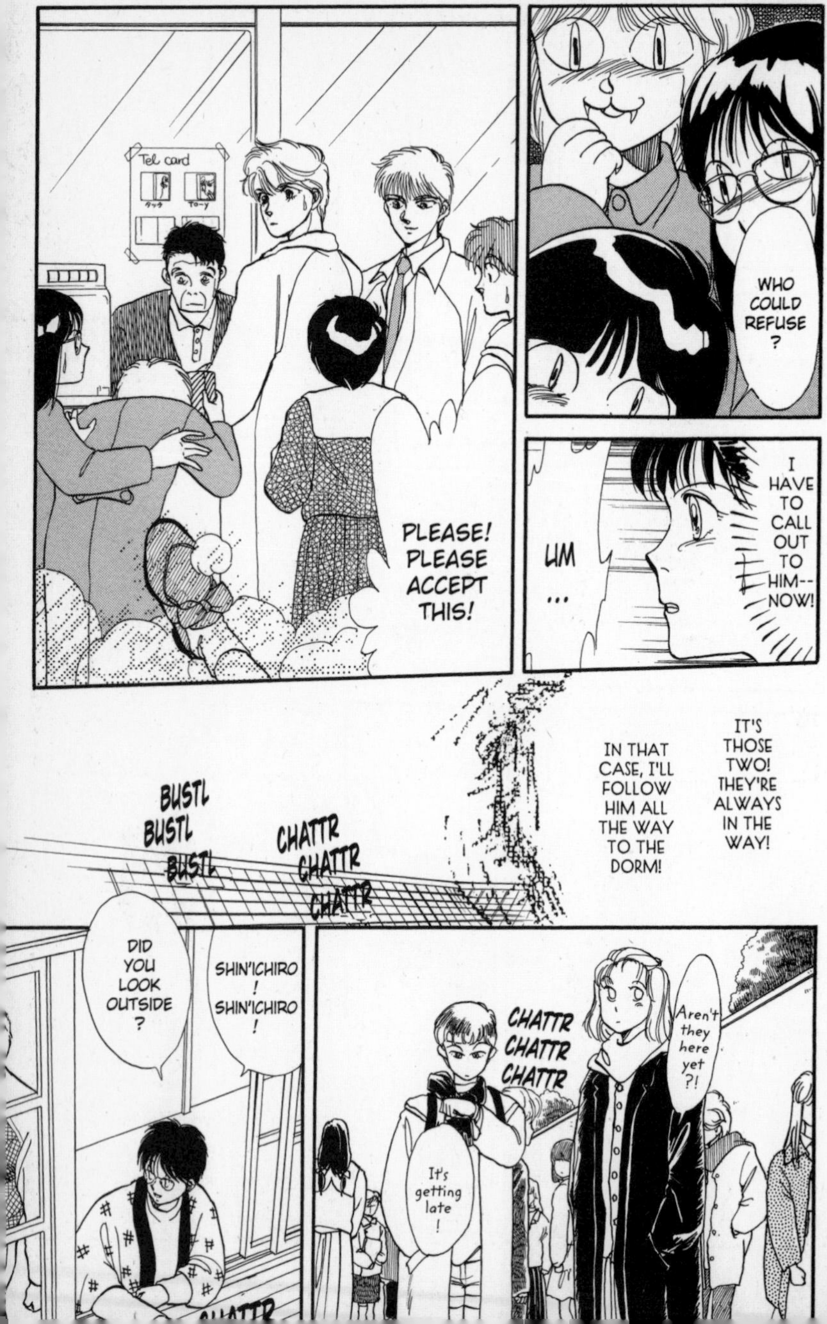
WHO COULD REFUSE?
UM ...
I HAVE TO CALL OUT TO HIM--NOW!
Tel card
PLEASE! PLEASE ACCEPT THIS!
IT'S THOSE TWO! THEY'RE ALWAYS IN THE WAY!
IN THAT CASE, I'LL FOLLOW HIM ALL THE WAY TO THE DORM!
CHATTR CHATTR CHATTR
BUSTL BUSTL BUSTL
Aren't they here yet?!
CHATTR CHATTR CHATTR
It's getting late!
SHIN'ICHIRO! SHIN'ICHIRO!
DID YOU LOOK OUTSIDE?

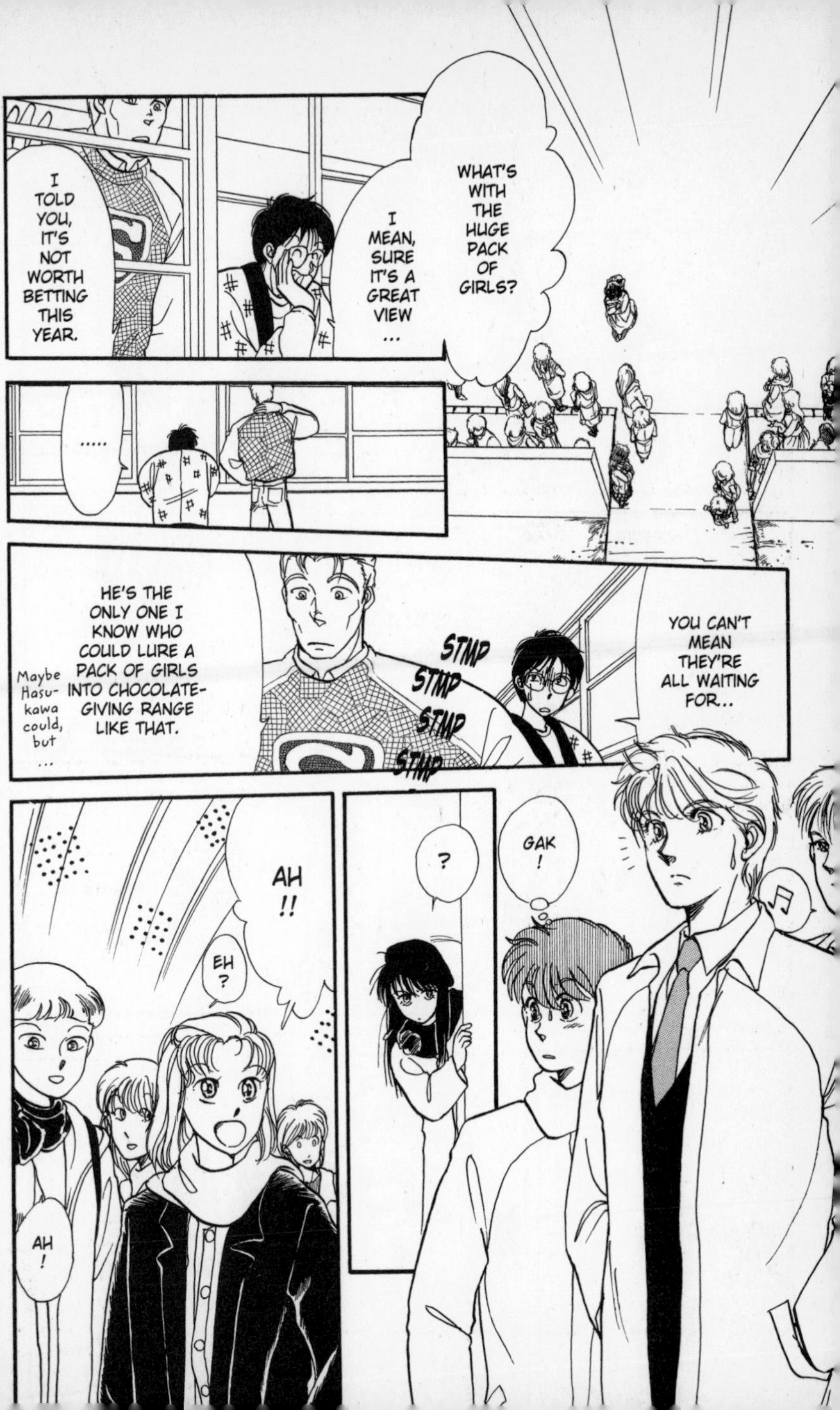
WHAT'S WITH THE HUGE PACK OF GIRLS?
I MEAN, SURE IT'S A GREAT VIEW ...
I TOLD YOU, IT'S NOT WORTH BETTING THIS YEAR.
.....
YOU CAN'T MEAN THEY'RE ALL WAITING FOR...
STMP STMP STMP STMP
HE'S THE ONLY ONE I KNOW WHO COULD LURE A PACK OF GIRLS INTO CHOCOLATE-GIVING RANGE LIKE THAT.
Maybe Hasu-kawa could, but ...
♪
GAK !
?
AH !!
EH ?
AH !

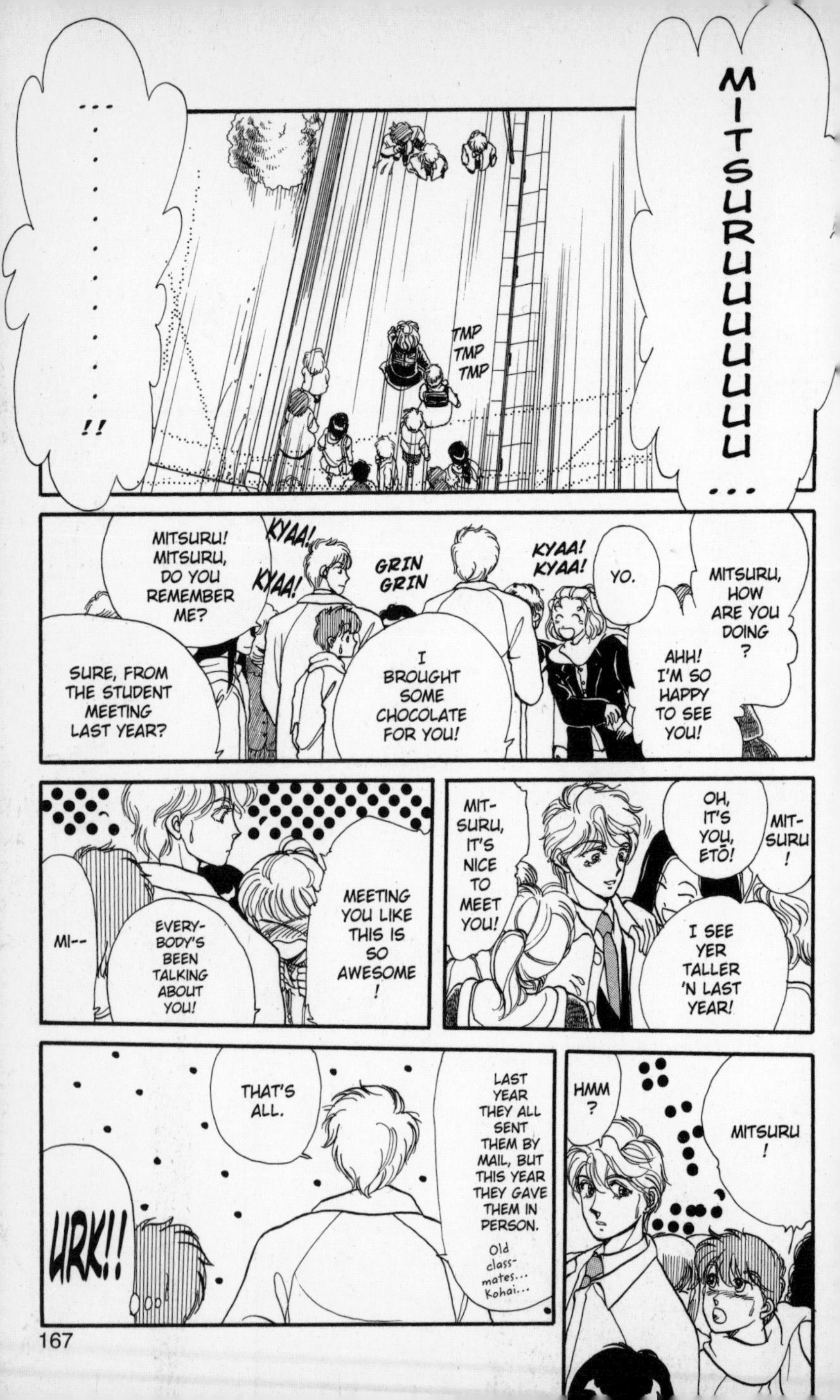
MITSURUUUUUU...
TMP TMP TMP
........!!
MITSURU, HOW ARE YOU DOING?
YO.
AHH! I'M SO HAPPY TO SEE YOU!
KYAA! KYAA!
I BROUGHT SOME CHOCOLATE FOR YOU!
GRIN GRIN
KYAA! KYAA!
MITSURU! MITSURU, DO YOU REMEMBER ME?
SURE, FROM THE STUDENT MEETING LAST YEAR?
MIT-SURU!
OH, IT'S YOU, ETŌ!
I SEE YER TALLER 'N LAST YEAR!
MIT-SURU, IT'S NICE TO MEET YOU!
MEETING YOU LIKE THIS IS SO AWESOME!
EVERY-BODY'S BEEN TALKING ABOUT YOU!
MI--
MITSURU!
HMM?
LAST YEAR THEY ALL SENT THEM BY MAIL, BUT THIS YEAR THEY GAVE THEM IN PERSON.
Old class-mates... Kohai...
THAT'S ALL.
URK!!

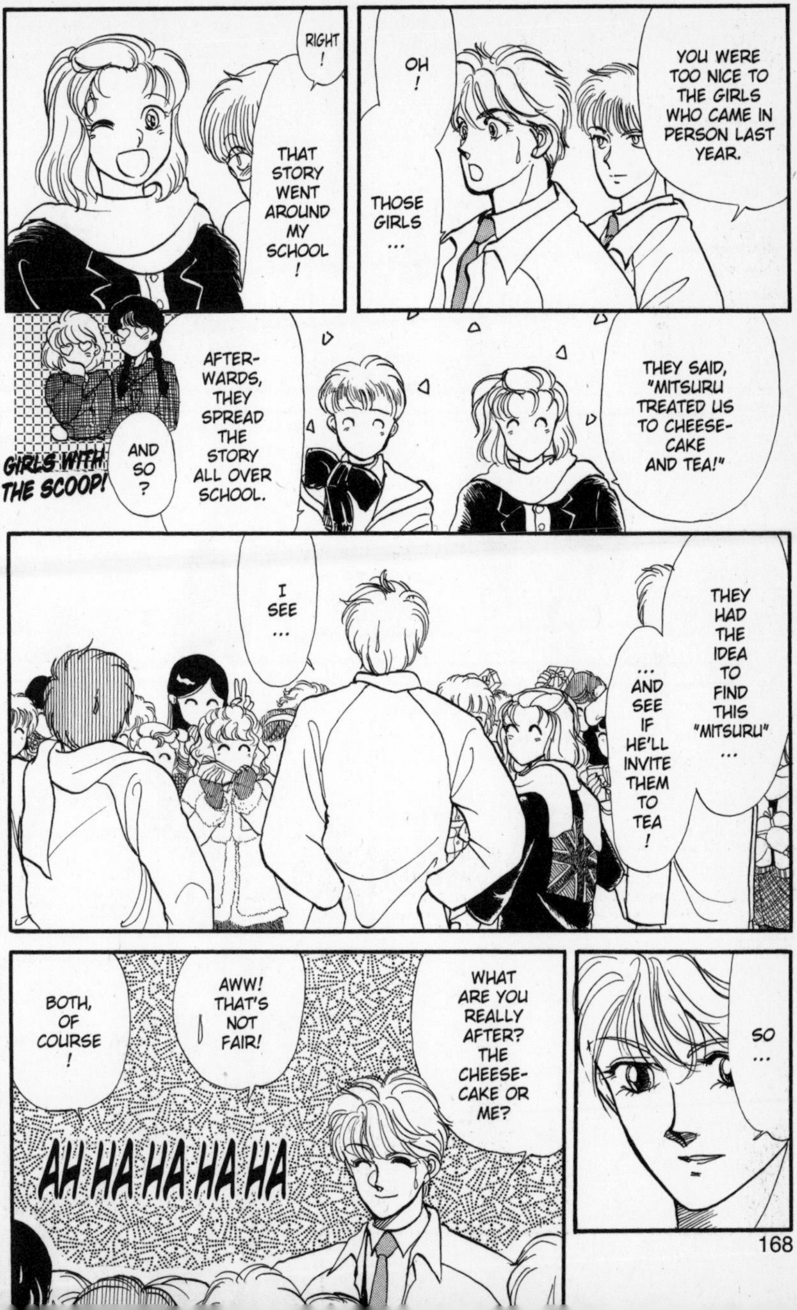
YOU WERE TOO NICE TO THE GIRLS WHO CAME IN PERSON LAST YEAR.
OH!
THOSE GIRLS...
RIGHT!
THAT STORY WENT AROUND MY SCHOOL!
THEY SAID, "MITSURU TREATED US TO CHEESE-CAKE AND TEA!"
AFTER-WARDS, THEY SPREAD THE STORY ALL OVER SCHOOL.
AND SO?
GIRLS WITH THE SCOOP!
THEY HAD THE IDEA TO FIND THIS "MITSURU"...
...AND SEE IF HE'LL INVITE THEM TO TEA!
I SEE...
SO...
WHAT ARE YOU REALLY AFTER? THE CHEESE-CAKE OR ME?
AWW! THAT'S NOT FAIR!
BOTH, OF COURSE!
AH HA HA HA HA

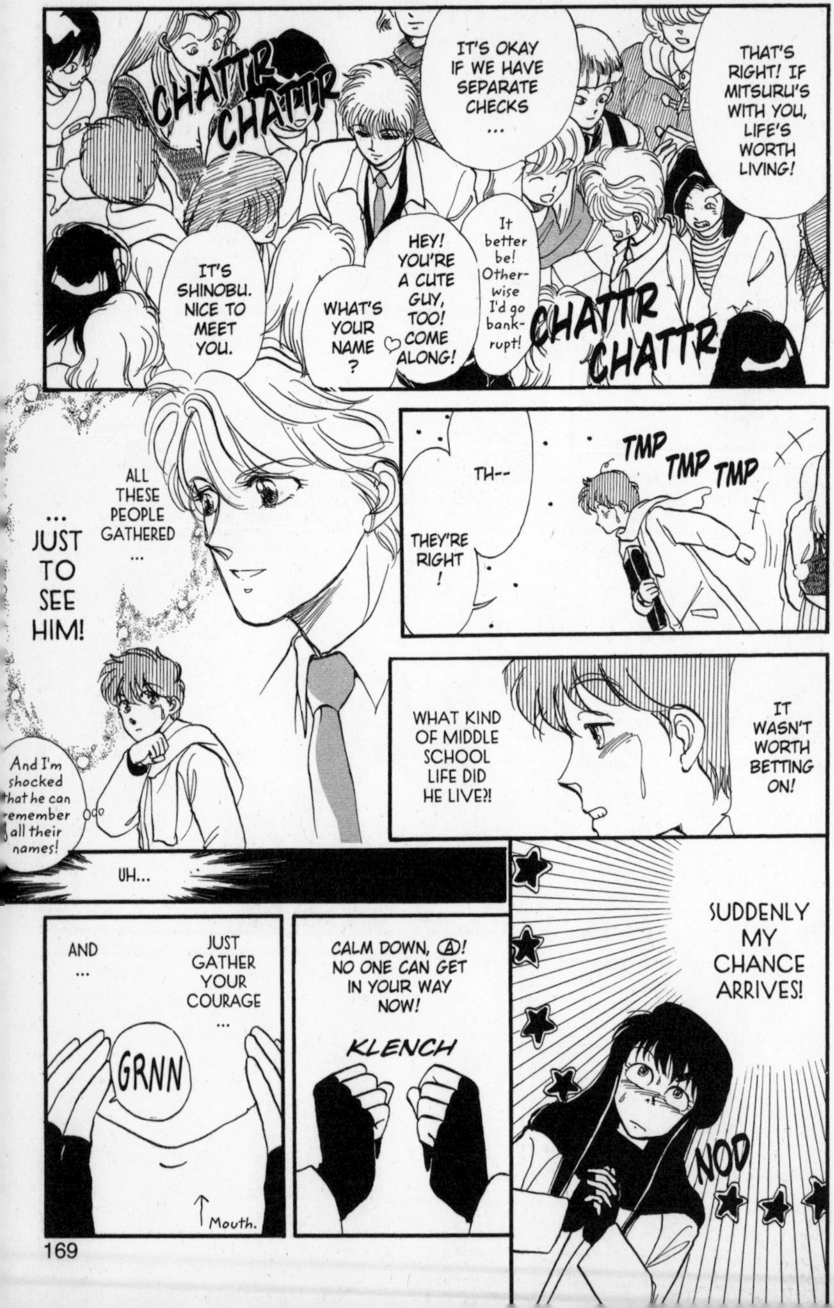

THAT'S RIGHT! IF MITSURU'S WITH YOU, LIFE'S WORTH LIVING!
IT'S OKAY IF WE HAVE SEPARATE CHECKS ...
CHATTR CHATTR
CHATTR CHATTR
It better be! Otherwise I'd go bankrupt!
HEY! YOU'RE A CUTE GUY, TOO! COME ALONG!
WHAT'S YOUR NAME♡?
IT'S SHINOBU. NICE TO MEET YOU.
TMP TMP TMP
TH-- THEY'RE RIGHT!
IT WASN'T WORTH BETTING ON!
WHAT KIND OF MIDDLE SCHOOL LIFE DID HE LIVE?!
ALL THESE PEOPLE GATHERED ...
... JUST TO SEE HIM!
And I'm shocked that he can remember all their names!
SUDDENLY MY CHANCE ARRIVES!
NOD
UH...
CALM DOWN, Ⓐ! NO ONE CAN GET IN YOUR WAY NOW!
KLENCH
JUST GATHER YOUR COURAGE ...
AND ...
GRNN
Mouth.

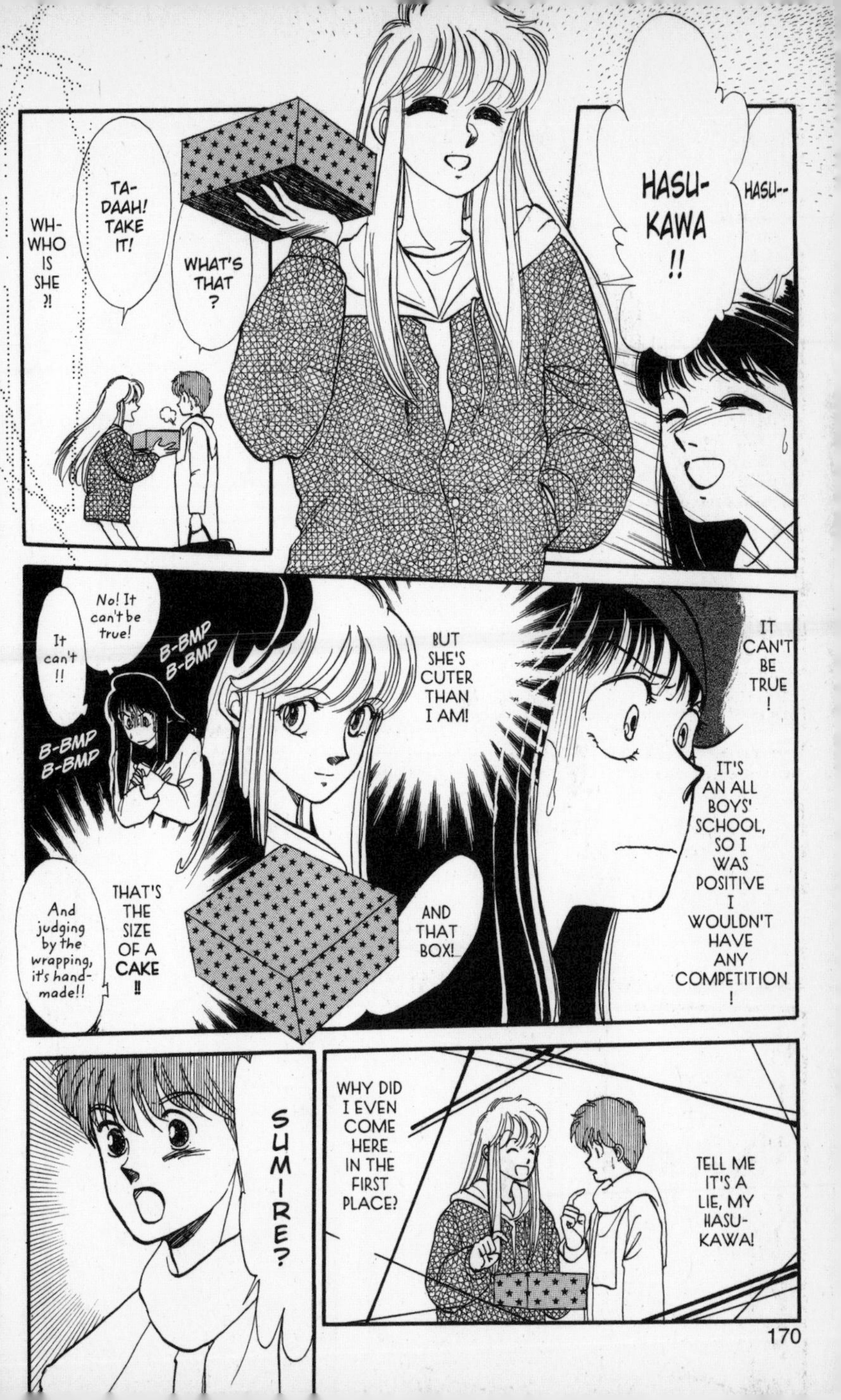
HASU--
HASU-KAWA!!
TA-DAAH! TAKE IT!
WHAT'S THAT?
WH-WHO IS SHE?!
IT CAN'T BE TRUE!
IT'S AN ALL BOYS' SCHOOL, SO I WAS POSITIVE I WOULDN'T HAVE ANY COMPETITION!
BUT SHE'S CUTER THAN I AM!
AND THAT BOX!
THAT'S THE SIZE OF A CAKE!!
And judging by the wrapping, it's hand-made!!
No! It can't be true!
It can't!!
B-BMP B-BMP
B-BMP B-BMP
TELL ME IT'S A LIE, MY HASU-KAWA!
WHY DID I EVEN COME HERE IN THE FIRST PLACE?
SUMIRE?

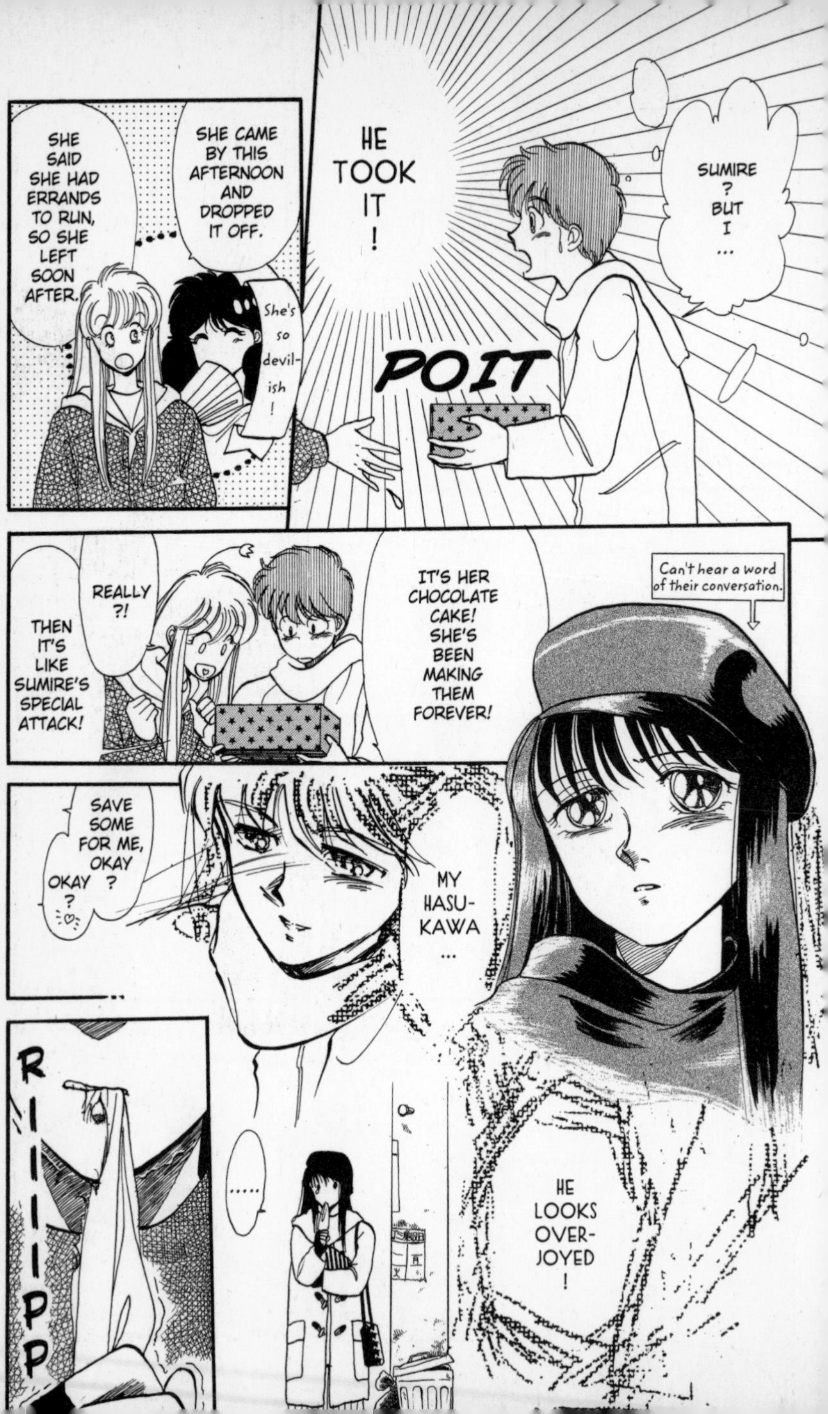
SUMIRE? BUT I...
HE TOOK IT!
POIT
SHE CAME BY THIS AFTERNOON AND DROPPED IT OFF.
SHE SAID SHE HAD ERRANDS TO RUN, SO SHE LEFT SOON AFTER.
She's so devil-ish!
Can't hear a word of their conversation.
HE LOOKS OVER-JOYED!
IT'S HER CHOCOLATE CAKE! SHE'S BEEN MAKING THEM FOREVER!
REALLY?!
THEN IT'S LIKE SUMIRE'S SPECIAL ATTACK!
MY HASU-KAWA...
SAVE SOME FOR ME, OKAY?
OKAY?
......
RIIIPP

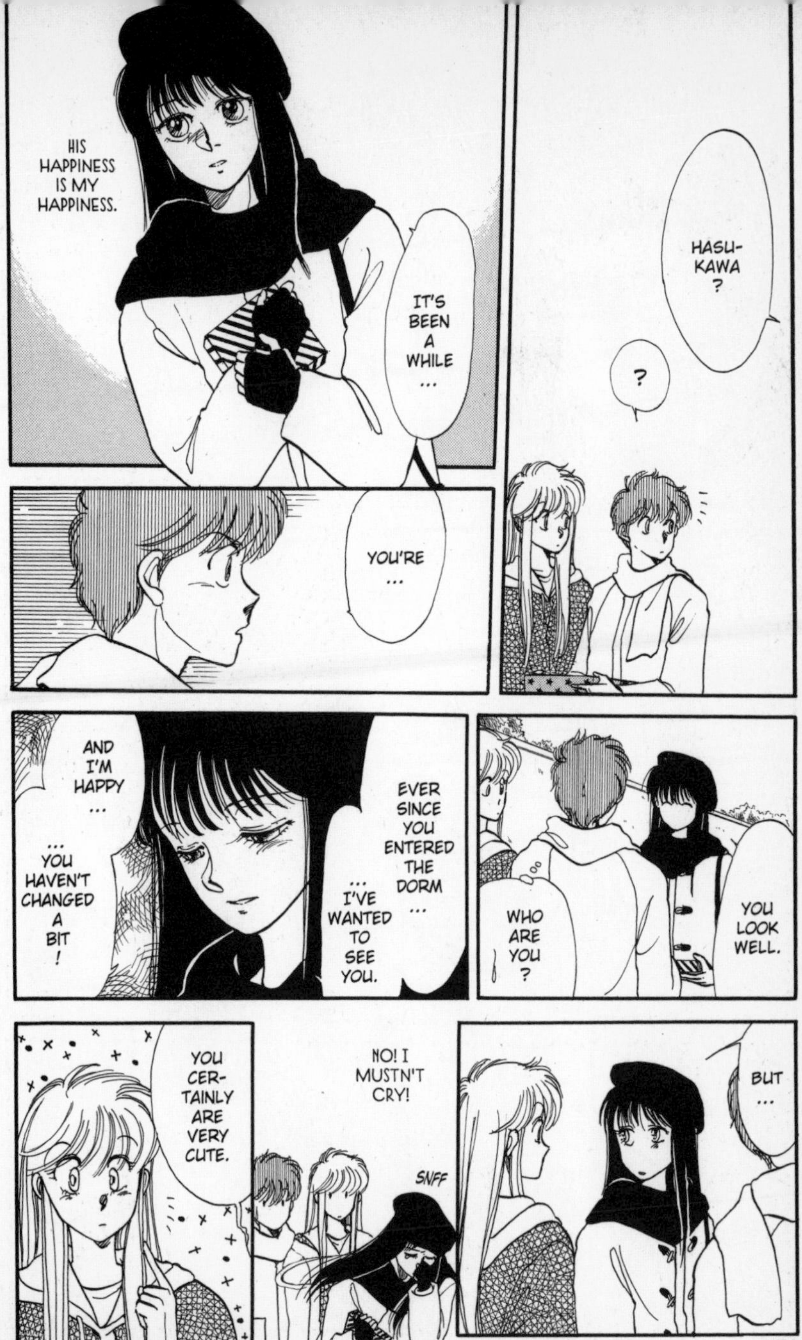

HASU-KAWA?
?
HIS HAPPINESS IS MY HAPPINESS.
IT'S BEEN A WHILE...
YOU'RE...
YOU LOOK WELL.
WHO ARE YOU?
EVER SINCE YOU ENTERED THE DORM...
...I'VE WANTED TO SEE YOU.
AND I'M HAPPY...
...YOU HAVEN'T CHANGED A BIT!
BUT...
NO! I MUSTN'T CRY!
SNFF
YOU CERTAINLY ARE VERY CUTE.

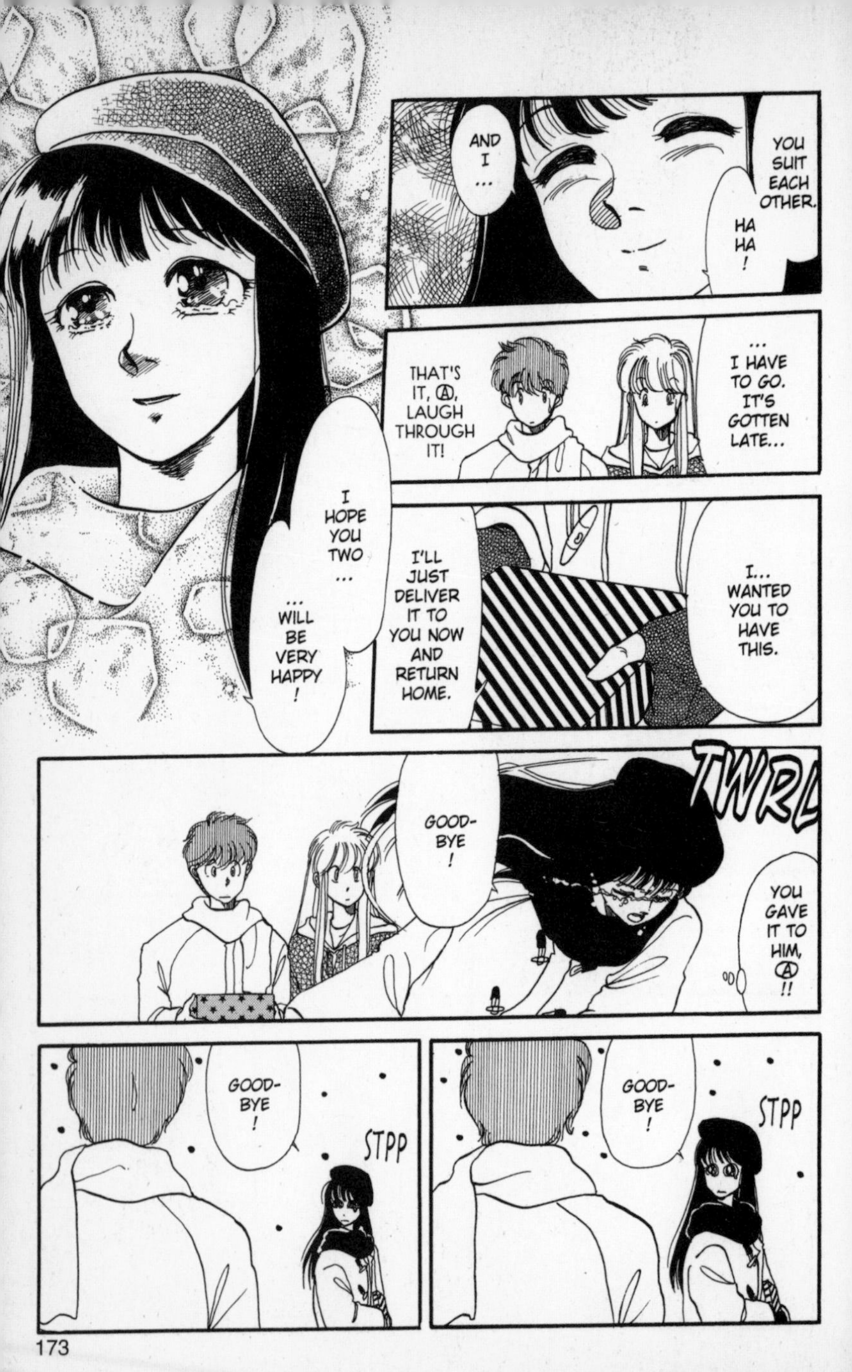
YOU SUIT EACH OTHER.
HA HA!
AND I ...
... I HAVE TO GO. IT'S GOTTEN LATE...
THAT'S IT, Ⓐ, LAUGH THROUGH IT!
I... WANTED YOU TO HAVE THIS.
I'LL JUST DELIVER IT TO YOU NOW AND RETURN HOME.
I HOPE YOU TWO ...
... WILL BE VERY HAPPY!
TWRL
YOU GAVE IT TO HIM, Ⓐ!!
GOOD-BYE!
GOOD-BYE!
STPP
GOOD-BYE!
STPP

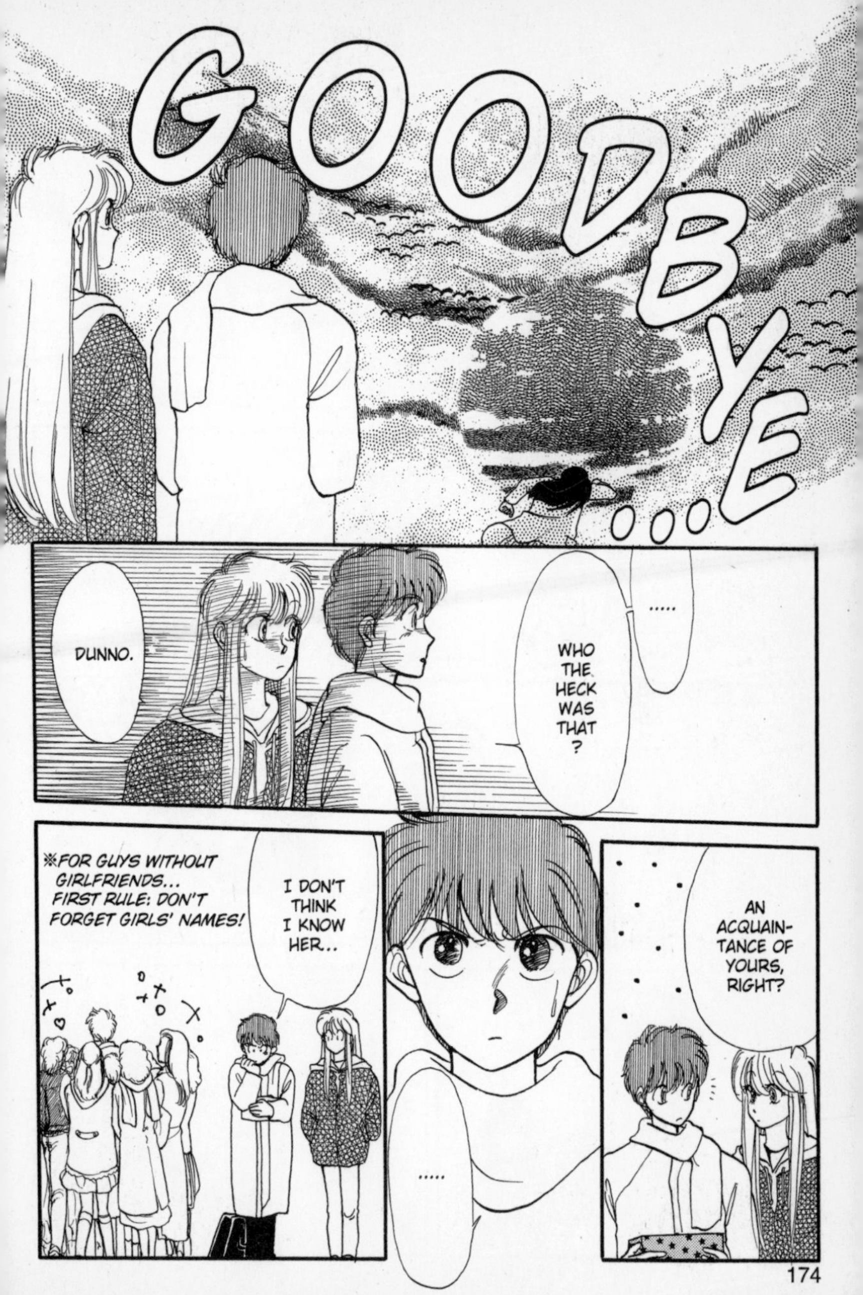
GOODBYE...E
.....
WHO THE HECK WAS THAT?
DUNNO.
AN ACQUAINTANCE OF YOURS, RIGHT?
.....
I DON'T THINK I KNOW HER...
※FOR GUYS WITHOUT GIRLFRIENDS... FIRST RULE: DON'T FORGET GIRLS' NAMES!

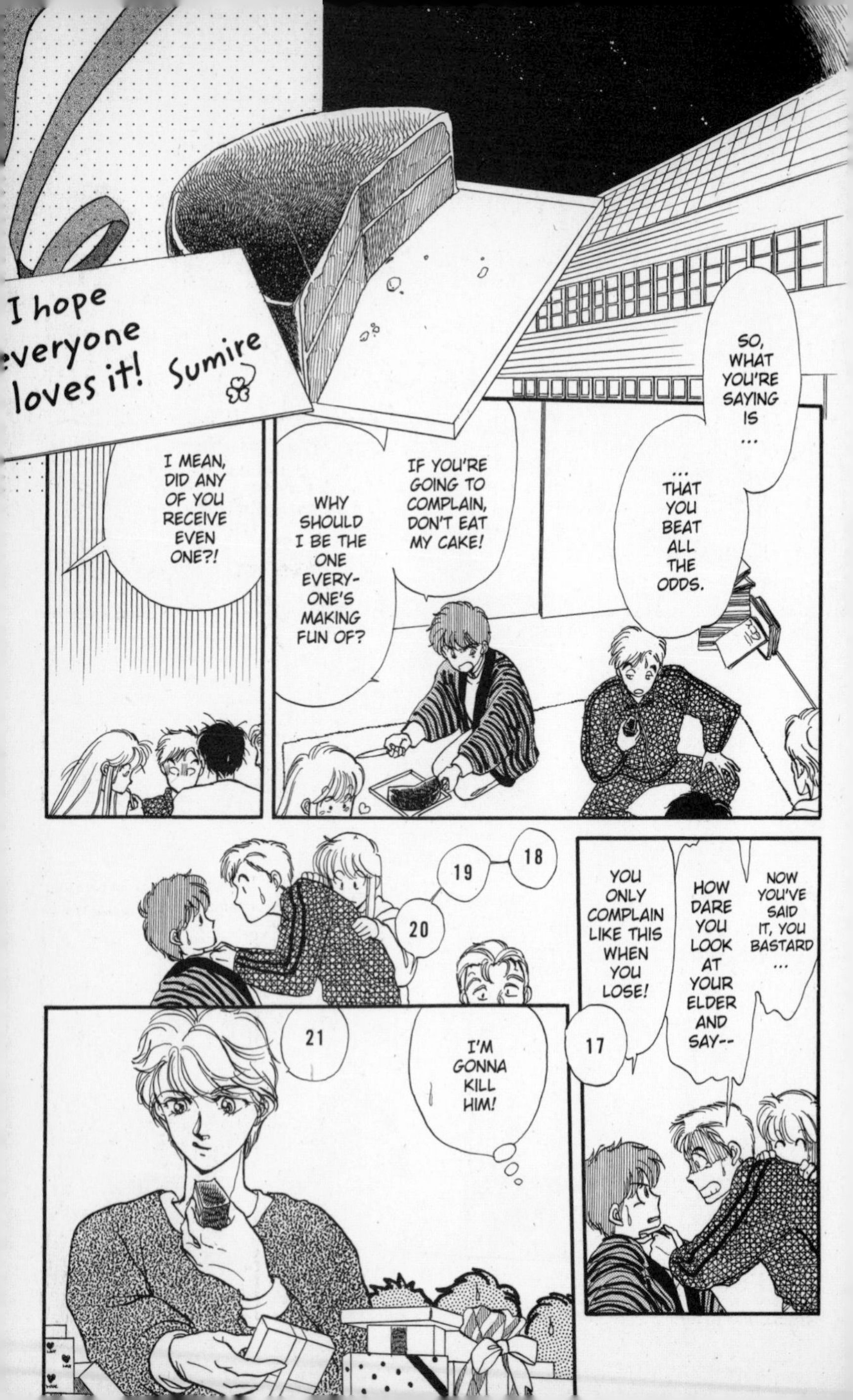
I hope everyone loves it! Sumire
SO, WHAT YOU'RE SAYING IS ...
... THAT YOU BEAT ALL THE ODDS.
IF YOU'RE GOING TO COMPLAIN, DON'T EAT MY CAKE!
WHY SHOULD I BE THE ONE EVERYONE'S MAKING FUN OF?
I MEAN, DID ANY OF YOU RECEIVE EVEN ONE?!
NOW YOU'VE SAID IT, YOU BASTARD ...
HOW DARE YOU LOOK AT YOUR ELDER AND SAY--
YOU ONLY COMPLAIN LIKE THIS WHEN YOU LOSE!
17
18
19
20
21
I'M GONNA KILL HIM!

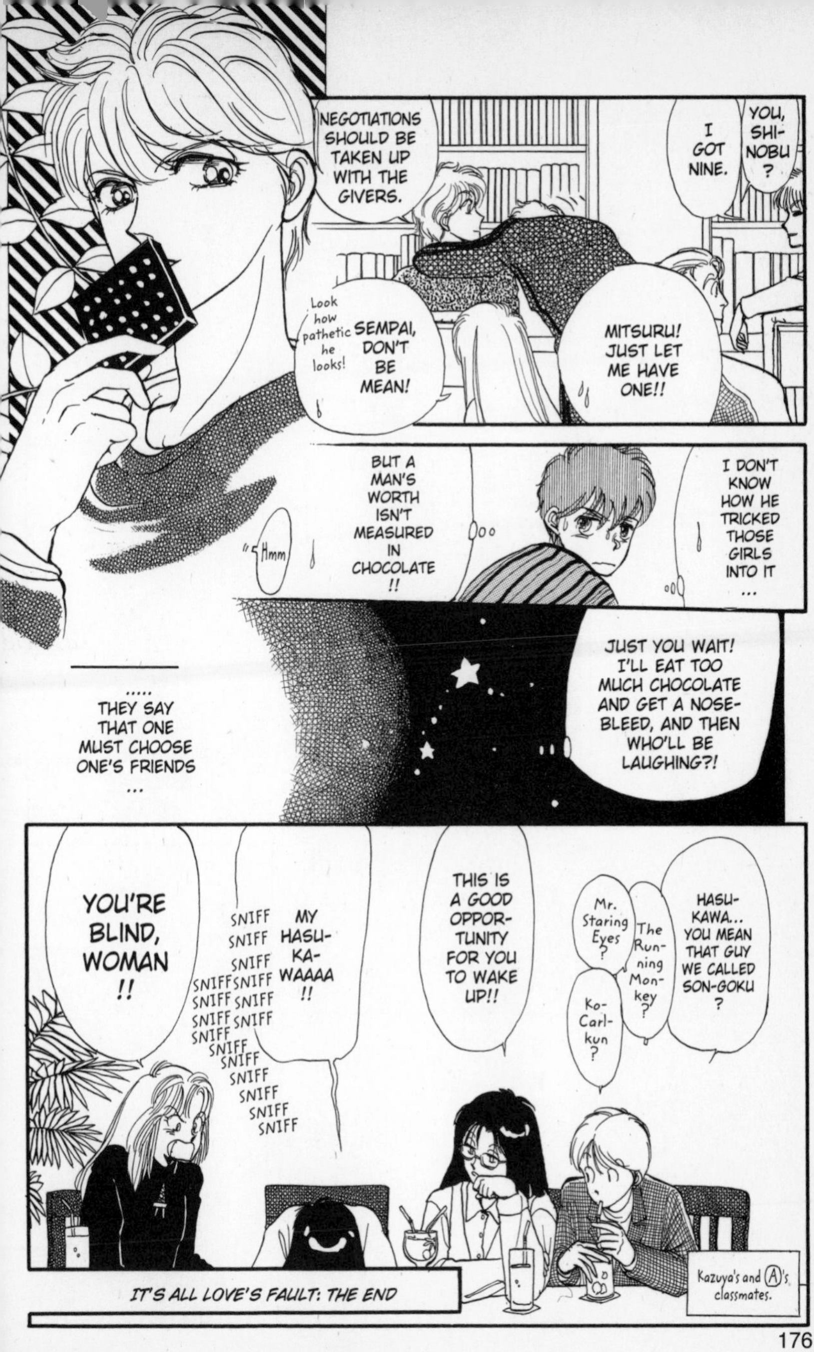
YOU, SHI-NOBU?
I GOT NINE.
NEGOTIATIONS SHOULD BE TAKEN UP WITH THE GIVERS.
MITSURU! JUST LET ME HAVE ONE!!
SEMPAI, DON'T BE MEAN!
Look how pathetic he looks!
I DON'T KNOW HOW HE TRICKED THOSE GIRLS INTO IT ...
BUT A MAN'S WORTH ISN'T MEASURED IN CHOCOLATE !!
Hmm
JUST YOU WAIT! I'LL EAT TOO MUCH CHOCOLATE AND GET A NOSE-BLEED, AND THEN WHO'LL BE LAUGHING?!
..... THEY SAY THAT ONE MUST CHOOSE ONE'S FRIENDS ...
Kazuya's and Ⓐ's classmates.
HASU-KAWA... YOU MEAN THAT GUY WE CALLED SON-GOKU?
The Run-ning Mon-key?
Mr. Staring Eyes?
Ko-Carl-kun?
THIS IS A GOOD OPPOR-TUNITY FOR YOU TO WAKE UP!!
MY HASU-KA-WAAAA!!
SNIFF SNIFF SNIFF SNIFF SNIFF SNIFF SNIFF SNIFF SNIFF SNIFF SNIFF SNIFF SNIFF SNIFF SNIFF SNIFF SNIFF
YOU'RE BLIND, WOMAN!!
IT'S ALL LOVE'S FAULT: THE END

WHITE DAY

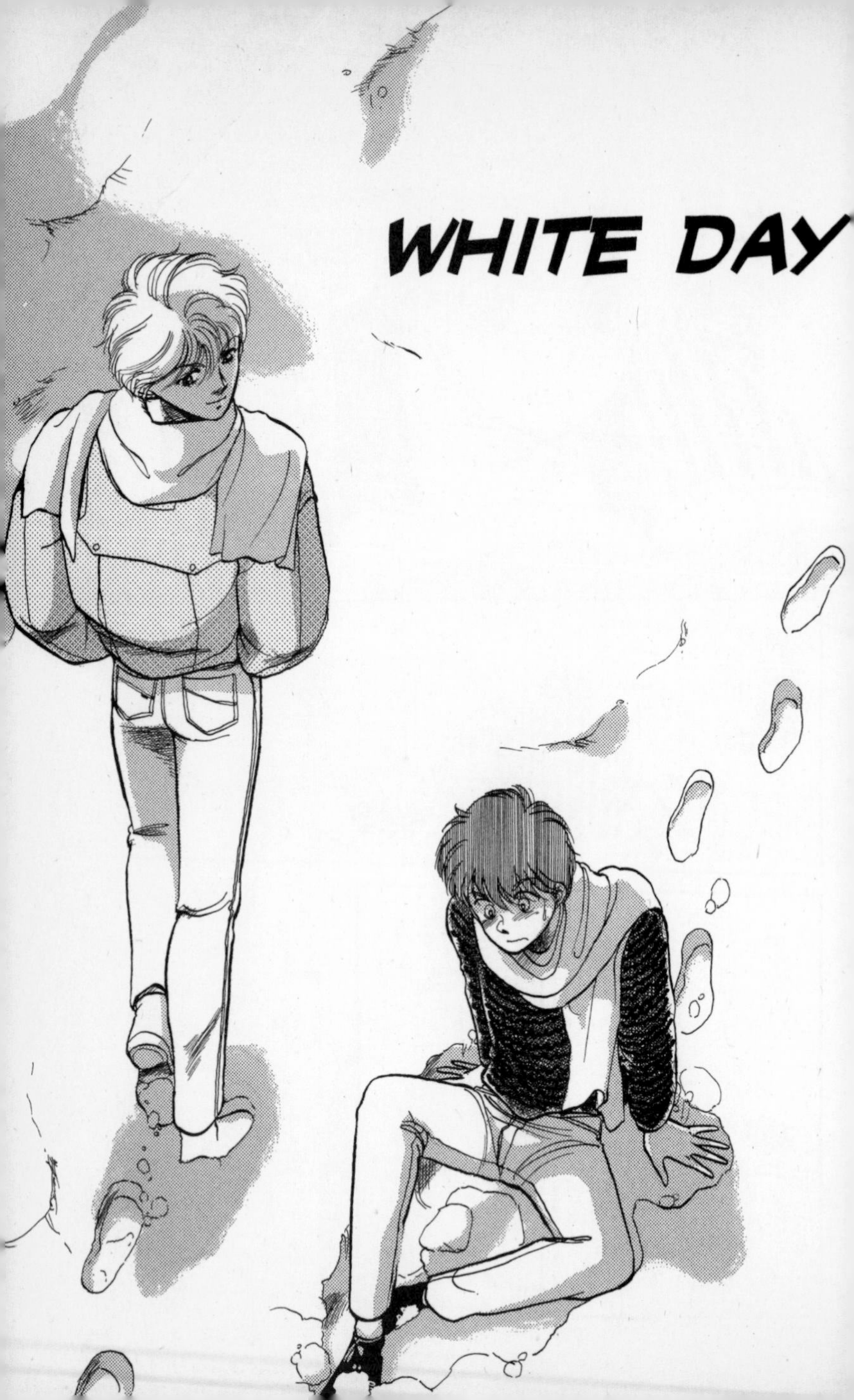
WHITE DAY

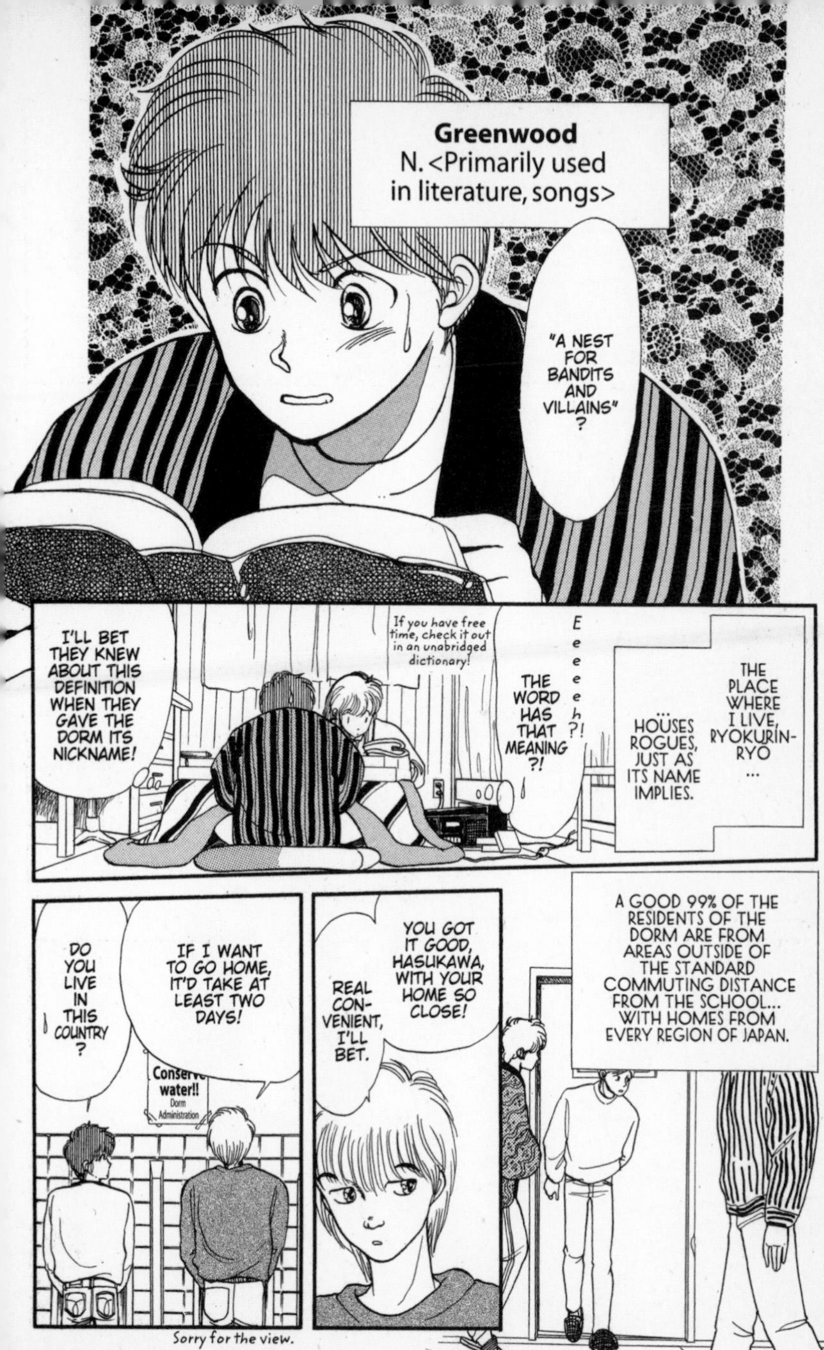
Greenwood
N. <Primarily used in literature, songs>
"A NEST FOR BANDITS AND VILLAINS"?
THE PLACE WHERE I LIVE, RYOKURIN-RYO...
...HOUSES ROGUES, JUST AS ITS NAME IMPLIES.
Eeeeeh?!
THE WORD HAS THAT MEANING?!
If you have free time, check it out in an unabridged dictionary!
I'LL BET THEY KNEW ABOUT THIS DEFINITION WHEN THEY GAVE THE DORM ITS NICKNAME!
A GOOD 99% OF THE RESIDENTS OF THE DORM ARE FROM AREAS OUTSIDE OF THE STANDARD COMMUTING DISTANCE FROM THE SCHOOL... WITH HOMES FROM EVERY REGION OF JAPAN.
YOU GOT IT GOOD, HASUKAWA, WITH YOUR HOME SO CLOSE!
REAL CON-VENIENT, I'LL BET.
IF I WANT TO GO HOME, IT'D TAKE AT LEAST TWO DAYS!
DO YOU LIVE IN THIS COUNTRY?
Conserve water!!
Dorm Administration
Sorry for the view.

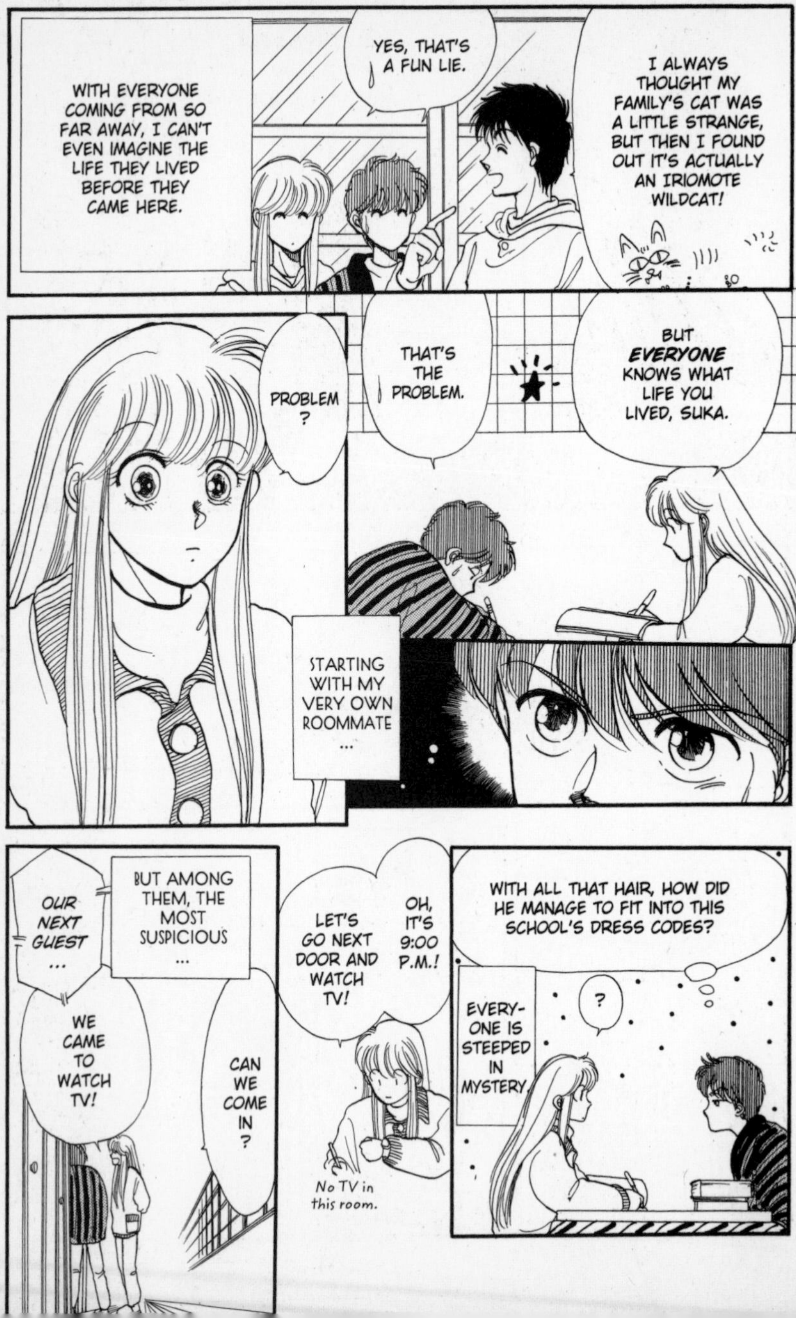
I ALWAYS THOUGHT MY FAMILY'S CAT WAS A LITTLE STRANGE, BUT THEN I FOUND OUT IT'S ACTUALLY AN IRIOMOTE WILDCAT!
YES, THAT'S A FUN LIE.
WITH EVERYONE COMING FROM SO FAR AWAY, I CAN'T EVEN IMAGINE THE LIFE THEY LIVED BEFORE THEY CAME HERE.
BUT *EVERYONE* KNOWS WHAT LIFE YOU LIVED, SUKA.
THAT'S THE PROBLEM.
STARTING WITH MY VERY OWN ROOMMATE ...
PROBLEM ?
WITH ALL THAT HAIR, HOW DID HE MANAGE TO FIT INTO THIS SCHOOL'S DRESS CODES?
?
EVERY-ONE IS STEEPED IN MYSTERY.
OH, IT'S 9:00 P.M.!
LET'S GO NEXT DOOR AND WATCH TV!
No TV in this room.
BUT AMONG THEM, THE MOST SUSPICIOUS ...
OUR NEXT GUEST ...
CAN WE COME IN ?
WE CAME TO WATCH TV!

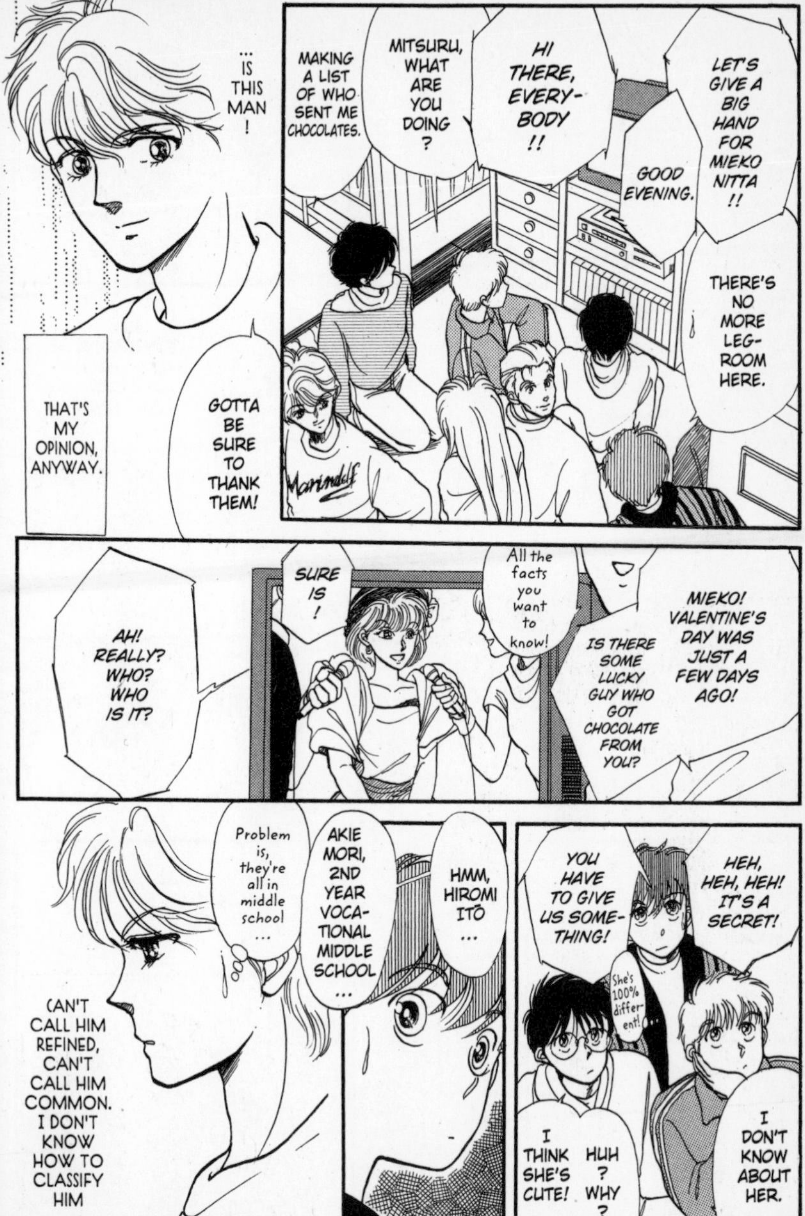
LET'S GIVE A BIG HAND FOR MIEKO NITTA!!
HI THERE, EVERY-BODY!!
GOOD EVENING.
MITSURU, WHAT ARE YOU DOING?
MAKING A LIST OF WHO SENT ME CHOCOLATES.
THERE'S NO MORE LEG-ROOM HERE.
GOTTA BE SURE TO THANK THEM!
... IS THIS MAN!
THAT'S MY OPINION, ANYWAY.
MIEKO! VALENTINE'S DAY WAS JUST A FEW DAYS AGO!
IS THERE SOME LUCKY GUY WHO GOT CHOCOLATE FROM YOU?
All the facts you want to know!
SURE IS!
AH! REALLY? WHO? WHO IS IT?
HEH, HEH, HEH! IT'S A SECRET!
YOU HAVE TO GIVE US SOME-THING!
She's 100% differ-ent!
I DON'T KNOW ABOUT HER.
HUH? WHY?
I THINK SHE'S CUTE!
HMM, HIROMI ITO...
AKIE MORI, 2ND YEAR VOCA-TIONAL MIDDLE SCHOOL...
Problem is, they're all in middle school...
CAN'T CALL HIM REFINED, CAN'T CALL HIM COMMON. I DON'T KNOW HOW TO CLASSIFY HIM...

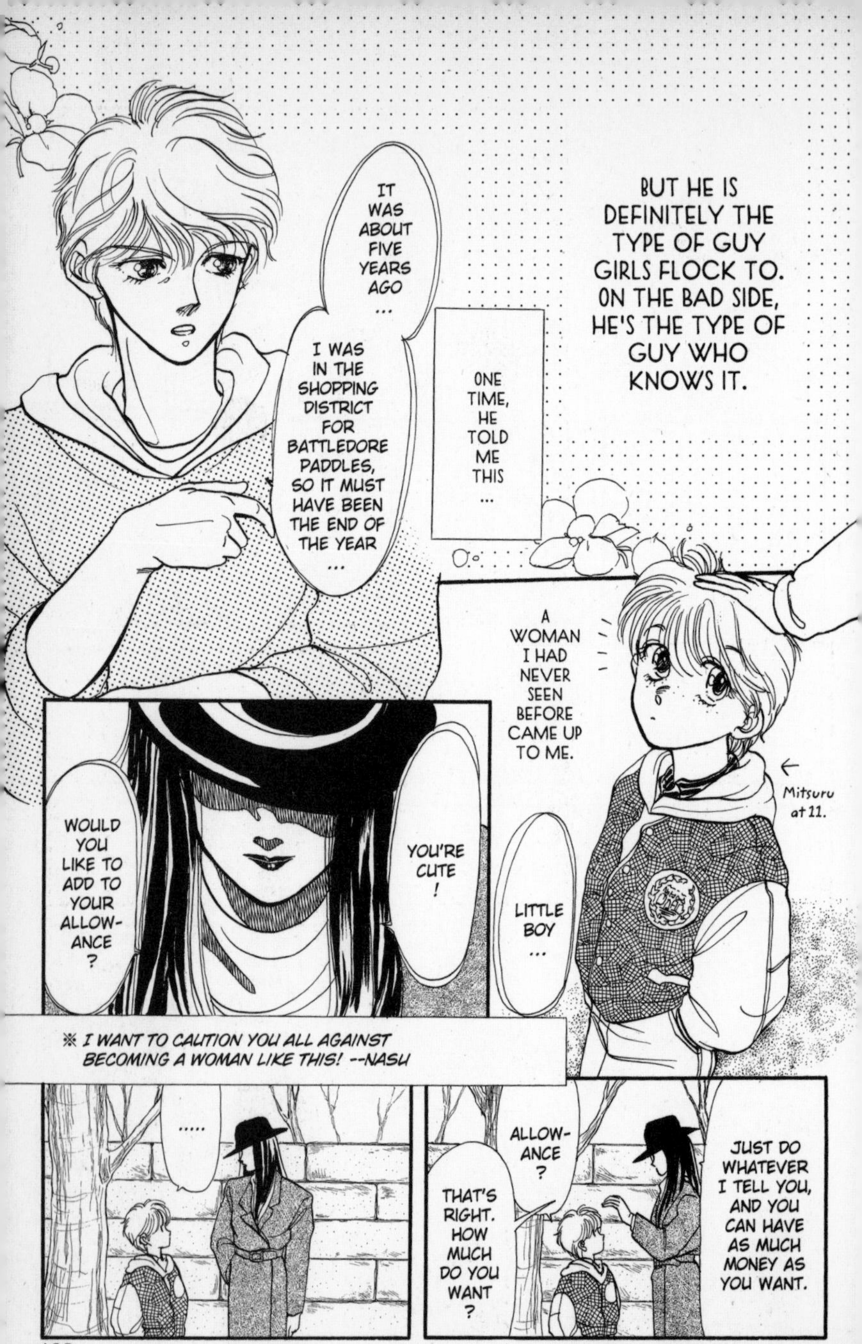
BUT HE IS DEFINITELY THE TYPE OF GUY GIRLS FLOCK TO. ON THE BAD SIDE, HE'S THE TYPE OF GUY WHO KNOWS IT.
ONE TIME, HE TOLD ME THIS ...
IT WAS ABOUT FIVE YEARS AGO ...
I WAS IN THE SHOPPING DISTRICT FOR BATTLEDORE PADDLES, SO IT MUST HAVE BEEN THE END OF THE YEAR ...
A WOMAN I HAD NEVER SEEN BEFORE CAME UP TO ME.
Mitsuru at 11.
LITTLE BOY ...
YOU'RE CUTE!
WOULD YOU LIKE TO ADD TO YOUR ALLOWANCE?
※ I WANT TO CAUTION YOU ALL AGAINST BECOMING A WOMAN LIKE THIS! --NASU
ALLOWANCE?
THAT'S RIGHT. HOW MUCH DO YOU WANT?
JUST DO WHATEVER I TELL YOU, AND YOU CAN HAVE AS MUCH MONEY AS YOU WANT.
.....

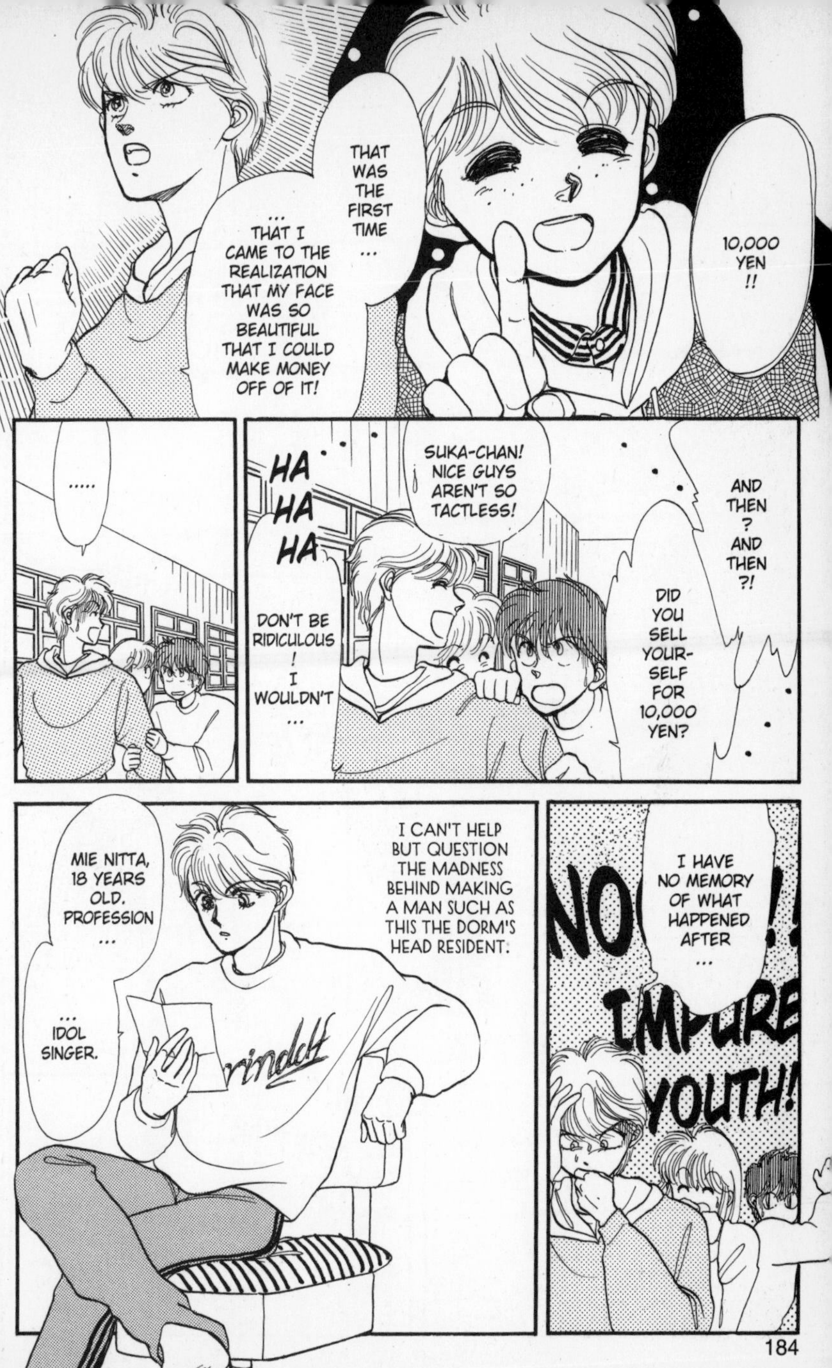
10,000 YEN !!
THAT WAS THE FIRST TIME ...
... THAT I CAME TO THE REALIZATION THAT MY FACE WAS SO BEAUTIFUL THAT I COULD MAKE MONEY OFF OF IT!
AND THEN? AND THEN?!
DID YOU SELL YOUR-SELF FOR 10,000 YEN?
SUKA-CHAN! NICE GUYS AREN'T SO TACTLESS!
HA HA HA
DON'T BE RIDICULOUS! I WOULDN'T ...
.....
NO!!
I HAVE NO MEMORY OF WHAT HAPPENED AFTER ...
IMPURE YOUTH!
I CAN'T HELP BUT QUESTION THE MADNESS BEHIND MAKING A MAN SUCH AS THIS THE DORM'S HEAD RESIDENT.
MIE NITTA, 18 YEARS OLD. PROFESSION ...
... IDOL SINGER.

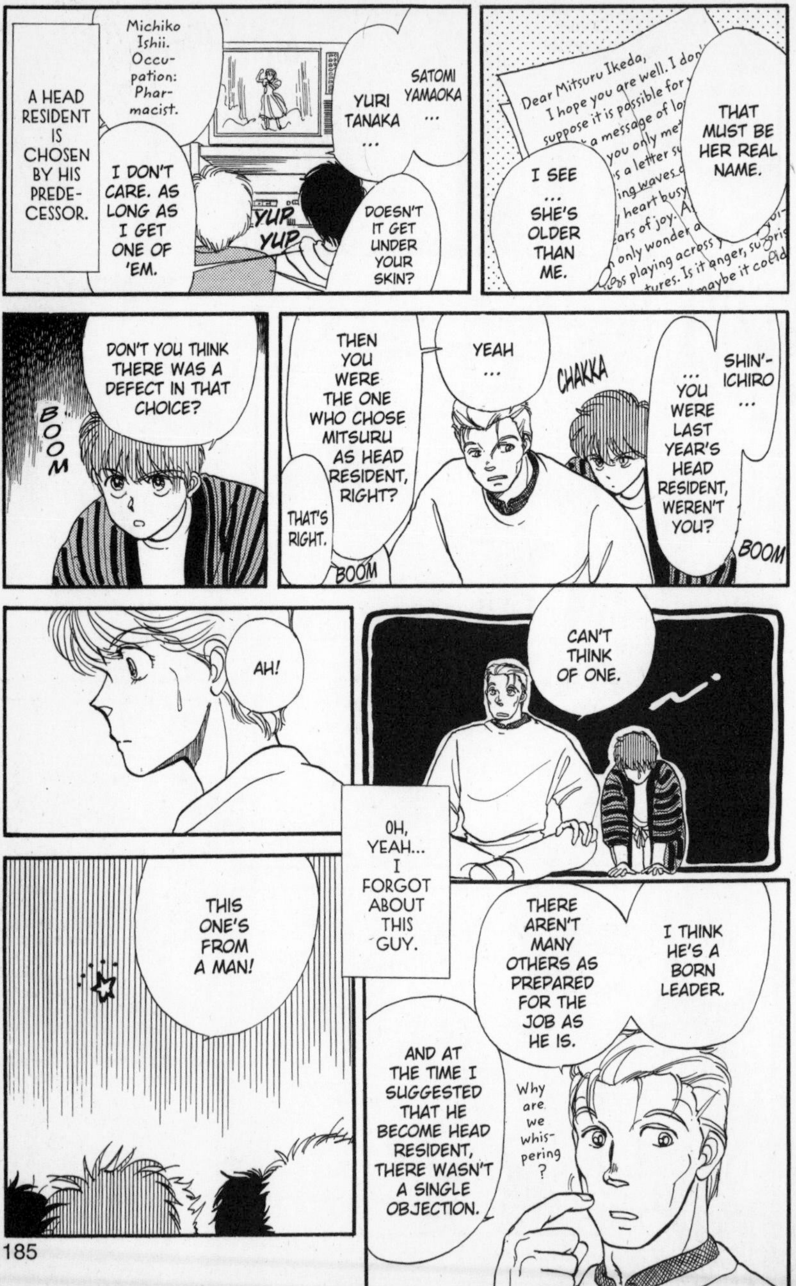
THAT MUST BE HER REAL NAME.
Dear Mitsuru Ikeda,
I hope you are well.
I SEE ... SHE'S OLDER THAN ME.
SATOMI YAMAOKA ...
YURI TANAKA ...
DOESN'T IT GET UNDER YOUR SKIN?
YUP YUP
Michiko Ishii. Occupation: Pharmacist.
I DON'T CARE. AS LONG AS I GET ONE OF 'EM.
A HEAD RESIDENT IS CHOSEN BY HIS PREDECESSOR.
SHIN'-ICHIRO ...
... YOU WERE LAST YEAR'S HEAD RESIDENT, WEREN'T YOU?
BOOM
CHAKKA
YEAH ...
THEN YOU WERE THE ONE WHO CHOSE MITSURU AS HEAD RESIDENT, RIGHT?
THAT'S RIGHT.
BOOM
DON'T YOU THINK THERE WAS A DEFECT IN THAT CHOICE?
BOOM
CAN'T THINK OF ONE.
OH, YEAH... I FORGOT ABOUT THIS GUY.
AH!
I THINK HE'S A BORN LEADER.
THERE AREN'T MANY OTHERS AS PREPARED FOR THE JOB AS HE IS.
Why are we whispering?
AND AT THE TIME I SUGGESTED THAT HE BECOME HEAD RESIDENT, THERE WASN'T A SINGLE OBJECTION.
THIS ONE'S FROM A MAN!

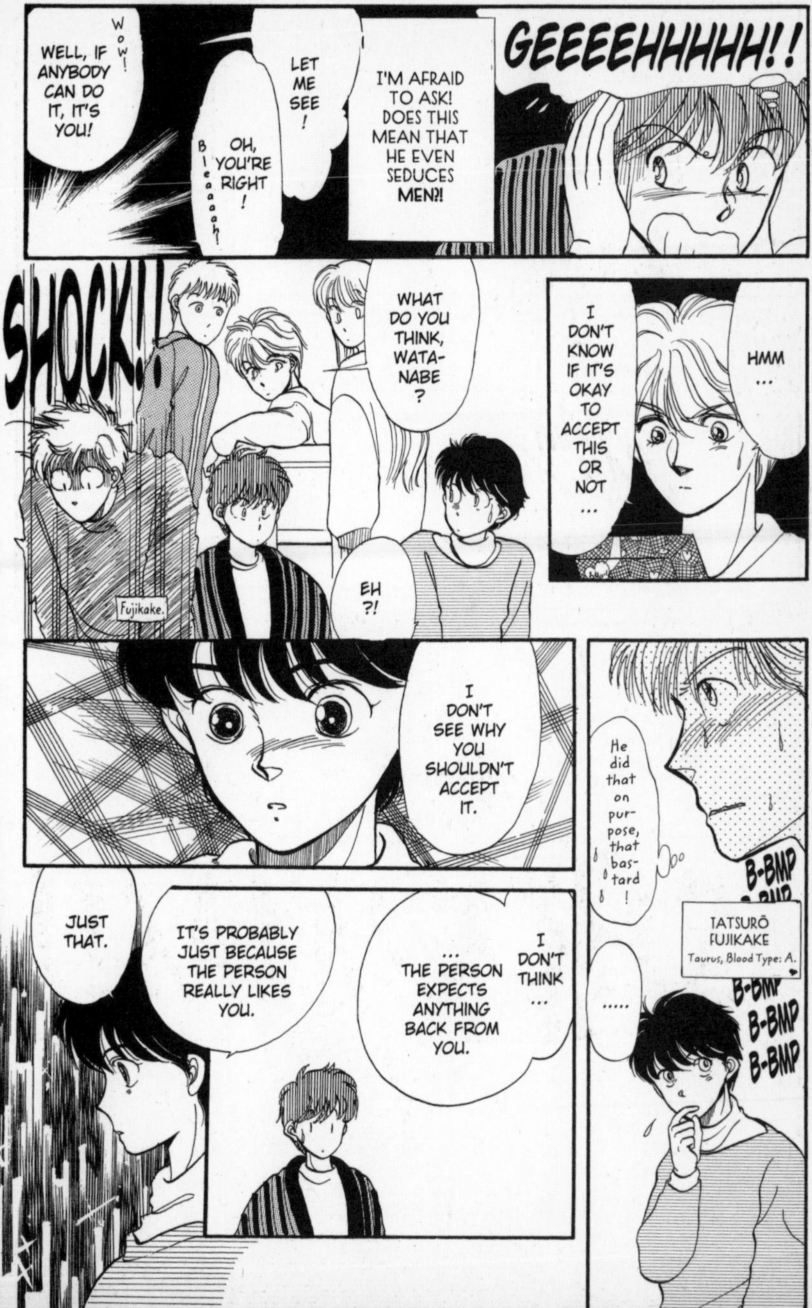
GEEEEHHHHH!!
I'M AFRAID TO ASK! DOES THIS MEAN THAT HE EVEN SEDUCES MEN?!
LET ME SEE!
OH, YOU'RE RIGHT!
Bleaaaaah!
Wow!
WELL, IF ANYBODY CAN DO IT, IT'S YOU!
HMM...
I DON'T KNOW IF IT'S OKAY TO ACCEPT THIS OR NOT...
WHAT DO YOU THINK, WATANABE?
EH?!
SHOCK!!
Fujikake.
He did that on purpose, that bastard!
B-BMP
B-BMP
TATSURŌ FUJIKAKE
Taurus, Blood Type: A.
.....
B-BMP
B-BMP
B-BMP
I DON'T SEE WHY YOU SHOULDN'T ACCEPT IT.
I DON'T THINK...
...THE PERSON EXPECTS ANYTHING BACK FROM YOU.
IT'S PROBABLY JUST BECAUSE THE PERSON REALLY LIKES YOU.
JUST THAT.

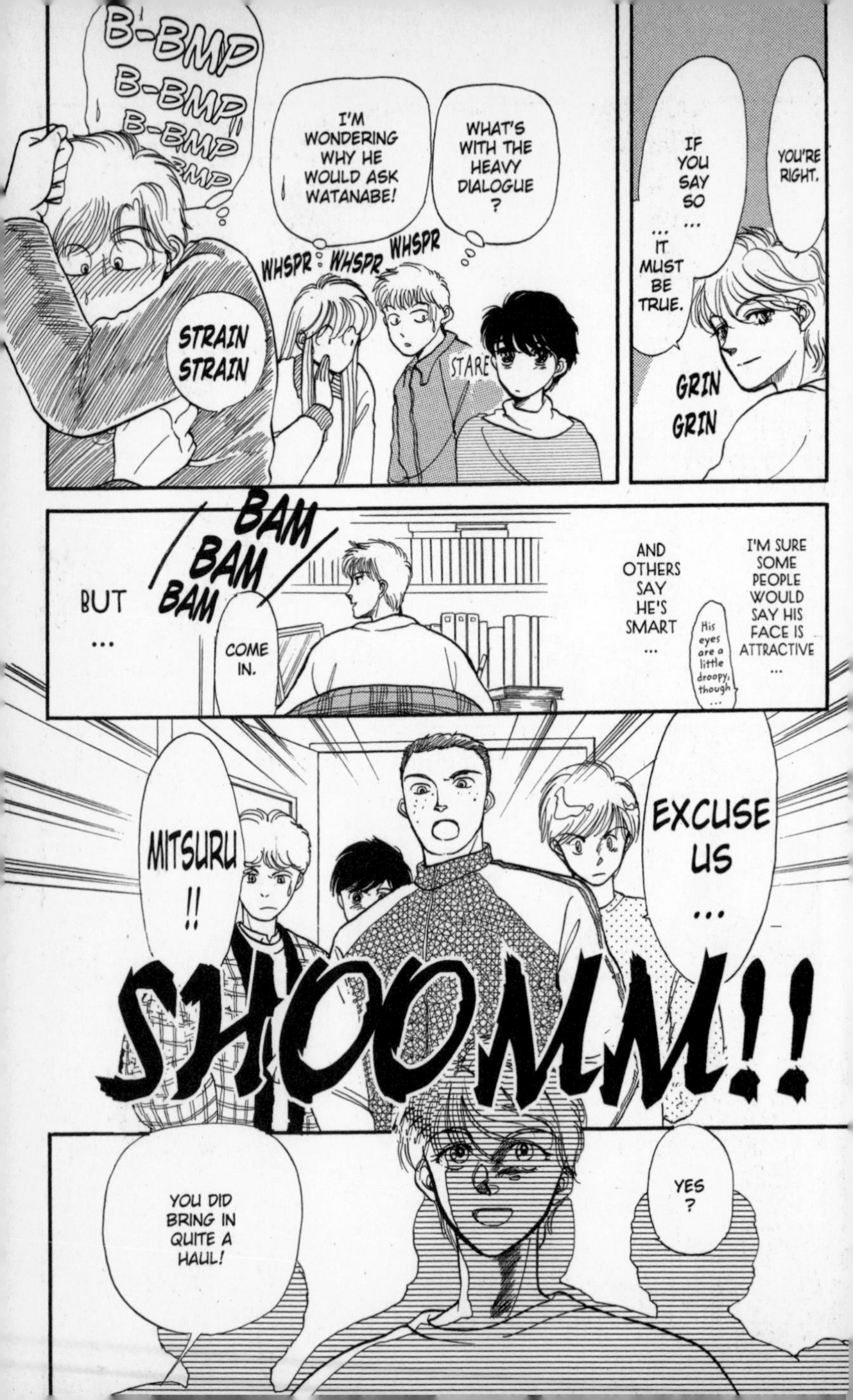
YOU'RE RIGHT.
IF YOU SAY SO ... IT MUST BE TRUE.
GRIN GRIN
WHAT'S WITH THE HEAVY DIALOGUE ?
I'M WONDERING WHY HE WOULD ASK WATANABE!
WHSPR WHSPR WHSPR
STARE
B-BMP B-BMP B-BMP
STRAIN STRAIN
I'M SURE SOME PEOPLE WOULD SAY HIS FACE IS ATTRACTIVE ...
His eyes are a little droopy, though ...
AND OTHERS SAY HE'S SMART ...
COME IN.
BAM BAM BAM
BUT ...
EXCUSE US ...
MITSURU !!
SHOOMM!!
YES ?
YOU DID BRING IN QUITE A HAUL!

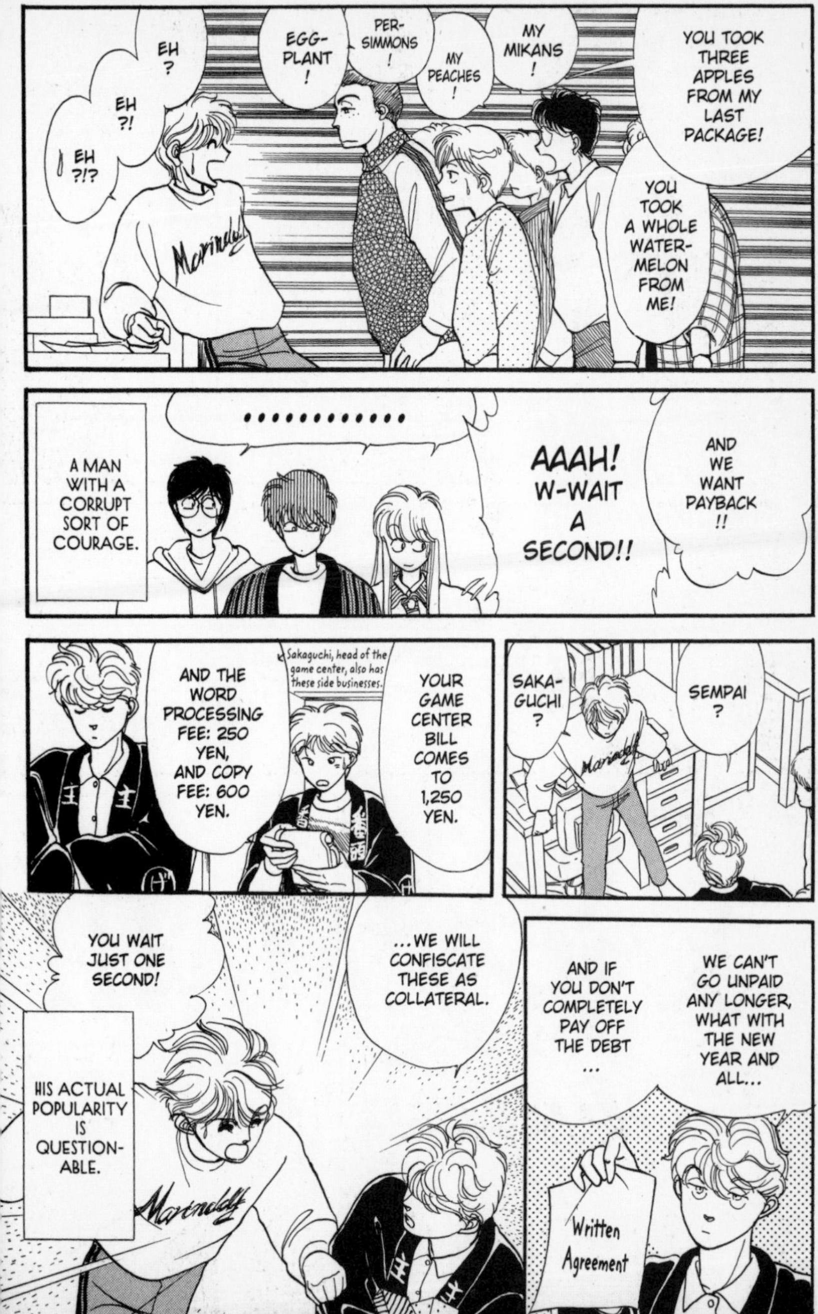
YOU TOOK THREE APPLES FROM MY LAST PACKAGE!
YOU TOOK A WHOLE WATER-MELON FROM ME!
MY MIKANS!
MY PEACHES!
PER-SIMMONS!
EGG-PLANT!
EH?
EH?!
EH?!?
AND WE WANT PAYBACK!!
AAAH! W-WAIT A SECOND!!
....
A MAN WITH A CORRUPT SORT OF COURAGE.
SEMPAI?
SAKA-GUCHI?
YOUR GAME CENTER BILL COMES TO 1,250 YEN.
Sakaguchi, head of the game center, also has these side businesses.
AND THE WORD PROCESSING FEE: 250 YEN, AND COPY FEE: 600 YEN.
WE CAN'T GO UNPAID ANY LONGER, WHAT WITH THE NEW YEAR AND ALL...
AND IF YOU DON'T COMPLETELY PAY OFF THE DEBT ...
Written Agreement
...WE WILL CONFISCATE THESE AS COLLATERAL.
YOU WAIT JUST ONE SECOND!
HIS ACTUAL POPULARITY IS QUESTIONABLE.

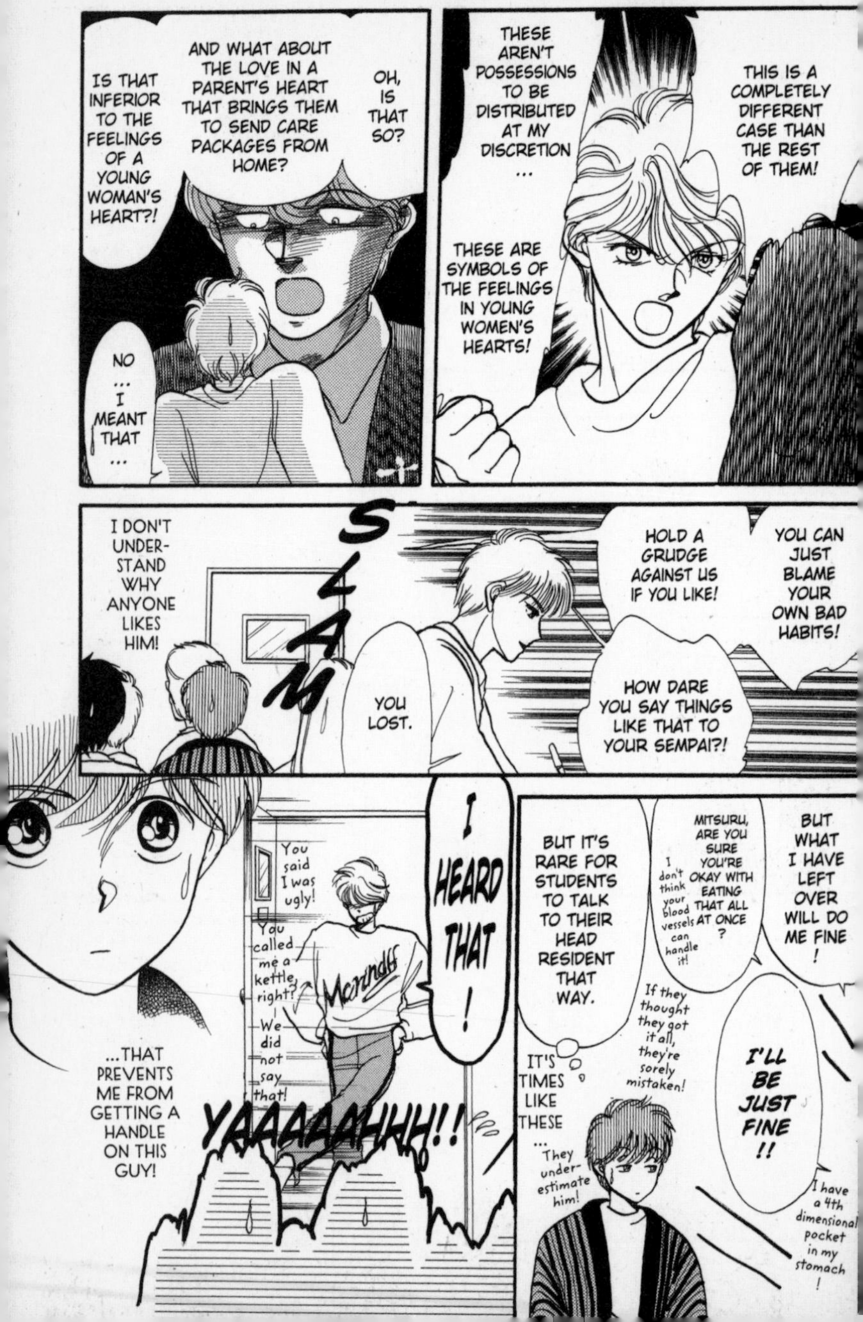
THIS IS A COMPLETELY DIFFERENT CASE THAN THE REST OF THEM!
THESE AREN'T POSSESSIONS TO BE DISTRIBUTED AT MY DISCRETION ...
THESE ARE SYMBOLS OF THE FEELINGS IN YOUNG WOMEN'S HEARTS!
OH, IS THAT SO?
AND WHAT ABOUT THE LOVE IN A PARENT'S HEART THAT BRINGS THEM TO SEND CARE PACKAGES FROM HOME?
IS THAT INFERIOR TO THE FEELINGS OF A YOUNG WOMAN'S HEART?!
NO ... I MEANT THAT ...
YOU CAN JUST BLAME YOUR OWN BAD HABITS!
HOLD A GRUDGE AGAINST US IF YOU LIKE!
HOW DARE YOU SAY THINGS LIKE THAT TO YOUR SEMPAI?!
YOU LOST.
SLAM
I DON'T UNDER-STAND WHY ANYONE LIKES HIM!
BUT WHAT I HAVE LEFT OVER WILL DO ME FINE!
I have a 4th dimensional pocket in my stomach!
MITSURU, ARE YOU SURE YOU'RE OKAY WITH EATING THAT ALL AT ONCE?
I don't think your blood vessels can handle it!
I'LL BE JUST FINE!!
BUT IT'S RARE FOR STUDENTS TO TALK TO THEIR HEAD RESIDENT THAT WAY.
If they thought they got it all, they're sorely mistaken!
IT'S TIMES LIKE THESE ...
They under-estimate him!
I HEARD THAT!
You said I was ugly!
You called me a kettle, right?!
We did not say that!
YAAAAAHHH!!
...THAT PREVENTS ME FROM GETTING A HANDLE ON THIS GUY!

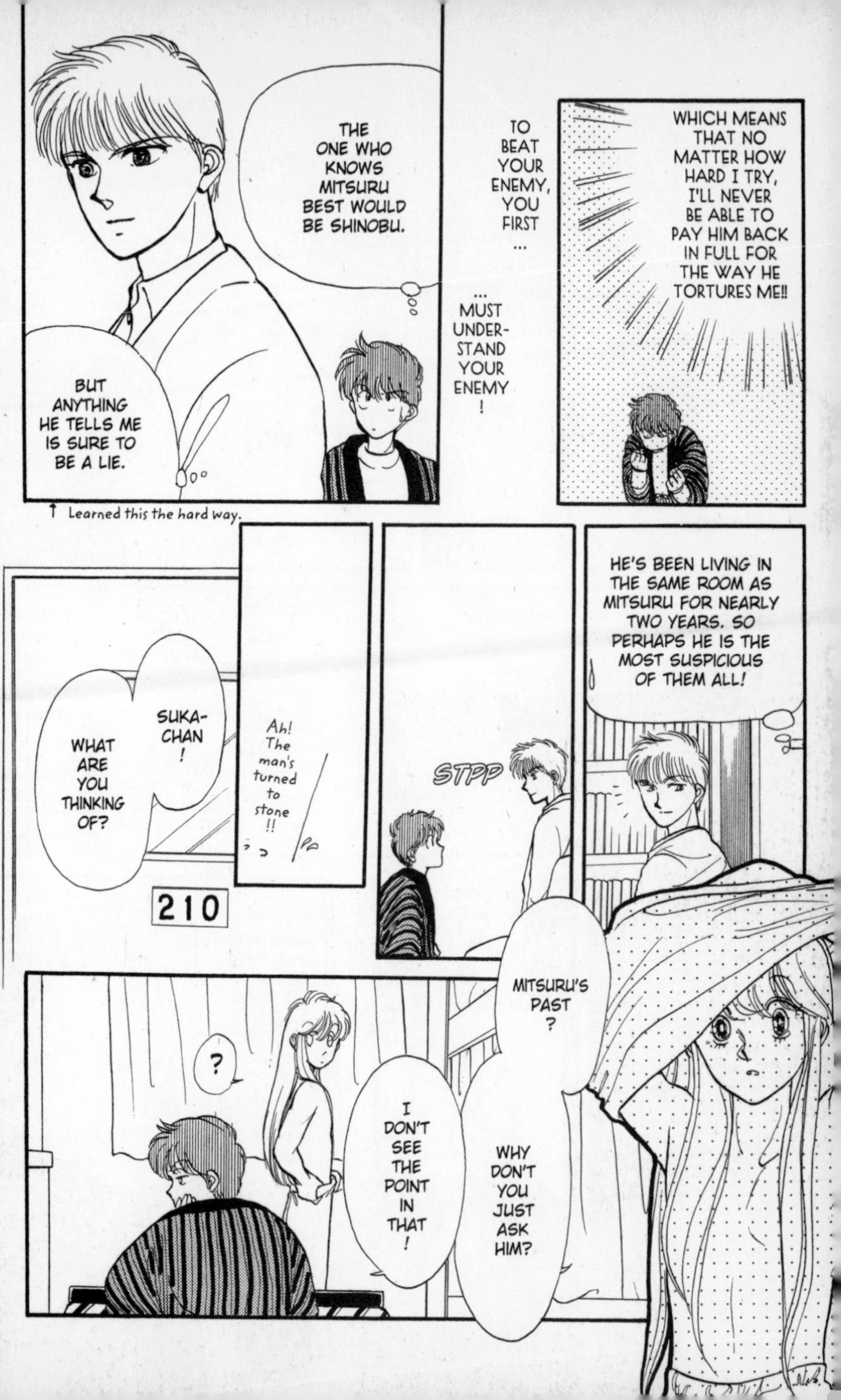
WHICH MEANS THAT NO MATTER HOW HARD I TRY, I'LL NEVER BE ABLE TO PAY HIM BACK IN FULL FOR THE WAY HE TORTURES ME!!
TO BEAT YOUR ENEMY, YOU FIRST ...
... MUST UNDER-STAND YOUR ENEMY!
THE ONE WHO KNOWS MITSURU BEST WOULD BE SHINOBU.
BUT ANYTHING HE TELLS ME IS SURE TO BE A LIE.
↑ Learned this the hard way.
HE'S BEEN LIVING IN THE SAME ROOM AS MITSURU FOR NEARLY TWO YEARS. SO PERHAPS HE IS THE MOST SUSPICIOUS OF THEM ALL!
STPP
Ah! The man's turned to stone!!
SUKA-CHAN!
WHAT ARE YOU THINKING OF?
210
MITSURU'S PAST?
WHY DON'T YOU JUST ASK HIM?
I DON'T SEE THE POINT IN THAT!
?

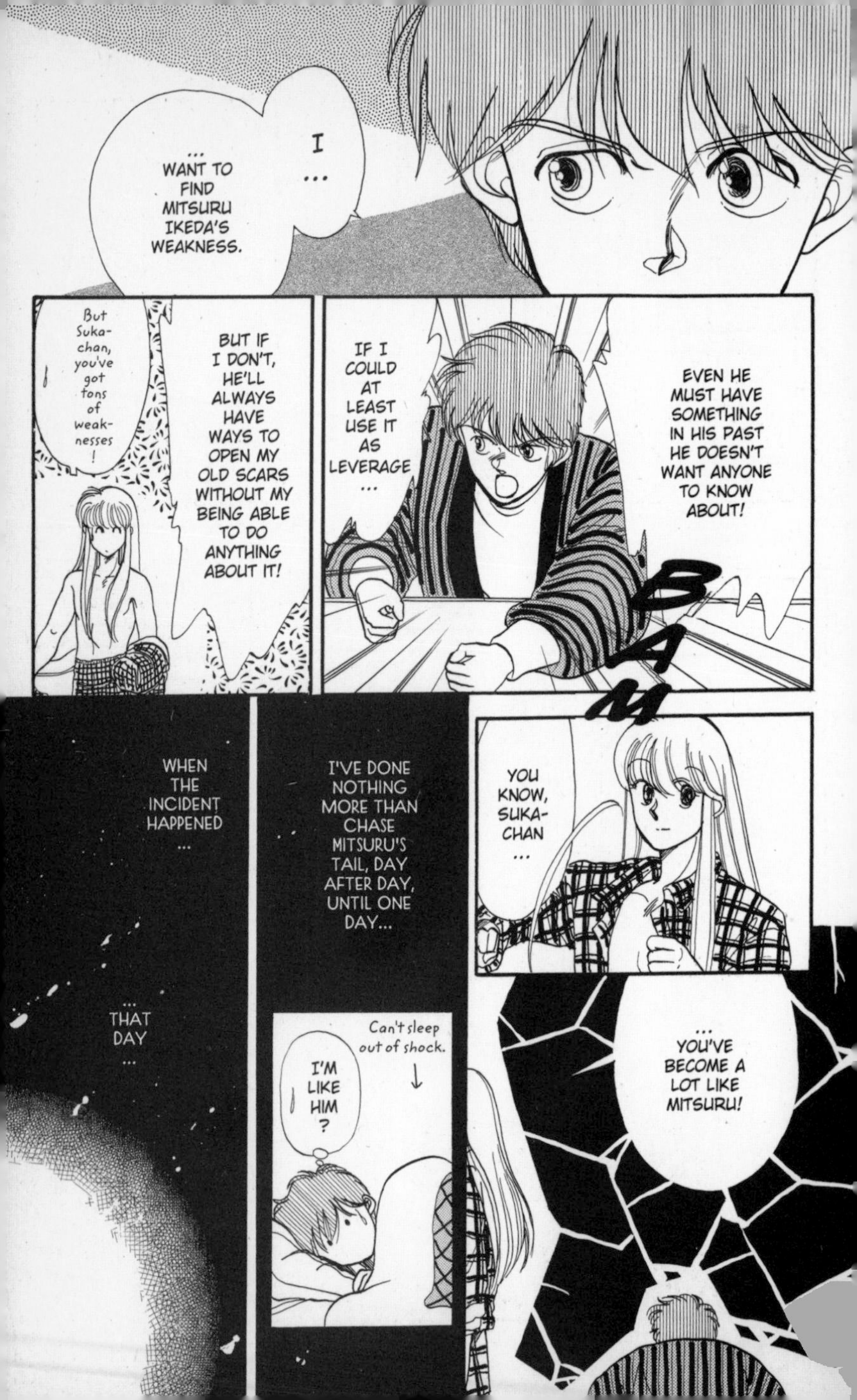
I ...
... WANT TO FIND MITSURU IKEDA'S WEAKNESS.
EVEN HE MUST HAVE SOMETHING IN HIS PAST HE DOESN'T WANT ANYONE TO KNOW ABOUT!
IF I COULD AT LEAST USE IT AS LEVERAGE ...
BAM
BUT IF I DON'T, HE'LL ALWAYS HAVE WAYS TO OPEN MY OLD SCARS WITHOUT MY BEING ABLE TO DO ANYTHING ABOUT IT!
But Suka-chan, you've got tons of weak-nesses!
YOU KNOW, SUKA-CHAN ...
... YOU'VE BECOME A LOT LIKE MITSURU!
I'VE DONE NOTHING MORE THAN CHASE MITSURU'S TAIL, DAY AFTER DAY, UNTIL ONE DAY...
Can't sleep out of shock.
I'M LIKE HIM?
WHEN THE INCIDENT HAPPENED ...
... THAT DAY ...

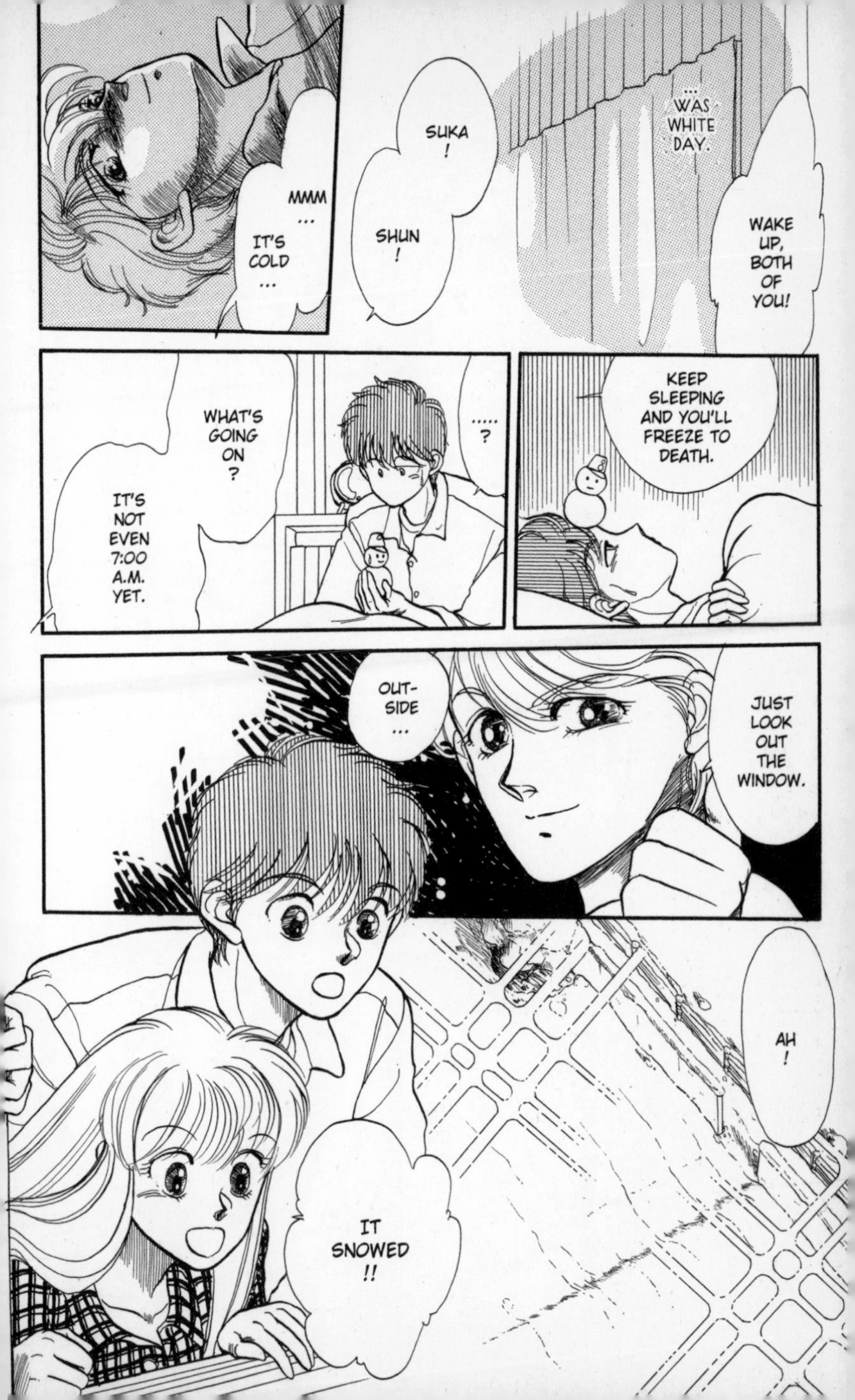
...WAS WHITE DAY.
WAKE UP, BOTH OF YOU!
SUKA!
SHUN!
MMM... IT'S COLD...
KEEP SLEEPING AND YOU'LL FREEZE TO DEATH.
.....?
WHAT'S GOING ON?
IT'S NOT EVEN 7:00 A.M. YET.
JUST LOOK OUT THE WINDOW.
OUT-SIDE...
AH!
IT SNOWED!!

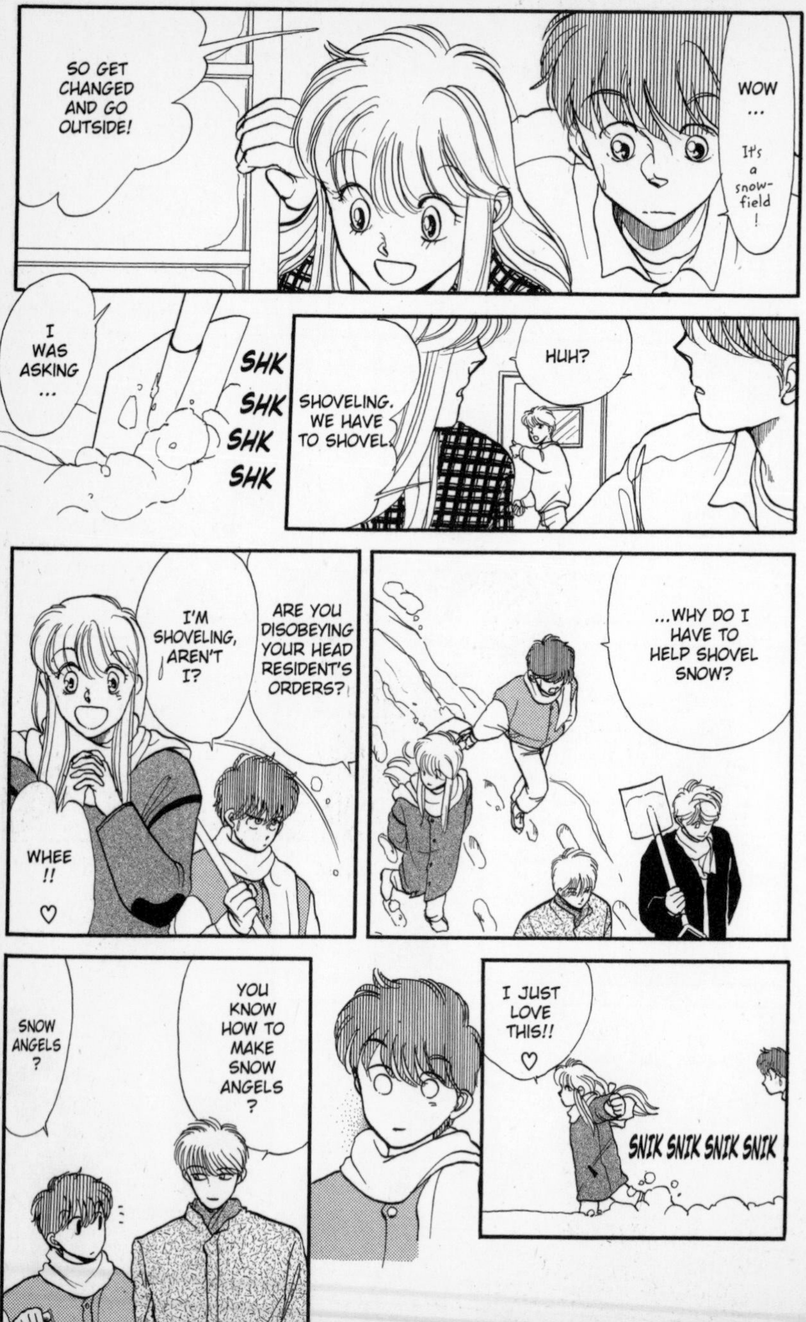
WOW ... It's a snow-field !
SO GET CHANGED AND GO OUTSIDE!
HUH?
SHOVELING. WE HAVE TO SHOVEL.
SHK SHK SHK SHK
I WAS ASKING ...
...WHY DO I HAVE TO HELP SHOVEL SNOW?
ARE YOU DISOBEYING YOUR HEAD RESIDENT'S ORDERS?
I'M SHOVELING, AREN'T I?
WHEE !! ♡
I JUST LOVE THIS!! ♡
SNIK SNIK SNIK SNIK
YOU KNOW HOW TO MAKE SNOW ANGELS ?
SNOW ANGELS ?

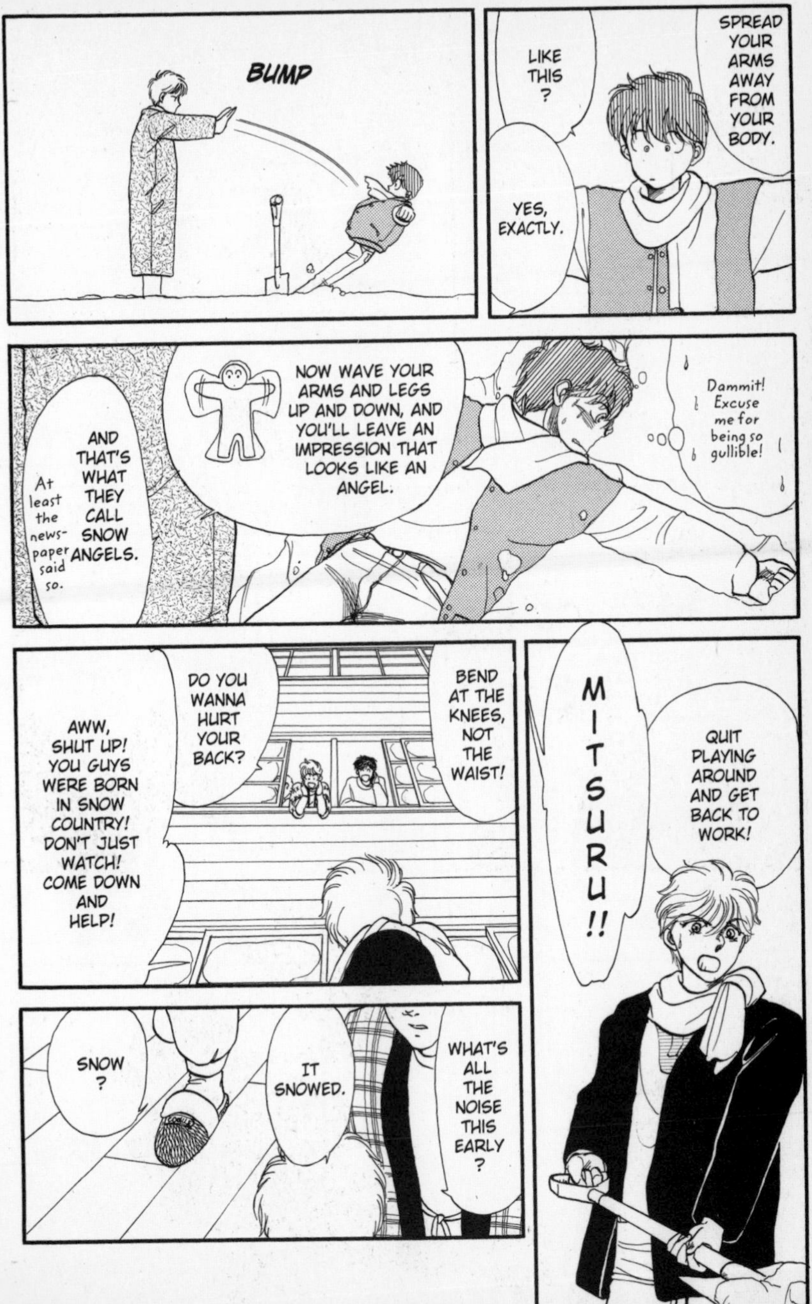
SPREAD YOUR ARMS AWAY FROM YOUR BODY.
LIKE THIS?
YES, EXACTLY.
BUMP
Dammit! Excuse me for being so gullible!
NOW WAVE YOUR ARMS AND LEGS UP AND DOWN, AND YOU'LL LEAVE AN IMPRESSION THAT LOOKS LIKE AN ANGEL.
AND THAT'S WHAT THEY CALL SNOW ANGELS.
At least the news-paper said so.
MITSURU!!
QUIT PLAYING AROUND AND GET BACK TO WORK!
BEND AT THE KNEES, NOT THE WAIST!
DO YOU WANNA HURT YOUR BACK?
AWW, SHUT UP! YOU GUYS WERE BORN IN SNOW COUNTRY! DON'T JUST WATCH! COME DOWN AND HELP!
WHAT'S ALL THE NOISE THIS EARLY?
IT SNOWED.
SNOW?

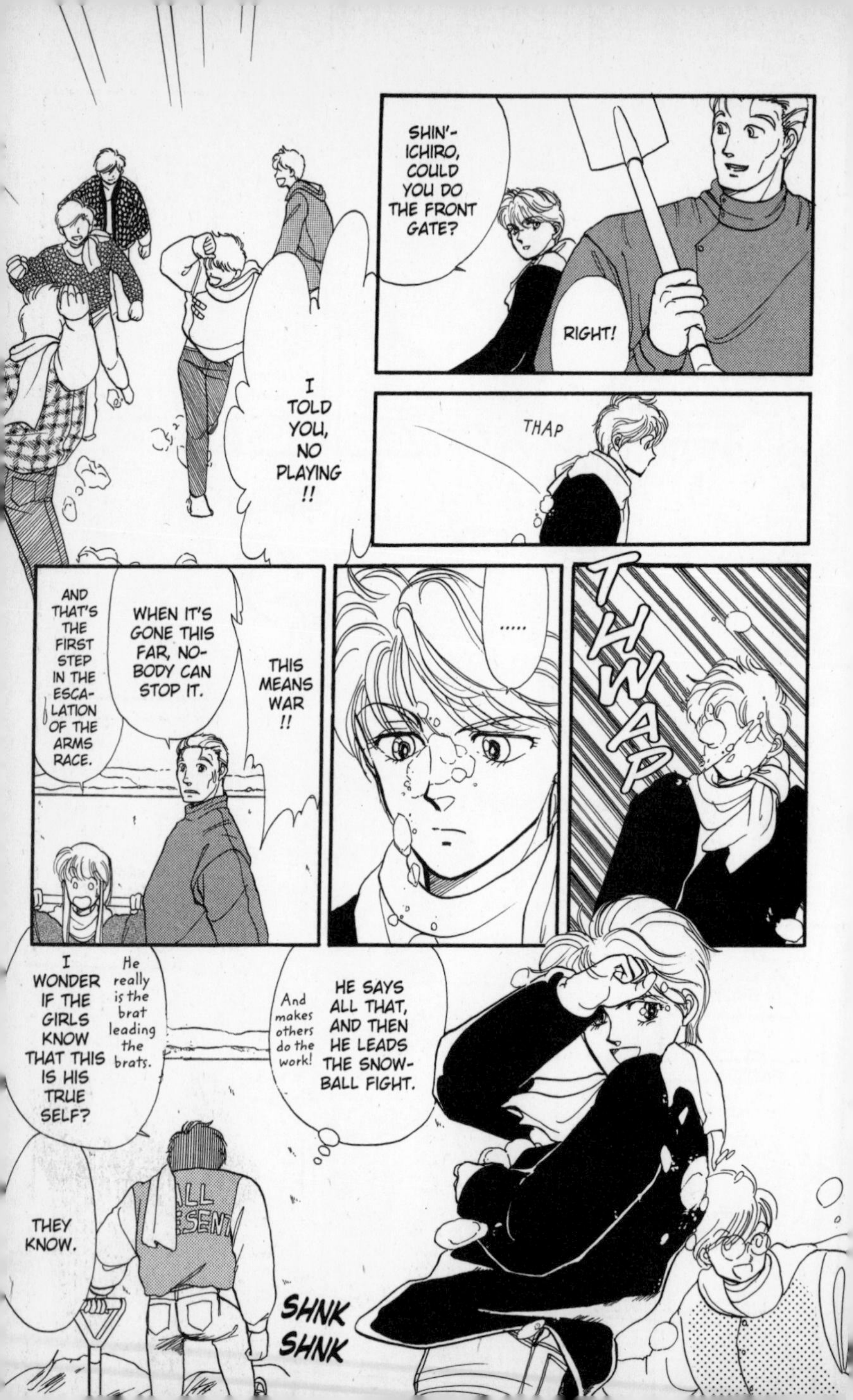

SHIN'-ICHIRO, COULD YOU DO THE FRONT GATE?
RIGHT!
THAP
I TOLD YOU, NO PLAYING!!
TWAP
......
THIS MEANS WAR!!
WHEN IT'S GONE THIS FAR, NO-BODY CAN STOP IT.
AND THAT'S THE FIRST STEP IN THE ESCA-LATION OF THE ARMS RACE.
HE SAYS ALL THAT, AND THEN HE LEADS THE SNOW-BALL FIGHT.
And makes others do the work!
I WONDER IF THE GIRLS KNOW THAT THIS IS HIS TRUE SELF?
He really is the brat leading the brats.
SHNK SHNK
THEY KNOW.

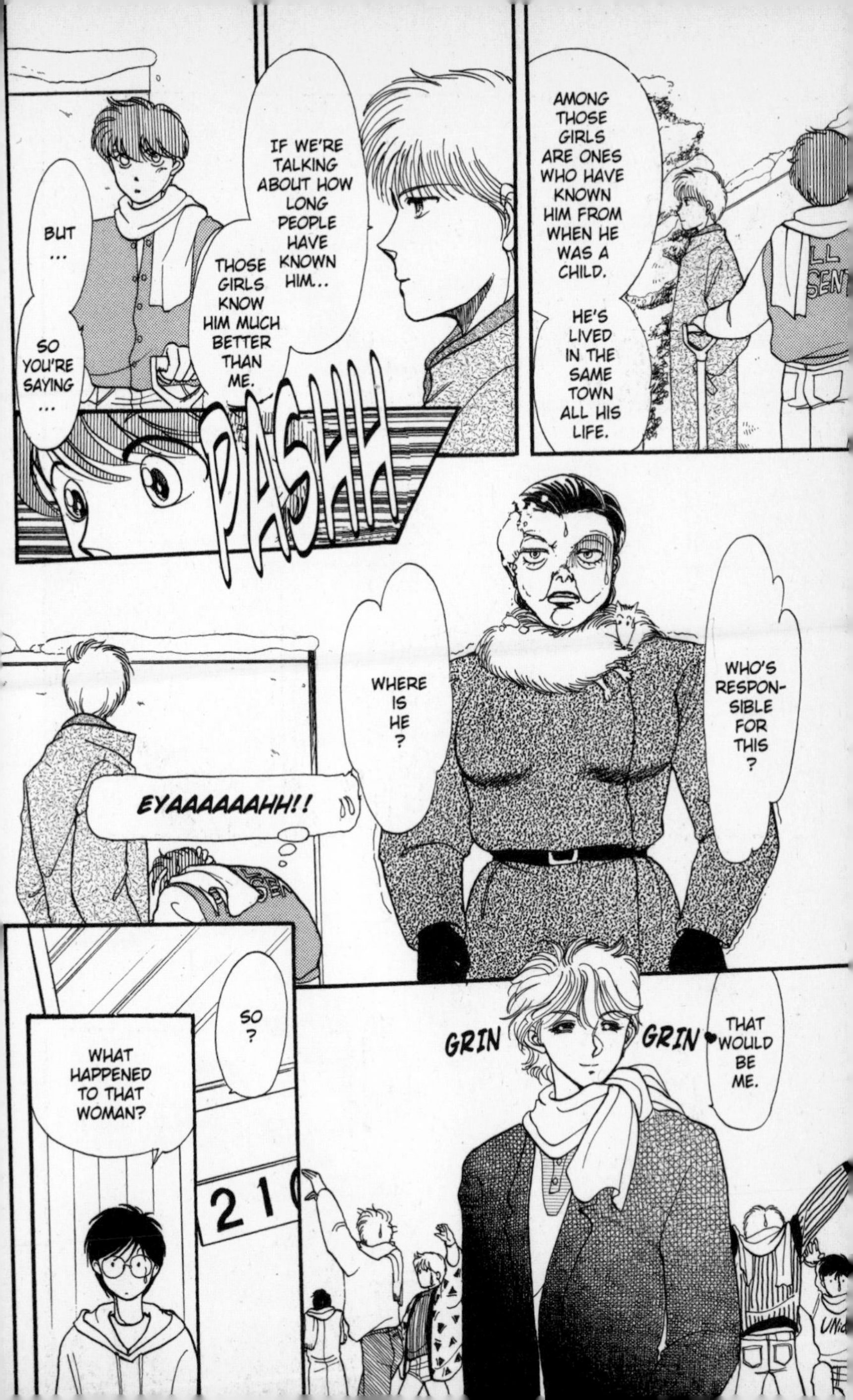
AMONG THOSE GIRLS ARE ONES WHO HAVE KNOWN HIM FROM WHEN HE WAS A CHILD.
HE'S LIVED IN THE SAME TOWN ALL HIS LIFE.
IF WE'RE TALKING ABOUT HOW LONG PEOPLE HAVE KNOWN HIM...
THOSE GIRLS KNOW HIM MUCH BETTER THAN ME.
BUT ...
SO YOU'RE SAYING ...
PASHH
WHO'S RESPON-SIBLE FOR THIS?
WHERE IS HE?
EYAAAAAAHH!!
GRIN GRIN
THAT WOULD BE ME.
SO?
WHAT HAPPENED TO THAT WOMAN?
21

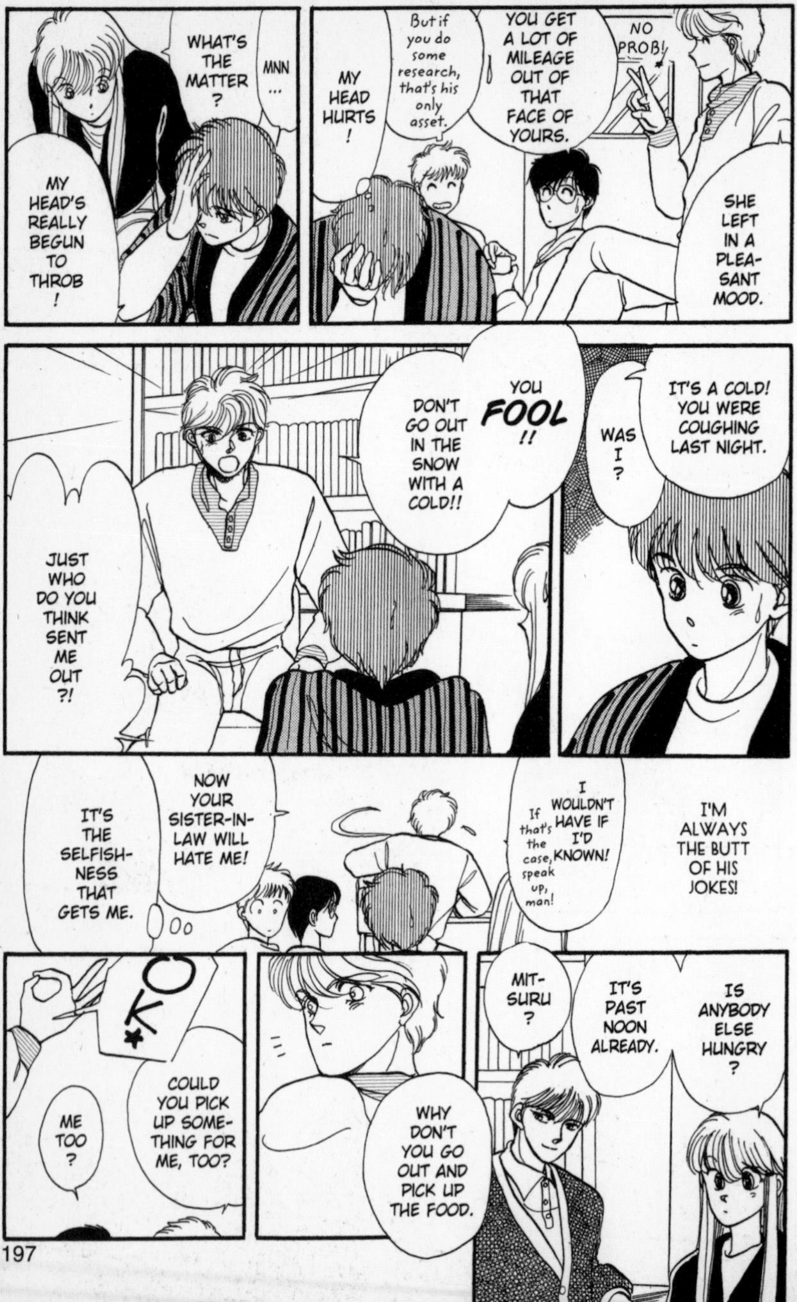
NO PROB!
SHE LEFT IN A PLEASANT MOOD.
YOU GET A LOT OF MILEAGE OUT OF THAT FACE OF YOURS.
But if you do some research, that's his only asset.
MY HEAD HURTS!
MNN...
WHAT'S THE MATTER?
MY HEAD'S REALLY BEGUN TO THROB!
IT'S A COLD! YOU WERE COUGHING LAST NIGHT.
WAS I?
YOU FOOL!!
DON'T GO OUT IN THE SNOW WITH A COLD!!
JUST WHO DO YOU THINK SENT ME OUT?!
I'M ALWAYS THE BUTT OF HIS JOKES!
I WOULDN'T HAVE IF I'D KNOWN!
If that's the case, speak up, man!
NOW YOUR SISTER-IN-LAW WILL HATE ME!
IT'S THE SELFISHNESS THAT GETS ME.
IS ANYBODY ELSE HUNGRY?
IT'S PAST NOON ALREADY.
MIT-SURU?
WHY DON'T YOU GO OUT AND PICK UP THE FOOD.
OK
COULD YOU PICK UP SOMETHING FOR ME, TOO?
ME TOO?

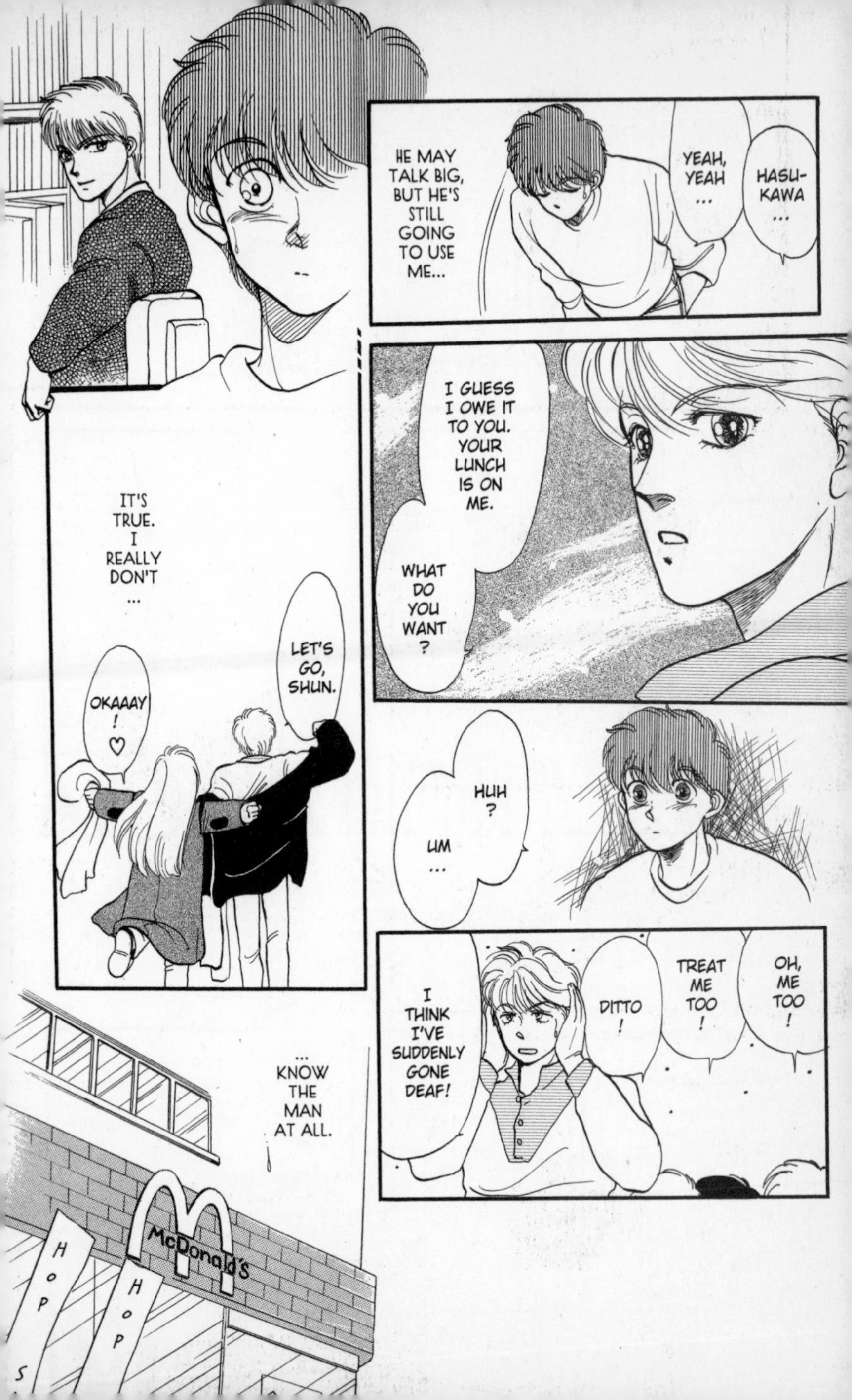
HASU-KAWA ...
YEAH, YEAH ...
HE MAY TALK BIG, BUT HE'S STILL GOING TO USE ME...
I GUESS I OWE IT TO YOU. YOUR LUNCH IS ON ME.
WHAT DO YOU WANT?
HUH?
UM ...
OH, ME TOO!
TREAT ME TOO!
DITTO!
I THINK I'VE SUDDENLY GONE DEAF!
--
LET'S GO, SHUN.
OKAAAY! ♡
IT'S TRUE. I REALLY DON'T ...
... KNOW THE MAN AT ALL.
McDonald's
HOP
HOP

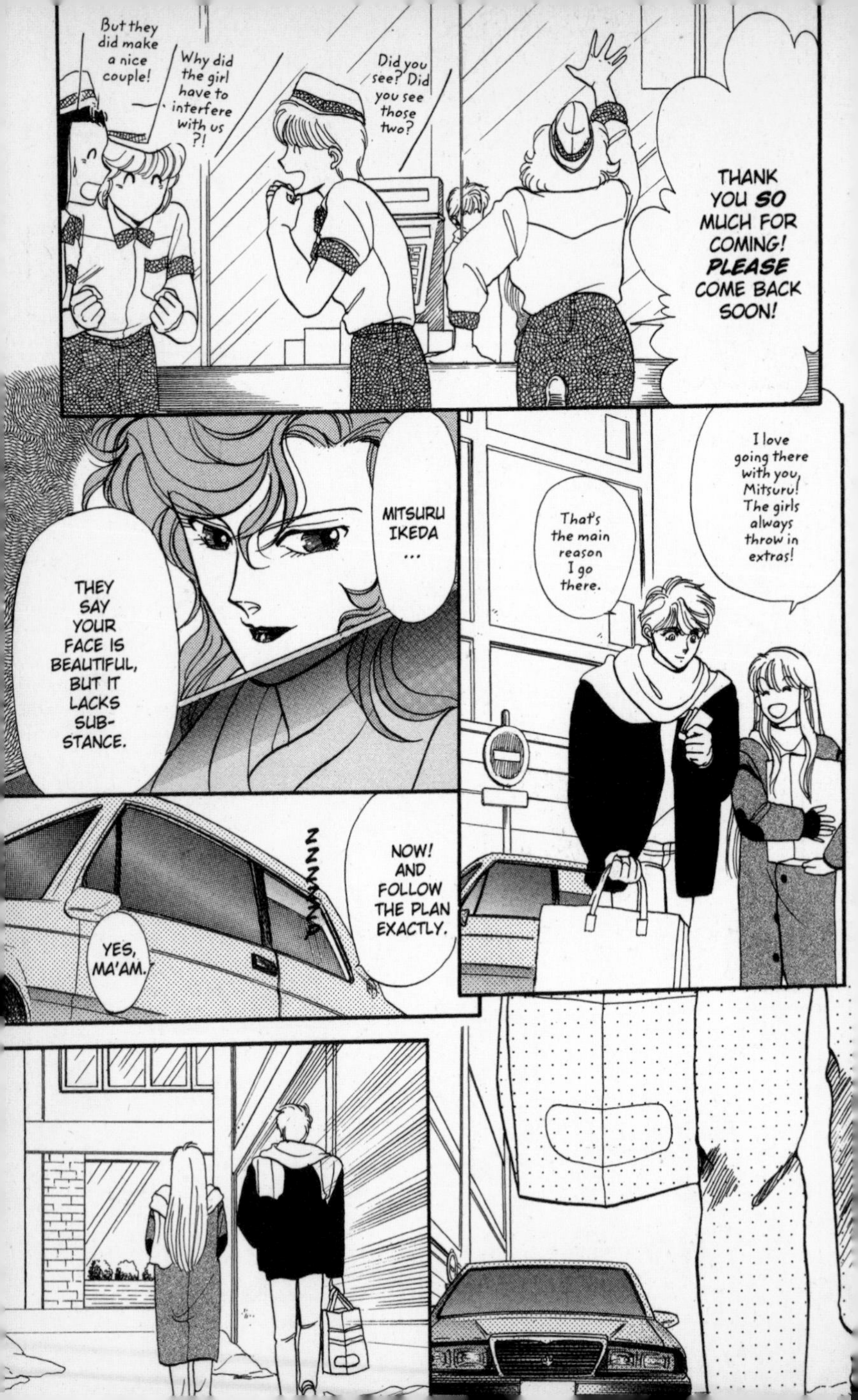
THANK YOU SO MUCH FOR COMING! PLEASE COME BACK SOON!
Did you see? Did you see those two?
Why did the girl have to interfere with us ?!
But they did make a nice couple!
I love going there with you, Mitsuru! The girls always throw in extras!
That's the main reason I go there.
MITSURU IKEDA ...
THEY SAY YOUR FACE IS BEAUTIFUL, BUT IT LACKS SUB-STANCE.
NOW! AND FOLLOW THE PLAN EXACTLY.
YES, MA'AM.

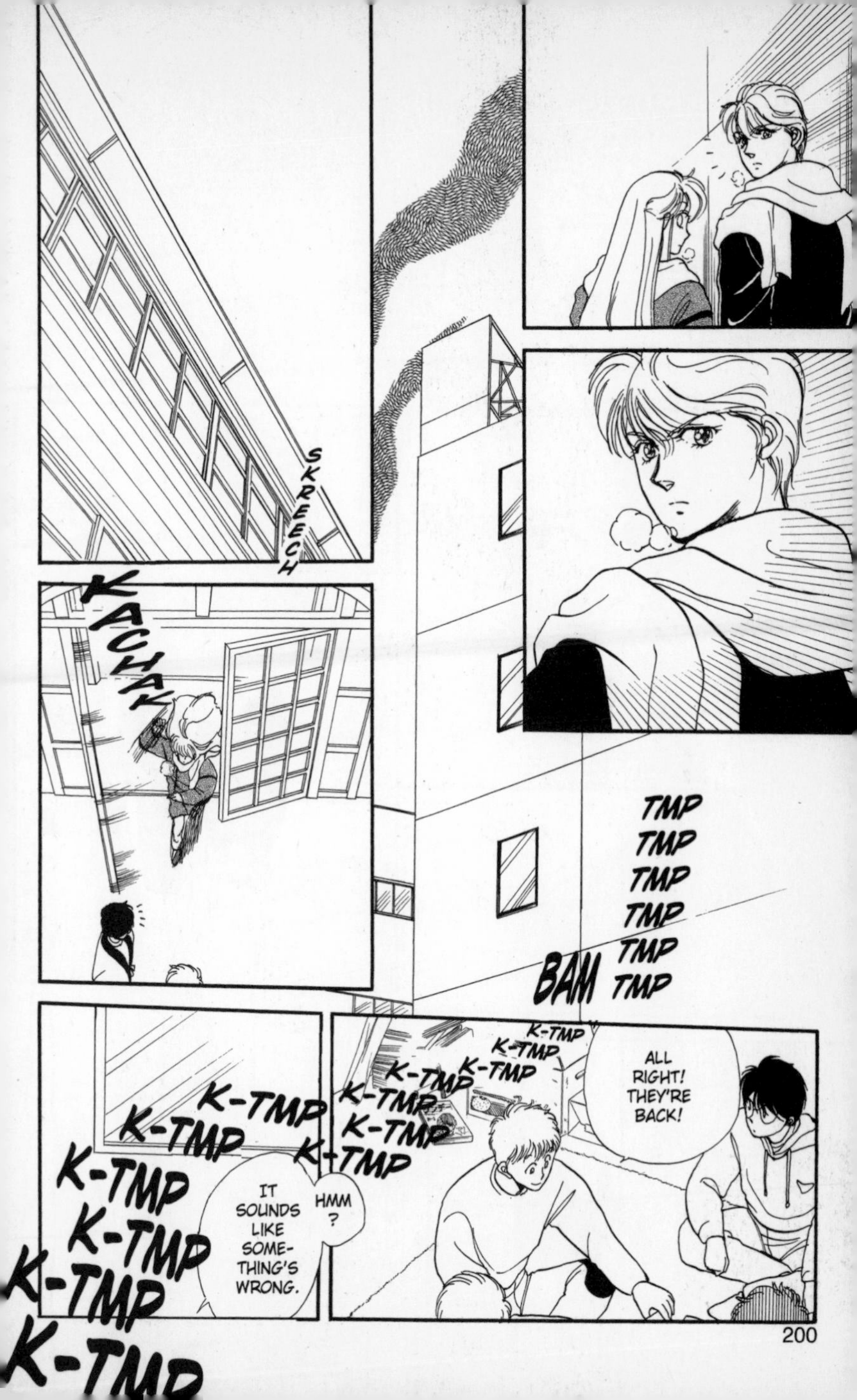
SKREECH
KACHAK
TMP TMP TMP TMP TMP TMP
BAM
K-TMP K-TMP K-TMP K-TMP K-TMP K-TMP
ALL RIGHT! THEY'RE BACK!
K-TMP K-TMP K-TMP K-TMP K-TMP K-TMP K-TMP K-TMP
HMM?
IT SOUNDS LIKE SOME-THING'S WRONG.

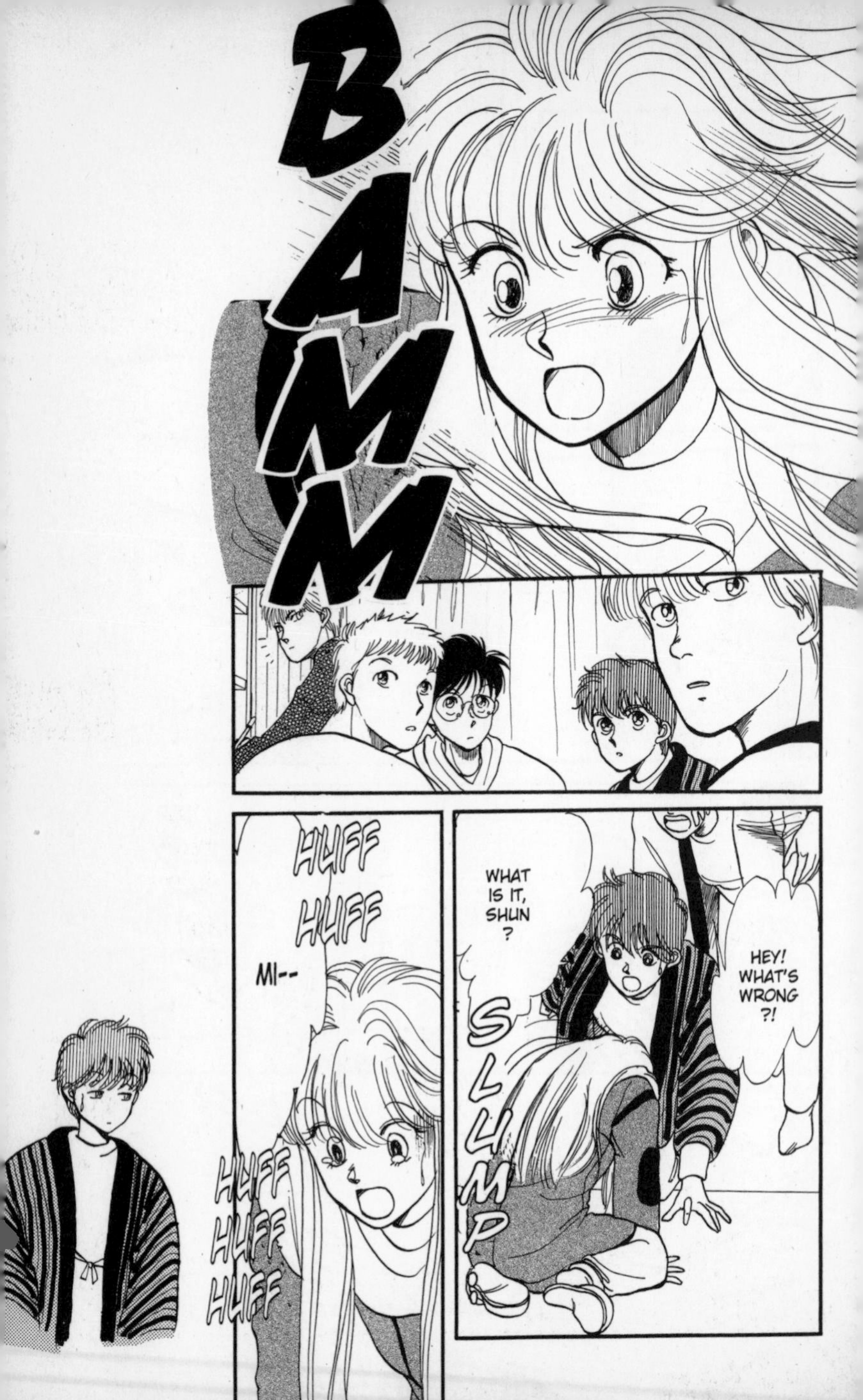
BAMM
HEY! WHAT'S WRONG?!
WHAT IS IT, SHUN?
SLUMP
HUFF HUFF
MI--
HUFF HUFF HUFF

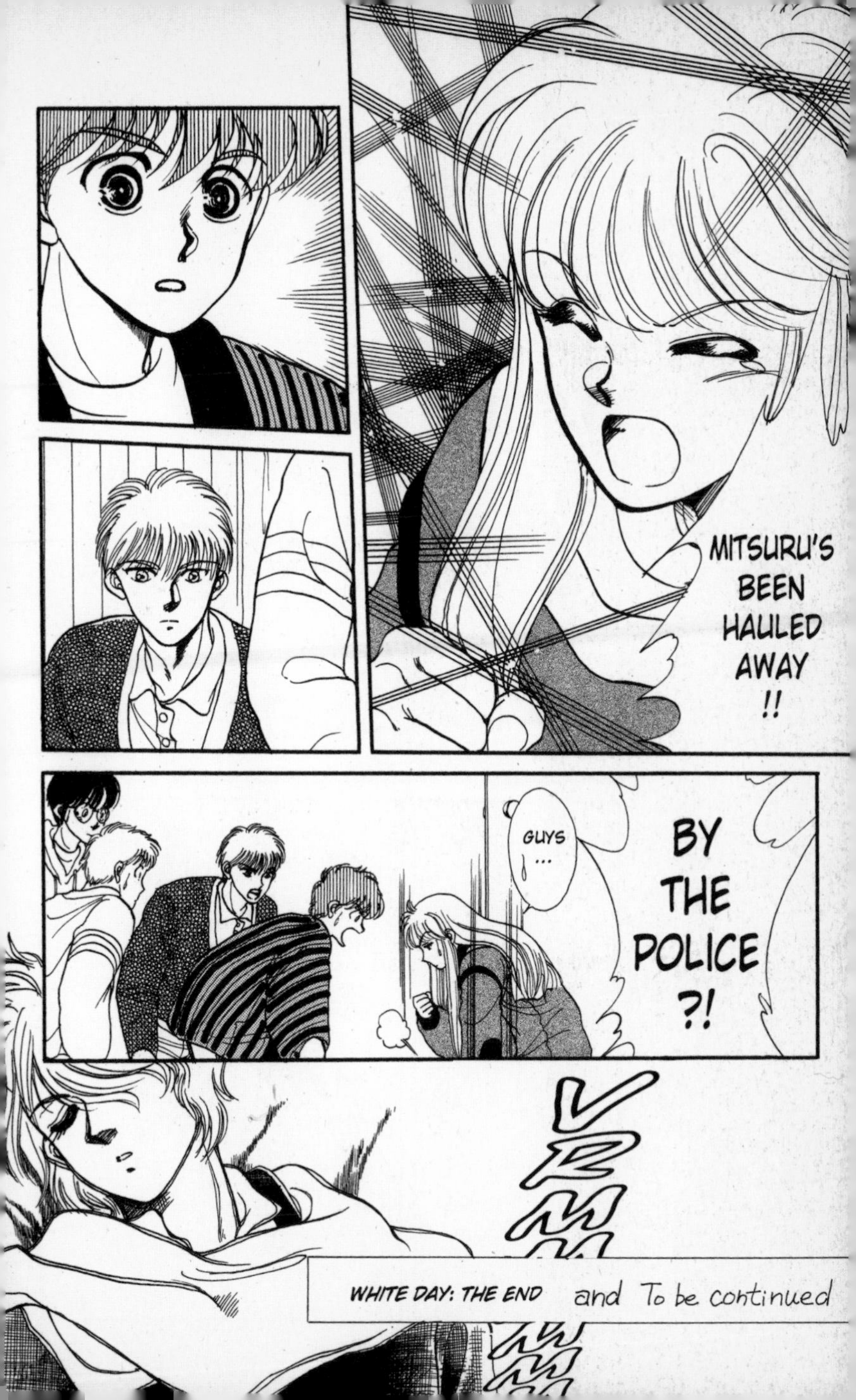
MITSURU'S BEEN HAULED AWAY !!
BY THE POLICE ?!
GUYS ...
WHITE DAY: THE END and To be continued

EDITOR'S RECOMMENDATIONS

More manga!
More manga!

If you enjoyed this volume of

Here is Greenwood™

then here's some more manga you might be interested in.

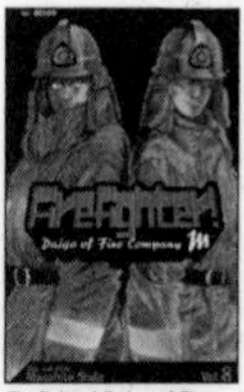
Firefighter!
Daigo of Fire Company
M
Firefighter! Daigo of Fire Company M © 1996 Masahito Soda/Shogakukan, Inc.

FIREFIGHTER! DAIGO OF FIRE COMPANY M

Daigo Asahina is a cocky and idealistic young man fresh out of firefighting academy, and the more assignments he gets sent on, the more he realizes that he has much to learn, develop and accept in order to become the firefighter he has always wanted to be!

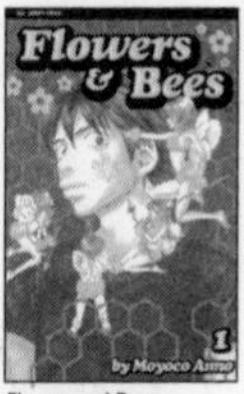
Flowers & Bees
1
by Moyoco Anno
Flowers and Bees © 2000 Moyoco Anno/Kodansha Ltd.

FLOWERS AND BEES

Masao Komatsu might deem himself a complete and utter loser, but high-school life is never terrible enough that it can't get any worse. Gorgeous sisters Kiyoko and Harumi Sakurai are more than happy to bring out what's left of this shell of a young man—with each and every visit Masao pays World of Beautiful Men, the men's beauty salon they own!

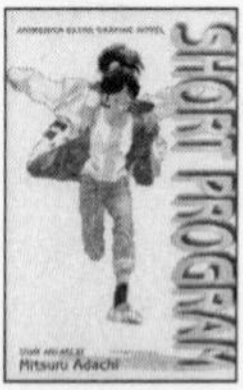
SHORT PROGRAM
Mitsuru Adachi
Short Program ©1996 Mitsuru Adachi/Shogakukan, Inc.

SHORT PROGRAM

Short Program is the first graphic novel collecting the short stories of Mitsuru Adachi, one of the masters of the art of storytelling. This graphic novel contains all the *Short Program* installments from *Animerica Extra* Vol. 2, No. 2, to Vol. 2, No. 11.

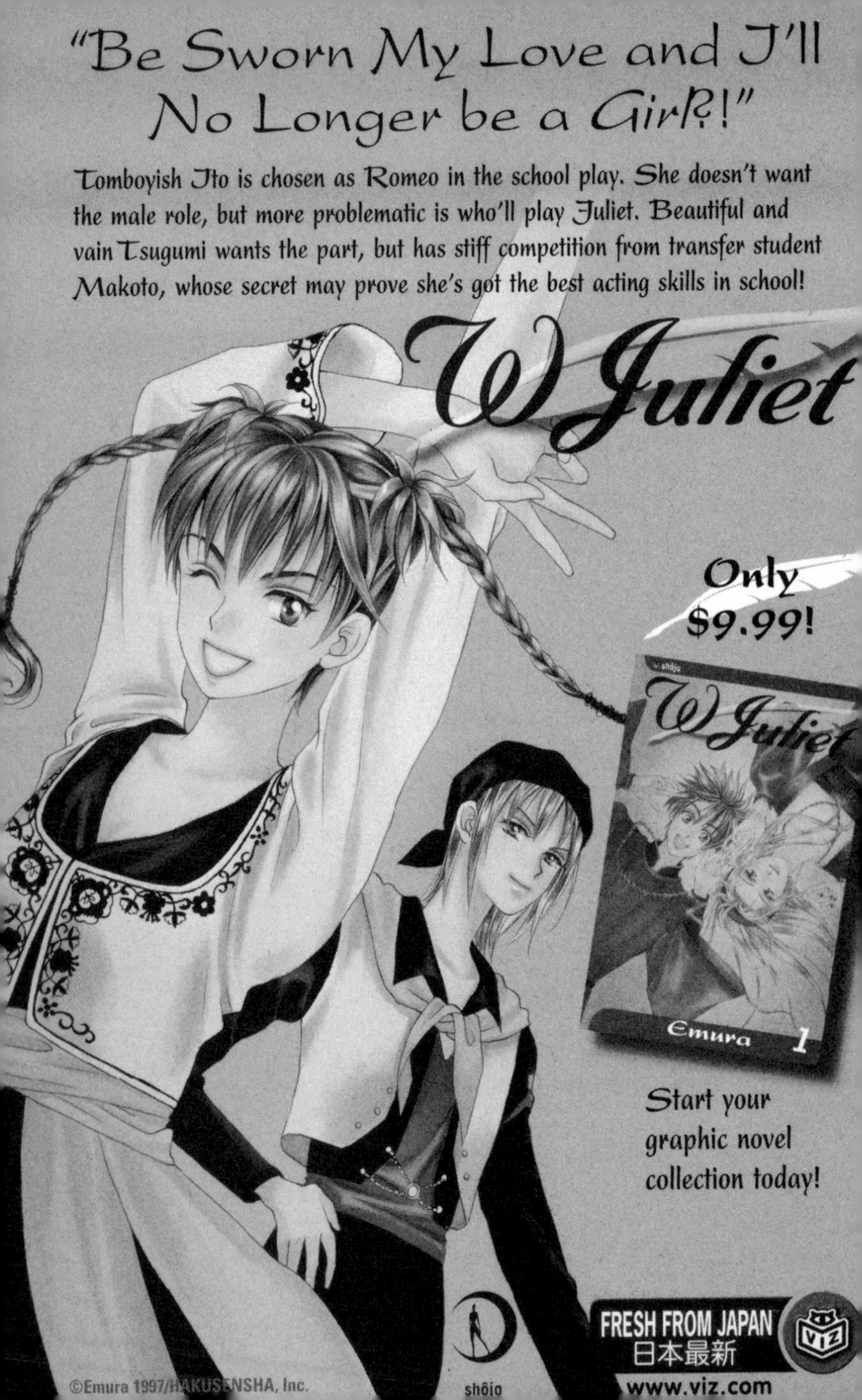
"Be Sworn My Love and I'll No Longer be a Girl?!"
Tomboyish Ito is chosen as Romeo in the school play. She doesn't want the male role, but more problematic is who'll play Juliet. Beautiful and vain Tsugumi wants the part, but has stiff competition from transfer student Makoto, whose secret may prove she's got the best acting skills in school!
W Juliet
Only $9.99!
W Juliet
Emura 1
Start your graphic novel collection today!
FRESH FROM JAPAN
日本最新
VIZ
www.viz.com
shôjo
©Emura 1997/HAKUSENSHA, Inc.

Here is Greenwood
Vol. 1
Shôjo Edition
Story and Art by Yukie Nasu

English Adaptation/William Flanagan
Touch-up Art & Lettering/Walden Wong
Cover and Interior Design/Izumi Evers
Editor/Michelle Pangilinan

Managing Editor/Annette Roman
Director of Production/Noboru Watanabe
Editorial Director/Alvin Lu
Sr. Director of Licensing & Acquisitions/Rika Inouye
Vice President of Sales & Marketing/Liza Coppola
Executive Vice President/Hyoe Narita
Publisher/Seiji Horibuchi

Published by VIZ, LLC
P.O. Box 77010
San Francisco, CA 94107

10 9 8 7 6 5 4 3 2 1
First printing, October 2004

 store.viz.com

www.viz.com

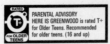

Here is
Greenwood™

Vol. 1
Story and Art by
Yukie Nasu